DISCOVERING LANGUAGE

DISCOVERING LANGUAGE

William Vesterman
RUTGERS UNIVERSITY

ALLYN AND BACON
Boston London Toronto Sydney Tokyo Singapore

Executive Editor: Joseph Opiela
Series Editorial Assistant: Amy Capute
Editorial-Production Administrator: Rowena Dores
Editorial-Production Service: Editorial Inc.
Cover Administrator: Linda Dickinson
Manufacturing Buyer: Louise Richardson

A Division of Simon & Schuster, Inc.
160 Gould Street
Needham Heights, Massachusetts 02194

Library of Congress Cataloging-in-Publication Data

Vesterman, William
Discovering language / William Vesterman.
p. cm.
Includes index.
ISBN 0-205-12829-7
1. Readers—Language and languages. 2. English language—Rhetoric. 3. Readers—English language. 4. English language—Usage. 5. College readers. I. Title.
PE1127.L47V47 1992
400—dc20 91-13058
CIP

Printed in the United States of America

10 9 8 7 6 5 4 3 2 1 96 95 94 93 92 91

CREDITS

Chapter 1

Credits continued on page 461, which constitutes an extension of the copyright page.

CONTENTS

RHETORICAL CONTENTS

ANALOGY

ARGUMENT AND PERSUASION

CAUSE AND EFFECT

COMPARISON AND CONTRAST

DEFINITION

DESCRIPTION

DIVISION AND CLASSIFICATION

EXAMPLE AND ILLUSTRATION

NARRATION

PROCESS ANALYSIS

PREFACE

Discovering Language is a thematic reader of sixty-three essays. It is designed primarily for courses in first-year composition. Not only is it intended to foster awareness, appreciation, and understanding of the many powers of language, but also to improve a student's own power of language in writing skills by offering pertinent instruction and analysis and an example of student writing in each chapter. The book aims to bring the students face to face with the complexities of language—the one subject college graduates in all walks of life, from agronomy to zoning, will need to master.

The editorial apparatus in this book is designed to assist a student in coming to terms with its subject and includes:

- An annotated contents for easy orientation.
- A rhetorical table of contents to assist in focusing on particular writing skills.
- Section introductions that link the individual essays to the chapter's particular theme.
- Headnotes that introduce the author and create a context for the essay.
- A student essay in each chapter responding to its theme.
- Discussion questions on both the style and the content of each selection.
- Two suggested writing assignments for each piece, including intertextual assignments.

The arrangement of the chapters leads students from the study of individual words to larger topics and applications. Overall, *Discovering Language* is a book that can bring its audience to an awareness of the power and glory inherent in the English language and to improve their own masteries of reading and writing.

ACKNOWLEDGMENTS

Many people have helped with this project throughout its development. In particular, I thank Patricia Loughran who helped with the book's editorial apparatus and who wrote its Instructor's Manual. I am grateful to Joseph Opiela, the Executive Editor at Allyn and Bacon, and to Amy Capute, his assistant. I thank Rowena Dores, head of production at Allyn and Bacon, and my production editor Marilyn Rash.

Many helpful comments have improved the manuscript. I thank Therese Brychta, Truckee Meadows Community College; David Covington, North Carolina State University; Terrance Kearns, University of Central Arkansas; William Lutz, Rutgers University, Camden Campus; James Porter, Indiana Purdue University at Fort Wayne; Gerald Poulin, Roane State Community College; Robert Shorter, Wake Forest University; Thomas Young, Purdue University North Central; Frank Shivers, Towson State University; Gratia Murphy, Youngstown State University.

DISCOVERING LANGUAGE

CHAPTER 1

Proper Words in Proper Places: What Is Good English?

Most people begin to learn "the right way" to say things from their parents and from their friends. Children are usually quite fluent by the time they get to school. But once there they sometimes find that the way they are saying things does not seem to be "the right way" after all. Surely no one would ever learn to speak and write coherently unless someone guided him or her, and everyone learns that there are right and wrong ways of saying things; but who is to decide the standards of proper English?

Most people would think first of the dictionary as a way of answering this question. But who gives authority to the compilers of a dictionary? The famous linguist S. I. Hayakawa answers indirectly by showing us how a dictionary is made. In doing so, he points out something that may be very surprising—that dictionaries are more like history books than books of rules.

Whether or not the dictionary can supply the proper authority for proper speech, people still want to know the right way to express themselves. Individual words and phrases make up the most obvious modes of expression. But obvious to whom? English speakers from different regions disagree on this issue. Although everyone is comfortable with the words used by friends and neighbors, most people find a stranger's expressions odd at best. In "Out-of-Town Words," James Kilpatrick comments that "American English is not as common a tongue as we may suppose it to be."

One way of talking that unites groups from all over the country is the language of sport. But even such a common language has shades of meaning. In "Crush vs. Whip," novelist and sports fan John Updike explores some of the subtler forms of fine tuning in the never-ending quest to avoid tedium in reporting similar sports scores at the same time.

Everyone agrees that (as the *Reader's Digest* says) it pays to increase your word power. This self-improvement usually means learning new words, and, for adults, new words are almost by definition big words. But are big words better or more powerful words? Many people seem to think so, among them writers in learned professions; Malcolm Cowley pokes fun at a notorious manifestation of this belief in "Sociological Habit Patterns in Linguistic Transmogrification." Here Cowley looks into the language used by many sociologists and finds that "so far as it has an effect on standard English, the effect is largely pernicious."

We see contrasting views of correctness in the last two professional essays in the section. John Simon makes an unambiguous claim for the power of proper language in "Why Good English Is Good for You." Simon bases his case on a proposition that the reader of this book should by now be in a position to discuss intelligently: "There is a close connection between the ability to think and the ability to use English correctly."

But even granting much of Simon's conclusion, "correctness" is still a troublesome issue. In "The Definition and Determination of 'Correct' English," Robert Pooley looks at attempts to satisfy the demand for correct standards of usage. The issue becomes clearer as he explores the idea that most people can and do speak and understand various levels of English and that the relations among these levels are often surprising.

Finally, student Patricia Loughran looks at a word important in academia—the term "grade." Her assignment was to argue for the grade she deserved in a writing course; as her analysis proceeded, her style, by attention to proper words in proper places, makes the best argument of all.

How Dictionaries Are Made

S. I. HAYAKAWA

Born in 1906, Samuel Ichiye Hayakawa has led a distinguished career in public life, serving as president of San Francisco State University and later as a United States Senator. He is also a respected scholar of semantics: he is, for instance, the founder and editor of ETC.: A Review of General Semantics. *This essay, taken from Hayakawa's* Language in Thought and Action *(1949), describes the painstaking compiling of a dictionary and argues that the ultimate authority in any language is not the dictionary, but the common speaker.*

It is widely believed that every word has a correct meaning, that we learn these meanings principally from teachers and grammarians (except that most of the time we don't bother to, so that we ordinarily speak "sloppy English"), and that dictionaries and grammars are the supreme authority in matters of meaning and usage. Few people ask by what authority the writers of dictionaries and grammars say what they say. I once got into a dispute with an Englishwoman over the pronunciation of a word and offered to look it up in the dictionary. The Englishwoman said firmly "What for? I am English. I was born and brought up in England. The way I speak *is* English." Such self-assurance about one's own language is not uncommon among the English. In the United States, however, anyone who is willing to quarrel with the dictionary is regarded as either eccentric or mad.

Let us see how dictionaries are made and how the editors arrive at definitions. What follows applies, incidentally, only to those dictionary offices where first-hand, original research goes on—not those in which editors simply copy existing dictionaries. The task of writing a dictionary begins with the reading of vast amounts of the literature of the period or subject that the dictionary is to cover. As the editors read, they copy on cards every interesting or rare word, every unusual or peculiar occurrence of a common word, a large number of common words in their ordinary uses, and also the sentences in which each of these words appears, thus:

> pail
> The dairy *pails* bring home increase of milk
>
> Keats, Endymion
> 1, 44–45

That is to say, the context of each word is collected, along with the word itself. For a really big job of dictionary writing, such as the *Oxford English Dictionary* (usually bound in about twenty-five volumes), millions of such cards are collected, and the task of editing occupies decades. As the cards are collected, they are alphabetized and sorted. When the sorting is completed, there will be for each word anywhere from two to three to several hundred illustrative quotations, each on its card.

To define a word, then, the dictionary editor places before him the stack of cards illustrating that word; each of the cards represents an actual use of the word by a writer of some literary or historical importance. He reads the cards carefully, discards some, rereads the rest, and divides up the stack according to what he thinks are the several senses of the word. Finally, he writes his definitions, following the hard-and-fast rule that each definition *must* be based on what the quotations in front of him reveal about the meaning of the word. The editor cannot be influenced by what *he* thinks a given word *ought* to mean. He must work according to the cards or not at all.

The writing of the dictionary, therefore, is not a task of setting up authoritative statements about the "true meanings" of words, but a task of *recording*, to the best of one's ability, what various words *have meant* to authors in the distant or immediate past. *The writer of a dictionary is a historian, not a lawgiver.* If, for example, we had been writing a dictionary in 1890, or even as late as 1919, we could have said that the word "broadcast" means "to scatter" (seed, for example), but we could not have decreed that from 1921 on, the most common meaning of the word should become "to disseminate audible messages, etc., by radio transmission." To regard the dictionary as an "authority," therefore, is to credit the dictionary writer with gifts of prophecy which neither he nor anyone else possesses. In choosing our words when we speak or write, we can be *guided* by the historical record afforded us by the dictionary, but we cannot be *bound* by it, because new situations, new experiences, new inventions, new feelings, are always compelling us to give new uses to old words. Looking under a "hood," we should ordinarily have found, five hundred years ago, a monk; today, we find a motorcar engine.

Discussing Ideas and Themes

1. How often do you use the dictionary? Does Hayakawa's essay change your ideas about what a dictionary is and how it should be used? Explain.
2. Hayakawa suggests that the dictionary is a "historical record" rather than an absolute "authority." What is the difference between these two things? How is Hayakawa's separation of them central to his ideas about language?
3. Who would Hayakawa say "owns" any given language? No one? Everyone? Poets? Scholars? Students? Why?
4. Have you ever considered your use of your language the "right" one? Have you ever found yourself in another country or in a new region of the United States in which people thought you talked funny? How do such experiences affect you?

Discussing Rhetoric and Style

1. What kind of an essay does Hayakawa's title seem to promise the reader? For example, what does the word "how" make you expect? Explain.
2. Does Hayakawa prove anything here, or is he simply describing a scholarly process? What rhetorical differences can you find between argument and description?
3. Why does Hayakawa draw a picture of the card for us? Is this an effective technique or just a nicety? For instance, what does the essay gain by including this picture? What would it lose if it were excluded?
4. Study Hayakawa's use of italics. Why and when are they effective? How do they help you to hear Hayakawa's voice, and in what ways is this voice a compelling and convincing one?
5. Consider Hayakawa's use of first-person pronouns. What does an essay—particularly an essay that describes what most of us

would consider a very scholarly and perhaps a boring procedure—gain by the use of such personable personal pronouns?

Ideas for Writing

1. One thing that Hayakawa accomplishes here is a step-by-step description of how something is done. Pick an activity that you think most people might not know about (stringing a guitar, making candles, canning tomatoes) and describe it in detail in fewer than two pages, as Hayakawa describes the making of dictionaries here. Feel free, as Hayakawa does, to use graphic designs.
2. Hayakawa writes that "the writer of a dictionary is a historian, not a lawgiver," but traditionally the lawgiver is someone who defines right and wrong and often creates meaning and morality from that definition. When a word is included in a prestigious dictionary, it becomes "legitimate"—it enters the lexicon through the front door. Write an essay in which you discuss the role of dictionaries in legitimizing words. You may wish to focus on a controversy, such as the furor over the inclusion of the word "ain't" in *Webster's Third New International Dictionary.*

Out-of-Town Words

JAMES J. KILPATRICK

Born in Oklahoma City in 1920, James Kilpatrick began his career in journalism with the Richmond News Leader *in 1941, rising in ten years' time from reporter to editor-in-chief and eventually syndicating his thrice-weekly column, "A Conservative View," to hundreds of newspapers around the country. Having left the* Richmond News *in 1966, Kilpatrick now resides in Washington, D.C., where he devotes most of his time to writing. The following piece, from a 1985 column, explores regional and colloquial varieties of language, offering as examples such linguistic curiosities as "pungling up" and "lagniappe." Characteristic of Kilpatrick's chatty style, the essay pokes fun at America's paranoia about "Correct English" while celebrating the variety of "out-of-town words."*

Not long ago I expressed my delight at discovering, through the Portland *Oregonian*, what was to me a brand-new verb: to pungle, or as it generally is used, to pungle up. In that same column I remarked that the recasting of an awkward sentence had given us a little lagniappe. I wound up with the admonition against the use of out-of-town words.

The consequences might have been anticipated. The mail brought half a dozen letters from Oregon, almost all of them to the same effect: Everybody out here knows "to pungle up," but what in the world is "lagniappe"?

The best letter came from Clara B. Salzman of Aloha, Ore., who remarked that she is 88 years old and has been hearing "pungled" all her life. The verb, she says, conveys a feeling of outrage or surprise, and she provided examples:

"We paid $15 apiece for our tickets, and then had to pungle up $7.50 to park the car. . . ."

"Their permanents are surely going up. Last time I paid $32.50 and this time I had to pungle up $39.50 for the same permanent."

"Their pizzas may be good, but they should be: Roy pungled up $9.50 for those two little pizzas."

I am much educated, and am reminded once more that American English is not as common a tongue as we suppose it to be. For my own part, I have been hearing "lagniappe" all my life. It is a French Creole word that once was part of the patois of New Orleans. If you bought a pound of shrimp for gumbo, the seafood merchant might first weigh the pound and then throw in a few more for lagniappe. Something extra.

Some years ago, as I recall, the papers carried a story about a team of philologists at work on a linguistic atlas of the United States. In the fashion of Shaw's Henry Higgins, they were seeking to pinpoint not only regional but even local usages. In some parts of the United States, we carry groceries home in a tote; in other areas, we use a bag; in still others, it's a poke. When the clock says 9:45, some of us say it's a "quarter to" 10; others say it's a "quarter of" 10.

Let us pray that these charming regionalisms and colloquialisms never get wiped out by the wet eraser of TV. Learning about "pungle up" was lagniappe for this columnist.

The mail brings some splendid mangles. This one comes from a publication of British Airways promoting a visit to London: "Sitting in Kew Gardens' outdoor cafe the other day, suddenly a fleeting shadow passed overhead. It was the Concorde."

This one comes from the *Daily News* of Johnson County, Kan., in a story about an explosion that destroyed a house but did not injure the occupants: "Bundled up in a borrowed coat, tears rolled down Mrs. Hayes' face as her teeth chattered in the freezing temperatures."

And how about this one from the AP's man in Poland, covering the trial of the thugs who murdered Father Popieluszko: "Pekala said Piotrowski beat the priest with his fists and a club wrapped in a rag at least four times."

These things ought not to happen, but they do happen, and they will keep on happening if we neglect to read our copy one more time before turning it in.

Discussing Issues and Themes

1. What were the "out-of-town" words that Kilpatrick discussed? What did they mean? Had you ever heard of them? Do you know any similar regional words?

2. How does Kilpatrick's correspondence with his readers around the nation qualify him to write on regionalisms? Do you see any shortcomings that make him less qualified? Explain.
3. What is a "linguistic atlas"? Does Kilpatrick think such an atlas would be a good thing? Is his opinion on this subject implicit or explicit? Explain.
4. After discussing some word histories, Kilpatrick comments, "let us pray that these charming regionalisms and colloquialisms never get wiped out by the wet eraser of TV." Why does Kilpatrick call television a "wet eraser"? Why would it threaten regionalisms?

Discussing Rhetoric and Style

1. As you probably noticed, there is an abrupt split in the essay. Where does it occur, and why? What relation does the second half of the essay have to the first? Do you think this split is a weakness or a strength?
2. Kilpatrick moves easily along the spectrum of personal pronouns, shifting from "I" to "we" to "you." What do you think this usage says about Kilpatrick's sense of voice and audience in this essay? Who is speaking here, and who is being spoken to?
3. Consider Kilpatrick's use of the examples in this essay. How does he manipulate outside material to enlighten and enliven his essay? Why does he *have* to use examples?
4. Did you understand the three "mangles" that Kilpatrick offered at the end of the essay? For reference, try to look each one up in a usage handbook and learn its name. Can you find similar mangles in your own writing?
5. Kilpatrick presents himself as an expert on usage and an advocate for regional linguistic curiosities. Do you find that his own style is peppered with regionalisms (his region's own—not ones he's discovered), or is it rather plain? What kind of diction does he use? What kind of tone does his diction create?

Ideas for Writing

1. Read your local newspaper and a national newspaper (such as *The New York Times* or *The Washington Post*) in order to track

down some home-town as well as out-of-town words. After you've found ten or fifteen, pick five of your favorites and write up a column, approximating Kilpatrick's style.

2. How does Kilpatrick's approach to his subject—proper and present English usage—differ from Hayakawa's treatment of a similar subject? Write an essay in which you compare these two writers' linguistic ideologies. Where do their ideas about language overlap?

Crush vs. Whip

JOHN UPDIKE

Born in 1932, John Updike grew up in Pennsylvania and studied at Harvard and Oxford as well as at the Ruskin School of Drawing and Fine Art. One of the most prolific writers of our time, Updike has published poetry, essays, and stories as well as numerous novels and a play. His most famous novels, the Rabbit *series, include* Rabbit Is Rich, Rabbit Redux, Rabbit Run, *and* Rabbit at Rest. *More recent works include* The Witches of Eastwick, *which was made into a motion picture;* Roger's Version; *and the 1988 book,* S. *In this essay he ruminates on one of his favorite pastimes other than writing—baseball, and the language thereof.*

Apparently, the St. Louis Cardinals are much more friable than they used to be, for a paper in San Francisco recently ran the headline "GIANTS CRUSH CARDINALS, 3–1." Now, we don't want to suggest that our city's eldest franchise has got in with a group of orange squeezers who don't know real pulverization when they see it. There's been too much of such carping already. When a boy leaves home, a mother's duty is to hold her tongue, we always say. While voices around us cried that the West Coast was, variously, a vile limbo, an obscure religious sect, a figment of Walter O'Malley's fevered imagination, and a tar pit of busherism certain to fossilize whatever it enveloped, we kept mum. As a reward to ourself for restraint, therefore, we *will* offer some advice about the science or art of baseball-headline verbs. These we have seen evolve from a simple matter of "WIN" and "LOSE" into a structure of periphrasis as complex as heraldry in feudalism's decadence. New York City, now a quaint port known principally for her historical monuments, once boasted three—we swear it, *three*—baseball teams and a dozen daily newspapers. The lore accumulated here should be passed on to headline writers in all the fresh, brash towns likely to be visited as the major leagues, driven by a dark fatality, continue their migration toward Asia.

The correct verb, San Francisco, is "WHIP." Notice the vigor, force, and scorn obtained, quite without hyperbole. This table may prove helpful:

3–1—WHIP
3–2—SHADE
2–1—EDGE
1–0—(Pitcher's name) BLANKS*

Turning back and working upward, we come to 4–2, known professionally as "the golden mean," or "absolute zero." The score is uniquely characterless. The bland terms "BEAT" and "DEFEAT" are called in from the bullpen (meaning an area in which pitchers not actually in the game may "warm up"). However, 4–1 gets the coveted verb "VANQUISH." Rule: Any three-run margin, *provided the winning total does not exceed ten,* may be described as a vanquishing. If, however, the margin is a mere two runs and the losing total is five or more, "OUTSLUG" is considered very tasty. You will notice, S.F., the trend called Mounting Polysyllabism, which culminates, at the altitude of double digits, in that trio of Latin-root rhymers, "ANNIHILATE," "OBLITERATE," and "HUMILIATE." E.g., "A's ANNIHILATE O's, 13–2."

Special cases:

1. If the home team is on the short end of the score, certain laws of mutation apply. "SHADE" becomes "SQUEAK BY." For "OUTSLUG," put "WIN OUT IN SLOPPY CONTEST." By a judicious exploitation of "BOW," the home team, while losing, can be given the active position in the sentence and an appearance of graciousness as well.
2. Many novice banner writers, elevated from the 2-col. obscurity of Class A ball to the black-cap. screamers of the big leagues, fumble the concept of "SWEEP." It *always* takes a plural object. Doubleheaders and series can be swept, but not regulation single games. (The minimal "WIN STREAK" is three games long; five makes a "SURGE.") A team that neither sweeps nor is swept splits. A headline familiar to New Englanders is "SOX SPLIT."
3. Which brings up the delicate matter of punning, or paronomasia. Each Baltimore journal is restricted by secret covenant to

* Below, in smaller type, you may have "Twirls 3- (4-, 5-) Hitter." Two-hitters are "spun." For a one-hitter, write "Robbed of No-hitter."

one "BIRDS SOAR" every two weeks. Milwaukee, with a stronger team, is permitted twelve instances of "braves scalp" before the All-Star game. "TIGERS CLAW" and "CUBS LICK" tend to take care of themselves. As for you, San Francisco, the lack of any synonyms for "giant" briefer than "behemoth" and "Brobdingnagian," together with the long-standing failure of New York's own writers to figure out exactly what giants *do* (intimidate? stomp?), rather lets you out of the fun. In view of this, and in view of the team's present surprising record, you may therefore write "GIANTS A-MAYS." But don't do it more than once a month: moderation in all things, S.F.

Discussing Issues and Themes

1. What does Updike claim to be the difference between "crush" and "whip"? How does he make that difference funny (or doesn't he)?
2. What is periphrasis? Why does Updike refer to it? Does he ever use it?
3. What is Updike's attitude toward the West Coast, and how do you know? How does this attitude differ from his attitude toward newspaper headlines, for example? What is his attitude toward language?
4. What is paronomasia? Does Updike give any examples of it? Can you think of any of your own?

Discussing Rhetoric and Style

1. List some of the characteristic words in this essay. How does Updike's diction create the tone here? How would you characterize that tone? Support your answer with references to the text.
2. Why does Updike use classical rhetorical terms (such as periphrasis and paronomasia) to describe baseball headlines? That is, what is the effect of his use of these terms—satire, irony, humor? Or all three?
3. How would you describe Updike's address to the West Coast in the first paragraph? Who is the real audience of this "address"? How do you know?

4. Why does Updike use a footnote? How is this technique in keeping with the style of the essay and the essayist? Again, cite the text.

Ideas for Writing

1. Can you do for football or soccer—or even for the Sears catalog—what Updike does here for baseball? That is, cite "typical" words that appear in headlines, articles, or advertising copy, and playfully analyze this specialized rhetoric. Keep your essay short: two or three pages.
2. Write an essay in which you discuss a piece of writing by any essayist or humorist (you can discuss this essay, if you don't have a special attachment to another author). What techniques make the essay so enjoyable? What does the writer do with language to make you laugh?

Sociological Habit Patterns in Linguistic Transmogrification

MALCOLM COWLEY

Malcolm Cowley is a critically acclaimed poet and critic, whose books include The Flower and the Leaf, The Many-Windowed House, A Second Flowering, *and* Think Back on Us. *An expert in the field of critical biography and literary memoir, Cowley worked in publishing, advising Viking Press on literary topics. A lover of the English language, Cowley possessed a shrewd eye for prose foibles of any sort. In the following essay, he zeroes in on the language peculiar to sociologists. As Cowley points out, specialized jargon can lead to the need for a specialized audience. The essay first appeared in the* Reporter *in September 1956.*

I have a friend who started as a poet and then decided to take a postgraduate degree in sociology. For his doctoral dissertation he combined his two interests by writing on the social psychology of poets. He had visited poets by the dozen, asking each of them a graded series of questions, and his conclusions from the interviews were modest and useful, though reported in what seemed to me a barbarous jargon. After reading the dissertation I wrote and scolded him. "You have such a fine sense of the poet's craft," I said, "that you shouldn't have allowed the sociologists to seduce you into writing their professional slang—or at least that's my judgmental response to your role selection."

My friend didn't write to defend himself; he waited until we met again. Then, dropping his voice, he said: "I knew my dissertation was badly written, but I had to get my degree. If I had written it in English, Professor Blank"—he mentioned a rather distinguished name—"would have rejected it. He would have said it was merely belletristic."

From that time I began to study the verbal folkways of the sociologists. I read what they call "the literature." A few sociologists write the best English they are capable of writing, and I suspect that they are the best men in the field. There is no mystery about them. If they go wrong, their mistakes can be seen and corrected. Others, however—and a vast majority—write in a language that has to be learned almost like Esperanto. It has a private vocabulary which, in addition to strictly sociological terms, includes new words for the commonest actions, feelings, and circumstances. It has the beginnings of a new grammar and syntax, much inferior to English grammar in force and precision. So far as it has an effect on standard English, the effect is largely pernicious.

Sometimes it misleads the sociologists themselves, by making them think they are profoundly scientific at points where they are merely being verbose. I can illustrate by trying a simple exercise in translation, that is, by expressing an idea first in English and then seeing what it looks like in the language of sociology.

An example that comes to hand is the central idea of an article by Norman E. Green, printed in the February, 1956, issue of the *American Sociological Review.* In English his argument might read as follows:

"Rich people live in big houses set farther apart than those of poor people. By looking at an aerial photograph of any American city, we can distinguish the richer from the poorer neighborhoods."

I won't have to labor over a sociological expression of the same idea, because Mr. Green has saved me the trouble. Here is part of his contribution to comparative linguistics. "In effect, it was hypothesized," he says—a sociologist must never say "I assumed," much less "I guessed"—"that certain physical data categories including housing types and densities, land use characteristics, and ecological location"—not just "location," mind you, but "ecological location," which is almost equivalent to locational location—"constitute a scalable content area. This could be called a continuum of residential desirability. Likewise, it was hypothesized that several social data categories, describing the same census tracts, and referring generally to the social stratification system of the city, would also be scalable. This scale could be called a continuum of socio-economic status. Thirdly, it was hypothesized that there would be a high positive correlation between the scale types on each continuum."

Here, after ninety-four words, Mr. Green is stating, or concealing, an assumption with which most laymen would have started, that rich people live in good neighborhoods. He is now almost ready for his deduction, or snapper:

"This relationship would define certain linkages between the social and physical structure of the city. It would also provide a precise definition of the commonalities among several spatial distributions. By the same token, the correlation between the residential desirability scale and the continuum of socio-economic status would provide an estimate of the predictive value of aerial photographic data relative to the social ecology of the city."

Mr. Green has used 160 words—counting "socio-economic" as only one—to express an idea that a layman would have stated in thirty-three. As a matter of fact, he has used many more than 160 words, since the whole article is an elaboration of this one thesis. Whatever may be the virtues of the sociological style—or Socspeak, as George Orwell might have called it—it is not specifically designed to save ink and paper. Let us briefly examine some of its other characteristics.

A layman's first impression of sociological prose, as compared with English prose, is that it contains a very large proportion of abstract words, most of them built on Greek or Latin roots. Often—as in the example just quoted—they are used to inflate or transmogrify a meaning that could be clearly expressed in shorter words surviving from King Alfred's time.

These Old English or Anglo-Saxon words are in number less than one-tenth of the entries in the largest dictionaries. But they are the names of everyday objects, attributes, and actions, and they are also the pronouns, the auxiliary verbs, and most of the prepositions and conjunctions, so that they form the grammatical structure of the language. The result is that most novelists use six Anglo-Saxon words for every one derived from French, Latin, or Greek, and that is probably close to the percentage that would be found in spoken English.

For comparison or contrast, I counted derivations in the passage quoted from the *American Sociological Review,* which is a typical example of "the literature." No less than 49 percent of Mr. Green's prose consists of words from foreign or classical languages. By this standard of measurement, his article is more abstruse than most textbooks of advanced chemistry and higher mathematics, which are said to contain only 40 percent of such words.

In addition to being abstruse, the language of the sociologists is also rich in neologisms. Apparently they like nothing better than inventing a word, deforming a word, or using a technical word in a strange context. Among their favorite nouns are "ambit," "extensity" (for "extent"), "scapegoating," "socializee," "ethnicity," "directionality," "cathexis," "affect" (for "feeling"), "maturation" (for both "maturing" and "maturity"), and "commonalities" (for "points in common"). Among their favorite adjectives are "processual," "prestigeful," and "insightful"—which last is insightful to murder—and perhaps their favorite adverb is "minimally," which seems to mean "in some measure." Their maximal pleasure seems to lie in making new combinations of nouns and adjectives and nouns used as adjectives, until the reader feels that he is picking his way through a field of huge boulders, lost among "universalistic-specific achievement patterns" and "complementary role-expectation-sanction systems," as he struggles vainly toward "ego-integrative action orientation," guided only by "orientation to improvement of the gratification-deprivation balance of the actor"—which last is Professor Talcott Parsons's rather involved way of saying "the pleasure principle."

But Professor Parsons, head of the Sociology Department at Harvard, is not the only delinquent recidivist, convicted time and again of corrupting the language. Among sociologists in general there is a criminal fondness for using complicated terms when there are simple ones available. A child says "Do it again," a teacher says "Repeat the exercise," but the sociologist says "It was determined to replicate the investigation." Instead of saying two things are alike or similar, as a layman would do, the sociologist describes them as being either isomorphic or homologous. Instead of saying that they are different, he calls them allotropic. Every form of leadership or influence is called a hegemony.

A sociologist never cuts anything in half or divides it in two like a layman. Instead he dichotomizes it, bifurcates it, subjects it to a process of binary fission, or restructures it in a dyadic conformation—around polar foci.

So far I have been dealing with the vocabulary of sociologists, but their private language has a grammar too, and one that should be the subject of intensive research by the staff of a very well-endowed foundation. I have space to mention only a few of its more striking features.

The first of these is the preponderance of nouns over all the other parts of speech. Nouns are used in hyphenated pairs of dyads, and sometimes in triads, tetrads, and pentads. Nouns are used as adjectives without change of form, and they are often used as verbs, with or without the suffix "ize." The sociological language is gritty with nouns, like sanded sugar.

On the other hand, it is poor in pronouns. The singular pronoun of the first person has entirely disappeared, except in case histories, for the sociologist never comes forward as "I." Sometimes he refers to himself as "the author" or "the investigator," or as "many sociologists," or even as "the best sociologists," when he is advancing a debatable opinion. On rare occasions he calls himself "we," like Queen Elizabeth speaking from the throne, but he usually avoids any personal form and writes as if he were a force of nature.

The second-personal pronoun has also disappeared, for the sociologist pretends to be speaking not to living persons but merely for the record. Masculine and feminine pronouns of the third person are used with parsimony, and most sociologists prefer to say "the subject," or "X———," or "the interviewee," where a layman would use the simple "he" or "she." As for the neuter pronoun of the third person, it survives chiefly as the impersonal subject of a passive verb. "It was hypothesized," we read, or "It was found to be the case." Found by *whom?*

The neglect and debasement of the verb is another striking feature of "the literature." The sociologist likes to reduce a transitive verb to an intransitive, so that he speaks of people's adapting, adjusting, transferring, relating, and identifying, with no more of a grammatical object than if they were coming or going. He seldom uses transitive verbs of action, like "break," "injure," "help," and "adore." Instead he uses verbs of relation, verbs which imply that one series of nouns and adjectives, used as the compound subject of a sentence, is larger or smaller than, dominant over, subordinate to, causative of, or resultant from another series of nouns and adjectives.

Considering this degradation of the verb, I have wondered how one of Julius Caesar's boasts could be translated into Socspeak. What Caesar wrote was *"Veni, vidi, vici"*—only three words, all of them verbs. The English translation is in six words: "I came, I saw, I conquered," and three of the words are first-personal pronouns, which the sociologist is taught to avoid. I suspect that he would have to write: "Upon the advent of the investigator, his hegemony became minimally coextensive with the areal unit rendered visible by his successive displacements in space."

The whole sad situation leads me to dream of a vast allegorical painting called "The Triumph of the Nouns." It would depict a chariot of victory drawn by the other conquered parts of speech—the adverbs and adjectives still robust, if yoked and harnessed; the prepositions bloated and pale; the conjunctions tortured; the pronouns reduced to sexless skeletons; the verbs dichotomized and feebly tottering—while behind them, arrogant, overfed, roseate, spilling over the triumphal car, would be the company of nouns in Roman togas and Greek chitons, adorned with laurel branches and flowering hegemonies.

Discussing Ideas and Themes

1. What characterizes Socspeak? Do you recognize any of these characteristics in your own prose? Have you encountered them anywhere else?
2. Do novelists use more or less Latin than sociologists, according to Cowley? Why?
3. What distinction does Cowley make between vocabulary and grammar? Give examples of each from Cowley's essay.
4. What is a "neologism"? Can you find any in Cowley's prose?

Discussing Rhetoric and Style

1. Consider the diction of the title. What makes it so funny? Can you translate it into lay language?
2. How effective are Cowley's "translations" of Socspeak into lay talk? Can you translate one of his sentences into Socspeak? What changes do you have to make to do it?
3. How does Cowley's editing of Green's text affect you?
4. Locate some of Cowley's spicier prose moments—similes, analogies, jokes. Would you expect to find these in a sociology book? What would be the effect if you did?
5. Is Cowley's last paragraph necessary? Does it achieve what the Greeks called *peroration* (a climactic conclusion)? Do you enjoy his "allegory" of personified grammar?

Ideas for Writing

1. Analyze Cowley's vocabulary and grammar, paying careful attention to dictions, parts of speech, and etymology (Latin, Anglo-Saxon, and so on). One good way to start doing this analysis is to list nouns, dividing your list into words of one or two syllables versus words of more than two syllables (the longest words will generally have Latin roots). Then look at the sentence structure in two or three of Cowley's paragraphs; does he write simple sentences or complex ones? Are his verbs active or passive? How many adverbs and adjectives does he typically use in a paragraph? Once you have done all these exercises, write a

short paper comparing and contrasting Cowley's prose and Socspeak.

2. Choose any field other than sociology (such as literary criticism, psychology, or anthropology), and find in the library an article written by and for people in this field. Then write an essay in which you do a close stylistic analysis of the causes and effects of this field's jargon. Try when you can to imitate Cowley's method, translating the words when you can to show how and why you think they are unnecessary.

Why Good English Is Good for You

JOHN SIMON

John Simon, theater reviewer for New York *magazine as well as a former columnist for* Esquire, *is well known for his witty pieces on the uses and abuses of language. In the following essay, excerpted from the collection* Paradigms Lost: Reflections on Literacy and Its Decline *(1980), Simon considers the hot debate that now surrounds the use of "Standard" English: Can standardized punctuation, spelling, and usage help to narrow communication gaps among English speakers? Can "Standard" English benefit its disciple? Simon thinks it can; according to him, sloppy language is often the sign of a sloppy mind, whereas disciplined use of language can lead to lifelong discipline, a quality he finds hopelessly lacking today in young students of the language.*

What's good English to you that . . . you should grieve for it? What good is correct speech and writing, you may ask, in an age in which hardly anyone seems to know, and no one seems to care? Why shouldn't you just fling bloopers, bloopers riotously with the throng, and not stick out from the rest like a sore thumb by using the language correctly? Isn't grammar really a thing of the past, and isn't the new idea to communicate in *any* way as long as you can make yourself understood?

The usual, basic defense of good English (and here, again, let us not worry about nomenclature—for all I care, you may call it "Standard English," "correct American," or anything else) is that it helps communication, that it is perhaps even a *sine qua non* of mutual understanding. Although this is a crude truth of sorts, it strikes me as, in some ways, both more and less than the truth. Suppose you say,

"Everyone in their right mind would cross on the green light" or "Hopefully, it won't rain tomorrow," chances are very good that the person you say this to will understand you, even though you are committing obvious solecisms or creating needless ambiguities. Similarly, if you write in a letter, "The baby has finally ceased it's howling" (spelling *its* as *it's*), the recipient will be able to figure out what was meant. But "figuring out" is precisely what a listener or reader should not have to do. There is, of course, the fundamental matter of courtesy to the other person, but it goes beyond that: Why waste time on unscrambling simple meaning when there are more complex questions that should receive our undivided attention? If the many cooks had to worry first about which out of a large number of pots had no leak in it, the broth, whether spoiled or not, would take forever to be ready.

It is, I repeat, only initially a matter of clarity. It is also a matter of concision. Space today is as limited as time. If you have only a thousand words in which to convey an important message it helps to know that "overcomplicated" is correct and "overly complicated" is incorrect. Never mind the grammatical explanations; the two extra characters and one space between words are reason enough. But what about the more advanced forms of word-mongering that hold sway nowadays? Take redundancy, like the "hopes and aspirations" of Jimmy Carter, quoted by Edwin Newman as having "a deeply profound religious experience"; or elaborate jargon, as when Charles G. Walcutt, a graduate professor of English at CUNY, writes (again as quoted by Newman): "The colleges, trying to remediate increasing numbers of . . . illiterates up to college levels, are being highschoolized"; or just obfuscatory verbiage of the pretentious sort, such as this fragment from a letter I received: "It is my impression that effective interpersonal verbal communication depends on prior effective intrapersonal verbal communication." What this means is that if you think clearly, you can speak and write clearly—except if you are a "certified speech and language pathologist," like the writer of the letter I quote. (By the way, she adds the letters Ph.D. after her name, though she is not even from Germany, where *Herr* and *Frau Doktor* are in common, not to say vulgar, use.)

But except for her ghastly verbiage, our certified language pathologist (whatever that means) is perfectly right: there is a close connection between the ability to think and the ability to use English correctly. After all, we think in words, we conceptualize in words, we work out our problems inwardly with words, and using them correctly is comparable to a craftsman's treating his tools with care, keeping his materials in good shape. Would you trust a weaver who hangs her wet laundry on her loom, or lets her cats bed down in her yarn? The person who does not respect words and their proper relationships cannot have much respect for ideas—very possibly cannot have ideas at all. My quarrel is not so much with minor errors that we all fall into from time to time even if we know better as it is with basic sloppiness or ignorance or defiance of good English.

Training yourself to speak and write correctly—and I say "training yourself" because nowadays, unfortunately, you cannot depend on other people or on institutions to give you the proper training, for reasons I shall discuss later—training yourself, then, in language, means developing at the very least two extremely useful faculties: your sense of discipline and your memory. Discipline because language is with us always, as nothing else is: it follows us much as, in the old morality play, Good Deeds followed Everyman, all the way to the grave; and, if the language is written, even beyond. Let me explain: if you can keep an orderly apartment, if you can see to it that your correspondence and bill-paying are attended to regularly, if your diet and wardrobe are maintained with the necessary care—good enough; you a disciplined person.

But the preliminary discipline underlying all others is nevertheless your speech: the words that come out of you almost as frequently and—if you are tidy—as regularly as your breath. I would go so far as to say that, immediately after your bodily functions, language is first, unless you happen to be an ascetic, an anchorite, or a stylite; but unless you are a styl*ite*, you had better be a styl*ist*.

Most of us—almost all—must take in and give out language as we do breath, and we had better consider the seriousness of language pollution as second only to air pollution. For the linguistically disciplined, to misuse or mispronounce a word is an unnecessary and unhealthy contribution to the surrounding smog. To have taught ourselves not to do this, or—being human and thus also imperfect—to do it as little as possible, means deriving from every speaking moment the satisfaction we get from a cap that snaps on to a container perfectly, an elevator that stops flush with the landing, a roulette ball that comes to rest exactly on the number on which we have placed our bet. It gives us the pleasure of hearing or seeing our words—because they are abiding by the rules—snapping, sliding, falling precisely into place, expressing with perfect lucidity and symmetry just what we wanted them to express. This is comparable to the satisfaction of the athlete or ballet dancer or pianist finding his body or legs or fingers doing his bidding with unimpeachable accuracy.

And if someone now says that "in George Eliot's lesser novels, she is not completely in command" is perfectly comprehensible even if it is ungrammatical, the "she" having no antecedent in the nominative (*Eliot's* is a genitive), I say, "Comprehensible, perhaps, but lopsided," for the civilized and orderly mind does not feel comfortable with that "she"—does not hear that desired and satisfying click of correctness—unless the sentence is restructured as "George Eliot, in her lesser novels, is not . . ." or in some similar way. In fact, the fully literate ear can be thrown by this error in syntax; it may look for the antecedent of that "she" elsewhere than in the preceding possessive case. Be that as it may, playing without rules and winning—in this instance, managing to communicate without using good English—is no more satisfactory than winning in a sport or game by accident or by disregarding the rules: which is really cheating.

The second faculty good speech develops is, as I have mentioned before, our memory. Grammar and syntax are partly logical—and to that extent they are also good exercisers and developers of our logical faculty—but they are also partly arbitrary, conventional, irrational. For example, the correct "compared to" and "contrasted with" could, from the logical point of view, just as well be "contrasted to" and "compared with" ("compared with," of course, is correct, but in a different sense from the one that concerns us here, namely, the antithesis of "contrasted with"). And, apropos *different,* logic would have to strain desperately to explain the exclusive correctness of "different from," given the exclusive correctness of "other than," which would seem to justify "different than," jarring though that is to the cultivated ear.

But there it is: some things are so because tradition, usage, the best speakers and writers, the grammar books and dictionaries have made them so. There may even exist some hidden historical explanation: something, perhaps, in the Sanskrit, Greek, Latin, or other origins of a word or construction that you and I may very easily never know. We can, however, memorize; and memorization can be a wonderfully useful thing—surely the Greeks were right to consider Mnemosyne (memory) the mother of the Muses, for without her there would be no art and no science. And what better place to practice one's mnemonic skills than in the study of one's language?

There is something particularly useful about speaking correctly and precisely because language is always there as a foundation—or, if you prefer a more fluid image, an undercurrent—beneath what is going on. Now, it seems to me that the great difficulty of life lies in the fact that we must almost always do two things at a time. If, for example, we are walking and conversing, we must keep our mouths as well as feet from stumbling. If we are driving while listening to music, we must not allow the siren song of the cassette to prevent us from watching the road and the speedometer (otherwise the less endearing siren of the police car or the ambulance will follow apace). Well, it is just this sort of bifurcation of attention that care for precise, clear expression fosters in us. By learning early in life to pay attention both to what we are saying and to how we are saying it, we develop the much-needed life skill of doing two things simultaneously.

Put another way, we foster our awareness of, and ability to deal with, form and content. If there is any verity that modern criticism has fought for, it is the recognition of the indissolubility of content and form. Criticism won the battle, won it so resoundingly that this oneness has become a contemporary commonplace. And shall the fact that form *is* content be a platitude in all the arts but go unrecognized in the art of self-expression, whether in conversation or correspondence, or whatever form of spoken or written utterance a human being resorts to? Accordingly, you are going to be judged, whether you like it or not, by the correctness of your English as much as by the correctness of your thinking; there are some people to whose ear bad English is as offensive as gibberish, or as your picking your nose in public would be to their eyes and stomachs. The fact that people of linguistic sensibilities may be a dying breed does not mean that they are wholly extinct, and it is best not to take any unnecessary chances.

To be sure, if you are a member of a currently favored minority, many of your linguistic failings may be forgiven you—whether rightly or wrongly is not my concern here. But if you cannot change your sex or color to the one that is getting preferential treatment—Bakke case or no Bakke case—you might as well learn good English and profit by it in your career, your social relations, perhaps even in your basic self-confidence. That, if you will, is the ultimate practical application of good English; but now let me tell you about the ultimate impractical one, which strikes me as being possibly even more important.

Somewhere in the prose writings of Charles Péguy, who was a very fine poet and prose writer—and, what is perhaps even more remarkable, as good a human being as he was an artist—somewhere in those writings is a passage about the decline of pride in workmanship among French artisans, which, as you can deduce, set in even before World War I, wherein Péguy was killed. In the passage I refer to, Péguy bemoans the fact that cabinetmakers no longer finish the backs of furniture—the sides that go against the wall—in the same way as they do the exposed sides. What is not seen was just as important to the old artisans as what is seen—it was a moral issue with them. And so, I think, it ought to be with language. Even if no one else notices the niceties, the precision, the impeccable sense of grammar and syntax you deploy in your utterances, you yourself should be aware of them and take pride in them as in pieces of work well done.

Now, I realize that there are two possible reactions among you to what I have said up to this point. Some of you will say to yourselves: what utter nonsense! Language is a flexible, changing, living organism that belongs to the people who speak it. It has always been changed according to the ways in which people chose to speak it, and the dictionaries and books on grammar had to, and will have to, adjust themselves to the people and not the other way around. For isn't it the glory of language that it keeps throwing up new inventions as surf tosses out differently polished pebbles and bits of bottle glass onto the shore, and that in this inexhaustible variety, in this refusal to kowtow to dry-as-dust scholars, lies its vitality, its beauty?

Others among you, perhaps fewer in number, will say to yourselves: quite so, there is such a thing as Standard English, or purity of speech, or correctness of expression—something worth safeguarding and fostering; but how the devil is one to accomplish that under the prevailing conditions: in a democratic society full of minorities that have their own dialects or linguistic preferences, and in a world in which television, advertising, and other mass media manage daily to corrupt the language a little further? Let me try to answer the first group first, and then come back to the questions of the second.

Of course language is, and must be, a living organism to the extent that new inventions, discoveries, ideas enter the scene and clamor rightfully for designations. Political, social, and psychological changes may also affect our mode of expression, and new words or phrases may have to be found to reflect what we might call historical changes. It is also quite natural for slang terms to be invented, become popular, and, in some cases, remain permanently in the language. It is perhaps equally inevitable (though here we are on more speculative ground) for certain words to become obsolescent and obsolete, and drop out of the language. But does that mean that grammar and syntax have to keep changing, that pronunciations and meanings of words must shift, that more complex or elegant forms are obliged to yield to simpler or cruder ones that often are not fully synonymous with them and not capable of expressing certain fine distinctions? Should, for instance, "terrestrial" disappear entirely in favor of "earthly," or are there shades of meaning involved that need to remain available to us? Must we sacrifice "notwithstanding" because we have "in spite of" or "despite"? Need we forfeit "jettison" just because we have "throw overboard"? And what about "disinterested," which is becoming a synonym for "uninterested," even though that means something else, and though we have no other word for "disinterested"?

"Language has *always* changed," say these people, and they might with equal justice say that there has always been war or sickness or insanity. But the truth is that some sicknesses that formerly killed millions have been eliminated, that some so-called insanity can today be treated, and that just because there have always been wars does not mean that someday a cure cannot be found even for that scourge. And if it cannot, it is only by striving to put an absolute end to war, by pretending that it can be licked, that we can at least partly control it. Without such assumptions and efforts, the evil would be so widespread that, given our current weaponry, we would no longer be here to worry about the future of language.

But we are here, and having evolved linguistically this far, and having the means—books of grammar, dictionaries, education for all—to arrest unnecessary change, why not endeavor with might and mind to arrest it? Certain cataclysms cannot be prevented: earthquakes and droughts, for example, can scarcely, if at all, be controlled; but we can prevent floods, for which purpose we have invented dams. And dams are precisely what we can construct to prevent floods of ignorance from eroding our language, and, beyond that, to provide irrigation for areas that would otherwise remain linguistically arid.

For consider that what some people are pleased to call linguistic evolution was almost always a matter of ignorance prevailing over knowledge. There is no valid reason, for example, for the word *nice* to have changed its meaning so many times—except ignorance of its exact definition. Had the change never occurred, or had it been stopped at any intermediate stage, we would have had just as good a word as we have now and saved some people a heap of confusion along the way. But if *nice* means what it does today—and it has two principal meanings, one of them, as in "nice distinction," alas, obsolescent—let us, for heaven's sake, keep it where it is, now that we have the means with which to hold it there.

If, for instance, we lose the accusative case *whom*—and we are in great danger of losing it—our language will be the poorer for it. Obviously, "The man, whom I had never known, was a thief" means something other than "The man who I had never known was a thief." Now, you can object that it would be just as easy in the first instance to use some other construction; but what happens if *this* one is used incorrectly? Ambiguity and confusion. And why should we lose this useful distinction? Just because a million or ten million or a billion people less educated than we are cannot master the difference? Surely it behooves us to try to educate the ignorant up to our level rather than to stultify ourselves down to theirs. Yes, you say, but suppose they refuse to or are unable to learn? In that case, I say, there is a doubly good reason for not going along with them. Ah, you reply, but they are the majority, and we must accept their way or, if the revolution is merely linguistic, lose our "credibility" (as the current parlance, rather confusingly, has it) or, if the revolution is political, lose our heads. Well, I consider a sufficient number of people to be educable enough to be capable of using *who* and *whom* correctly, and to derive satisfaction from this capability—a sufficient number, I mean, to enable us to preserve *whom,* and not to have to ask "for who the bell tolls."

The main problem with education, actually, is not those who need it and cannot get it, but those who should impart it and, for various reasons, do not. In short, the enemies of education are the educators themselves: miseducated, underpaid, overburdened, and intimidated teachers (frightened because, though the pen is supposed to be mightier than the sword, the switchblade is surely more powerful than the ferrule), and professors who—because they are structural linguists, democratic respecters of alleged minority rights, or otherwise misguided folk—believe in the sacrosanct privilege of any culturally underprivileged minority or majority to dictate its ignorance to the rest of the world. For, I submit, an English improvised by slaves and other strangers to the culture—to whom my heart goes out in every human way—under dreadfully deprived conditions can nowise equal an English that the best literary and linguistic talents have, over the centuries, perceptively and painstakingly brought to a high level of excellence.

So my answer to the scoffers in this or any audience is, in simplest terms, the following: contrary to popular misconception, language does not belong to the people, or at least not in the sense in which *belong* is usually construed. For things can rightfully belong only to those who invent or earn them. But we do not know who invented language: is it the people who first made up the words for *father* and *mother,* for *I* and *thou,* for *hand* and *foot;* or is it the people who evolved the subtler shadings of language, its poetic variety and suggestiveness, but also its unambiguousness, its accurate and telling details? Those are two very different groups of people and two very different languages, and I, as you must have guessed by now, consider the latter group at least as important as the former. As for *earning* language, it has surely been earned by those who have striven to learn it properly, and here even economic and social circumstances are but an imperfect excuse for bad usage; history is full of examples of people rising from humble origins to learn, against all kinds of odds, to speak and write correctly—even brilliantly.

Belong, then, should be construed in the sense that parks, national forests, monuments, and public utilities are said to belong to the people: available for properly respectful use but not for defacement and destruction. And all that we propose to teach is how to use and enjoy the gardens of language to their utmost aesthetic and salubrious potential. Still, I must now address myself to the group that, while agreeing with my aims, despairs of finding practical methods for their implementation.

True enough, after a certain age speakers not aware of Standard

English or not exceptionally gifted will find it hard or impossible to change their ways. Nevertheless, if there were available funds for advanced methods in teaching; if teachers themselves were better trained and paid, and had smaller classes and more assistants; if, furthermore, college entrance requirements were heightened and the motivation of students accordingly strengthened; if there were no structural linguists and National Councils of Teachers of English filling instructors' heads with notions about "Students' Rights to Their Own Language" (they have every right to it as a *second* language, but none as a *first*); if teachers in all disciplines, including the sciences and social sciences, graded on English usage as well as on specific proficiencies; if aptitude tests for various jobs stressed good English more than they do; and, above all, if parents were better educated and more aware of the need to set a good example to their children, and to encourage them to learn correct usage, the situation could improve enormously.

Clearly, to expect all this to come to pass is utopian; some of it, however, is well within the realm of possibility. For example, even if parents do not speak very good English, many of them at least can manage an English that is good enough to correct a very young child's mistakes; in other words, most adults can speak a good enough four-year-old's idiom. They would thus start kids out on the right path; the rest could be done by the schools.

But the problem is what to do in the most underprivileged homes: those of blacks, Hispanics, immigrants from various Asian and European countries. This is where day-care centers could come in. If the fathers and mothers could be gainfully employed, their small children would be looked after by day-care centers where—is this asking too much?—good English could be inculcated in them. The difficulty, of course, is what to do about the discrepancy the little ones would note between the speech of the day-care people and that of their parents. Now, it seems to me that small children have a far greater ability to learn things, including languages, than some people give them credit for. Much of it is indeed rote learning, but, where languages are concerned, that is one of the basic learning methods even for adults. There is no reason for not teaching kids another language, to wit, Standard English, and turning this, if desirable, into a game: "At home you speak one way; here we have another language," at which point the instructor can make up names and explanations for Standard English that would appeal to pupils of that particular place, time, and background.

At this stage of the game, as well as later on in school, care should be exercised to avoid insulting the language spoken in the youngsters' homes. There must be ways to convey that both home and school languages have their validity and uses and that knowing both enables one to accomplish more in life. This would be hard to achieve if the children's parents were, say, militant blacks of the Geneva Smitherman sort, who execrate Standard English as a weapon of capitalist oppression against the poor of all races, colors, and religions. But, happily, there is evidence that most black, Hispanic, and other non-Standard English-speaking parents want their children to learn correct English so as to get ahead in the world.

Yet how do we defend ourselves against the charge that we are old fogeys who cannot emotionally adjust to the new directions an ever-living and changing language must inevitably take? Here I would want to redefine or, at any rate, clarify, what "living and changing" means, and also explain where we old fogeys stand. Misinformed attacks on Old Fogeydom, I have noticed, invariably represent us as people who shudder at a split infinitive and would sooner kill or be killed than tolerate a sentence that ends with a preposition. Actually, despite all my travels through Old Fogeydom, I have yet to meet one inhabitant who would not stick a preposition onto the tail of a sentence; as for splitting infinitives, most of us O.F.'s are perfectly willing to do that, too, but tactfully and sparingly, where it feels right. There is no earthly reason, for example, for saying "to dangerously live," when "to live dangerously" sounds so much better; but it does seem right to say (and write) "What a delight to sweetly breathe in your sleeping lover's breath"; that sounds smoother, indeed sweeter, than "to breathe in sweetly" or "sweetly to breathe in." But infinitives begging to be split are relatively rare; a sensitive ear, a good eye for shades of meaning will alert you whenever the need to split arises; without that ear and eye, you had better stick to the rules.

About the sense in which language is, and must be, alive, let me speak while donning another of my several hats—actually it is not a hat but a cap, for there exists in Greenwich Village an inscription on a factory that reads "CRITIC CAPS." So with my drama critic's cap on, let me present you with an analogy. The world theater today is full of directors who wreak havoc on classic plays to demonstrate their own ingenuity, their superiority, as it were, to the author. These directors—aborted playwrights, for the most part—will stage productions of *Hamlet* in which the prince is a woman, a flaming homosexual, or a one-eyed hunchback.

Well, it seems to me that the same spirit prevails in our approach to linguistics, with every newfangled, ill-informed, know-nothing construction, definition, pronunciation enshrined by the joint efforts of structural linguists, permissive dictionaries, and allegedly democratic but actually demagogic educators. What really makes a production of, say, *Hamlet* different, and therefore alive, is that the director, while trying to get as faithfully as possible at Shakespeare's meanings, nevertheless ends up stressing things in the play that strike him most forcefully; and the same individuality in production design and performances (the Hamlet of Gielgud versus the Hamlet of Olivier, for instance—what a world of difference!) further differentiates one production from another, and bestows on each its particular vitality. So, too, language remains alive because each speaker (or writer) can and must, *within the framework of accepted grammar, syntax, and pronunciation,* produce a style that is his very own, that is as personal as his posture, way of walking, mode of dress, and so on. It is such stylistic differences that make a person's—or a nation's—language flavorous, pungent, alive, and all this without having to play fast and loose with the existing rules.

But to have this, we need, among other things, good teachers and, beyond them, enlightened educators. I shudder when I read in the *Birmingham* (Alabama) *Post-Herald* of October 6, 1978, an account of a talk given to eight hundred English teachers by Dr. Alan C. Purves, vice-president of the National Council of Teachers of English. Dr. Purves is quoted as saying things like "We are in a situation with respect to reading where . . . ," and culminating in the following truly horrifying sentence: "I am going to suggest that when we go back to the basics, I think what we should be dealing with is our charge to help students to be more proficient in producing meaningful language—language that says what it means." Notice all the deadwood, the tautology, the anacoluthon in the first part of that sentence; but notice especially the absurdity of the latter part, in which the dubious word "meaningful"—a poor relation of "significant"—is thought to require explaining to an audience of English teachers.

Given such leadership from the N.C.T.E., the time must be at hand when we shall hear—not just "Don't ask for who the bell rings" (*ask not* and *tolls* being, of course, archaic, elitist language), but also "It rings for you and I."

Discussing Ideas and Themes

1. Answer the title's implied question: Why is good English good for you?
2. Simon comments in his fourth paragraph that "there is a close connection between the ability to think and the ability to use English correctly." Does Simon support this assertion with examples, and, if so, what are they? Can you think of an argument for the other side?
3. What does Simon think are the "ultimate practical" and "imprac-

tical" applications of good English? Do you agree? Why or why not?

4. Simon makes a powerful case for "good English," but is his argument always persuasive? For example, Simon suggests that "redundancy" is a form of "word mongering." When might "redundancy" be a virtue in prose or speech?

Discussing Rhetoric and Style

1. Simon opens with a rhetorical question and proceeds throughout the essay to use this technique. Why might this technique be particularly appropriate to his casual, often sardonic tone? That is, what is the tone of most rhetorical questions, and how does that tone match the overall tone of the essay?
2. Simon's method of proving his point often includes token consideration of both sides of the argument. Find an example of this technique in the essay, and then study it closely. Is it an effective tactic? An honest one? Before deciding, try it on your own: Write a few paragraphs on why Simon's essay is either good or bad, carefully providing both sides of the argument but clearly siding with only one.
3. What did you think of Simon's treatment of the speech pathologist's letter? How does he express his dislike for her? Does he object to the content or to the tone of her letter? Did you object at all to the content or tone of his response?
4. Simon uses a traditional analogy, comparing writers to craftsmen. Find the analogy, and then look for others like it in the essay. At what moments in Simon's prose do these analogies pop up? Can you identify a pattern in when and why they appear? Explain.
5. Consider the range of Simon's examples—Jimmy Carter, George Eliot, Charles Péguy, Shakespeare, the NCTE, and so on. Why is such a broad range helpful in an essay like this one? What does it establish about the speaker's character?

Ideas for Writing

1. James Kilpatrick ("Out-of-Town Words") might say that Simon's position on language is snobbish and elitist. Write a brief essay on why Simon is or is not a snob.

2. What does Simon seem to believe about the power and uses of language? How do his ideas about language differ from those of Kilpatrick? Write an essay in which you compare and contrast Kilpatrick's approach to language and Simon's approach. Do these two essayists ever agree?

The Definition and Determination of "Correct" English

ROBERT C. POOLEY

Born in 1898 in Brooklyn, NY, Robert C. Pooley led a distinguished career in education, teaching English at several universities around the country as well as serving as a civilian specialist in teaching and training techniques for the army's pre-induction training unit. An authority on the English language, Pooley wrote Teaching English Usage *and* Teaching English Grammar. *In the following essay, Pooley argues that "in establishing the laws of language, our personal desires, preferences, and prejudices must give way to the scientific determination and interpretation of the facts of language." In following this empirical thread, Pooley goes on to determine and classify several "levels" of present usage—the illiterate, the homely, the informal, the formal, and the literary. Knowing these levels, he suggests, can help guide us all in knowing the right thing to say at the right time. The essay first appeared in* Teaching English Usage *(1946). Pooley died in 1978.*

In the year 1712 Dean Swift wrote a letter to the Earl of Oxford outlining a plan for the foundation of an English academy similar to the French Academy for the purpose of regularizing and establishing correct English. Although his plan was received with interest, it was never acted upon, and many later attempts to found an academy have failed. The purists of the later eighteenth century did much of what Swift desired, but fortunately for the life and vigor of our tongue it has never been submitted to the restraint of a board of authorities. Several theories of "correctness" in English have therefore been formulated and have influenced writers and teachers of the past and present. One of the most important of these theories was that enunciated by George Campbell in 1776, that "correctness" rests in good custom, defined as "national," "reputable," and "present." This definition was accepted by practically all the nineteenth-century grammarians (although they frequently did it violence in specific instances), and may be found in a number of the high-school composition books of the present day. Another theory, really a modification of Campbell's, proposed by Fitzedward Hall and other nineteenth-century students of language, is that "good usage is the usage of the best writers and speakers." This definition is also very widely used in the textbooks of today, and is probably the expressed or implied standard of good English in almost every American school room. Both of these definitions, useful as they have been and are, present many difficulties in application to the teaching of current usage.

The chief difficulty lies in the interpretation of the terms "reputable" and "the best writers and speakers." For example, nearly all grammar books list as undesirable English the use of the split infinitive, the dangling participle or gerund, the possessive case of the noun with inanimate objects, the objective case of the pronoun with the gerund, the use of *whose* as a neuter relative pronoun, and many others; yet all of these uses may be found in the authors who form the very backbone of English literature and who are "reputable" and the "best writers" in every sense of the words. If the standard-makers defy the standards, to whom shall we turn for authority? Moreover, the use of literary models tends to ignore the canon of *present* usage, for by the time an author has come to be generally recognized as *standard* his usage is no longer *present*. And among present speakers, who are best? The writer has heard a large number of the most prominent platform speakers of the day, yet he has still to hear one who did not in some manner violate the rules of the books. Are all great writers and speakers at fault, or is it possible that the rules are inaccurate?

The way out of this perplexity is to shift the search for standards away from "authorities" and traditional rules to the language itself as it is spoken and written today. Just as the chemist draws his deductions from the results of laboratory experiments, the biologist from his observation of forms of life, and the astronomer from his telescope, so must students of language draw their deductions from an observation of the facts of language. In establishing the laws of language, our personal desires, preferences, and prejudices must give way to the scientific determination and interpretation of the facts of language. What language we use ourselves may take any form we desire, but the making of rules and the teaching of rules must rest upon objective facts. We must take the attitude of a distinguished scholar who said recently of *due to,* "I don't like it, but there is no doubt about its establishment in English."

If we discard the authority of rules and of "reputable" writers, to what can we turn for a definition of "correct" English? At the outset it must be acknowledged that there can be no absolute, positive definition. "Correct English" is an approximate term used to describe a series of evaluations of usage dependent upon appropriateness, locality, social level, purpose, and other variables. It is a relative term, in decided contrast with the positive nature of (1) *reputability,* the determination of good usage by reference to standard authors; (2) *preservation,* the obligation to defend and maintain language uses because they are traditional, or are felt to be more elegant; (3) *literary,* the identification of good usage with formal literary usage. By discarding these traditional conceptions, and turning to the language itself as its own standard of good usage, we may find the following definition adequate for our present needs. *Good English is that form of speech which is appropriate to the purpose of the speaker, true to the language as it is, and comfortable to speaker and listener. It is the product of custom, neither cramped by rule nor freed from all restraint; it is never fixed, but changes with the organic life of the language.*

Such a definition is linguistically sound because it recognizes the living, organic nature of language; it is historically sound, for the language of the present is seen to be the product of established custom; it is socially sound in recognizing the purpose of language and its social acceptability in *comfort* to speaker and writer.

Teachers of English will recognize that the acceptance of this or a similar definition of good English necessitates great changes in the presentation of usage in textbooks and in the classroom. Those who are accustomed to rule and authority, to an absolute right and wrong in language, will find great difficulty in making the mental readjustment imperative for a relative rather than an absolute standard of usage. Much of the conventional teaching of grammar and correctness will have to be vastly modified or discarded. There will be much confusion and some distress. But eventually, there will grow up in the schools a new theory of good English so closely knit with the language itself that the perplexity now arising from the discrepancies between rule and usage will no longer have cause for existence. But in discarding an absolute right and wrong for a relative standard of appropriateness and social acceptability, we shall have to determine the areas or levels of language usage, to define and illustrate them, and to apply them as standards for the written and spoken English in the schools. . . .

It is obvious that when such terms as *appropriate, customary, comfortable,* or *socially desirable* are used in defining the nature of good English usage, the conception of a single standard or level of correctness can no longer prevail. Speech is a form of human behavior, and like all forms of human behavior, is subject to almost infinite variety. But in even the most primitive societies human behavior is made subject to certain restraints, determined and maintained by the social group. Some of these are fundamental, essential to the life of the group, like the prohibition of murder; others are ceremonial in character, applying to all members of the group at certain times, or to some members of the group at all times. In somewhat similar fashion language usages are subjected to the restraints of society. At all times those who speak a language are required to keep within the limits of intelligibility in order to be understood; language which departs from custom so far as to be incomprehensible defeats its own purpose. But in addition to fundamental understanding there are ceremonial distinctions in language to be found in the most primitive societies; the language of the council fire or religious observance differs in vocabulary and tone from that of the hunt or the harvest. In civilized societies the same principle prevails, except that greater complexity of life calls forth a wider range of differentiations in usage. It will cause no surprise upon reflection to realize that we all more or less unconsciously distinguish three or more gradations or levels in our language usage; there is the informal intimate speech of the home and of our hours of recreation; the slightly restrained speech of semi-public occasions, like conversation with strangers; and the carefully chosen, deliberate language of public address on formal occasions. Each of these has its analogue in writing. Moreover, business and professional people are very apt to employ a technical vocabulary among their colleagues, sometimes almost incomprehensible to the uninitiated. It seems beyond doubt reasonable, therefore, that this differentiation of language usage, a fundamental law of language, should be our first consideration in the study of "correct" English and in the presentation of English usage in the classroom. The purpose of this chapter is to define and illustrate the levels of English usage and to point out their relative values in the social group.

THE ILLITERATE LEVEL

The words and phrases typical of this level of English usage mark the user as belonging definitely outside the pale of cultivated, educated society. They have no standing whatever in literature, except in the dialect conversation of characters deliberately portrayed as illiterate or uncultivated. Although comparatively few in number, they are widespread and extremely common in the speech of the uneducated. They cannot be tolerated in the classroom except in deliberate attempts to reproduce the conversation of illiterate characters.

Examples

If I had *of* come, he wouldn't *of* done it.

I got the measles *off* Jimmie.

He *give* me the book. (past tense)

They *was*, we *was*, you *was*

I *is*, you *is*, they *is*, them *is*

He *come, done, seen, run,* etc.

Have went, have came, have did, have saw, have ran, have drank, etc.

The double negative, as in: *didn't have no, won't never, can't never, couldn't get no,* etc.

Them books

Youse

I *ain't*, you *ain't*, etc.

Growed, knowed, blowed, seed, etc.

That there, this here

He looked at me and *says*

Leave me to do it.

He did *noble, good, swell,* etc.

THE HOMELY LEVEL

The words and phrases typical of this level are outside the limits of standard, cultivated usage, yet are not completely illiterate. They characterize the speech of many worthy men and women with some claim to literacy, who by the accident of birth, occupation, or geographical location are denied the society of more cultivated persons. The children in many of our rural schools come from homes in which the parents speak the English of this level. It behooves the teacher, therefore, to have an understanding sympathy for this type of speech, and while zealously seeking to build up in the children a dialect more closely approaching standard English, to refrain from ridiculing the speech of the home or from characterizing it unreservedly as "bad English." Tactful understanding will do far more than rigid purism in creating among these children a respect for the more standard forms of speech and a desire to attain a higher standard of usage.

Examples

He *don't* come here any more.

I *expect* you're hungry.

Stop the bus; I *want out.*

Mary's mother, *she* isn't very smart.

I *got* an apple right here in my hand.

I *haven't hardly* time.

We *can't scarcely* do it.

Just where are we *at?*

He *begun, sung, drunk, eat,* etc.

The various forms of confusion in *lie* and *lay, sit* and *set, rise* and *raise.*

I *want for* you to do it.

The dessert was made with *whip cream.*

He comes *of a Sunday.*

John *was raised* in Kentucky.

This is *all the farther* we can go.

Calculate (or cal'late, reckon) for *guess, suppose*

A light-*complected* girl

Hadn't he ought to do it?

To this homely level of English speech belong also the local dialect uses not generally recognized over the United States, like the *to home,* for *at home,* of New England; the *admire* for *like* of the South; the *loco* for *crazy* of the West; and the characteristic idioms of the mountaineers in the Blue Ridge and Ozark ranges.

STANDARD ENGLISH, INFORMAL LEVEL

The range of standard English is necessarily very wide. It must include all the words, phrases, forms, and idioms employed by the great mass of English-speaking people in the United States whose dialect lies between the homely level and the decidedly literary level. It must be wide enough to include the variations of language usage common among people of education; the speech of the home, of the hours of business and recreation, as well as that of the party and formal reception. In written form it must include the most informal of personal correspondence to the formal phrasing of the business and social note. Standard English is, in fact, *the language;* it is present, ordinary, comfortable usage, with sufficient breadth in limits to permit the shades of difference appropriate to specific occasions.

The informal level of standard English includes words and phrases commonly used by people of culture and education in their more informal moments, but which are generally excluded from formal public address, social conversation with strangers, and formal social correspondence. Informal standard English should be the normal usage of the teacher in the classroom and the goal which is set for the pupils to attain. A large part of the confusion arising from the teaching of usage in schools has been the result of trying to maintain the formal standard dialect, appropriate to careful writing, for the conversational needs of the schoolroom. There is no more need for children to be bookish in their schoolroom speech than for the teacher herself to be bookish in her intimate conversation.

The examples listed here for the informal standard level include only those items which may be employed informally but which are generally excluded from formal standard English.

Examples

He *blamed* the accident on me.

The *picnic* was a failure, *due to* a heavy shower.

No one knows what *transpires* in Washington.

Does anyone know *if* he *was* there?

I have never seen anyone act *like* he does.

His attack on my paper was most *aggravating.*

Most everyone is familiar with this picture.

Where can you get *these kind* of gloves?

We had just two dollars *between* the four of us.

I *can't help but* go to the store.

Who did you send for?

John is the *quickest* of the two.

They were *very pleased* with the new house.

It was *good and cold (nice and warm)* in the room.

I *will try and do* it.

They invited John and *myself.*

Did you *get through with* your work?

As long as you have come, we can start.

STANDARD ENGLISH, FORMAL LEVEL

It is quite in accord with the customs of language usage that "correct" English have considerable variety in range of appropriateness, two levels of which are distinguished in this study by the terms *informal* and *formal* standard English. In general the leading characteristics of the more formal level of standard English are (1) greater restraint in vocabulary, with the avoidance of words distinctly informal in tone; (2) greater attention to formal agreement in number, both in subject-verb and pronoun-antecedent relationships, in tense sequence, and in case-agreement of pronouns; (3) greater attention to word order, particularly with respect to the position of modifying words, phrases, and clauses, and the use of a more complex sentence structure.

In the schoolroom this formal level of standard English should be the goal set for careful theme-writing, especially in what is commonly called the "thought theme," whether expository or argumentative. Narration and the various kinds of informal essays, as well as friendly letters, need not be held to the more exacting requirements of the formal standard level. It is, however, of great importance that children recognize the characteristics of both levels, and are able to use either appropriately.

To this level of English usage belong not only the public speech and formal writing of educated people, but also much of the printed material generally classed as "literature." Writing designed primarily for communication, as for example news articles, editorials, textbooks, and other expository compositions, unless distinctly technical or artistic in aim, employ the usages of the formal standard level.

It is rather difficult to offer many distinctive examples of formal standard usage, inasmuch as it is characterized by a general tone of restraint and care more than by the use of certain expressions. A few examples, however, may be found which are quite typical of the formal standard level.

Examples

I *shall* be glad to help you.

Neither of the parties *was* injured.

Here are three *whom* we have omitted from the list.

I *had rather* stay at home.

We *had* better complete this investigation.

Under the circumstances, he did as well as might be expected.

The use of connectives like *furthermore, notwithstanding, despite, inasmuch as, on the contrary*

THE LITERARY LEVEL

It must be granted at the outset that the definition of the literary level of English usage employed in this study is somewhat arbitrary, and is more narrow in scope than the definitions of many textbooks. But since much of the difficulty in the teaching of English usage centers about the confusion of the terms *literary, standard,* and *correct* English, a most earnest attempt has been made here to differentiate the terms and to clarify their meanings and applications. It is therefore assumed that what is commonly called "correct" English includes the usages of at least three levels: the informal standard, the formal standard, and the literary levels, the correctness of any specific item in any given instance being dependent upon its appropriateness. The first two levels have been defined; it remains to describe the third.

Literary English is taken to mean that form of speech or writing which in aim goes beyond mere utility to achieve beauty. It differs from formal standard English not so much in kind as in purpose and effect. In diction it seeks not only accuracy in meaning but also a subjective quality of suggestion aroused by the sound of the word or the associated ideas and feelings. In form it goes beyond mere orderliness to achieve rhythm, symmetry, and balance. In every respect it surpasses the ordinary prose of communication in the attainment of aesthetic values transcending the needs of everyday expression.

An illustration of the difference between standard formal English and literary English may be seen in the opening sentence of Lincoln's "Gettysburg Address." Had Lincoln said, "Eighty-seven years ago our ancestors established on this continent a new nation, inspired by the spirit of liberty, and actuated by the theory that all men are created equal," he would have met adequately the demands of clear, formal communication. But in his phrasing, "Four score and seven years ago, our fathers brought forth on this continent a new nation, conceived in liberty, and dedicated to the proposition that all men are created equal," there are to be found those characteristics of the literary style which transcend communication. The literary tone of *four score and seven, fathers, dedicated to the proposition* is at once apparent; the associations awakened by the words *brought forth, conceived,* and *dedicated* give them emotional depths unsounded by *established, inspired,* or *actuated;* moreover, the sentence as a whole moves with an effect of solemnity achieved only by the happy arrangement of accents and the sonorous quality of the vowels employed. These qualities combine to make this sentence artistic, literary prose of the highest order.

It is obvious that the literary level cannot be made a requirement for all students in schoolroom composition. It is too much the product of mental maturity and highly developed skill to be attainable by the average student, or indeed, by the average teacher. Therefore, while examples of beautiful prose should be given to pupils to study, and the few who are gifted should be encouraged to strive toward the development of a literary tone and style, the great body of school children should be expected to do no more than to cultivate the clear, direct English of communication, together with a feeling for the appropriateness of word and idiom to the purpose intended. Students in whom these perceptions have been engendered will always use "correct," adequate English.

Discussing Ideas and Themes

1. What is Pooley's definition of "correct" English? Is it what you expected? Do you agree with it? Why or why not?
2. How does Pooley historicize his argument from the very start? What moments in history does he see as most important to "the definition and determination of 'correct' English"? Explain.
3. Why does Pooley think "correct" English is a relative concept? Compare his ideas about the relativity of language with James Baldwin's ("If Black English Isn't a Language . . ."). What does each writer say about the need for open-mindedness in the speakers and classifiers of the English language?
4. Reread the third paragraph of Pooley's essay. What does he think determines the use of language? What examples does he give to support his idea? Are they persuasive?
4. Name the levels Pooley outlines here, and give an example of each. Why does he think this kind of distinction is helpful? Can you think of any levels he has left out?

Discussing Rhetoric and Style

1. Why is Pooley's opening paragraph effective? What audience does it appeal to? What sources does he draw on to attract this audience?
2. Pooley, always the empiricist, makes an extended analogy between the "facts of language" and scientific facts. How well does the analogy hold up? Can you think of any big differences between these two kinds of "facts"? What are they?

3. Can you hear Pooley's voice in this essay? What is his tone? Do you think this is just a speaking voice or a real personality? Explain.

4. Did you enjoy Pooley's examples? What did they add to the essay? Were they better than the examples you have found in usage handbooks? Why or why not?

5. Take one of Pooley's sentences, and rewrite it according to his classification of the "levels" of language. That is, rewrite it at the illiterate, homely, informal, formal, and literary levels. Are the distinctions between these levels clearer to you after performing this exercise?

Ideas for Writing

1. As does Hayakawa ("How Dictionaries Are Made"), this essayist disputes the absolute value of any authority over the fluid and relative nature of language. Compare and contrast the two essays in a few pages, mentioning similar ideas and the differing techniques each author uses in proving those ideas.

2. Pick one of your favorite writers and examine his usage. Consider his departures from standard usage—punctuation, spelling, split infinitives, and so on. If correct English were to be determined by this writer's prose style, what would be some of the new rules? Write an essay in which you describe your stylistic investigations and then offer conclusions about what is "right" and what seems "good."

STUDENT ESSAY

Meditation
An Argument for My Grade

TRICIA LOUGHRAN

Tricia Loughran, a 1990 graduate of Rutgers University, intends to pursue a graduate degree in English. In 1988, as a student in an upper-level writing course, she was asked at the end of the term to construct an argument for her grade. Her response, rather than straightforwardly answering the question, focuses on another issue, moving away from an argument for a specific grade and toward the more general discussion of the grading system that, Loughran charges, fails to assess real talent and achievement. Is a grade the proper evaluation—or even the proper word for an evaluation—of our experience in school?

Etymologically, the word "grade" comes down to us from the Latin word *gradus*, which once meant "step" and has since derived into our modern day "grade"—a grade, that is, in the sense of a degree or level—and which eventually trickled down into the verb that will allow our professor, in a few days, to "grade" us—to assign a letter which describes what level of excellence we have achieved (or failed to achieve) over the past fourteen weeks.

The etymology is a useful one: it urges us to set aside our concepts of grades as practical (certainly abstract but nonetheless real) quantities and to consider them instead as metaphor: that is, the word grade, coming down from a word which means "step," implies that learning is a staircase, and when our teacher grades us, he looks down from his step far above us and reports to the world what he sees us doing below—some of us loitering down at the bottom of the staircase, others bounding up quickly.

The metaphor is a lovely one (consider the golden handrail, the rich, red carpet decorated with the paisley swirls of this or that idea). It is also, unfortunately, an inaccurate one when applied to the grading system which is used almost universally in higher education today, for our system, even in these enlightened times, remains a crude one, positing learning as a limited number of steps (five to be exact: A, B, C, D, and F).

If we were to take this five-step educational staircase to its literal extreme, we would find it not only stingy (depriving my metaphor of all its grace) but blatantly, logically impossible as well. After all, if there are only five steps, which one does the teacher occupy? It can't be the step labeled "A" because I have received many A's without ever challenging the skills of my teachers. With this in mind, we might suppose, then, that there is an implied step above the "A" step and that this step belongs to the teacher. But this too seems rigid. How could we argue, for instance, that all teachers occupy a single step? This is impossible, for I have been taught by many teachers, some far more gifted than others. In the end, we must recognize that there are many steps above the "A" step, and various teachers occupy various steps. But if this is so, why are these steps closed to the student? There are, after all, those students who eclipse their teachers, even while they are still students, as Wittgenstein, for example, surpassed Bertrand Russell and as Aristotle (some might argue) surpassed Plato. And if such progress is the ultimate goal of the educator—that is, to nurture the student, as Quintilian urged, so that he will eventually become self-sufficient, sharing first his teacher's step and then going on to the next, following the long bead chain of intellectual evolution (and it *is* more of a bead chain than a staircase)—if such progress is the goal of education, then how can we justify the startlingly inaccurate metaphor on which our grading system is based?

When I think about it this way, I find myself perplexed. An "A" seems frighteningly final, leaving me nowhere else to go but down; an "F," on the other hand, would give me room to grow, but I'd probably be kicked out of school before I got the chance to do so. Perhaps the best option is to get a lemon and an old-fashioned quill. An invisible grade: that way I'd never have to know.

Discussing Issues and Themes

1. What is the etymology of "grade"? Why does Loughran consider this etymology "metaphorical"?
2. Why does Loughran criticize the grading system? What are the

faults in this system? Can you think of any others that Loughran omits?

3. What does Loughran suggest is "the ultimate goal of the educator"? How does she support her ideas? Do you agree? Why or why not?
4. In the end, Loughran asks for "an invisible grade." What qualities of grades does she wish to avoid? Why does she want any kind of grade at all?

Discussing Rhetoric and Style

1. Study Loughran's word choice—particularly the verbs—in two or three paragraphs. What would make these sentences better? Rewrite a few of them.
2. Loughran often shifts tone and diction—parentheses, for instance, usually mark such shifts in this essay. Where else can you hear such a shift? Find two or three examples.
3. How does Loughran garnish the initial metaphor of a "step"? How does she expand the metaphor, and what does this expansion do for her argument?
4. Grading is a serious subject, but Loughran treats it lightly. What does she accomplish by doing this?
5. Why, according to Loughran, is the "five-step educational staircase . . . blatantly, logically impossible"? Can you follow her argument? Explain.

Ideas for Writing

1. Choose several words for which to look up etymologies (you might look up the words in this sentence: several, words, etymologies, sentence, and so on). Do you find, as Loughran did, any basis for metaphor in the words you looked up? Following Loughran's model, discuss your findings in a brief paper.
2. Loughran approaches language historically, as does Hayakawa ("How Dictionaries Are Made"). How does her treatment of the word "grade" reflect Hayakawa's interest in the history and contemporary usage of language? Compare these two writers' approaches to definition.

CHAPTER 2

The Word That Dare Not Speak Its Name: Euphemism, Jargon, and Taboo

"Why don't people just say what they think?" One answer to this much-asked question begins with the observation that thoughts expressed in words have style as well as content. Because the ways in which language is used convey subtle connotations of personal attitude, emotional weight, and social context, few people speak about any subject to their grandmothers (for example) in the same way as they speak about the subject to their friends. Anxieties about self-presentation—fears of having one's words express the wrong attitude, emotion, or social background—are among the motives that have led to the usages explored in this section. The equally common desire to defy such fears often results in the willful use of words considered taboo.

The section begins with an account of euphemism, a kind of language that many people find foolishly indirect, and ends with discussions of a kind of language that many people find too direct to allow its public utterance. Hugh Rawson's "Euphemism" introduces the first topic: he traces euphemism as a common habit of social discourse from its etymology ("beautiful speech") through the many ways in which the desire for "beauty" hides reality behind "speech" by attempting either to diminish or to magnify that reality. For example, when people say that someone has "passed away," they speak euphemistically. The attempt here is to diminish the horror of death by describing it as travel. Carefully read, Rawson's essay will provide a framework for understanding the ways in which the essays that follow are related to one another.

As Rawson points out, each period of history has its own topics that it wishes to diminish or magnify. In "New Age Babble," the well-known humorist Russell Baker makes fun of some current topics and the language invented to describe them. Though annoyed, Baker charitably suggests that silly talk ceases even to annoy when it is used so often that people come to forget how silly it sounds. It may be characteristic of the age that several of the terms that Baker finds in general use come from the world of business.

In the next essay, language watcher William Safire takes a witty though close look at some of the terms originating in today's commerce. He relies partly on his own sense of the language and fashions in the world of affairs, but he also cites the authority of corporate officials and editors of *The Harvard Business Review* to make his case.

The study of literature is often considered incompatible with the study of business. But the survival of literature posits the existence of books, and the making and selling of books is undeniably a business. One implication of this fact is shown in Dorothy Wickenden's essay, "Bowdlerizing the Bard: How to Protect Your Kids from Shakespeare." Wickenden demonstrates how some of the same motives that produce euphemism in other areas of life lead to editorial alteration of the language of Shakespeare, even though he is included in textbooks exclusively because of his authority as a great writer.

Shakespeare is bowdlerized or censored by people who are offended by "dirty language," which many euphemisms are invented to avoid. But what is dirty language, how does it work, and why do people wish either to use it or to avoid it? These questions of psychological motivation are addressed by the psychologist Dr. Joyce Brothers in "What Dirty Words Really Mean." Dr. Brothers generally takes a positive view of the subject and finds that, oddly, a healthier attitude is often reflected in the occasional use (rather than scrupulous avoidance) of words that many people consider the sign of unhealthy minds.

The columnist and editor William Buckley tries to take a balanced view of the same issue in "On the Use of Dirty Words." Buckley focuses less on words themselves than on their users, and he divides the world of speakers into saints and sinners. He concludes that because most of us are neither, a range in the use of language is appropriately expressive of who we are.

In the final essay of the section, student writer M. K. Tucker describes how moving from a euphemism to a taboo word became for her a rite of passage. By allowing herself to define her "Aunt Ethel" by the name that seemed to fit her nature, Tucker locates the moment in which her adulthood was recognized within her family—the same moment in which she began to make peace with her aunt's personality.

Euphemism

HUGH RAWSON

"Euphemism," which serves as the introduction to Hugh Rawson's Dictionary of Euphemisms and Other Double-talk *(1981), discusses the nature of euphemism, the practice of which is "embedded so deeply in our language that few of us, even those who pride themselves on being plain-spoken, ever get through a day without using them." The author goes on to divide euphemism into two major categories, offering six principles with which to spot and classify euphemisms of every kind. He claims (perhaps with tongue in cheek) that "with quantification, the study of euphemism has at last been put on a firm scientific footing." This observation aside, however, perhaps his most useful and earnest advice to the would-be euphemist (or non-euphemist) is this simple formula: "Choose words with care."*

Mr. Milquetoast gets up from the table, explaining that he has to go to the *little boys' room* or *see a man about a dog;* a young woman announces that she is *enceinte.* A secretary complains that her boss is a pain in the *derrière;* an undertaker (or *mortician*) asks delicately where to ship the *loved one.* These are euphemisms—mild, agreeable, or roundabout words used in place of coarse, painful, or offensive ones. The term comes from the Greek *eu,* meaning "well" or "sounding good," and *phēmē,* "speech."

Many euphemisms are so delightfully ridiculous that everyone laughs at them. (Well, almost everyone: The people who call themselves the National Selected Morticians usually manage to keep from smiling.) Yet euphemisms have very serious reasons for being. They conceal the things people fear the most—death, the dead, the supernatural. They cover up the facts of life—of sex and reproduction and excretion—which inevitably remind even the most refined people that they are made of clay, or worse. They are beloved by individuals and institutions (governments, especially) who are anxious to present only the handsomest possible images of themselves to the world. And they are embedded so deeply in our language that few of us, even those who pride themselves on being plain-spoken, ever get through a day without using them.

The same sophisticates who look down their noses at *little boys' room* and other euphemisms of that ilk will nevertheless say that they are going to the *bathroom* when no bath is intended; that Mary has been *sleeping* around even though she has been getting precious little shut-eye; that John has *passed away* or even *departed* (as if he'd just made the last train to Darien); and that Sam and Janet are *friends*, which sounds a lot better than "illicit lovers."

Thus, euphemisms are society's basic *lingua non franca*. As such, they are outward and visible signs of our inward anxieties, conflicts, fears, and shames. They are like radioactive isotopes. By tracing them, it is possible to see what has been (and is) going on in our language, our minds, and our culture.

Euphemisms can be divided into two general types—positive and negative. The positive ones inflate and magnify, making the euphemized items seem altogether grander and more important than they really are. The negative euphemisms deflate and diminish. They are defensive in nature, offsetting the power of tabooed terms and otherwise eradicating from the language everything that people prefer not to deal with directly.

Positive euphemisms include the many fancy occupational titles, which salve the egos of workers by elevating their job status: *custodian* for janitor (itself a euphemism for caretaker), *counsel* for lawyer, the many kinds of *engineer* (*exterminating engineer, mattress engineer, publicity engineer,* ad infinitum), *help* for servant (itself an old euphemism for slave), *hooker* and *working girl* for whore, and so forth. A common approach is to try to turn one's trade into a profession, usually in imitation of the medical profession. *Beautician* and the aforementioned *mortician* are the classic examples, but the same imitative instinct is responsible for social workers calling welfare recipients *clients*, for football coaches conducting *clinics*, and for undertakers referring to corpses as *cases* or even *patients*.

Other kinds of positive euphemisms include personal honorifics such as *colonel*, the *honorable*, and *major*, and the many institutional euphemisms, which convert madhouses into *mental hospitals*, colleges into *universities*, and small business establishments into *emporiums, parlors, salons,* and *shoppes*. The desire to improve one's surroundings also is evident in geographical place names, most prominently in the case of the distinctly nongreen *Greenland* (attributed to an early real estate developer named Eric the Red), but also in the designation of many small burgs as *cities*, and in the names of some cities, such as *Troy*, New York (*née* Vanderheyden's Ferry; its name-change in 1789 began a fad for adopting classical place names in the United States).

Negative, defensive euphemisms are extremely ancient. It was the Greeks, for example, who transformed the Furies into the *Eumenides* (the Kindly Ones). In many cultures, it is forbidden to pronounce the name of God (hence, pious Jews say *Adonai*) or of Satan (giving rise to the *deuce*, the *good man*, the *great fellow*, the generalized *Devil*, and many other roundabouts). The names of the dead, and of animals that are hunted or feared, may also be euphemized this way. The bear is called *grandfather* by many peoples and the tiger is alluded to as the *striped one*. The common motivation seems to be a confusion between the names of things and the things themselves: The name is viewed as an extension of the thing. Thus, to know the name is to give one power over the thing (as in the Rumpelstiltskin story). But such power may be dangerous: "Speak of the Devil and he appears." For mere mortals, then, the safest policy is to use another name, usually a flattering, euphemistic one, in place of the supernatural being's true name.

As strong as—or stronger than—the taboos against names are the taboos against particular words, especially the infamous *four-letter words*. (According to a recent Supreme Court decision, the set of *four-letter words* actually contains some words with as few as three and as many as 12 letters, but the logic of Supreme Court decisions is not always immediately apparent.) These words form part of the vocabulary of practically everyone above the age of six or seven. They are not slang terms, but legitimate Standard English of the oldest stock, and they are euphemized in many ways, typically by conversion into pseudo-Latin (e.g., *copulation, defecation, urination*), into slang (*make love, number two, pee*), or into socially acceptable dashes (*f*——, *s*——, *p*——, etc.). In the electronic media, the function of the dash is fulfilled by the *bleep* (sometimes pronounced *blip*), which has completed the circle and found its way into print.

The taboo against words frequently degenerates into mere prudery. At least—though the defensive principle is the same—the primitive (or *preliterate*) hunter's use of *grandfather* seems to operate on a more elemental level than the excessive modesty that has produced *abdomen for* belly, *afterpart* for ass, bosom for breast, *limb* for leg, *white meat* for breast (of a chicken), and so on.

When carried too far, which is what always seems to happen, positive and negative euphemisms tend finally to coalesce into an unappetizing mush of elegancies and genteelisms, in which the underlying terms are hardly worth the trouble of euphemizing, e.g., *ablutions* for washing, *bender* for knee, *dentures* for false teeth, *expectorate* for spit, *home* for house, *honorarium* for fee, *ill* for sick, *libation* for drink, *perspire* for sweat, *position* for job, etc., etc., etc.

All euphemisms, whether positive or negative, may be used either unconsciously or consciously. Unconscious euphemisms consist mainly of words that were developed as euphemisms, but so long ago that hardly anyone remembers the original motivation. Examples in this category include such now-standard terms as *cemetery* (from the Greek word for "sleeping place," it replaced the more deathly "graveyard"), and the names of various barnyard animals, including the *donkey* (the erstwhile ass), the *sire* (or studhorse), and the *rooster* (for cock, and one of many similar evasions, e.g., *haystack* for haycock, *weather vane* for weathercock, and Louisa May *Alcott*, whose father changed the family name from the nasty-sounding Alcox). Into this category, too, fall such watered-down swear words as *cripes, Jiminy Cricket, gee,* and *gosh,* all designed to avoid taking holy names in vain and now commonly used without much awareness of their original meaning, particularly by youngsters and by those who fill in the balloons in comic strips. Then there are the words for which no honest *Anglo-Saxon* (often a euphemism for "dirty") equivalents exist, e.g., *brassiere,* which has hardly anything to do with the French *bras* (arm) from which it derives, and *toilet,* from the diminutive of *toile* (cloth).

Conscious euphemisms constitute a much more complex category, which is hardly surprising, given the ingenuity, not to say the deviousness, of the human mind. This is not to imply that euphemisms cannot be employed more or less honestly as well as knowingly. For example, garbage men are upgraded routinely into *sanitation men,* but to say "Here come the sanitation men" is a comparatively venial sin. The meaning does come across intelligibly, and the listener understands that it is time to get out the garbage cans. By the same token, it is honest enough to offer a woman condolences upon "the loss of her husband," where *loss* stands for death. Not only are amenities preserved: By avoiding the troublesome term, the euphemism actually facilitates social discourse.

Conscious euphemisms also lead to social double-thinking, however. They form a kind of code. The euphemism stands for "something else," and everyone pretends that the "something else" doesn't exist. It is the essentially duplicitous nature of euphemisms that makes them so attractive to those people and institutions who have something to hide, who don't want to say what they are thinking, and who find it convenient to lie about what they are doing.

It is at this point, when speakers and writers seek not so much to avoid offense as to deceive, that we pass into the universe of dishonest euphemisms, where the conscious elements of circumlocution and double-talk loom large. Here are the murky worlds of the CIA, the FBI, and the military, where murder is translated into *executive action*, an illegal break-in into a *black bag job*, and napalm into *soft* or *selective ordnance*. Here are the Wonderlands in which Alice would feel so much at home: advertising, where small becomes *medium* if not *large*, and politics, where gross errors are passed off as *misspeaking* and lies that won't wash anymore are called *inoperative*. Here, too, are our great industries: the prison business, where solitary confinement cells are disguised as *adjustment centers, quiet cells*, or *seclusion;* the atomic power business, where nuclear accidents become *core rearrangements* or simply *events;* the death business, where *remains* (not bodies) are *interred* (not buried) in *caskets* (not coffins); and, finally, of murder on its largest scale, where people are put into *protective custody* (imprisonment) in *concentration camps* (prison camps) as a first step toward achieving the *Final Solution* (genocide). George Orwell wrote in a famous essay ("Politics and the English Language," 1946) that "political language . . . is designed to make lies sound truthful and murder respectable, and to give an appearance of solidity to pure wind." His dictum applies equally through the full range of dishonest euphemisms.

Such doubletalk is doubly dangerous. Besides deceiving those on the receiving end, it helps the users fool themselves. As John W. Dean III has noted "If . . . Richard Nixon has said to me, 'John, I want you to do a little crime for me. I want you to obstruct justice,' I would have told him he was crazy and disappeared from sight. No one thought about the Watergate coverup in those terms—at first, anyway. Rather, it was 'containing' Watergate or keeping the defendants 'on the reservation' or coming up with the right public relations 'scenario' and the like" (*New York Times*, 4/6/75). And as the Senate Intelligence Committee observed in 1975, after wading through a morass of euphemisms and circumlocutions in its investigation of American plots to kill foreign leaders: " 'Assassinate,' 'murder,' and 'kill' are words many people do not want to speak or hear. They describe acts which should not even be proposed, let alone plotted. Failing to call dirty business by its rightful name may have increased the risk of dirty business being done." It is probably no coincidence that the conversations and internal memos of the Nixon White House were liberally studded with terms that had been popularized in the underworld and in the cloak-and-dagger business, where few, if any, holds are barred, e.g., *caper* (burglary), *covert operation* (burglary), *launder* (cleaning dirty money), *neutralize* (murder or, as used in the White

House, character assassination), *plausible denial* (official lying), and so forth.

Euphemisms are in a constant state of flux. New ones are created almost daily. Many of them prove to be nonce terms—one-day wonders that are never repeated. Of those that are ratified through reuse as true euphemisms, some may last for generations, even centuries, while others fade away or develop into unconscious euphemisms, still used, but reflexively, without thought of their checkered origins. The ebb and flow of euphemisms is governed to a large extent by two basic rules: Gresham's Law of Language and the Law of Succession.

In monetary theory, where it originated, Gresham's Law can be summarized as "bad money drives out good"—meaning that debased or underweight coins will drive good, full-weight coins out of circulation. (By the by: Though Sir Thomas Gresham, 1519–1579, has gotten all the credit, the effect was noticed and explained by earlier monetary experts, including Nicolaus Koppernick, 1473–1543, who doubled as an astronomer and who is better known as Copernicus.) In the field of language, on the same principle, "bad" meanings or associations of words tend to drive competing "good" meanings out of circulation. Thus, *coition, copulation,* and *intercourse* once were general terms for, respectively, coming together, coupling, and communication, but after the words were drawn into service as euphemisms, their sexual meanings became dominant, so that the other senses are hardly ever encountered nowadays except in very special situations. The same thing happened to *crap* (formerly a general term for chaff, residue, or dregs), *feces* (also dregs, as of wine or salad oil), and *manure* (literally: "to work with the hands").

Gresham's Law remains very much in force, of course. Witness what has happened to *gay*, whose homosexual meaning has recently preempted all others. The law is by no means limited to euphemisms, and its application to other words helps explain why some euphemisms are formed. Thus, the incorrect and pejorative uses of "Jew" as a verb and adjective caused many people, Jews as well as Gentiles, to shift to *Hebrew* even though that term should, in theory, be reserved for the Jews of ancient times or their language. A similar example is "girl," whose pejorative meanings have recently been brought to the fore, with the result that anxiety-ridden men sometimes fall into the worse error of referring to their *lady* friends.

Gresham's Law is the engine that powers the second of the two great euphemistic principles: the Law of Succession. After a euphemism becomes tainted by association with its underlying "bad" word, people will tend to shun it. For example, the seemingly innocent *occupy* was virtually banned by polite society for most of the seventeenth and eighteenth centuries because of its use as a euphemism for engaging in sex. (A man might be said to *occupy* his wife or to go to an *occupying* house.) Once people begin to shun a term, it usually is necessary to develop a new euphemism to replace the one that has failed. Then the second will become tainted and a third will appear. In this way, chains of euphemisms evolve. Thus, "mad" has been euphemized successively as *crazy, insane, lunatic, mentally deranged,* and just plain *mental.* Then there are the poor and backward nations that have metamorphosed from *underdeveloped* to *developing* to *emergent.* (*Fledgling* nations never really took hold despite the imprimatur of Eleanor Roosevelt.) A new chain seems to be evolving from the FBI's *black bag job,* which has fallen into sufficient disrepute that agents who condone break-ins are more likely now to talk in terms of *surreptitious entries, technical trespasses, uncontested physical searches,* or *warrantless investigations.*

Extraordinary collections of euphemisms have formed around some topics over the years as a result of the continual creation of new terms, and it seems safe to say that the sizes of these collections reflect the strength of the underlying taboos. Nowhere is this more evident than in the case of the *private parts,* male and female, whose Anglo-Saxon names are rarely used in mixed company, except by those who are on intimate terms. Thus, the monumental *Slang and Its Analogues* (J. S. Farmer and W. E. Henley, 1890–94) lists some 650 synonyms for *vagina,* most of them euphemistic, and about half that number for *penis.* (These are just the English synonyms; for *vagina,* for example, Farmer and Henley include perhaps another 900 synonyms in other languages.) Other anatomical parts that have inspired more than their share of euphemisms include the *bosom, bottom, limb,* and *testicles.* All forms of sexual *intercourse* and the subjects of *defecation, urination,* and the *toilet* also are richly euphemistic, as are *menstruation* (well over 100 terms have been noted), all aspects of death and dying, or *passing away,* and disease (it used to be *TB* and the sexual, *social diseases* that were euphemized; now it is cancer, usually referred to in *obituaries,* or death notices, as a *long illness*).

The incidence of euphemisms may also reflect society's ambivalent feelings on certain subjects. Alcohol, for example, is responsible for a great many euphemisms: There are 356 synonyms for "drunk"—more than for any other term—in the appendixes to the *Dictionary of American Slang* (Harold Wentworth and Stuart Berg Flexner, 1976). The practice of punishing criminals with death *(capital punishment)* also makes many people uncomfortable, judging from the number of linguistic evasions for it, both in the United States, where the electric chair may be humorously downplayed as a *hot seat,* and in other countries, such as France, where the condemned are introduced to *Madame la guillotine.* Meanwhile, the so-called victimless crime of prostitution has inspired an inordinate number of euphemisms, with some 70 listed in this book under *prostitute* (a sixteenth-century Latinate euphemism for "whore," which itself may have begun as a euphemism for some now-forgotten word, the Old English *hōre* being cognate with the Latin *cara,* darling). The precarious position of *minorities* (a code term for blacks and/or Hispanics) and other oft-oppressed groups (e.g., homosexuals, servants, women) also is revealed by the variety of terms that have been devised to characterize them.

Just as the clustering of euphemisms around a given term or topic appears to reflect the strength of a particular taboo, so the unusual accumulation of euphemisms around an institution is strongly indicative of interior rot. Thus, the Spanish Inquisition featured an extensive vocabulary of words with double meanings (e.g., *auto-da-fé* for act of faith, and the *question* for torture). In our own time, the number of euphemisms that have collected around the CIA and its attempts at *assassination,* the FBI and its reliance on break-ins and *informants,* and the prison business and its noncorrectional *correctional facilities,* all tend to confirm one's darker suspicions. This is true, too, of the *Defense* (not War) *Department,* with its *enhanced radiation weapons* (neutron bombs) and its *reconnaissance in force* (search-and-destroy) missions. The military tradition, though, is very old. As long ago as ca. 250 B.C., a Macedonian general, Antigonus Gonatas, parlayed a "retreat" into a *strategic movement to the rear.* And, finally, there is politics, always a fertile source of doubletalk, but especially so during the Watergate period when euphemisms surfaced at a rate that is unlikely (one hopes) ever to be matched again: *Deep Six, expletive deleted, inoperative, sign off,* and *stonewall* are only a few of the highpoints (or lowpoints, depending upon one's perspective) of this remarkably fecund period. . . .

The ancient Egyptians called the deadhouse, where bodies were turned into mummies, the *beautiful house,* and the ways of expunging offensive expressions from language have not changed since. Simplest is to make a straight substitution, using a word that has happier connotations than the term one wishes to avoid. Frequently, a legitimate synonym will do. Thus, *agent, speculator,* and *thrifty* have better vibes than "spy," "gambler," and "tight," although the literal meanings, or denotations, of each pair of words are the same. On this level, all the euphemist has to do is select words with care. Other principles may be applied, however, a half dozen of which are basic to creating—and deciphering—euphemisms. They are:

Foreign languages sound finer. It is permissible for speakers and writers of English to express almost any thought they wish, as long as the more risqué parts of the discussion are rendered in another language, usually French or Latin. The versatility of French (and the influence of French culture) is evident in such diverse fields as love (*affair, amour, liaison*), war (*matériel, personnel, sortie, triage*), women's underwear (*brassiere, chemise, lingerie*), and dining (goat, cow, deer, and other animals with English names when they are alive and kicking are served up on the dinner table as the more palatable *chevon, filet mignon*, and *venison*). *French* itself is a euphemistic prefix word for a variety of "wrong" and/or "sexy" things, such as the *French disease* (syphilis) and one of the methods of guarding against it, the *French letter* (condom). Latin is almost equally popular as a source of euphemisms, especially for the body's sexual and other functions. Thus, such words as *copulation, fellatio, masturbation, pudendum*, and *urination* are regarded as printable and even broadcastable by people (including United States Supreme Court justices) who become exercised at the sight and sound of their English counterparts. Other languages have contributed. For example, the Dutch *boss* (master), the Spanish *cojones* (balls), and the Yiddish *tushie* (the ass). Not strictly speaking a foreign language is potty talk, a distinct idiom that has furnished many euphemisms, i.e., *number one, number two, pee, piddle*, and other relics of the nursery, often used by adults when speaking to one another as well as when addressing children.

Bad words are not so bad when abbreviated. Words that otherwise would create consternation if used in mixed company or in public are acceptable when reduced to their initial letters. Essentially, such abbreviations as *BS* and *SOB* work the same way as the dash in *f*——. Everyone knows what letters have been deleted, but no one is seriously offended because the taboo word has not been paraded in all its glory. Dean Acheson even got away with *snafu* when he was secretary of state, though the acronym did cause some comment among the British, not all of whom felt this to be a very diplomatic way of apologizing for an American—er—*foul up*. This acronym also is noteworthy for spawning a host of picturesque albeit short-lived descendants, including *fubar* (where *bar* stands for Beyond All Recognition), *janfu* (Joint Army-Navy), *tarfu* (Things Are Really), and *tuifu* (The Ultimate In). Abbreviations function as euphemisms in many fields, e.g., the child's *BM*, the advertiser's *BO*, the hypochondriac's *Big C*, and the various shortenings for offbeat sex, such as *AC/DC* for those who swing both says, *bd* for bondage and discipline, and *S/M*.

Abstractions are not objectionable. The strength of particular taboos may be dissipated by casting ideas in the most general possible terms; also, abstractions, being quite opaque to the uninformed eye (and meaningless to the untrained ear) make ideal cover-up words. Often, it is only a matter of finding the lowest common denominator. Thus, *it, problem, situation,* and *thing* may refer to anything under the sun: the child who keeps playing with *it* and the girl who is said to be doing *it, problem* days and *problem* drinking; the *situation* at the Three Mile Island, Pennsylvania, nuclear power plant; an economic *thing* (slump, recession, or depression), *our thing* (i.e., the Costa Nostra), or the Watergate *thing* (elaborated by the president himself into the *pre-thing* and the *post-thing*). The American tendency toward abstraction was noted early on by de Tocqueville, who believed that democratic nations as a class were "addicted to generic terms and abstract expressions because these modes of speech enlarge thought and assist the operation of the mind by enabling it to include many objects in a small compass." The dark side of this is that abstractions are inherently fuzzy. As de Tocqueville also noted: "An abstract term is like a box with a false bottom; you may put in what ideas you please, and take them out again without being observed" [*Democracy in America*]. Bureaucrats, engineers, scientists, and those who like to be regarded as scientists, are particularly good at generalizing details out of existence. They have produced such expressions as *aerodynamic personnel decelerator* for parachute, *energy release* for radiation release (as from a nuclear reactor), *episode* and *event* for disasters of different sorts and sizes, *impact attenuation device* for a crash cushion, and *Vertical Transportation Corps* for a group of elevator operators.

Indirection is better than direction. Topics and terms that are too touchy to be dealt with openly may be alluded to in a variety of ways, most often by mentioning one aspect of the subject, a circumstance involving it, a related subject, or even by saying what it is not. Thus, people really do come together in an *assembly center* and soldiers do stop fighting when they *break off contact with the enemy,* but these are indirect euphemisms for "prison" and "retreat," respectively. *Bite the dust* is a classic of this kind, and the adjective is used advisedly, since the expression appears in Homer's *Iliad,* circa 750 B.C. Many of the common anatomical euphemisms also depend on indirection—the general, locational, it's-somewhere-back-there allusions to the *behind,* the *bottom,* and the *rear,* for example. A special category of anatomical euphemisms are those that conform to the Rule of the Displaced Referent, whereby "unmentionable" parts of the human body are euphemized by referring to nearby "mentionable" parts, e.g., *chest* for breasts; *fanny,* a word of unknown origin whose meaning has not always been restricted to the back end of a person; *tail,* which also has had frontal meanings (in Latin, *penis* means "tail"), and *thigh,* a biblical euphemism for the balls. Quaintest of the indirect euphemisms are those that are prefaced with a negative adjective, telling us what they are not, such as *unnatural, unthinkable,* and *unmentionable.* (The latter also appears as a noun in the plural; some women wear *upper unmentionables* and *lower unmentionables.*) An especially famous negative euphemism is the dread *love that dare not speak its name,* but the phrase was not totally dishonest in the beginning, since it dates to 1894 (from a poem by Oscar Wilde's young *friend,* Alfred, Lord Douglas), when "homosexual" was still so new a word as not to be known to many people, regardless of their *sexual orientation.*

Understatement reduces risks. Since a euphemism is, by definition, a mild, agreeable, or roundabout word or phrase, it follows logically that its real meaning is always worse than its apparent meaning. But this is not always obvious to the uninitiated, especially in constructions that acknowledge part of the truth while concealing the extent of its grimness. Thus, a nuclear reactor that is said to be *above critical* is actually out of control, *active defense* is attack, *area bombing* is terror bombing, *collateral damage* is civilian damage (as from nuclear bombs), and so on. The soft sell also is basic to such euphemisms as *companion, partner,* and *roommate,* all of which downplay "lover"; to *pro-choice* for pro-abortion, and to *senior citizen* for old person. The danger with understatement is that it may hide the true meaning completely. As a result, euphemists often erect signposts in front of the basic term, e.g., *close personal friend, constant companion, criminal conversation* (a legalism for adultery), *meaningful relationship,* etc. The signposts ensure that even a dullard would get the message.

The longer the euphemism the better. As a rule, to which there are very few exceptions (*hit* for murder, for instance), euphemisms are longer than the words they replace. They have more letters, they have more syllables, and frequently, two or more words will be deployed in place of a single one. This is partly because the tabooed Anglo-Saxon words tend to be short and partly because it almost always takes more words to evade an idea than to state it directly and honestly. The effect is seen in euphemisms of every type. Thus, *Middle Eastern* dancing is what better "belly" dancers do; more advertisers agree that *medication* gives faster relief than "medicine"; the writers of financial reports eschew "drop" in favor of *adjustment downward*, and those poor souls who are required to give testimony under oath prefer *at this point in time* to "now." The list is practically endless. Until this very point in time, however, it was impossible for anyone to say exactly *how much* longer was *how much* better. That important question has now been resolved with the development of the Fog or Pomposity Index (FOP Index, for short).

The FOP Index compares the length of the euphemism or circumlocution to the word or phrase for which it stands, with an additional point being awarded for each additional letter, syllable, or word in the substitute expression. Thus, "medicine" has 8 letters and 3 syllables, while *medication* has 10 letters and an extra, fourth syllable, giving it a point count of 11. Dividing 8 into 11 produces a FOP Index of 1.4. By the same token, *adjustment downward* has a FOP Index of 5.75 compared to "drop" (18 letters, plus 4 extra syllables, plus 1 extra word, for a total of 23, divided by the 4 letters of the euphemized term).

Like most breakthroughs in the social (or soft) sciences, the FOP Index doesn't really tell you anything you didn't already know. Everyone (well, almost everyone) has always sensed that *medication* is on the pretentious side. The index, however, arms users with a number to back up their intuition, thus enabling them to crush opponents in debate. It can now be said authoritatively that *lower extremity* (FOP Index of 6.6) outdoes *limb* (1.3) as a euphemism for leg. In much the same way, *prostitute* (2.4) improves upon *harlot* (1.4) for whore. In another field: *Oval Office* (2.6) is better than *Presidency* (2.4) is better than "Nixon," but both pale in comparison to the 17.8 of former HEW Secretary Joe Califano's *Personal Assistant to the Secretary (Special Activities)*, who was a "cook." (Califano's *Personal Assistant* illustrates a basic rule of bureaucracies: the longer the title, the lower the rank.) And so it goes: *Active defense* has a FOP Index of 2.5 for attack; *benign neglect* rates 2.3 for neglect (the "benign" being an example of a Meaningless Modifier); *categorical inaccuracy* is a whopping 10.3 compared to lie; *intestinal fortitude* is 6.5 for guts.

With quantification, the study of euphemisms has at last been put on a firm scientific footing. . . .

Discussing Ideas and Themes

1. What is the etymology of "euphemism"? Why does Rawson include it in his discussion? How important are the origins of words? How useful is the information?

2. Where, according to Rawson, are we most likely to encounter euphemisms? Who uses them the most and in what situations? Do you ever find yourself using them? When? Where?

3. Why does Rawson find euphemisms funny? Are they ever not funny, in his view? Do you agree? Why or why not?

4. What two categories does Rawson provide for euphemisms? What sub-groups does he invent for each of his two categories? Give examples of each, both from the essay and from your experience.

5. What are some of the principles on which euphemism is based? How does Rawson introduce them, and why? Are there any you can think of that he has missed? Make up your own list of principles with illustrative examples.

Discussing Rhetoric and Style

1. How would you characterize the overall style of the essay—journalistic, scholarly, anecdotal, or a mixture? Reread the essay again before answering, jotting a note in the margins whenever you recognize a shift of viewpoint. How capable is Rawson of handling such shifts?

2. Compare Rawson's use of division as an argumentative method with John Simon's ("Why Good English Is Good for You"). In what ways do their techniques overlap? In what ways do they differ? Provide examples to support your view.

3. What are the *least* interesting moments in Rawson's essay? Write them in the margins, and then compose a few brief paragraphs on how these sections could be improved. Remember, as always, to cite the text.

4. What is the thesis of Rawson's essay? Is it explicit or implicit? Is he successful in proving it? Explain.

5. Any discussion of euphemism must implicitly consider diction and tone. With this in mind, study Rawson's diction and tone. Does Rawson provide us with any euphemistic moments? Any ironic ones? What, in the end, is the difference between the two? Or isn't there any?

Ideas for Writing

1. Pretend your best friend has fallen in love with a dope, bought a bomb of a car, or gotten a disastrous haircut. Write a few paragraphs of dialogue in which you exchange comments about the

new acquisition. Your friend, of course, should be proud and boastful; you should be euphemistic. Then, after your sketch is done, mark off your euphemisms (try to include at least ten) and write in the margins the principle (according to Rawson's essay) on which each is based.

2. Write a detailed summary of all the euphemisms you hear in one day—in the classroom, on television, at home, on the street. When is euphemism most appropriate? When is it dangerous? Write an essay in which you explain in detail your own ideas about these euphemisms.

New Age Babble

RUSSELL BAKER

Born in Virginia in 1925, Russell Baker studied at Johns Hopkins University and later became a reporter for the Baltimore Sun. *After serving as political correspondent and bureau chief for the* Sun's *office in London, he was hired by* The New York Times *to cover Washington politics. As the longtime author of the Sunday* Magazine's "Observer" *column, he received a Pulitzer Prize for distinguished commentary in 1979. Baker has written several autobiographical books, including the best-selling* Growing Up *and* The Good Times *(1989). In "New Age Babble," written for the* Times *in 1988, Baker takes a brief, humorous look at the prose style currently used by the United States government, television news shows, and would-be savants of all sorts. According to Baker, "people who talk New Age Babble nowadays are forced to use it to get ahead and, after talking it among themselves long enough, forget that they are talking silly."*

The company providing our cable-television service has just accessed me with a print communication, or, as the old-timers used to say, "sent me a letter."

It says the price of the cable service has been "adjusted." It doesn't say who adjusted it. Could the watchman have fallen asleep, permitting some rascal to sneak in and adjust the price?

Hah! I know what "the price has been adjusted" means in New Age Babble. It means "price is going up." I don't whine about prices going up. That's what prices do. What I object to is being told the price has been "adjusted."

What's wrong with companies that can't come right out and say, "Folks, the price is going up again"? They can't believe we're so dumb we don't know that "price adjustment" is New Age Babble meaning "price rise."

My theory is that companies are run nowadays by people who enjoy talking New Age Babble. Maybe they now have to talk that way to get to the top, the way you had to talk weird in advertising agencies in the old, old days to show you were on the ball.

Yes, there really was a time when adult human beings could be taken seriously after saying, "Let's run it up the flagpole and see if anybody salutes."

My theory is that people who talk New Age Babble nowadays are forced to use it to get ahead and, after talking it among themselves long enough, forget that they are talking silly.

Fellow Americans, do we really want to be accessed by communications? Send me a letter or call me on the telephone, but access me not by communication devices: This is my plea, and I might as well be talking to the west wall.

Or as a New Age Babbler might put it, "might as well try to impact the west wall." The New Age is the age of impacting.

Systems are constantly not only impacting, but also being impacted. Processes also get a lot of action, impactwise. For instance, not long ago I was startled to hear a man on "The MacNeil/Lehrer NewsHour" call a cigarette a "nicotine-delivery system."

In New Age Babble, however, I was not startled; something far more ponderous had happened. My impression-input system had been impacted by the man's long-winded synonym for "cigarette."

There's hardly anything that a New Age Babbler can't convert into a dreary, dull, mind-numbing, excruciatingly boring system. Take the automobile. In New Age Babble it is not a car; it's an individually operable, quadri-wheeled, internal-combustion, surface transportation system.

This curiosity constantly experiences processes. If it sits at the curb, it is because it has undergone the parking process. If it balks and refuses to work, into the garage it goes for the repair process. The repair process ends with the owner's bank account being impacted by a bill.

The New Age Babbler spends much of his life in situations. If the mechanic's bill bankrupts him, he enters a bankruptcy situation. If he resorts to embezzlement to save himself, he is involved in an embezzlement situation.

If he escapes with millions to South America, he settles into a South American situation. There he probably enters the language-study process so he can figure out how big a price adjustment will follow the latest print communication to impact his mail slot.

There is another theory, incidentally, about why people speak New Age Babble. This is, that its speakers really do think we're too dumb to know what they're saying.

The evidence always adduced for this theory is the Reagan Administration's invention of the term "revenue enhancement." I always assumed this was a joke produced by some wise guy at the Treasury who had to talk about getting more tax money in an era when the President had said he wouldn't let taxes rise.

Joke or not, every American smart enough to cope with Form 1040 instantly knew that "revenue enhancement" was just a flannelmouth synonym for "tax boosts."

Speaking of taxes, "Read my lips" is not New Age Babble but something quite different, though perhaps equally annoying—especially to President-elect Bush, who must now live with it. It is the kind of talk that seems vital and dynamic during campaign excitements, but is seen as merely tiresome or embarrassing when political fever subsides.

Another example: "The (insert letter of alphabet) Word." Before the campaign, it was "the C word," referring to cancer; in the campaign, "the L word." Recently I've seen "the M word" (referring to Minimalist") and "the R word" ("Recession"). It's become "the E. A. phrase" ("Enough already!").

Discussing Ideas and Themes

1. Give a few examples of New Age Babble. What characterizes this kind of talking? Where, according to Baker, are you most likely to encounter it?
2. Who speaks this way? Does Baker suggest that it has any political implications? Do you see any? Explain.
3. To what other kind of "silly" talk does Baker compare his subject? Why is the spread of such babble so distressing to him?
4. How would you translate this sentence out of New Age Babble? "In his journalistic survey, Mr. Baker accesses a theory of an impacted verbal process."

Discussing Rhetoric and Style

1. New Age Babble seems to be the language of sprawling social systems—for example, large corporations and the United States government. How does Baker attempt to set himself in opposition to these strong forces—as a little guy, an everyday regular person? How appealing is his persona? How useful?

2. Compare the style of these two sentences:

   a. Our cable-television service has just accessed me with a print communication.

   b. It has sent me a letter.

   What effect does Baker get by placing these two statements side by side? Why does he put the first one first? Are you pleasantly surprised by the second? Explain.

3. Study the verbs: "access," "adjust," "impact." Can you think of any others? Use each in a sentence, both in the active and in the passive. What do New Age verbs have in common?

4. Do you ever find Baker's essay repetitive? Can this iteration be considered a rhetorical technique? For instance, is there anything funny about Baker's use of repetition? How does it (or doesn't it) enhance his satire?

5. Baker describes the style he examines as "dreary, dull, mind-numbing, [and] excruciatingly boring. . . ." How would you describe Baker's prose? Does he ever "babble"?

Ideas for Writing

1. Take the first paragraph of any essay in this text and translate it into New Age Babble. What does this exercise teach you about the rules of the style? Once you have a few ideas, write them down in the form of a brief critique entitled "A User's Guide to New Age Babble."

2. Compare the style Baker examines to Malcolm Cowley's essay. Are sociologists New Age Babblers? Do they intend to fool us or exclude us? Explain the difference in detail.

Bizbuzz

WILLIAM SAFIRE

Born in 1929, William Safire first worked in public relations, but between 1968 and 1973, he moved out of business and into public service, acting as President Nixon's chief speechwriter. After Nixon's resignation, Safire was hired by The New York Times *to write its "Essay" column and has since become the popular author of the weekly "On Language" column, which appears each Sunday in the* Magazine. *The author of many books, including* Safire's Political Dictionary, On Language, Good Advice, *and* I Stand Corrected, *Safire won a Pulitzer Prize for distinguished commentary in 1978. In this essay, a 1982 "On Language" column, he discusses a linguistic phenomenon that everyone in the business world today experiences: bizbuzz, a pop trend in yuppie language. According to Safire, up-to-date buzz words like "impact" and "interface" can make or break the climber of corporate ladders: "Nobody can apply for a job these days," he remarks, "without a degree in 'bizbuzz,' the jargon that prioritizes the career path of the rising young ballpark figurer." With characteristic style, Safire impacts on upscale bizbuzz, giving us the bottom line, wordwise.*

Nobody can apply for a job these days—or interface with a personnel recruiter in the hopes of impacting on his bottom line—without a degree in "bizbuzz," the jargon that prioritizes the career path of the rising young ballpark figurer.

I have already flunked. The figures of speech used in the preceding paragraph are already business archaisms that might as well have been the patois of Commodore Vanderbilt or Andrew Carnegie.

"The biggest 'bad' corporate word," opines Walter Kiechel 3d, associate editor of Fortune magazine, "is *impact* as a verb." The former noun has been used so often in its verb form in bored rooms that *impact on* has lost its punch, and rising executives are now testing the effect of *affect.*

"*Interface* is a dying word in management," adds John F. Lubin, professor of management at the University of Pennsylvania's Wharton School. "It was taken from systems engineering, where it meant the juncture between two pieces. For a while, *system* was taking over the language of management, but this, too, is dying."

Bottom line is still kicking around, but too many outsiders have been using it, and in jargon, freshness is all. "The *bottom line* originally referred to earnings figures," reports Timothy B. Blodgett of the Harvard Business Review. "Bottom-line responsibility is responsibility for the economic welfare of a division or subsidiary that is supposed to turn a profit. However, the phrase has expanded to include more than just earnings and profits; it can mean, 'The onus is on us' for just about anything." Mr. Blodgett is a senior editor; he has a *straight-line responsibility* to the editor in chief, and a *dotted-line responsibility* to a bunch of other editors. Life follows chart. While we're entangled in lines, Prof. Michael Porter at the Harvard Business School defines *dotted-line responsibility* as "when two people consult with or interact with each other, but one does not report to the other." In olden times, the "dotted line" was where the customer signed; now it is where the responsibility is diffused, and even that expression is fading fast.

Ballpark figure is developing a paunch, too. This derivation of "in the ballpark," an indication of proximity (in contrast to a ball hit clear out of the stadium), is being replaced by one of the new triple hyphenations that make up adjectival phrases dear to bizbuzz: *back-of-the-envelope.* There is a quickly figured difference in meaning, however: "A *ballpark figure* is a rough estimate," explains lexicographer Sol Steinmetz, "while a *back-of-the-envelope sum* is one simply or easily arrived at without the need of a pocket calculator."

Another example of the triple hyphenator is *top-of-the-line,* a compound adjective launched in the late 1960's by auto manufacturers to describe their most expensive models. The British equivalent is *top-of-the-market,* and the phrase is not considered run-down or ramshackle by bizbuzz linguists on top of the state of the art, which is the bottom line on *top-of-the-line.*

Now that we know what is out, what is in?

If you are sad about the loss of *impact on,* try the new *abstract away.* "This means to dwindle into nothing," says the H.B.R.'s Blodgett. "If something *abstracts away,* it has ceased to be definable." Nice phrase; to move from the concrete to the abstract and then to vanish, like the Cheshire cat, leaving only the grin.

Hands-on, a compound adjective with one measly hyphen, has a stranglehold on the throats of businesspeople today. (I almost wrote "businessmen." Somebody must be getting to me.) The original meaning was "vocational," and the first citation in the Barnhart files is "hands-on instruction" for vocational schools, and was a play on "hands off," or so theoretical that it abstracted away. Now it means "practical"; nobody with hands-on experience, in a job interview, would claim anything as outdated as "practical experience." A synonym is *line* experience; this time, the metaphor is probably not from accounting, as in *bottom line,* but from the military, which contrasts *line* (from "front line") and *staff* (or headquarters) experience.

When in need of a modern mystifier, and tired of systems and the same old interfaces, reach for the favorite new management noun: *matrix.* "This came out of organizational behavior," says Professor Lubin, "and was used to describe orthogonal relationships." Asked to put that on a dotted-line basis, Professor Lubin explained: "That's when you have two bosses, or when responsibility is shared between divisions. Came from mathematics, and it's overused." He can hands-on that again. In the Wharton 1980 catalogue, a course in matrix management is advertised in this way: "The unique problem of changing, implementing and fine-tuning matrix forms will be highlighted." According to J. M. Rosenberg's Dictionary of Business and Management, "a matrix organization exists when organizational members have a dual allegiance—to a particular assignment or task and also to their department." O.K.: two bosses, a matrix and (soon to come) a patrix.

Students of bizbuzz (not to be confused with jargon scholars, who are in buzzbiz) search for topical combining forms. For a generation, combination-oriented linguists were studying the use of *-wise,* while formwise lexicographers were collecting the usages of *-oriented.* You could be *job-oriented, leisure-oriented,* or even *Occident-oriented;* similarly, languagewise, you could be *advertisingwise, careerwise* or even *smartswise.*

Forget all that. The new combining forms are *-wide,* and *-intensive.* According to Judy Uhl, senior editor of the division of research for the Harvard Business School, about whose dotted-line responsibilities I have not inquired: "A very common thing is to add *-wide* at the end of things to mean 'a totality,' such as *corporate-wide, industry-wide.* This can also be done without a hyphen, as in *personnelwide.*"

On the *-intensive* front, the earliest entries were *labor-intensive* and *capital-intensive,* but Steinmetz has pockets bulging with citations for *profit-intensive, energy-intensive, people-intensive, assets-*

intensive and *technology-inensive.* His work is neologism-intensive, and applies dictionary-wide.

Vision is a hot word in executive aeries, usually defined as "the ability to see around corners," rather than off into the distance. *Style* is equally sought after, and what *manager style* a corporation prefers determines its character. Fortune's Kiechel points to the popular *earthquake style,* "which is when a manager comes in and shakes everything up."

Bailout has replaced *rescue* in bizbuzz: A dispute is raging among etymologists about its derivation. One school holds that it is from the act of a pilot donning a parachute and leaping out of a falling airplane; another points to the frenzied activity of a fisherman bailing out a boat that is taking in water.

If a bailout fails, a company no longer goes bankrupt; it goes *belly up,* also a fishing metaphor, perhaps influenced by "belly up to the bar." At Forbes magazine, such a term is frowned upon. Geoffrey Smith, an assistant managing editor, who has a wavy-line responsibility to Malcolm Forbes, points to a memo directing writers to stay away from such bizbuzz as *clobber, plummet* and *soar* (trite descriptions of earnings gains or losses), along with *on stream, game plan, shortfall* and *upscale.*

My top-of-the-line model has just intersected with my bottom-line judgment, forming a dotted-line responsibility to all those who want to bellow at bizbuzz and outplace all its speakers. That's earthquake style.

Discussing Ideas and Themes

1. How does Safire define bizbuzz? Does he stick completely to business language? Do you recognize any of these business buzzwords from common usage? Give examples.
2. According to Safire, why do words like "impact" and "interface" become boring or obsolete? What criterion does this short-lived fame establish for vogue bizbuzz words?
3. What relationships can you see between language as a system and business as a system? Does Safire comment on this relationship explicitly? For instance, how does he feel about jargon? About big business? What is the lure of each?
4. What is "earthquake style"? Why does Safire use this term? Why is it funny?

5. What is the difference between Safire's bizbuzz and Baker's New Age Babble? Cite examples.

Discussing Rhetoric and Style

1. Safire's essay is a series of definitions of bizbuzz phrases. Does he ever stop to analyze the language of bizbuzz? Is his critique explicit or implicit? Explain.
2. How effective is Safire's use of quotations from business publications? How does he make these quotations funny just by repeating them? In answering, consider one such passage.
3. Describe Safire's tone throughout the essay. How does it cue you to his aims? For instance, how does the tone of the first paragraph imply that this will not be a serious discussion of the social ramifications of bizbuzz?
4. Do you like the end of the essay? Is it appropriate? Explain.

Ideas for Writing

1. Find a copy of the *Harvard Business Review* in the library and write a critique, modeled on Safire's, on the newest trends in bizbuzz.
2. Although Safire takes bizbuzz lightly here, jargon is a problem that some believe is contributing to America's literacy crisis. Write an essay in which you discuss the ways in which bizbuzz and similar jargon either help or hinder communication among classes and social groups around the country. Do you think bizbuzz is a serious problem? Why or why not?

Bowdlerizing the Bard

How to Protect Your Kids from Shakespeare

DOROTHY WICKENDEN

Born in 1954, Dorothy Wickenden has worked for both the Folger Shakespeare Library and the Shakespeare Review *and is currently a managing editor for* The New Republic, *a popular magazine of politics and culture, in which the following essay first appeared in 1985. In her essay, Wickenden discusses the common and often surreptitious censorship of Shakespeare texts at the high-school level. According to Wickenden, "textbook publishers and school boards have become so accustomed to covert bowdlerization that they apparently came to forget that it was even going on." Thus, even while such censorship is rampant, it is rarely acknowledged on the title page. Wickenden's solution? Alert readers to alterations by using ellipses, and then let them find the original versions in the library.*

It was a studious ninth grader, not an anti-censorship brigade, who set off the most recent flurry about what kids ought to be reading in school. The culprits were not fervid fundamentalists but staid corporate publishers. And the object of censorship was not a science or history text or an obscene novel, but the work of the most revered playwright in the world.

Daniel Blum, a student at Madison High School in Vienna, Virginia, had seen a Folger Theatre production of *Romeo and Juliet,* and when he sat down with his Scott, Foresman *America Reads* textbook to write a paper about Mercutio's Queen Mab speech, he noticed that some of the lines were missing. For example, the "fairies' midwife" who "gallops night by night / Through lovers' brains" is no longer characterized as the hag who "when maids lie on their backs, / . . . presses them and learns them first to bear, / Making them women of good carriage."

Around the time the story broke in Virginia, a parent in Minneapolis discovered that the same anthology had been altered as well as abridged. Romeo's line in Act V, "Well, Juliet, I will lie with thee tonight," was changed to read, "Well, Juliet, I will *be* with thee tonight." Investigations by a Fairfax County textbook advisory committee, school boards, columnists, and People for the American Way revealed not only that more than 300 lines had been eliminated from Scott, Foresman's *Romeo and Juliet*—most of them sexual allusions—but that high school textbook publishers routinely expurgate Shakespeare. Some, including Scott, Foresman, note in teachers' editions that "abridgments" have been made. Most do not.

The overwhelming reaction was one of astonished indignation. Scott, Foresman has received over 2,000 letters deploring the practice of "self-censorship." Yet there is nothing new or surprising about the bowdlerization of Shakespeare. On the contrary, the current batch of "censored" textbooks is resolutely faithful to the traditions of Dr. Bowdler and his sister Harriet, who published their first edition of *Family Shakespeare* in 1807. And publishers of literature anthologies for the public schools have always felt constrained to abridge and excerpt—keeping in mind both the sophistication of the students who will be reading them and the requirements of parents and school districts that will be buying them.

Marlene Blum, a member of the Fairfax County textbook advisory committee and the mother of Daniel, complained to Sandra Sugawara of *The Washington Post*, "It's as if [the publishers] have become the arbiter of what children are to read and not read." Yet if anything, textbook publishers have become more fearful over the years about making their own determinations of what children are to read and not read. They have found that they cannot afford to dismiss the bedrock fundamentalism of people like Mel and Norma Gabler, Texas's notorious textbook scourges, any more than they can the clamoring of countless other political, religious, and ethnic groups to cleanse their books of sexual and racial stereotyping. Jane Bachman, an editorial vice president at Scott, Foresman, guardedly told me, "Textbook publishers anticipate what may be a troublesome matter. We might be a little paranoid when we put a book together."

Clearly some things have changed since the heyday of bowdlerism. There is no comfortable consensus, as there was in the Victorian era, about matters of propriety, church, and state. In its absence, the public schools have become a stage for various special interest groups to perform their political dramas. As the requirements for textbooks have multiplied, publishers have honed their marketing skills, and the role of the editor has dwindled. No single sentinel trims the text and upholds moral and literary standards. Indeed, it is almost irrelevant what the editor believes. Before a textbook comes into being, surveys are conducted, focus groups are convened, and outside consultants are hired. As the book is prepared, armies of reading specialists, instructional designers, teachers, and computers zealously watch over it. They guard against unattractive book covers and ethnic slurs; they monitor "curricular congruence" (text, workbook, and teachers' guide must complement each other) and "readability" levels (vocabulary words and number of syllables per sentence are tabulated according to grade). When the book is finally published, it is subject to review and complaint by concerned citizens and put up for "adoption" by state and local textbook advisory committees equipped with complicated checklists of requirements.

In this Byzantine method of patching together textbooks, the integrity of any single story or play—not to mention the needs of students—often gets lost. Certain particularly troublesome items have been virtually abandoned—among them Shirley Jackson's famous short story, "The Lottery" (too violent), and *The Merchant of Venice* (anti-Semitic). Publishers have gone to absurd lengths to accommodate disparate interest groups and varying state guidelines. Elsa Walsh reported in *The Washington Post* that in a chapter from *Tom Sawyer,* which appears in Ginn and Company's sixth-grade reader *Flights of Color,* the colloquialisms have vanished, the grammar has been cleaned up, Tom's oath of "honest Injun" has been removed, and most references to boys or men have been changed to children or people. A story called "A Perfect Day for Ice Cream" was included in Scott, Foresman's 1985 eighth-grade anthology only after the words "ice cream" had been deleted from the title and a scene about a trip to the ice-cream parlor had been eliminated. The reason, apparently, was California's "social content guidelines" for textbooks, which warn against references to junk food. McGraw-Hill's seventh-grade *Focus* anthology has expunged from "Rip Van Winkle" not only difficult vocabulary words here and there such as "dismembered," but the reference to "obsequious and conciliatory" men who go home to "shrews" and "termagant" wives.

And yet, this is an old story. As Jane Bachman of Scott, Foresman aptly, if perhaps inadvertently, punned in a letter to a man who had written to express dismay at the censoring of the Bard, "Stage and film directors have had their way with Shakespeare since his plays were first performed." One of those they have taken particular liberties with is *Romeo and Juliet.* In *Dr. Bowdler's Legacy* Noel Perrin describes David Garrick in 1750 preparing an acting version of the play in which he decided to dampen Juliet's ardent soliloquy in Act II. "He wasn't trying to spare the audience, though; he just thought it out of character for such a nice girl to speak of maidenheads, much less to wish openly that Romeo would hurry up and take hers." In the 1818 edition of *Family Shakespeare,* Dr. Bowdler removed almost exactly the same lines. Today's textbook publishers too have banished the stuff about maidenheads, both in the banter between Capulet's servants Samson and Gregory in Act I and in Juliet's soliloquy. Harcourt Brace Jovanovich; Scott, Foresman; Macmillan; Ginn; McDougal, Littell and Company; and McGraw-Hill have all eliminated the lines:

> Lovers can see to do their amorous rites
> By their own beauties, or, if love be blind,
> It best agrees with night. Come, civil night,
> Thou sober-suited matron all in black
> And learn me how to lose a winning match,
> Play'd for a pair of stainless maidenhoods.
> Hood my unmann'd blood, bating in my cheeks,
> With thy black mantle, till strange love grow bold,
> Think true love acted simple modesty . . .

as well as,

> O, I have bought the mansion of a love,
> But not possess'd it, and though I am sold,
> Not yet enjoy'd. . . .

Bowdlerizers have long recognized that *Romeo and Juliet,* with its arousing themes of young love, sex, drugs, and death, is particularly appealing to adolescents, and thus a perfect candidate for the curriculum—and for excisions. In editions for the tender reader, it isn't just the impassioned words of a young girl that are generally deemed unprintable, but references to the body (notably nipples and genitals) and its natural functions (particularly childbearing and sexual desire or activity).

One of the salacious lines that has been consistently singled out over the years is Mercutio's remark in Act II, in which he teasingly replies to the Nurse's question about the time: " 'Tis no less, I tell you, for the bawdy hand of the dial is now upon the prick of noon." The first great American expurgation of Shakespeare, published in 1872 by Ginn ("selected and prepared for use in Schools, Clubs, Classes, and Families"), scrupulously retained the word "prick," but omitted "bawdy." Perrin surmises that the book's editor—a Shakespearean scholar—hoped that without the clue his readers wouldn't catch the double entendre. A century later no major textbook publisher is so daring. All have removed the entire line from their ninth-grade anthologies.

Macbeth and *Hamlet* have fared somewhat better. Among the 12th-grade anthologies that include *Macbeth* as their Shakespeare selection, five of the big publishers, like a number of their 19th-century predecessors, have left the play virtually intact—except for the Porter's second speech, where he expounds upon drunken lechery, which "provokes the desire," but "takes away the performance." Scott, Foresman restored the speech in 1979, but continues to do some damage (100 lines' worth) to *Hamlet*. The scene in Act III where he viciously berates his mother for wallowing in incest has been robbed of some of the lines that would doubtless most appeal to teenagers, including: "Nay, but to live / In the rank sweat of an enseamed bed, / Stewed in corruption, honeying and making love / Over the nasty sty!"

As Perrin points out, the Victorians bowdlerized openly, secure in the belief that they were serving the cause of Christianity and assisting in society's moral progress. Today's textbook editors, by contrast, do it shamefully, defensively, on behalf of a cause that most of them don't fully believe in. Responding to the initial complaints about Scott, Foresman's fiddling with Shakespeare, Richard T. Morgan, the president, emphatically stated that "no language has been changed." That proved to be incorrect. It also skirts the tougher question about the line between abridgment and selective expurgation, and about the publisher's responsibility to state clearly what kinds of changes have been made. Jane Bachman insisted, "In no way has the basic nature of 'Romeo and Juliet' been altered." Ginn, which eliminated about 400 lines from *Romeo and Juliet* in its ninth-grade anthology, *Understanding Literature*, brazenly states in its teachers' edition, " 'The Tragedy of Romeo and Juiet' is presented here as Shakespeare wrote it."

Edmund Farrell, a professor of English education at the University of Texas at Austin who has been an author and outside editor for Scott, Foresman since 1958, says frankly: "We are putting out books for ninth graders, not for college students. Schools act in loco parentis. There is no way I know of that a publisher can print 'the bawdy hand of the dial is now upon the prick of noon.' The choice is between abridging the play or not including it at all." That may be understandable. What is not understandable, or acceptable, regardless of the book's market, is to purge and then insist that the basic nature of the play is unchanged. If certain passages must be trimmed, why not indicate with ellipses, as Scott, Foresman does in its 12th-grade *Hamlet?* Why not also point out in both the teachers' guide and the students' introduction that the play has been expurgated?

Textbook publishers and school boards have become so accustomed to covert bowdlerization that they apparently came to forget that it was even going on. The Virginia state board of education, for one, had been happily buying the disputed Scott, Foresman textbook series for years until a ninth grader and his mother objected to its cavalier treatment of Shakespeare. As for teachers, the good ones have always had more faith in their own judgment about what is suitable for their students than they have in the prepackaged selections of mass-market textbook publishers. Some have even taken advantage of their books' flaws. After Daniel Blum's discovery, his teacher supplied the students with the full text of *Romeo and Juliet,* and discussed the anthology's cuts in class. Covert or open, censorship is a doomed enterprise, for it stimulates precisely that dangerous urge it set out to crush: curiosity.

Discussing Ideas and Themes

1. Define "bowdlerization." What is the origin of the term? How has it developed? Does it have good or bad connotations? How does Wickenden use it? Explain in detail.
2. Why do textbook publishers alter texts? What is the origin of this practice? Is it more or less common today than it was a hundred years ago? Why or why not?
3. Why does Wickenden find the textbook process "Byzantine"? Does she ever define this term? Do you understand its use in context? And do you agree with her characterization? Give reasons to support your conclusions.
4. What differences does Wickenden see between modern censorship and Victorian censorship? How detailed is her description of the Victorian system? Is this description necessary to explain the modern system? Why does she include it?
5. What kinds of books are likely to be censored? What lines are likely to be altered? Can you relate these facts to other arguments in this section about euphemism and taboos in language?

Discussing Rhetoric and Style

1. Outline Wickenden's argument. Is her arrangement well chosen? Is it interesting? Explain with references to the essay.
2. How well does Wickenden describe the procedures of bookmaking and bookselling? List each step in the process. Is the list coherent?
3. Why does Wickenden choose to build her discussion on the censorship of Shakespeare? Does this strategy help to broaden her audience? Why or why not?
4. If you were an editor, would you alter any of Wickenden's text? Go through it once or twice, bowdlerizing what you will. Do your changes hurt the essay?

Ideas for Writing

1. Describe a procedure that you have often encountered—for instance, looking for a job, choosing a college, or even going shopping. Base your discussion on Wickenden's essay, imitating when you can the strategies she uses in describing the processes of bookselling.
2. Develop an essay on one of the Shakespearean passages cited in Wickenden's essay, arguing either for or against the alterations commonly made by publishers. What makes these lines important enough to keep or negligible enough to change?

What "Dirty Words" Really Mean

DR. JOYCE BROTHERS

Dr. Joyce Brothers is a well-known psychologist, author, and television personality who frequently appears on talk shows and game shows as well as occasionally cameoing for prime-time sitcoms and movies. In this essay, she turns to a less glamorous task, discussing what she considers to be the source of "gutter" language. Brothers suggests that although the use of dirty words can often be the sign of healthy liberation from stifling social restraints, it can also denote deeper problems and insecurities about sex, race, and self; ultimately, though such language is meant to defiantly shock, it more often becomes predictable and goes unnoticed: according to Brothers, "there is nothing more conventional than dirty words." The essay first appeared in an issue of Good Housekeeping.

We were talking, a group of us at a party, about a new book remarkable for its ferocious obscenity. "I couldn't read it," someone said. "All those dirty words." At that, an indignant young woman fixed the speaker with a withering glance and announced, "There are no dirty words—only dirty minds."

This extreme position, accepting any kind of language, however gross or violent, is not uncommon today. Individuals who pride themselves on their sophistication often feel it's important to be shockproof. ("I'm so enlightened, so aware, nothing fazes me.") Such an attitude betrays a misunderstanding of the nature of obscenity and, more seriously, of its emotional meaning. There have always been "dirty" words—and probably there always will be.

Of course, the words themselves change from one generation to another. In the Victorian period, a respectable woman would have hesitated to call a leg a *leg* ("limb" being both more refined and less suggestive). It was only a generation ago that Clark Gable, as Rhett Butler in the movie version of *Gone with the Wind,* created a sensation by declaring that he didn't give a *damn.* And Norman Mailer became notorious during the Forties for his free use of earthy terms denoting sexual intercourse.

What gives dirty words their shock power? Partly convention. We are startled by language that violates our sense of what may and may not be said. More important is the fact that such words are connected with emotions and experiences that both frighten and fascinate. "Hell" and "damn" have lost a good deal of their force as religion becomes a less potent influence in daily life. But sex, in spite of the much-heralded sexual revolution, remains a subject highly charged with emotion, and most dirty language which retains its power to disturb is sex-related.

One source of dirty talk about sex is simple awkwardness. There are situations in which the common coarse term is the easiest way to describe certain parts of the anatomy, certain physical functions. Any doctor knows that men or women with genital or excretory problems are often at a loss for words to explain the trouble. Even if the patient is familiar with medical terminology, he may feel self-conscious using it. (Can he pronounce the word correctly? Will he sound pretentious?) And lovers, understandably, may feel that such terms as "sexual intercourse" and "copulation" are a cold, impersonal way to describe the sex act.

Furthermore, there exists in most people a deep ambivalence about sex, a confusion that may express itself in deliberately ugly language. The fact that, as the poet Yeats says, "Love has pitched his mansion in the place of excrement" still muddles our feelings about sex. On an unconscious level, we may feel there is something dirty, something soiling about physical union. Semen and the lubricating fluids of the vagina are at one level regarded as if they were body wastes—when in fact they are nothing of the sort. For most, the sex drive is strong enough to overcome any squeamishness, but there remains a lingering unease.

This ambivalence turns the obscene word for intercourse into an insult, the thrust of the insult being directed at the person who receives the sexual attention. ("——you.") Although we no longer consider women passive participants in the sex act, much of the vehemence of obscenity has been directed against the female and her sexual role, as if being the receiver of semen was somehow humiliating.

Ultimately, dirty words are ugly not because they refer to sex but because they imply a narrow, mechanical master-and-victim concept of sexuality. Prohibiting the use of such words will not change basic attitudes that give rise to them. They lose their power only when we are able to see sex as neither exploitation nor salvation but a human, often imperfect, activity bringing a man and woman together in a loving way.

Of course some kinds of obscenity are only superficially sexual. The real emotional meaning of a dirty word can't be understood apart from the situation in which it occurs. A child's occasional filthy language is probably a kind of testing and self-assertion; he says the unspeakable to get a rise out of his parents. (And they would do well not to overreact.) A normally "refined" woman may at times need the release of profanity. (She's been driving in a rainstorm, say, hears the thump-thump of a flat tire—and pulling over to the side of the road, finds the spare is flat too.) In a wildly frustrating situation, there's something healthy about the defiant outpouring of gutter language; it's more positive than helpless weeping. Women who have serious responsibilities thrust upon them—supporting a whole family, running a business—are more likely to use dirty words than women with simpler lives. Few people would judge them harshly for that. And among some young people, the use of profanity is so constant as to be meaningless—like everything else, dirty words wear out with overuse.

Dirty words are often used by teenagers in telling off-color stories and this can be considered part of their sex education. As their bodies grow and change, both boys and girls wonder and worry. To keep from being overwhelmed by these fears, they turn them into jokes or dirty-word stories. By telling and retelling off-color stories, they gain a little information, more misinformation and a lot of reassurance. They learn that they aren't the only ones in the group disturbed about their future roles in courtship and marriage. Using dirty words and stories to laugh at sexual doubts and fears, may diminish their importance and make them less frightening.

Most of us are disturbed, though, when a bright, attractive young woman punctuates her every sentence with a four-letter word. Other women view such language as a threat to conventional notions of femininity. Men sense it as an implicit challenge. ("I have just as much right as any man to say what I feel like saying.") It's not surprising that college campuses, the scene of so many rebellions, are also centers of an almost total language freedom, with "nice" girls using words which were once the prerogative of truckdrivers. This phenomenon is a predictable reaction to the easing of social and sexual restraints on women, such restrictions having always been more severe for women than for men. (Psychologist Philip Zimbardo reports that among agitated mental patients, it's women who use the most obscene language. "The psychological controls we put on women are so tight that when they break through, they really let go.")

Obscene language serves as a tension-releaser for men too. And men cut off from women—in prison, during wartime, on submarines—are likely to employ an unusual amount of obscenity, partly to vent the fears about homosexual impulses aroused by such highly charged, intimate situations.

So far I've been talking about occasional, casual obscenity. But anyone who seems obsessed with the use of dirty words is not simply giving vent to healthy self-expression. The repeated, compulsive use of obscene language is a sign of psychological disturbance. The child who constantly assaults a parent with abusive language, the adolescent preoccupied with dirty words, the man or woman unable to become sexually aroused without a tirade of filthy language, the man who delights in muttering obscenities at female passersby—these people are using language in an aggressive, hostile way, expressing their own inner confusion.

Inner confusion also generates another large class of dirty words. These have nothing to do with bathroom or bedroom, but they are obscene in that they too are dehumanizing and distorting. Derogatory epithets applied to persons of different race, religion or culture are as hostile as sexual slurs. Like other kinds of obscenity, they stem from fear and ambivalence. An insecure individual easily feels threatened by differences in appearance and behavior; his instinctive defense, often, is foul language.

Such name-calling is not limited to ethnic groups. Calling policemen "pigs," men "male chauvinists" and feminists "bra burners" is using aggressive, deliberately insulting language to deny the individual uniqueness of another person.

Fortunately, this type of obscenity is being slowly drained of its power. One way to render it impotent is for the group in question to use the supposedly derogatory term for themselves. So, blacks may refer to themselves ironically as "niggers," policemen call themselves "pigs" and men laughingly speak of themselves as "male chauvinists." Or a group may adopt a term originally derisive and insist on its usage, a term which acknowledges differentness—with pride Mexican-Americans, for example, now often refer to themselves as Chicanos.

Even a TV program like *All in the Family* may help reduce fears and prejudices simply by airing them. Archie Bunker is funny because week after week his fears and misconceptions about minority groups are shown to be unrealistic and unreasonable, and we laugh at his narrow view of the world.

Ethnic, sexual or whatever, all forms of obscenity, as psychologist Renatus Hartogs observes, "have one thing in common: they are the mask of fear. They camouflage a reality too unbearable without the release obtained through the therapeutic four-letter word. . . . Because the mask hides our fears from ourselves, the obscene person rarely knows just what he is masking. The freedom he gains through his vernacular is illusory."

The real argument against the use of dirty words, then, is not that they shock or disturb the listener but that they are a limiting, self-deceiving form of expression that reveals insecurity rather than unconventionality. There is nothing *more* conventional than dirty words.

Discussing Ideas and Themes

1. What does Brothers feel to be the source of dirty language? Does she consider such language acceptable? Dangerous? Trivial? Explain.
2. Is the use of "gutter" language ever healthy? If so, cite examples.
3. Throughout her essay, Brothers seems particularly interested in women's use of dirty words. What connections does she see between language taboos and other social restraints placed on women? How, according to the author, do women react when released from such restraints? Do you agree with her analysis?
4. Describe the relationship between "dirty" sexual terms and ethnic epithets. What do they have in common? What makes them different? Explain, with a few brief examples.
5. Brothers claims that "prohibiting the use of such [dirty] words will not change basic attitudes that give rise to them." Compare this statement to one quoted at the beginning of the essay: "There are no dirty words—only dirty minds." Are the two statements at all similar? What does each imply about the nature of taboo language and about human nature in general? What conclusions about dirty words does each speaker eventually draw from these statements?

Discussing Rhetoric and Style

1. Consider Brothers's sexual vocabulary (such as her use of the phrases "the sex act" and "the receiver of semen"). Do you consider her vocabulary euphemistic? Is her choice of words ever motivated by any of the factors that supposedly motivate the use of "dirty" words? And if so, what does this choice say about the relationship between euphemism and taboo in language?

2. Study the examples in this essay—for example, the use of anecdotes, the reference to Yeats, the allusion to *All in the Family*, and so on. To what audiences does Brothers try to appeal with the use of such examples? How successful is she?

3. How does Brothers organize her essay? Can you see the major sections of her argument? How are these sections linked? How are they wrapped up in the conclusion?

4. Although Brothers's essay deals with the use of dirty language, it never actually uses any. Why do you think Brothers has opted *not* to list any dirty words? Does this omission bother you? How would you have handled the problem, and why?

Ideas for Writing

1. Write a brief essay in response to Brothers's assertion, "There is nothing *more* conventional than dirty words."

2. Write a history of your own experiences with dirty words, cataloguing and describing your earliest memories of language taboos. How has your sense of what is dirty and what isn't gradually changed over time? What do you consider the strongest influences on your use or non-use of dirty language (for instance, parents, teachers, television, peers)? As you map your verbal patterns, compare your behavior to the descriptions and analyses in Brothers's essay. If you ever used taboo language, were you motivated by the reasons Brothers discussed? Why or why not?

On the Use of "Dirty" Words

WILLIAM F. BUCKLEY, JR.

Joyce Brothers concludes that dirty language masks unhealthy insecurities; William F. Buckley maintains that dirty words are, on the contrary, often completely appropriate and even necessary to describe certain states of mind. Buckley emphasizes the importance of context, noting that even Shakespeare used obscene language to enrich his plays. Buckley, a prolific writer as well as an editor of the National Review *and the host of television's* Firing Line, *has published several books of nonfiction, such as* God and Man at Yale: The Superstition of Academic Freedom, *as well as many best-selling novels, including* High Jinx *and* Stained Glass. *This essay appeared in the* National Review *in 1973.*

I guess I was seven when I first heard the maxim that only people with a small vocabulary use "dirty" words. I am 47 and have just received a communication from a reader delivering that maxim as though he had invented it. The trouble with the cliché is (a) it isn't true; (b) it doesn't take into account the need to use the resources of language; and (c) the kind of people who use it are almost always engaged in irredentist ventures calculated to make "dirty," words and expressions that no longer are, and even some that never were.

The first point is easily disposed of by asking ourselves the question, Did Shakespeare have a good vocabulary? Yes; and he also used, however sparingly, profane and obscene words.

The second point raises the question of whether a certain kind of emotion is readily communicable with the use of other than certain kinds of words. Let us assume the only thing it is safe to assume about the matter, namely that every emotion is experienced by everyone, from the darkest sinner to the most uplifted saint. The sinner, having no care at all for people's feelings, let alone for propriety abstractly considered, lets loose a profanity not only on occasions when his emotions are acutely taxed, but even when they are mildly stirred. The saint—or so I take it from their published writings—manages to exclude the profane word from his vocabulary, and does not resort to it under any circumstances. It was for the saint that the tushery was invented. "Tush! tush!" the saint will say to his tormentors, as he is eased into the cauldron of boiling oil.

Non-saints, it is my thesis, have a difficult time adopting the manners of saints; and even if they succeed most of the time in suppressing obnoxious words, they will probably not succeed all of the time. Moreover, as suggested above, they are up against a community some of whose members are always seeking to repristinate the world of language back to the point where you could not even say, "Gosh, Babe Ruth was a good baseball player," because Gosh is quite clearly a sneaky way of saying God, the use of which the purists would hold to be impermissible under any circumstances—indeed they, plus the Supreme Court, reduce the permissible use of the word to the innermost tabernacles.

The context in which a bad word is used does much to determine the quality of its offensiveness, and the usefulness of the word. Reviewing Norman Mailer's first novel many years ago, Professor John Roche objected that the recurring use of barracks language, while it reproduced faithfully the language of the barracks, in fact distorts the prose for readers outside the barracks set who are emotionally or psychologically interrupted every time they run into a word they are not used to seeing on the printed page. It is as if a poet were handicapped by the miscadencing of his verse by a reader who suddenly paused at unexpected places, as if to walk around a puddle of water.

I had reason to reach, a while back, for a word to comment upon a line of argument I considered insufferably sanctimonious. "Crap," I wrote: And the irredentist hordes descended upon me in all their fury. I have replied to them that the word in question is defined in a current dictionary in several ways. That among these are meaning 2: "nonsense; drivel: *Man, don't hand me that crap.* 3. a lie; an exaggeration: *Bah, you don't believe that crap, do you?*" Notwithstanding that the word has these clearly non-scatological uses, there is an Anglo-Saxon earthiness to it which performs for the writer a function altogether different from such a retort as, say, "Flapdoodle."

There are those of us who feel very strongly that the cheapest and most indefensible way to give offense is to direct obscenities wantonly, and within the earshot of those who seek protection from that kind of thing. There will always be a certain healthy tension between Billingsgate and the convent, but in the interest of the language, neither side should win the war completely. Better a stalemate, with a DMZ that changes its bed meanderingly, like the Mississippi River.

Discussing Ideas and Themes

1. What does Buckley find wrong with the theory that "only people with a small vocabulary use 'dirty' words"? How does he prove otherwise?
2. What is the difference, in Buckley's essay, between saints and sinners? What examples does Buckley provide of each? Which does Buckley think he is? Which are you?
3. How important is a word's context in determining its appropriateness? Are certain words ever completely inappropriate? Cite several examples, both from the essay and from your own experience.
4. How is Buckley's argument essentially different from that of Brothers? Would she approve of his use of the word "crap"? Would he approve of her analysis of his use of "crap"?

Discussing Rhetoric and Style

1. Buckley immediately dismisses the initial maxim about dirty words as a "cliché," dividing the statement into three parts and then proving each one false. Outline Buckley's argument and method. Do you see a hole in his logic?
2. Pick an example of a funny moment in Buckley's essay, and then try to describe how the humor works. For example, why is his discussion of saints and sinners humorous? From what unstated facts does the irony in this discussion arise?
3. Buckley often creates winning arguments by using the topic of division. That is, he divides people into two groups (such as Saints versus Sinners or People-Who-Respect-Shakespeare versus People-Who-Don't), and he then makes one group more desirable to his audience than the other (usually by including himself in it). How effective is this technique in winning over an

intelligent audience? Does it ever annoy you? Does it always work?

4. Describe the tone of this essay. How does Buckley use tonal variations to imply unspoken conclusions about who uses dirty language and who doesn't? Cite an example.
5. Buckley is a popular writer. How would you characterize his prose style? Do you find it readable, confusing, enjoyable, annoying, dense? Make a list of adjectives, with examples of each cited from the essay.

Ideas for Writing

1. Pick a slightly taboo word like "crap," and then discuss its origin and use as Buckley does here. Are there situations in which the word you have chosen is the only one that can convey a particular meaning? And if so, does this fact sanction the use of this word? Why or why not?
2. Write an ironic response to Buckley, imitating his own humorous tone in order to support the argument that "only people with a small vocabulary use 'dirty' words."

STUDENT ESSAY

Aunt Ethel

M. K. TUCKER

Miriam Tucker returned to college after many years to brush up on her writing skills and to observe the goings-on in a college classroom. The following essay, written for an undergraduate class in Advanced Expository Writing at Rutgers University, describes her memories of her Aunt Ethel. Although she insists that she grew up with the conviction that "Aunt Ethel was a real bitch," Tucker never expressed her suspicions because she knew that her parents would disapprove. In this brief but finely detailed sketch, Tucker manages to catch the fantastic power that taboo words can have on children, who are not allowed to use them, as well as the responsibility they inspire in adults, who can.

My Aunt Ethel was what you'd call a real bitch.

Stating this is simple now, particularly now, four years after her death and many more since I made my peace with her. But it wasn't always.

Aunt Ethel was A Women Who Understood A Thing Or Two About What Was Best, and she behaved as if this burden of knowledge carried with it certain pedagogical duties and obligations. She advised everyone, and everyone's children. She told me how much excitement I could stand, how much sun, how much sleep and when. How much food and in what combinations. Her rightness was unending, and because she was always Clearly Correct, incontrovertible. She inspected every supper table I ever set, no matter how casual the occasion, to ensure the proper placement of the salt and pepper cellars. When offering round sweets, she held forth on the benefits of healthful eating, particularly in young girls who tended towards chubbiness.

Aunt Ethel never understood what drove children and adults

alike to resent her plentiful advice. She was, after all, "only trying to be helpful." She could never, in all truthfulness, "see the need for hypersensitivity." She was only "suggesting," and why a person wouldn't at least give some consideration to these suggestions was "at least a little peculiar." No. Nothing and no one was good enough for my Aunt Ethel. Most any circumstance disappointed, at least in part, as did most people, particularly the ones she loved.

On alternate weekends throughout the summers of my childhood, my family would make the drive from Philadelphia to the Atlantic City shore to visit Aunt Ethel. It is a measure of the greatness of my loathing for her that even the beach and the sea, even the boardwalk at twilight, its ringing arcades and splendid taffies, could not make up for the hours spent near her.

"Please," I would beg, "Please, Daddy. Let's stay home this weekend. I don't like it at Aunt Ethel's."

This was code. I could not bring myself to say outright "I hate this woman and would happily never see her again," could not risk the disapproval. Still, my father would take my tacit meaning, and answer the sentiment unspoken.

"Now, Miriam," he would say, "My sister has had a difficult time of it. You have to understand. She loves you very much."

And so we would go, year after year, alternate weekends, until I left for college and was let alone.

One summer night at dinner when I was nineteen, my parents suggested that perhaps I might like to join them on that weekend's expedition to Ethel's, and I thought this invitation over carefully in the silence that ensued.

"Dad," I finally said, "Dad, Aunt Ethel is a bitch."

My father pulled up from his soup in surprise.

"Miriam." he said. "You know as well as I do that your aunt has had a difficult time of it. You have to be a little more understanding. She loves you very much."

"I know, Dad. She loves me. But, Dad . . . she's still a bitch."

My father began to speak, but he didn't. He colored slightly and looked away from me. Then he looked back. He eyed me for what seemed a very long time.

"Well." he said, still looking sharply into my eyes. "Well. I suppose you could say she is."

And there it was. The truth. The truth made word. The word made speech and voiced for all of us to share. I was overwhelmed. I was giddy with release.

"YES!" I wanted to scream, "I KNEW IT! I'VE KNOWN IT FOR YEARS! WE'VE ALL KNOWN IT FOR YEARS AND YEARS AND YEARS!"

But I didn't. I restrained myself and we went on eating, my parents and I, eating, but not speaking. As we did, I played and replayed for myself the miraculous exchange with my father.

"Aunt Ethel's a bitch," I thought. "Well, what do you know. What do you know. Old Aunt Ethel. Stupid old Aunt Ethel. Poor old stupid old Aunt Ethel's a bitch."

"What I'm saying," said my father, "is that my sister may be . . . , but she has reasons."

"I know, Dad," I said. "I know. So, how about this. I'll call when you're down there. Okay? I'll say hello."

Discussing Ideas and Themes

1. Describe Aunt Ethel. Can you imagine any details that Tucker omits—for example, Aunt Ethel's wardrobe, her favorite television shows (if any), the books she might read? Would any of these details make the essay better? Why or why not?
2. Does Tucker stereotype her aunt? Do you recognize this character from anywhere else—television, books, everyday life? Do you have an "Aunt Ethel" of your own?
3. Why is it so hard for Tucker to admit out loud that Aunt Ethel is a bitch? What might Brothers make of Tucker's difficulty? What do you think?
4. Describe in a few sentences the author's "miraculous exchange" with her father. What makes the exchange so meaningful for her? Why is she surprised by her father's response? Does voicing her lifelong suspicion make it any more true for her? Why or why not?
5. What lesson does Tucker learn from Aunt Ethel and from her father? Where does the lesson become clear? Is it a lesson about love? Family? Language? Etiquette? Why?

Discussing Rhetoric and Style

1. Why, in light of the readings in this section, is the first sentence so striking? What are the elements—besides the word "bitch"—that contribute to its power (for example, its placement as a separate paragraph, or its tone)? Is it a good sentence, or just a sensationalist grabber?

2. Read Tucker's essay aloud, listening carefully to the rhythm of her prose and particularly watching her use of strategic pauses and interruptions. Then take an old essay of your own, and try to disrupt your sentence patterns in order to create an aural or spoken effect (as Tucker does here). Does your prose sound better this way? Offer reasons to support your position.

3. Consider Tucker's punctuation, for example, her use of capitalized letters and words. What effect does punctuation have on the way you read her sentences? Does punctuation such as this affect tone and meaning? Before answering, retype the sentences without the capitals. How or how aren't they different?

4. How do you relate to the author—do you like her at all? Does Tucker's rhetorical posture, her awareness of both her audience and her own persona, contribute to your feelings? Explain in a few sentences.

5. Does the end of this essay seem too didactic for your taste? Are we meant to learn a lesson? Does Tucker learn one? Is her treatment of the growth theme appropriate in its light-handedness? Why or why not?

Ideas for Writing

1. Write a brief letter to Tucker in the voice of her Aunt Ethel. Try, as much as you can, to stick to the characterization Tucker has given us here.

2. Using Tucker's essay as a model, write a memoir about someone you really don't or didn't like. Do you encounter any difficulties similar to Tucker's in admitting that you never liked this person? Why?

CHAPTER 3

Language and Gender: Is English Sexually Biased?

The power of language to elicit emotions by describing relations between the sexes is not limited to great literature. Everyday talk inevitably describes those who use it. And since language is both a public property—"belonging" to everyone who can use it, and at the same time a very personal matter—expressing an individual's thoughts and feelings, the possibilities for emotional conflict are always present. One such conflict involves the emotionally charged question of sexist language. The debate in this section deals with whether the English language as traditionally used is offensive to women and should therefore be modified.

Casey Miller and Kate Swift make a feminist case in their famous essay, "One Small Step for Genkind," whose publication made an early and thorough presentation of the claim of an inherent antifemale prejudice in English. The authors give their views of the origins and nature of the prejudice and make recommendations about overcoming it. Miller and Swift published their essay in 1972; in the following years many linguistic issues arose, none perhaps so touchy as those involving husband and wife. The question of a bride's surname became a topic that continues to be debated. In "The Name Is Mine" Anna Quindlen gives her personal testimony while acknowledging the difficulty of deciding the issue completely.

Susan Jacoby takes a hard, patient look at the word "feminism," one of the most debated words in recent history. In looking at the relations of "feminine" and "feminist" Jacoby finds that many women are, in the words of her title, "Misconstruing Feminism's Nature."

Richard Mitchell resists many of the changes in English that the arguments of earlier essays support. He finds the reasoning faulty, the claims disingenuous, and the results ugly. In "The Hand that Rocks the Helm," the case depends heavily on irony.

Eugene August seems to agree with Mitchell, but takes a different approach in "Real Men Don't: Anti-Male Bias in English." August adopts methods that imitate the thoroughness and historical depth of Miller and Swift but finds that the apparent prejudice of English is not one that favors men.

In the last professional essay of the section, Joseph Mehan addresses issues of public ceremony related to earlier essays on the language of marriage. Mehan sees unreasonable panic in the tendency to suppress "honorifics"—titles of respect like "Mr." and "Mrs."—merely because they identify the sex of the person described.

Student writer Anthony Maimone approaches the same issue more generally when he argues against a college resolution to change the designation "freshman" to "first-year student."

One Small Step for Genkind

CASEY MILLER and KATE SWIFT

Published in 1972 in The New York Times Magazine, *Casey Miller and Kate Swift's "One Small Step for Genkind" was the first analysis of sexist language to gain the recognition of a national audience. In it, the authors discuss the kinds of anti-female prejudices at work in our language today and explore their possible origins. They argue that even from the earliest eras of spoken and written language, women have been considered invisible: "the English language defines everyone as male," they tell us; "the hypothetical person ('If a man can walk ten miles in two hours . . .'), the average person ('the man in the street') and the active person ('the man on the move') are [all] male." With humor and scholarly precision, the two authors try to reconstruct history the way it should have been written—with women included. Miller and Swift are the editors of the* Handbook of Nonsexist Writing, *which first appeared in 1980.*

A riddle is making the rounds that goes like this: A man and his young son were in an automobile accident. The father was killed and the son, who was critically injured, was rushed to a hospital. As attendants wheeled the unconscious boy into the emergency room, the doctor on duty looked down at him and said, "My God, it's my son!" What was the relationship of the doctor to the injured boy?

If the answer doesn't jump to your mind, another riddle that has been around a lot longer might help: The blind beggar had a brother. The blind beggar's brother died. The brother who died had no brother. What relation was the blind beggar to the blind beggar's brother?

As with all riddles, the answers are obvious once you see them: The doctor was the boy's mother and the beggar was her brother's sister. Then why doesn't everyone solve them immediately? Mainly because our language, like the culture it reflects, is male oriented. To say that a woman in medicine is an exception is simply to confirm that statement. Thousands of doctors are women, but in order to be seen in the mind's eye, they must be called women doctors.

Except for words that refer to females by definition (mother, actress, Congresswoman), and words for occupations traditionally held by females (nurse, secretary, prostitute), the English language defines everyone as male. The hypothetical person ("If a man can walk 10 miles in two hours . . ."), the average person ("the man in the street") and the active person ("the man on the move") are male. The assumption is that unless otherwise identified, people in general—including doctors and beggars—are men. It is a semantic mechanism that operates to keep women invisible: *man* and *mankind* represent everyone; *he* in generalized use refers to either sex; the "land where our fathers died" is also the land of our mothers—although they go unsung. As the beetle-browed and mustachioed man in a Steig cartoon says to his two male drinking companions, "When I speak of mankind, one thing I *don't* mean is womankind."

Semantically speaking, woman is not one with the species of man, but a distinct subspecies. "Man," says the 1971 edition of the Britannica Junior Encyclopedia, "is the highest form of life on earth. His superior intelligence, combined with certain physical characteristics, have enabled man to achieve things that are impossible for other animals." (The prose style has something in common with the report of a research team describing its studies on "the development of the uterus in rats, guinea pigs and men.") As though quoting the Steig character, still speaking to his friends in McSorley's, the Junior Encyclopedia continues: "Man must invent most of his behavior, because he lacks the instincts of lower animals. . . . Most of the things he learns have been handed down from his ancestors by language and symbols rather than by biological inheritance."

Considering that for the last 5,000 years society has been patriarchal, that statement explains a lot. It explains why Eve was made from Adam's rib instead of the other way around, and who invented all those Adam-rib words like *fe*male and *wo*man in the first place. It also explains why, when it is necessary to mention woman, the language makes her a lower caste, a class separate from the rest of man; why it works to "keep her in her place."

This inheritance through language and other symbols begins in the home (also called a man's castle) where man and wife (not husband and wife, or man and woman) live for a while with their children. It is reinforced by religious training, the educational system, the press, government, commerce and the law. As Andrew Greeley wrote not long ago in his magazine, "Man is a symbol-creating animal. He orders and interprets his reality by his symbols, and he uses the symbols to reconstruct that reality."

Consider some of the reconstructed realities of American history. When school children learn from their textbooks that the early colonists gained valuable experience in governing themselves, they are not told that the early colonists who were women were denied the privilege of self-government; when they learn that in the 18th century the average man had to manufacture many of the things he and his family needed, they are not told that this "average man" was often a woman who manufactured much of what she and her family needed. Young people learn that intrepid pioneers crossed the country in covered wagons with their wives, children and cattle; they do not learn that women themselves were intrepid pioneers rather than part of the baggage.

In a paper published this year in Los Angeles as a guide for authors and editors of social-studies textbooks, Elizabeth Burr, Susan Dunn and Norma Farquhar document unintentional skewings of this kind that occur either because women are not specifically mentioned as affecting or being affected by historical events, or because they are discussed in terms of outdated assumptions. "One never sees a picture of women captioned simply 'farmers' or 'pioneers,'" they point out. The subspecies nomenclature that requires a caption to read "women farmers" or "women pioneers" is extended to impose certain jobs on women by definition. The textbook guide gives as an example the word *housewife,* which it says not only "suggests that domestic chores are the exclusive burden of females," but gives "female students the idea that they were born to keep house and teaches male students that they are automatically entitled to laundry, cooking and housecleaning services from the women in their families."

Sexist language is any language that expresses such stereotyped attitudes and expectations, or that assumes the inherent superiority of one sex over the other. When a woman says of her husband, who has drawn up plans for a new bedroom wing and left out closets, "Just like a man," her language is as sexist as the man's who says, after his wife has changed her mind about needing the new wing after all, "Just like a woman."

Male and female are not sexist words, but masculine and feminine almost always are. Male and female can be applied objectively to individual people and animals and, by extension, to things. When electricians and plumbers talk about male and female couplings, everyone knows or can figure out what they mean. The terms are graphic and culture free.

Masculine and feminine, however, are as sexist as any words

can be, since it is almost impossible to use them without invoking cultural stereotypes. When people construct lists of "masculine" and "feminine" traits they almost always end up making assumptions that have nothing to do with innate differences between the sexes. We have a friend who happens to be going through the process of pinning down this very phenomenon. He is 7 years old and his question concerns why his coats and shirts button left over right while his sister's button the other way. He assumes it must have something to do with the differences between boys and girls, but he can't see how.

What our friend has yet to grasp is that the way you button your coat, like most sex-differentiated customs, has nothing to do with real differences but much to do with what society wants you to feel about yourself as a male or female person. Society decrees that it is appropriate for girls to dress differently from boys, to act differently, and to think differently. Boys must be masculine, whatever that means, and girls must be feminine.

Unabridged dictionaries are a good source for finding out what society decrees to be appropriate, though less by definition than by their choice of associations and illustrations. Words associated with males—*manly, virile* and *masculine,* for example—are defined through a broad range of positive attributes like strength, courage, directness and independence, and they are illustrated through such examples of contemporary usage as "a manly determination to face what comes," "a virile literary style," "a masculine love of sports." Corresponding words associated with females are defined with fewer attributes (though weakness is often one of them) and the examples given are generally negative if not clearly pejorative: "feminine wiles," "womanish tears," "a womanlike lack of promptness," "convinced that drawing was a waste of time, if not downright womanly."

Male-associated words are frequently applied to females to describe something that is either incongruous ("a mannish voice") or presumably commendable ("a masculine mind," "she took it like a man"), but female-associated words are unreservedly derogatory when applied to males, and are sometimes abusive to females as well. The opposite of "masculine" is "effeminate," although the opposite of "feminine" is simply "unfeminine."

One dictionary, after defining the word *womanish* as "suitable to or resembling a woman," further defines it as "unsuitable to a man or to a strong character of either sex." Words derived from "sister" and "brother" provide another apt example, for whereas "sissy," applied either to a male or female, conveys the message that sisters are expected to be timid and cowardly, "buddy" makes clear that brothers are friends.

The subtle disparagement of females and corresponding approbation of males wrapped up in many English words is painfully illustrated by "tomboy." Here is an instance where a girl who likes sports and the out-of-doors, who is curious about how things work, who is adventurous and bold instead of passive, is defined in terms of something she is not—a boy. By denying that she can be the person she is and still be a girl, the word surreptitiously undermines her sense of identity: it says she is unnatural. A "tomboy," as defined by one dictionary, is a "girl, especially a young girl, who behaves like a spirited boy." But who makes the judgment that she is acting like a spirited boy, not a spirited girl? Can it be a coincidence that in the case of the dictionary just quoted the editor, executive editor, managing editor, general manager, all six members of the Board of Linguists, the usage editor, science editor, all six general editors of definitions, and 94 out of the 104 distinguished experts consulted on usage—are men?

It isn't enough to say that any invidious comparisons and stereotypes lexicographers perpetuate are already present in the culture. There are ways to define words like womanly and tomboy that don't put women down, though the tradition has been otherwise. Samuel Johnson, the lexicographer, was the same Dr. Johnson who said, "A woman preaching is like a dog's walking on his hind legs. It is not done well; but you are surprised to find it done at all."

Possibly because of the negative images associated with womanish and womanlike, and with expressions like "woman driver" and "woman of the street," the word woman dropped out of fashion for a time. The women at the office and the women on the assembly line and the women one first knew in school all became ladies or girls or gals. Now a countermovement, supported by the very term women's liberation, is putting back into words like woman and sister and sisterhood the meaning they were losing by default. It is as though, in the nick of time, women had seen that the language itself could destroy them.

Some long-standing conventions of the news media add insult to injury. When a woman or girl makes news, her sex is identified at the beginning of a story, if possible in the headline or its equivalent. The assumption, apparently, is that whatever event or action is being reported, a woman's involvement is less common and therefore more newsworthy than a man's. If the story is about achievement, the implication is: "pretty good for a woman." And because people are assumed to be male unless otherwise identified, the media have developed a special and extensive vocabulary to avoid the constant repetition of "woman." The results, "Grandmother Wins Nobel Prize," "Blonde Hijacks Airliner," "Housewife to Run for Congress," convey the kind of information that would be ludicrous in comparable headlines if the subjects were men. Why, if "Unsalaried Husband to Run for Congress" is unacceptable to editors, do women have to keep explaining that to describe them through external or superficial concerns reflects a sexist view of women as decorative objects, breeding machines and extensions of men, not real people?

Members of the Chicago chapter of the National Organization for Women recently studied the newspapers in their area and drew up a set of guidelines for the press. These include cutting out descriptions of the "clothes, physical features, dating life and marital status of women where such references would be considered inappropriate if about men"; using language in such a way as to include women in copy that refers to homeowners, scientists and business people where "newspaper descriptions often convey the idea that all such persons are male"; and displaying the same discretion in printing generalizations about women as would be shown toward racial, religious and ethnic groups. "Our concern with what we are called may seem trivial to some people," the women said, "but we regard the old usages as symbolic of women's position within this society."

The assumption that an adult woman is flattered by being called a girl is matched by the notion that a woman in a menial or poorly paid job finds compensation in being called a lady. Ethel Strainchamps has pointed out that since lady is used as an adjective with nouns designating both high and low occupations (lady wrestler, lady barber, lady doctor, lady judge), some writers assume they can use the noun form without betraying value judgments. Not so, Strainchamps says, rolling the issue into a spitball: "You may write, 'He addressed the Republican ladies,' or 'The Democratic ladies convened' . . . but I have never seen 'the Communist ladies' or 'the Black Panther ladies' in print."

Thoughtful writers and editors have begun to repudiate some of the old usages. "Divorcée," "grandmother" and "blonde," along with "vivacious," "pert," "dimpled" and "cute," were dumped by the Washington Post in the spring of 1970 by the executive editor, Benjamin Bradlee. In a memo to his staff, Bradlee wrote, "The meaningful equality and dignity of women is properly under scrutiny today . . . because this equality has been less than meaningful and the dignity not always free of stereotype and condescension."

What women have been called in the press—or at least the part that operates above ground—is only a fraction of the infinite variety of alternatives to "women" used in the subcultures of the English-speaking world. Beyond "chicks," "dolls," "dames," "babes," "skirts" and "broads" are the words and phrases in which women are reduced to their sexuality and nothing more. It would be hard to think of another area of language in which the human mind has been so fertile in devising and borrowing abusive terms. In "The Female Eunuch," Germaine Greer devotes four pages to anatomical terms and words for animals, vegetables, fruits, baked goods, implements and receptacles, all of which are used to dehumanize the female person. Jean Faust, in an article aptly called "Words That Oppress," suggests that the effort to diminish women through language is rooted in a male fear of sexual inadequacy. "Woman is made to feel guilty for and akin to natural disasters," she writes; "hurricanes and typhoons are named after her. Any negative or threatening force is given a feminine name. If a man runs into bad luck climbing up the ladder of success (a male-invented game), he refers to the 'bitch goddess' success."

The sexual overtones in the ancient and no doubt honorable custom of calling ships "she" have become more explicit and less honorable in an age of air travel. "I'm Karen. Fly me." Attitudes of ridicule, contempt and disgust toward female sexuality have spawned a rich glossary of insults and epithets not found in dictionaries. And the usage in which four-letter words meaning copulate are interchangeable with cheat, attack and destroy can scarcely be unrelated to the savagery of rape.

In her updating of Ibsen's "A Doll's House," Clare Booth Luce has Nora tell her husband she is pregnant—"In the way only men are supposed to get pregnant." "Men, pregnant?" he says, and she nods; "With ideas. Pregnancies there [*she taps his head*] are masculine. And a very superior form of labor. Pregnancies here [*taps her tummy*] are feminine—a very inferior form of labor."

Public outcry followed a revised translation of the New Testament describing Mary as "pregnant" instead of "great with child." The objections were made in part on esthetic grounds: there is no attractive adjective in modern English for a woman who is about to give birth. A less obvious reason was that replacing the euphemism with a biological term undermined religious teaching. The initiative and generative power in the conception of Jesus are understood to be God's; Mary, the mother, was a vessel only.

Whether influenced by this teaching or not, the language of human reproduction lags several centuries behind scientific understanding. The male's contribution to procreation is still described as though it were the entire seed from which a new life grows: the initiative and generative power involved in the process are thought of as masculine, receptivity and nurturance as feminine. "Seminal" remains a synonym for "highly original," and there is no comparable word to describe the female's equivalent contribution.

An entire mythology has grown from this biological misunderstanding and its semantic legacy; its embodiment in laws that for centuries made women nonpersons was a key target of the 19th-century feminist movement. Today, more than 50 years after women finally won the basic democratic right to vote, the word "liberation" itself, when applied to women, means something less than when used of other groups of people. An advertisement for the NBC news department listed Women's Liberation along with crime in the streets and the Vietnam war as "bad news." Asked for his views on Women's Liberation, a highly placed politician was quoted as saying, "Let me make one thing perfectly clear. I wouldn't want to wake up next to a lady pipe-fitter."

One of the most surprising challenges to our male-dominated culture is coming from within organized religion, where the issues are being stated, in part, by confronting the implications of traditional language. What a growing number of theologians and scholars are saying is that the myths of the Judeo-Christian tradition, being the products of patriarchy, must be reexamined, and that the concept of an exclusively male ministry and the image of a male god have become idolatrous.

Women are naturally in the forefront of this movement, both in their efforts to gain ordination and full equality and through their contributions to theological reform, although both these efforts are often subtly diminished. When the Rev. Barbara Anderson was ordained by the American Lutheran Church, one newspaper printed her picture over a caption headed "Happy Girl." Newsweek's report of a protest staged last December by women divinity students at Harvard was jocular ("another tilt at the windmill") and sarcastic: "Every time anyone in the room lapsed into what [the students] regarded as male chauvinism—such as using the word 'mankind' to describe the human race in general—the outraged women . . . drowned out the offender with earpiercing blasts from party-favor kazoos. . . . What annoyed the women most was the universal custom of referring to God as 'He.' "

The tone of the report was not merely unfunny; it missed the connection between increasingly outmoded theological language and the accelerating number of women (and men) who are dropping out of organized religion, both Jewish and Christian. For language, including pronouns, can be used to construct a reality that simply mirrors society's assumptions. To women who are committed to the reality of religious faith, the effect is doubly painful. Professor Harvey Cox, in whose classroom the protest took place, stated the issue directly: The women, he said, were raising the "basic theological question of whether God is more adequately thought of in personal or suprapersonal terms."

Toward the end of Don McLean's remarkable ballad "American Pie," a song filled with the imagery of abandonment and disillusion, there is a stanza that must strike many women to the quick. The church bells are broken, the music has died; then:

And the three men I admire most,
The Father, Son and the Holy Ghost,
They caught the last train for the Coast—
The day the music died.

Three men I admired most. There they go, briefcases in hand and topcoats buttoned left over right, walking down the long cold platform under the city, past the baggage wagons and the hissing steam onto the Pullman. Bye, bye God—all three of you—made in the image of male supremacy. Maybe out there in L.A. where the weather is warmer, someone can believe in you again.

The Roman Catholic theologian Elizabeth Farians says "the bad theology of an overmasculinized church continues to be one of the root causes of women's oppression." The definition of oppression is "to crush or burden by abuse of power or authority; burden spiritually or mentally as if by pressure."

When language oppresses, it does so by any means that disparage and belittle. Until well into the 20th century, one of the ways English was manipulated to disparage women was through the addition of feminine endings to nonsexual words. Thus a woman who aspired to be a poet was excluded from the company of real poets by the label poetess, and a woman who piloted an airplane was denied full status as an aviator by being called an aviatrix. At about the time poetess, aviatrix, and similar Adam-ribbisms were dropping out of use, H. W. Fowler was urging that they be revived. "With the coming expansion of women's vocations," he wrote in the first edition (1926) of "Modern English Usage," "feminines for vocation-words are a special need of the future." There can be no doubt he subconsciously recognized the relative status implied in the *-ess* designations. His criticism of a woman who wished to be known as an author rather than an authoress was that she had no need "to raise herself to the level of the male author by asserting her right to his name."

Who has the prior right to a name? The question has an interesting bearing on words that were once applied to men alone, or to both men and women, but now, having acquired abusive associations, are assigned to women exclusively. Spinster is a gentle case in point. Prostitute and many of its synonyms illustrate the phenomenon better. If Fowler had chosen to record the changing usage of harlot from hired man (in Chaucer's time) through rascal and entertainer to its present definition, would he have maintained that the female harlot is trying to raise herself to the level of the male harlot by asserting her right to his name? Or would he have plugged for harlotress?

The demise of most *-ess* endings came about before the start of the new feminist movement. In the second edition of *Modern English Usage*, published in 1965, Sir Ernest Gowers frankly admitted what his predecessors had been up to. "Feminine designations," he wrote, "seem now to be falling into disuse. Perhaps the explanation of this paradox is that it symbolizes the victory of women in their struggle for equal rights; it reflects the abandonment by men of those ideas about women in the professions that moved Dr. Johnson to his rude remark about women preachers."

If Sir Ernest's optimism can be justified, why is there a movement back to feminine endings in such words as chairwoman, councilwoman and congresswoman? Betty Hudson, of Madison, Conn., is campaigning for the adoption of "selectwoman" as the legal title for a female member of that town's executive body. To have to address a woman as "Selectman," she maintains, "is not only bad grammar and bad biology, but it implies that politics is still, or should be, a man's business." A valid argument, and one that was, predictably, countered by ridicule, the surefire weapon for undercutting achievement. When the head of the Federal Maritime Commission, Helen D. Bentley, was named "Man of the Year" by an association of shipping interests, she wisely refused to be drawn into light-hearted debate with interviewers who wanted to make the award's name a humorous issue. Some women, of course, have yet to learn they are invisible. An 8-year-old who visited the American Museum of Natural History with her Brownie scout troop went through the impressive exhibit on pollution and overpopulation called "Can Man Survive?" Asked afterward, "Well, can he?" she answered, "I don't know about him, but we're working on it in Brownies."

Nowhere are women rendered more invisible by language than in politics. The United States Constitution, in describing the qualifications for Representative, Senator and President, refers to each as *he*. No wonder Shirley Chisholm, the first woman since 1888 to make a try for the Presidential nomination of a major party, has found it difficult to be taken seriously.

The observation by Andrew Greeley already quoted—that "man" uses "his symbols" to reconstruct "his reality"—was not made in reference to the symbols of language but to the symbolic impact the "nomination of a black man for the Vice-Presidency" would have on race relations in the United States. Did the author assume the generic term "man" would of course be construed to include "woman"? Or did he deliberately use a semantic device to exclude Shirley Chisholm without having to be explicit?

Either way, his words construct a reality in which women are ignored. As much as any other factor in our language, the ambiguous meaning of *man* serves to deny women recognition as people. In a recent magazine article, we discussed the similar effect on women of the generic pronoun *he*, which we proposed to replace by a new common gender pronoun *tey*. We were immediately told, by a number of authorities, that we were dabbling in the serious business of linguistics, and the message that reached us from these scholars was loud and clear: It-is-absolutely-impossible-for-anyone-to-introduce-a-new-word-into-the-language-just-because-there-is-a-need-for-it-so-stop-wasting-your-time.

When words are suggested like "herstory" (for history), "sportsoneship" (for sportsmanship) and "mistresspiece" (for the work of a Virginia Woolf) one suspects a not-too-subtle attempt to make the whole language problem look silly. But unless Alexander Pope, when he wrote "The proper study of mankind is man," meant that women should be relegated to the footnotes (or, as George Orwell might have put it, "All men are equal, but men are more equal than women"), viable new words will surely someday supersede the old.

Without apologies to Freud, the great majority of women do not wish in their hearts that they were men. If having grown up with a language that tells them they are at the same time men and not men raises psychic doubts for women, the doubts are not of their sexual identity but of their human identity. Perhaps the present unrest surfacing in the Women's Movement is part of an evolutionary change in our particular form of life—the one form of all in the animal and plant kingdoms that orders and interprets its reality by symbols. The achievements of the species called man have brought us to the brink of self-destruction. If the species survives into the next century with the expectation of going on, it may only be because we have become part of what Harlow Shapley calls the psychozoic kingdom, where brain overshadows brawn and rationality has replaced superstition.

Searching the roots of Western civilization for a word to call this new species of man and woman, someone might come up with *gen*, as in genesis and generic. With such a word, *man* could be used exclusively for males as *woman* is used for females, for gen would include both sexes. Like the words deer and bison, gen would be both plural and singular. Like progenitor, progeny, and generation, it would convey continuity. Gen would express the warmth and generalized sexuality of generous, gentle, and genuine; the specific sexuality of genital and genetic. In the new family of gen, girls and boys would grow to genhood, and to speak of genkind would be to include all the people of the earth.

Discussing Issues and Themes

1. The authors assert that "an entire mythology has grown" from a "biological misunderstanding and its semantic legacy." What do you understand them to mean? What are that "biological misunderstanding and its semantic legacy"? Can you describe the "mythology" that they suggest has sprung from them?
2. What do Miller and Swift have to say about theological language? Why is a consideration of religion and its language an important component in their discussion here? Would the essay be incomplete without this discussion? Explain.
3. What, according to the authors, is the origin of sexist assumptions in language? Do the authors feel that these assumptions are independent of the language in which they are expressed? Do you agree? Explain.
4. This essay was written in 1972. Does the issue of sexist language retain its sense of urgency and significance? Cite examples to support your view.
5. The authors argue that "except for words that refer to females by definition (mother, actress, Congresswoman), and words for occupations traditionally held by females (nurse, secretary, prostitute), the English language defines everyone as male." Do you agree? Respond from your own vantage point as either a man or a women, but whoever you are, don't forget to consider Miller and Swift's examples. Do they have a point or not?

Discussing Rhetoric and Style

1. The authors have the difficult job of tracing the evolution of a social and linguistic imbalance that dates back to the beginnings of civilization. How well do they achieve this overview? Do they do a lot of generalizing? Explain with examples from the essay.
2. Go through the essay, paying particular attention to the verbs. How often do the authors resort to passive constructions? How assertive is the style of the essay? Would you characterize it as verb-strong? As aggressive? Explain.
3. Study the authors' presentation and analysis of conventional phrases and the conclusions that they draw from these examples. Does the essay move from particular examples to gen-

eral conclusions (inductive reasoning) or does it begin with general assertions and then cite examples to demonstrate them (deductive reasoning)? Why do the authors choose to organize their argument as they do?

4. How well do the authors use riddles, jokes, puns, irony, and other types of humor to express their point of view and to hold their audience's interest? What do you like or not like about writers who can make light of serious issues and who can shed light on humorous ones?

Ideas for Writing

1. Break into groups of two—preferably one man and one woman—and prepare an essay on sexist assumptions or biases, either visual or verbal, that you have noticed in newspaper or magazine articles. Besides exploring the issues of language and gender that Miller and Swift discuss, invent research strategies and methods for writing a collaborative paper.

2. Miller and Swift believe that sexist language has allowed history to overlook women. Do some research in your university library, looking up turn-of-the-century newspapers and magazines or even old history books. Are women invisible—that is, not represented at all? Write a comparative study of these old magazines and books as they compare to newer ones. In what ways, if any, are women represented differently?

The Name Is Mine

ANNA QUINDLEN

Anna Quindlen, formerly the metropolitan editor of the New York Times, *is now at work on a novel. Her nationally syndicated columns often explore family issues of special interest to women—the experience, for example, of being a wife or a working mother. Often drawn from her personal experience, Quindlen's work reflects strong feminist principles and often focuses on the relation of a woman to her family and to the larger community. In the following piece, Quindlen explores the significance of the ancient ritual of name-taking—the convention whereby a woman accepts her husband's name when she marries him. Should a woman take a married name? Quindlen kept her name because, as she says, she "is not an adjunct to anybody, especially a husband." But while the decision sounds like a firm one, she does experience moments of ambivalence about the name she refused. The essay was originally published as a column in* The New York Times.

I am on the telephone to the emergency room of the local hospital. My elder son is getting stitches in his palm, and I have called to make myself feel better, because I am at home, waiting, and my husband is there, holding him. I am 34 years old, and I am crying like a child, making a slippery mess of my face. "Mrs. Krovatin?" says the nurse, and for the first time in my life I answer "Yes."

This is a story about a name. The name is mine. I was given it at birth, and I have never changed it, although I married. I could come up with lots of reasons why. It was a political decision, a simple statement that I was somebody and not an adjunct of anybody, especially a husband. As a friend of mine told her horrified mother, "He didn't adopt me, he married me."

It was a professional and a personal decision, too. I grew up with an ugly dog of a name, one I came to love because I thought it was weird and unlovable. Amid the Debbies and Kathys of my childhood, I had a first name only my grandmothers had and a last name that began with a strange letter. "Sorry, the letters I, O, Q, U, V, X, Y and Z are not available," the catalogues said about monogrammed key rings and cocktail napkins. Seeing my name in black on white at the top of a good story, suddenly it wasn't an ugly dog anymore.

But neither of these are honest reasons, because they assume rational consideration, and it so happens that when it came to changing my name, there was no consideration, rational or otherwise. It was mine. It belonged to me. I don't even share a checking account with my husband. Damned if I was going to be hidden beneath the umbrella of his identity.

It seemed like a simple decision. But nowadays I think the only simple decisions are whether to have grilled cheese or tuna fish for lunch. Last week, my older child wanted an explanation of why he, his dad and his brother have one name, and I have another.

My answer was long, philosophical and rambling—that is to say, unsatisfactory. What's in a name? I could have said disingenuously. But I was talking to a person who had just spent three torturous, exhilarating years learning names for things, and I wanted to communicate to him that mine meant something quite special to me, had seemed as form-fitting as my skin, and as painful to remove. Personal identity and independence, however, were not what he was looking for; he just wanted to make sure I was one of them. And I am—and then again, I am not. When I made this decision, I was part of a couple. Now, there are two me's, the me who is the individual and the me who is part of a family of four, a family of four in which, in a small way, I am left out.

A wise friend who finds herself in the same fix says she never wants to change her name, only to have a slightly different identity as a family member, an identity for pediatricians' offices and parent-teacher conferences. She also says that the entire situation reminds her of the women's movement as a whole. We did these things as individuals, made these decisions about ourselves and what we wanted to be and do. And they were good decisions, the right decisions. But we based them on individual choice, not on group dynamics. We thought in terms of our sense of ourselves, not our relationships with others.

Some people found alternative solutions: hyphenated names, merged names, matriarchal names for the girls and patriarchal ones for the boys, one name at work and another at home. I did not like those choices; I thought they were middle grounds, and I didn't live much in the middle ground at the time. I was once slightly disdainful of women who went all the way and changed their names. But I now know too many smart, independent, terrific women who have the same last names as their husbands to be disdainful anymore. (Besides, if I made this decision as part of a feminist world view, it seems dishonest to turn around and trash other women for deciding as they did.)

I made my choice. I haven't changed my mind. I've just changed my life. Sometimes I feel like one of those worms I used to hear about in biology, the ones that, chopped in half, walked off in different directions. My name works fine for one half, not quite as well for the other. I would never give it up. Except for that one morning when I talked to the nurse at the hospital, I always answer the question "Mrs. Krovatin?" with "No, this is Mr. Krovatin's wife." It's just that I understand the down side now.

When I decided not to disappear beneath my husband's umbrella, it did not occur to me that I would be the only one left outside. It did not occur to me that I would ever care—not enough to change, just enough to think about the things we do on our own and what they mean when we aren't on our own anymore.

Discussing Issues and Themes

1. Do you think a married woman should take her husband's name? Should their children take the father's name? What, according to Quindlen, is the significance of these acts?
2. Why did Quindlen keep her own name after marriage? Is she ambivalent about her choice? Explain.
3. Who are the "two me's" in Quindlen's essay? Compare them. Does Quindlen prefer one over the other? Why or why not?
4. What, according to Quindlen, are the rational reasons why a woman would want to keep her name? What are the "irrational" ones? Do you agree with Quindlen's characterizations?
5. Discuss why a woman might want to maintain a separate name from her husband's. Look to daily life as well as to Quindlen's essay.

Discussing Rhetoric and Style

1. Quindlen begins very personally, recounting a private moment in her life. How well does she treat this experience in her essay? What appeal does such an intimate memoir have on the reader?

Do you identify with the writer or feel that she is like other people you know?

2. What is Quindlen's thesis? Where and how does she express it?
3. Why does Quindlen begin her essay in the present tense? Study the shifts in tense throughout the essay. What is the effect of each?
4. Discuss the aptness of Quindlen's umbrella metaphor. How does Quindlen use that figure of speech to unify her essay?
5. How many viewpoints does Quindlen offer on this issue? Reread the essay, marking off each of the different solutions she discusses. Does she intend to persuade you that her preference is the only right one, or is her goal simply to describe the issue rather than to argue it? Cite the text to support your conclusions.

Ideas for Writing

1. Trace the origin of your name, and write a brief essay on its aptness. Does defining your name give you a stronger sense of who you are?
2. Discuss a critical moment in your life when you questioned your role within your family. Do you think your identity within and outside your family is influenced by language? Discuss your conclusion.

Too Many Women Are Misconstruing Feminism's Nature

SUSAN JACOBY

Susan Jacoby is a frequent freelance contributor to the New York Times. *Interested in both feminist ideology and foreign policy, Jacoby has written* The Possible She *and* Immigration and the News Media *as well as books about her three-year visit to the Soviet Union:* Moscow Conversations, The Friendship Barrier: Ten Russian Encounters, *and* Inside Soviet Schools. *In "Misconstruing Feminism's Nature," which appeared in* The New York Times, *Jacoby reflects on the status of "feminism" among today's young women. Her essay stands as a potent reminder that feminism still has a great deal to say (and to do) and that a dislike for labels may actually shield a dislike for what those labels represent.*

fem-i-nism, n. *1. the doctrine advocating social and political rights of women equal to those of men; 2.* (sometimes cap.) *an organized movement for the attainment of such rights for women.*

The Random House Dictionary
of the English Language

For many young women today, "feminism" is a word with a shady reputation. I first became aware of this depressing fact when I was teaching a magazine writing course at New York University and one of my brighter female students said: "I know from your lectures in class that you consider yourself a feminist. But that surprises me, because you look so feminine."

By "feminine" she meant what both the dictionary and ordinary people mean: that I looked the way women are usually expected to look: I wear lipstick, comb my hair (streak it, too!) and am as likely to be found in a skirt as in blue jeans. I don't wear combat boots or have bulging biceps. My student was really saying she didn't understand how someone who was committed to equal rights for women could also display conventional feminine attributes.

This point of view is held by a surprising number of well-educated young women in their early 20's, those who have benefited the most from the professional opportunities now open to them as a result of battles waged by the feminist movement over the past 15 years.

To a woman who is proud to call herself a feminist, the most disturbing aspect of this phenomenon is not its naïveté but its adoption of the age-old patriarchal assumption that a woman who wants the same intellectual, economic and professional opportunities as a man is rejecting her sex rather than the disabilities imposed on her because of her sex.

Among organized feminists of the older generation, a common response is to insist that young women are reacting not against feminism but only against the word and its "unfair" association with strident anger. This was typified by Eleanor Smeal, outgoing president of the National Organization for Women, in an interview with Susan Bolotin that appeared last fall in the *New York Times Magazine.*

"People don't even like the word 'discrimination,' " Mrs. Smeal said. "One of the reasons is that they don't want you to think they have a bellyache, that they are not O.K. And the word 'feminist' is still considered a militant word. The best way of dealing with all these things is not to use catch-words. Talk about actual situations."

This approach, which suggests that resistance to feminism is largely a question of semantics, evades the concrete issues raised by that resistance. The meanings people attach to words are of the utmost importance. When a political term becomes unpopular—whether the word is feminist, liberal, conservative, socialist or capitalist—the unpopularity arises not only from a misunderstanding of what the word actually means but from genuine distrust of the ideas it represents.

My students told me they objected to feminism because it made women bitter, angry and unattractive to men. They said they felt that feminists had placed too much emphasis on careers at the expense of both romance and family life. All of them planned to take 5 to 10 years off from work to raise their children and then return to rewarding, well-paid jobs.

Most significant, my students told me that any form of sex

discrimination could be overcome by individual effort and that older feminists tended to blame personal inadequacies on "the system."

Many of these beliefs can, of course, be attributed entirely to insufficient life experience. Recent college graduates do not know any more about what it takes to build a career than they know about bringing up children. The idea that one can take 10 years off from work without incurring adverse professional consequences is as phantasmagorical as the notion that one will give birth to a child who never gives its mother a moment's cause for worry.

Furthermore, these women have not experienced the entry-level discrimination that was taken for granted in the 1950's and '60's. They do not realize that their individual abilities would have counted for very little in a system in which women made up fewer than 5 percent of first-year law and medical school classes. The feminist movement has opened those doors; women in their early 20's have not had occasion to knock on doors still closed.

But it is no comfort for a feminist in her 30's to sit back, secure in the knowledge that life will change the minds of young women who do not now wish to identify themselves with feminism. The whole point of movements for social change is to make it unnecessary for each new generation to learn the same lessons over again. The older generation of feminists is in roughly the same position as scientists who have been pressured to teach creationism as a respectable alternative to the theory of evolution.

The question is: What can be done to rectify the situation?

One common response is to pretend not to be angry at all. The dishonesty of this posture is quickly, and correctly, perceived by the young. Feminism is concerned with justice, and anyone who cares about justice is bound to be angry at some of the people some of the time. There is nothing wrong with anger—and we should say so with no apologies—as long as it is directed at those who are responsible for special injustices, not at the whole world.

It is also unrealistic to adopt the position that the most obvious goals of the feminist movement, like equal pay for equal work, have already been achieved and we must now concentrate on achieving the nirvana of a more "human" workplace, in which both men and women will be able to enjoy the rewards of equal rights and responsibilities. A workplace that takes family and child-rearing needs into account is a laudable goal, but, as the defeat of the proposed Federal equal rights amendment clearly demonstrated, we are far from a consensus on the desirability of most basic forms of equality between the sexes.

I do not believe that the amendment was turned down solely because some people identified it with lesbian rights and unisex toilets or because the right wing spent enormous amounts of money to oppose it (although these elements certainly played a role in its defeat). The amendment was rejected because a great many people still do not believe in equal rights for women.

That is why I believe Eleanor Smeal is wrong in suggesting that opposition to feminism can be neutralized by avoiding the word. Feminism is considered "militant" by many members of both sexes because equal rights for women is in fact a radical idea. By "radical" I mean not the commonly used political pejorative but the original definition, derived from the Latin word for root. Feminists should not be reluctant to identify themselves with an honorable tradition rooted in issues that every woman—regardless of how much she might prefer to be seen solely as an individual rather than as a member of the sex—must eventually face.

Discussing Issues and Themes

1. Both Jacoby's title and the epigraph to her essay (the Random House definition) mention the word "feminism." What are your associations with that word? How do these associations differ, if they do, from the dictionary definition?

2. What is the difference between "feminine" and "feminist" in the minds of Jacoby's students? Does she see any way to reconcile these terms?

3. What problems does Jacoby see in her students' attitude towards feminism and women's rights in general? For example, she suggests that these women do not yet have "experience"; what does she think experience will teach them?

4. What do today's students owe to "the feminist movement"? Do you sense that most young women today think that feminism has done anything for them? Does Jacoby persuade you that they should think so?

5. Jacoby argues that the Equal Rights Amendment "was rejected because a great many people still do not believe in equal rights for women." Do you agree with this statement?

Discussing Rhetoric and Style

1. Why does Jacoby place a dictionary definition at the head of her essay? What message does the presence of a definition immediately after the title convey? Explain.

2. The body of the essay begins with an anecdote. Is it an effective opening? What do we learn about Jacoby's own career and personal appearance?
3. The author suggests that anger is not out of place when one is concerned with issues that involve "justice." How would you evaluate the tone in this essay? Does she sound "angry" or not? Cite examples that illustrate her tone.
4. Jacoby writes that "equal rights for women is in fact a radical idea." Compare her definition of "radical" with the Random House definition of "feminism." How is this definition different?

Ideas for Writing

1. Write an essay in which you discuss your own experiences with and responses to what you perceive to be feminism. Jacoby suggests that feminism is an issue that concerns justice rather than appearances; keep this distinction in mind as you write your own essay.
2. Jacoby suggests that resistance to feminism is not merely a matter of semantics. Choose another word, such as "liberal" or "communist," and analyze the popular response to that word as Jacoby analyzes the response to the word "feminism." Do you think that semantics plays a greater role than political conviction in people's resistance to your word?

The Hand That Rocks the Helm

RICHARD MITCHELL

Born in New York City in 1929, Richard Mitchell has taught at Glassboro State College in New Jersey since 1963 and has written several books on language issues, including Less Than Words Can Say *and* The Leaning Tower of Babble. *Responding to a letter to the editor, Mitchell discusses here the merits of replacing what Miller and Swift would call "male-exclusive" words (like "helmsman") with egalitarian equivalents (like "helmsperson"). He argues that nobody literally believes that a word such as "helmsman" denies the capability of women to steer a boat. He concludes that the political correctness of artificial gender-fair words could never make up for the ugliness and awkwardness they inspire. The essay appeared in* The Underground Grammarian, *a monthly newsletter that Mitchell himself prints on a hand-operated press.*

Writing about sailing, I had always used the word "helmsman" to describe the person who steers a boat. Finally seeing the light with my ninth book, I decided it was time to admit women can steer too, and changed the traditional, exclusive word to "helmsperson," or "steerer." Every alteration, I felt, was doubling the size of my potential readership.

We never miss the comics page of the Sunday *New York Times*, and it was there that we came across the Great Moral Awakening of one John Rousmaniere, from whose letter to the editor the passage above is taken. What a great moment in his inner life it must have been when it suddenly dawned on him, not only that women actually *can* steer, but even that his oblique admission of that hitherto unsuspected power, cleverly encoded in "helmsperson," would increase sales of his ninth book on sailing.

We can hear the excited phone calls now: Hello, Madge, it's Flo. Listen, you've just got to rush right out and buy this great new book, *Yet Another Book on Sailing,* by John Rousmaniere! You won't believe this, but he actually says, well, not right out, but just as good as, that women can *steer.* Steer boats! I'm not kidding. Yes, women! I'd lend you my copy, but I think that every woman should have her own, don't you? I mean, after all, it's time we took a stand!

But it is only *en passant* that Rousmaniere makes his astonishing discovery. He steers his course toward the undoing of an earlier letter writer who complained that he found ugliness and awkwardness in enlightened words like "helmsperson." Ha! To that feeble whimper, Rousmaniere exclaims, in what must have been a sprightly riposte that somehow got garbled by a sub-editor, "Yet given a choice between the risk of a little phonetic barbarism and the fact of a language that in a few simple nouns and pronouns minimizes (if not oppresses) about half our fellow human beings, who can choose?"

Who indeed? Not we. (Or maybe yes we, depending on what that question might mean.) We do not care to be counted among the uncountable who have minimized (if not oppressed) all female human beings ever born in the whole history of our species by falsely accusing them of the inability to steer a boat. And here and now, in print for all to see, we'd like to take a stand and join in the Great Affirmation, perhaps even doubling our readership thereby, by saying, "Women can steer a boat!"

However, while we would *like* to do that, if only for the sake of doubling our readership, we won't. We can't. We are ruled, and choose to be ruled, by the motto that we quote not often enough, the words of Ben Jonson: "Neither can his mind be thought to be in tune, whose words do jarre; nor his Reason in frame, whose sentence is preposterous." That sentence is preposterous. It is neither true nor false; it is simply without meaning, which must also be said of "Men can steer a boat."

Of making sense, there is one way. Preposterousness knows no limits. Its every appearance must be sniffed out anew, and the ability to smell the preposterous is alone worthy of the name of literacy. Anything less is illiteracy, at best the reception of communication, the recognition of the words. Nevertheless, preposterousness is most likely to appear in certain contexts, and one of those is what is called, and probably being taught in some school at this very moment, Social Thinking.

How sweet its sound, how kind and humanistic. But Social Thinking is in fact, both in and out of schools, a great inculcator of irreversible illiteracy, for it depends largely, and in the schools entirely, we would guess, on the recitation of seemingly amiable propositions of the sort that could not be tested even if the educationists wanted to test them, which they don't.

Consider the Social Thinking of Rousmaniere. One day, he claims, he "sees the light," and finds it "time to admit," as though he had obstinately denied it in the past, that "women can steer too." Wow. It is the sort of statement that seems at first, and here is the great snare of Social Thinking, too obviously true to be worth saying, and certainly indisputable. But around here we think enough of women to suspect that some Madge might find it neither.

Oh really? she might say to Flo. Well, that's nice of him to say, but, to tell the truth, Flo, I *can't* steer a boat. I know. I tried it for a while and we kept luffing. You should have heard the kids. I'm sure I could learn, but why bother? And in fact, I'm not the least bit offended when some purely hypothetical steerer of some equally hypothetical boat is called a "helmsman." As long as this fellow isn't talking about me, why should I care? But you know, I think that maybe I do care a little when he does talk about me and gets it wrong. After all, I am included in "women," and I think this guy has lots of brass to shoot off his mouth about what I can and what I can't do, which is, in any case, none of his damned business. So how about you, Flo? Can you steer a boat?

Language is not a person who can think and will and do, any more than "women" is a person who can think and will and do. It is preposterous to imply the presence of mind, will, and action in "women," or in "men," or in Eskimos or football players. It is just as preposterous to imply those powers in language. Pronouns do not minimize persons. Words do not oppress persons. Only persons can minimize or oppress, or praise or condemn, or lie or speak the truth. Such acts are possible only to individuals in whom there is, whether governed or not, the power to choose.

No sane person will find offense in the word "helmsman," whose equivalent was regularly used by plenty of Viking women who knew how to steer a boat. In the history of our species, no man before Rousmaniere has said "helmsman" in order to suggest that women can't steer boats. Nor did any woman imagine such absurdity.

If we can, and do, imagine such absurdity, it is because we are far more superstitious than our ancestors, which is to say that we are Social Thinkers. We imagine the possibility of agency in nonpersonal nonbeings, which is a step or two down from imagining agency in the spirits of the trees and rivers. Where a miscreant might once have had the good sense to blame his misbehavior on the Devil, a supposed person with a will and intentions, he now passes the buck to Society, a nothing, a word, in which neither will nor intention is possible. We are deprived where there is no depriver, oppressed where there is no oppressor, and affronted where there is no one who gives a damn whether or not we can steer a boat.

No one who knows any history at all can deny that many women have been subject to men and treated like property or dependent children, or even domestic animals, for most of recorded history on most of the face of the Earth. Shall we now treat them like simpletons, to be cajoled with puny offerings of words like "helmsperson" and "herstory"? Are they imbeciles, that we can con them into buying our books, and anything else we want to sell them, by changing a word here and there? Are they so dim of mind that we must make allowance for the fact that the poor things do indeed suppose that the word "helmsman" is a slur devised by men in order to remind them of their inadequacies? Can we buy them off with a few he/she's?

In "helmsman" there is no contempt, for there is no contemner. In "helmsperson" there is condescension, and a holier-than-thou condescender. If that is what "women" want, well, maybe the Patriarchs did know something after all.

Discussing Issues and Themes

1. What is the topic of this essay? Is it introduced explicitly or implicitly? Explain.
2. What does Mitchell object to in replacing words like "helmsman" with ones like "helmsperson"?
3. Why, according to Mitchell, did John Rousmaniere decide to adopt the word "helmsperson" after so many years and books? Do you feel Mitchell misrepresents Rousmaniere here? Why or why not?
4. Have you ever been offended by sexist language? Where are you most likely to encounter it? Do you try to avoid it in your own writing? Why or why not?
5. Can you think of any case in which language discriminates against men? Do you think that counter-discrimination is an important issue? Explain in a paragraph or two.

Discussing Rhetoric and Style

1. Who is the "we" to whom Mitchell refers throughout his essay, and how does his use of it strike you? Is he trying to include you? Why would he want to? Is he successful?

2. Why does Mitchell choose to include pieces of a fictional conversation between "Madge" and "Flo"? What is the effect of these exchanges? Do they support Mitchell's argument? Explain.

3. What persona does Mitchell adopt? Who is he trying to be, and who does he expect his audience to be?

4. Where is Mitchell's sarcasm most evident? How effective is it? Reread the essay, listening closely for shifts in tone. Does Mitchell's sarcasm ever get out of hand, and does it ever relax? If so, where?

5. In order to persuade his audience, Mitchell must shift emphasis from sexual discrimination to another issue. What is that issue, and how does Mitchell achieve the shift? Is his argument logical? Explain in detail.

Ideas for Writing

1. Write a brief essay in which you compare and contrast the rhetoric of Mitchell's essay with that of John Rousmaniere's letter. In what ways does each author's perception of his audience differ? What stylistic differences can you find? Differences in tone? Explain, using references to the texts.

2. Using Mitchell as your model, write an essay on another topic of your own choosing (defending or opposing, for example, political rhetoric, English as a national language, or bilingual education).

Real Men Don't
Anti-Male Bias in English

EUGENE R. AUGUST

An early spokesman in the emerging field of men's studies, Professor Eugene August has lectured extensively on the topic of reverse discrimination and is the author of Men's Studies: A Selected and Annotated Interdisciplinary Bibliography. *Although essays like Miller and Swift's "One Small Step for Genkind" argue that women are represented falsely or not at all in a male-dominated language, August argues that men are as often victimized by the language as women are. He asserts that men and women are engaged in "symbiotic" partnerships of mutual agreement; and if men are what feminists make them out to be, it is only because they have been trained to act that way: as Warren Farrell has said, "the more we make men the enemy, the more they will have to behave like the enemy." "Real Men Don't" appeared in the* University of Dayton Review.

Despite numerous studies of sex bias in language during the past fifteen years, only rarely has anti-male bias been examined. In part, this neglect occurs because many of these studies have been based upon assumptions which are questionable at best and which at worst exhibit their own form of sex bias. Whether explicitly or implicitly, many of these studies reduce human history to a tale of male oppressors and female victims or rebels. In this view of things, all societies become *patriarchal societies,* a familiar term used to suggest that for centuries males have conspired to exploit and demean females. Accordingly, it is alleged in many of these studies that men control language and that they use it to define women and women's roles as inferior.

Despite the popularity of such a view, it has received scant support from leading social scientists, including one of the giants of modern anthropology, Margaret Mead. Anticipating current ideology, Mead in *Male and Female* firmly rejected the notion of a "male conspiracy to keep women in their place," arguing instead that

> the historical trend that listed women among the abused minorities . . . lingers on to obscure the issue and gives apparent point to the contention that this is a man-made world in which women have always been abused and must always fight for their rights.
>
> It takes considerable effort on the part of both men and women to reorient ourselves to thinking—when we think basically—that this is a world not made by men alone, in which women are unwilling and helpless dupes and fools or else powerful schemers hiding their power under their ruffled petticoats, but a world made by mankind for human beings of both sexes. (298, 299–300)

The model described by Mead and other social scientists shows a world in which women and men have lived together throughout history in a symbiotic relationship, often mutually agreeing upon the definition of gender roles and the distribution of various powers and duties.

More importantly for the subject of bias in speech and writing, women—as well as men—have shaped language. As Walter J. Ong reminds us,

> Women talk and think as much as men do, and with few exceptions we all . . . learn to talk and think in the first instance largely from women, usually and predominantly our mothers. Our first tongue is called our "mother tongue" in English and in many other languages. . . . There are no father tongues. . . . (36)

Feminists like Dorothy Dinnerstein agree: "There seems no reason to doubt that the baby-tending sex contributed at least equally with the history-making one to the most fundamental of all human inventions: language" (22). Because gender roles and language are shaped by society in general—that is, by both men and women—anti-male bias in language is as possible as anti-female bias.

To say this, however, is emphatically not to blame women alone, or even primarily, for anti-male usage. If guilt must be assigned, it would have to be placed upon sexist people, both male and female, who use language to manipulate gender role behavior and to create negative social attitudes towards males. But often it is difficult to point a finger of blame: except where prejudiced gender stereotypes are deliberately fostered, most people evidently use sex-biased terminology without clearly understanding its import. In the long run, it is wiser to concentrate not on fixing blame, but on heightening public awareness of anti-male language and on discouraging its use. In particular, teachers and writers need to become aware of and to question language which denigrates or stereotypes males.

In modern English, three kinds of anti-male usage are evident: first, gender-exclusive language which omits males from certain kinds of consideration; second, gender-restrictive language which attempts to restrict males to an accepted gender role, some aspects of which may be outmoded, burdensome, or destructive; and third, negative stereotypes of males which are insulting, dehumanizing, and potentially dangerous.

Although gender-exclusive language which excludes females has often been studied, few students of language have noted usage which excludes males. Those academics, for example, who have protested *alumnus* and *alumni* as gender-exclusive terms to describe a university's male and female graduates have failed to notice that, by the same logic, *alma mater* (nourishing mother) is an equally gender-exclusive term to describe the university itself. Those who have protested *man* and *mankind* as generic terms have not begun to question *mammal* as a term of biological classification, but by categorizing animals according to the female's ability to suckle the young through her mammary glands, *mammal* clearly omits the male of the species. Consequently, it is as suspect as generic *man*.

In general, gender-exclusive usage in English excludes males as parents and as victims. Until recently, the equating of *mother* with *parent* in the social sciences was notorious: a major sociological study published in 1958 with the title *The Changing American Parent* was based upon interviews with 582 mothers and no fathers (Roman and Haddad 87). Although no longer prevalent in the social sciences, the interchangeability of *mother* and *parent* is still common, except for *noncustodial parent* which is almost always a synonym for *father*. A recent ad for *Parents* magazine begins: "To be the best mother you can be, you want practical, reliable answers to the questions a mother must face." Despite the large number of men now seen pushing shopping carts, advertisers still insist that "Choosy mothers choose Jif" and "My Mom's a Butternut Mom." Frequently, children are regarded as belonging solely to the mother, as in phrases like *women and their children*. The idea of the mother as primary parent can be glimpsed in such expressions as *mother tongue, mother wit, mother lode, mother of invention*, and *mothering* as a synonym for *parenting*.

The male as victim is ignored in such familiar expressions as *innocent women and children*. In June 1985, when President Reagan rejected a bombing strike to counter terrorist activities, newspapers reported that the decision had been made to prevent "the deaths of many innocent women and children in strife-torn Lebanon" (Glass). Presumably, strife-torn Lebanon contained no innocent men. Likewise, *rape victim* means females only, an assumption made explicit in the opening sentences of this newspaper article on rape: "Crime knows no gender. Yet, there is one offense that only women are prey to: rape" (Mougey). The thousands of males raped annually, in addition to the sexual assaults regularly inflicted upon males in prison, are here entirely overlooked. (That these males have been victimized mostly by other males does not disqualify them as victims of sexual violence, as some people assume.) Similarly, the term *wife and child abuse* conceals the existence of an estimated 282,000 husbands who are battered annually (O'Reilly et al. 23). According to many expressions in English, males are not parents and they are never victimized.

Unlike gender-exclusive language, gender-restrictive language is usually applied to males only, often to keep them within the confines of a socially prescribed gender role. When considering gender-restrictive language, one must keep in mind that—as Ruth E. Hartley has pointed out—the masculine gender role is enforced earlier and more harshly than the feminine role is (235). In addition, because the boy is often raised primarily by females in the virtual absence of close adult males, his grasp of what is required of him to *be a man* is often unsure. Likewise, prescriptions for male behavior are usually given in the negative, leading to the "Real Men Don't" syndrome, a process which further confuses the boy. Such circumstances leave many males extremely vulnerable to language which questions their sense of masculinity.

Furthermore, during the past twenty years an increasing number of men and women have been arguing that aspects of our society's masculine gender role are emotionally constrictive, unnecessarily stressful, and potentially lethal. Rejecting "the myth of masculine privilege," psychologist Herb Goldberg reports in *The Hazards of Being Male* that "every critical statistic in the area of [early death], disease, suicide, crime, accidents, childhood emotional disorders, alcoholism, and drug addiction shows a disproportionately higher male rate" (5). But changes in the masculine role are so disturbing to so many people that the male who attempts to break out of familiar gender patterns often finds himself facing hostile opposition which can be readily and powerfully expressed in a formidable array of sex-biased terms.

To see how the process works, let us begin early in the male life cycle. A boy quickly learns that, while it is usually acceptable for girls to be *tomboys,* God forbid that he should be a *sissy.* In *Sexual Signatures: On Being a Man or a Woman* John Money and Patricia Tucker note:

> The current feminine stereotype in our culture is flexible enough to let a girl behave "boyishly" if she wants to without bringing her femininity into question, but any boy who exhibits "girlish" behavior is promptly suspected of being queer. There isn't even a word corresponding to "tomboy" to describe such a boy. "Sissy" perhaps comes closest, or "artistic" and "sensitive," but unlike "tomboy," such terms are burdened with unfavorable connotations. (72)

Lacking a favorable or even neutral term to describe the boy who is quiet, gentle, and emotional, the English language has long had a rich vocabulary to insult and ridicule such boys—*mama's boy, mollycoddle, milksop, muff, twit, softy, creampuff, pantywaist, weenie, Miss Nancy,* and so on. Although sometimes used playfully, the currently popular *wimp* can be used to insult males from childhood right into adulthood.

Discussion of words like *sissy* as insults have been often one-sided: most commentators are content to argue that the female, not the male, is being insulted by such usage. "The implicit sexism" in such terms, writes one commentator, "disparages the woman, not the man" (Sorrels 87). Although the female is being slurred indirectly by these terms, a moment's reflection will show that the primary force of the insult is being directed against the male, specifically the male who cannot differentiate himself from the feminine. Ong argues in *Fighting for Life* that most societies place heavy pressure on males to differentiate themselves from females because the prevailing environment of human society is feminine (70–71). In English-speaking societies, terms like *sissy* and *weak sister,* which have been used by both females and males, are usually perceived not as insults to females but as ridicule of males who have allegedly failed to differentiate themselves from the feminine.

Being *all boy* carries penalties, however: for one thing, it means being less lovable. As the nursery rhyme tells children, little girls are made of "sugar and spice and all that's nice," while little boys are made of "frogs and snails and puppy-dogs' tails." Or, as an American version of the rhyme puts it:

Girls are dandy
Made of candy—
That's what little girls are made of.
Boys are rotten,
Made of cotton—
That's what little boys are made of.

Baring-Gould 176n116

When not enjoined to *be all boy,* our young lad will be urged to *be a big boy, be a brave soldier,* and (the ultimate appeal) *be a man.* These expressions almost invariably mean that the boy is about to suffer something painful or humiliating. The variant—*take it like a man*—provides the clue. As Paul Theroux defines it, *be a man* means: "Be stupid, be unfeeling, obedient and soldierly, and stop thinking."

Following our boy further into the life cycle, we discover that in school he will find himself in a cruel bind: girls his age will be biologically and socially more mature than he is, at least until around age eighteen. Until then, any ineptness in his social role will be castigated by a host of terms which are reserved almost entirely for males. "For all practical purposes," John Gordon remarks, "the word 'turkey' (or whatever the equivalent is now) can be translated as 'a boy spurned by influential girls' " (141). The equivalents of *turkey* are many: *jerk, nerd, clod, klutz, schmuck, dummy, goon, dork, square, dweeb, jackass, meathead, geek, zero, reject, goofball, drip,* and numerous others, including many obscene terms. Recently, a Michigan high school decided to do away with a scheduled "Nerd Day" after a fourteen-year-old male student, who apparently had been so harassed as a nerd by other students, committed suicide (" 'Nerd' day"). In this case, the ability of language to devastate the emotionally vulnerable young male is powerfully and pathetically dramatized.

As our boy grows, he faces threats and taunts if he does not take risks or endure pain to prove his manhood. *Coward,* for example, is a word applied almost exclusively to males in our society, as are its numerous variants—*chicken, chickenshit, yellow, yellow-bellied, lily-livered, weak-kneed, spineless, squirrelly, fraidy cat, gutless wonder, weakling, butterfly, jellyfish,* and so on. If our young man walks away from a stupid quarrel or prefers to settle differences more rationally than with a swift jab to the jaw, the English language is richly supplied with these and other expressions to call his masculinity into question.

Chief among the other expressions that question masculinity is a lengthy list of homophobic terms such as *queer, pansy, fag, faggot, queen, queeny, pervert, bugger, deviant, fairy, tinkerbell, puss, priss, flamer, feller, sweet, precious, fruit, sodomite,* and numerous others, many obscene. For many people, *gay* is an all-purpose word of ridicule and condemnation. Once again, although homosexuals are being insulted by these terms, the primary target is more often the heterosexual male who fails or refuses to live up to someone else's idea of masculinity. In "Homophobia Among Men" Gregory Lehne explains, "Homophobia is used as a technique of social control . . . to enforce the norms of male sex-role behavior. . . . [H]omosexuality is not the real threat, the real threat is change in the male sex-role" (77).

Nowhere is this threat more apparent than in challenges to our society's male-only military obligation. When a young man and a young woman reach the age of eighteen, both may register to vote; only the young man is required by law to register for military service. For the next decade at least, he must stand ready to be called into military service and even into combat duty in wars, "police actions," "peace-keeping missions," and "rescue missions," often initiated by legally dubious means. Should he resist this obligation, he may be called a *draft dodger, deserter, peacenik, traitor, shirker, slacker, malingerer,* and similar terms. Should he declare himself a conscientious objector, he may be labeled a *conchy* or any of the variants of *coward.*

In his relationships with women, he will find that the age of equality has not yet arrived. Usually, he will be expected to take the initiative, do the driving, pick up the tab, and in general show a deferential respect for women that is a left-over from the chivalric code. Should he behave in an *ungentlemanly* fashion, a host of words—which are applied almost always to males alone—can be used to tell him so: *louse, rat, creep, sleaze, scum, stain, worm, fink, heel, stinker, animal, savage, bounder, cad, wolf, gigolo, womanizer, Don Juan, pig, rotter, boor,* and so on.

In sexual matters he will usually be expected to take the initiative and to *perform.* If he does not, he will be labeled *impotent.* This word, writes Goldberg, "is clearly sexist because it implies a standard of acceptable masculine sexual performance that makes a man abnormal if he can't live up to it" (*New Male* 248). Metaphorically, *impotent* can be used to demean any male whose efforts in any area are deemed unacceptable. Even if our young man succeeds at his sexual performance, the sex manuals are ready to warn him that if he reaches orgasm before a specified time he is guilty of *premature ejaculation.*

When our young man marries, he will be required by law and social custom to support his wife and children. Should he not succeed as breadwinner or should he relax in his efforts, the language offers numerous terms to revile him: *loser, deadbeat, bum, freeloader, leech, parasite, goldbrick, sponge, mooch, ne'er-do-well, good for nothing,* and so on. If women in our society have been regarded as sex objects, men have been regarded as success objects, that is, judged by their ability to provide a standard of living. The title of a recent book—*How to Marry a Winner*—reveals immediately that the intended audience is female (Collier).

When he becomes a father, our young man will discover that he is a second-class parent, as the traditional interchangeability of *mother* and *parent* indicates. The law has been particularly obtuse in recognizing fathers as parents, as evidenced by the awarding of child custody to mothers in ninety percent of divorce cases. In 1975 a father's petition for custody of his four-year-old son was denied because, as the family court judge said, "Fathers don't make good mothers" (qtd. in Levine 21). The judge apparently never considered whether *fathers* make good *parents*.

And so it goes throughout our young man's life: if he deviates from society's gender role norm, he will be penalized and he will hear about it.

The final form of anti-male bias to be considered here is negative stereotyping. Sometimes this stereotyping is indirectly embedded in the language, sometimes it resides in people's assumptions about males and shapes their response to seemingly neutral words, and sometimes it is overtly created for political reasons. It is one thing to say that some aspects of the traditional masculine gender role are limiting and hurtful; it is quite another to gratuitously suspect males in general of being criminal and evil or to denounce them in wholesale fashion as oppressors, exploiters, and rapists. In *The New Male* Goldberg writes, "Men may very well be the last remaining subgroup in our society that can be blatantly, negatively and vilely stereotyped with little objection or resistance" (103). As our language demonstrates, such sexist stereotyping, whether unintentional or deliberate, is not only familiar but fashionable.

In English, crime and evil are usually attributed to the male. As an experiment I have compiled lists of nouns which I read to my composition students, asking them to check whether the words suggest "primarily females," "primarily males," or "could be either." Nearly all the words for law-breakers suggest males rather than females to most students. These words include *murderer, swindler, crook, criminal, burglar, thief, gangster, mobster, hood, hitman, killer, pickpocket, mugger*, and *terrorist*. Accounting for this phenomenon is not always easy. *Hitman* may obviously suggest "primarily males," and the *-er* in *murderer* may do the same, especially if it reminds students of the word's feminine form, *murderess*. Likewise, students may be aware that most murders are committed by males. Other words—like *criminal* and *thief*—are more clearly gender-neutral in form, and it is less clear why they should be so closely linked with "primarily males." Although the dynamics of the association may be unclear, English usage somehow conveys a subtle suggestion that males are to be regarded as guilty in matters of law-breaking.

This hint of male guilt extends to a term like *suspect*. When the person's gender is unknown, the suspect is usually presumed to be a male. For example, even before a definite suspect had been identified, the perpetrator of the 1980–1981 Atlanta child murders was popularly known as *The Man*. When a male and female are suspected of a crime, the male is usually presumed the guilty party. In a recent murder case, when two suspects—Debra Brown and Alton Coleman—were apprehended, police discovered *Brown's* fingerprint in a victim's car and interpreted this as evidence of *Coleman's* guilt. As the Associated Press reported:

> Authorities say for the first time they have evidence linking Alton Coleman with the death of an Indianapolis man.
>
> A fingerprint found in the car of Eugene Scott has been identified as that of Debra Brown, Coleman's traveling companion . . ." ("Police").

Nowhere does the article suggest that Brown's fingerprint found in the victim's car linked Brown with the death: the male suspect was presumed the guilty party, while the female was only a "traveling companion." Even after Brown had been convicted of two murders, the Associated Press was still describing her as "the accused accomplice of convicted killer Alton Coleman" ("Indiana").

In some cases, this presumption of male guilt extends to crimes in which males are not the principal offenders. As noted earlier, a term like *wife and child abuse* ignores battered husbands, but it does more: it suggests that males alone abuse children. In reality most child abuse is committed by mothers (Straus, Gelles, Steinmetz 71). Despite this fact, a 1978 study of child abuse bears the title *Sins of the Fathers* (Inglis).

The term *rape* creates special problems. While the majority of rapes are committed by males and the number of female rape victims outdistances the number of male rape victims, it is widely assumed—as evidenced by the newspaper article cited above—that rape is a crime committed only by males in which only females are victims. Consequently, the word *rape* is often used as a brush to tar all males. In *Against Our Will* Susan Brownmiller writes: "From prehistoric times to the present, I believe, rape . . . is nothing more or less than a conscious process of intimidation by which *all men* keep *all women* in a state of fear" (15; italics in original). Making the point explicitly, Marilyn French states, "All men are rapists and that's all they are" (qtd. in Jennes 33). Given this kind of smear tactic, *rape* can be used metaphorically to indict males alone and to exonerate females, as in this sentence: "The rape of nature—and the ecological disaster it presages—is part and parcel of a dominating masculinity gone out of control" (Hoch 137). The statement neatly blames males alone even when the damage to the environment has been caused in part by females like Anne Gorsuch Burford and Rita Lavelle.

Not only crimes but vices of all sorts have been typically attributed to males. As Muriel R. Schulz points out, "The synonyms for *inebriate* . . . seem to be coded primarily 'male': for example, *boozer, drunkard, tippler, toper, swiller, tosspot, guzzler, barfly, drunk, lush, boozehound, souse, tank, stew, rummy,* and *bum*" (126). Likewise, someone may be *drunk as a lord* but never *drunk as a lady.*

Sex bias or sexism itself is widely held to be a male-only fault. When *sexism* is defined as "contempt for women"—as if there were no such thing as contempt for men—the definition of *sexism* is itself sexist (Bardwick 34).

Part of the reason for this masculinization of evil may be that in the Western world the source of evil has long been depicted in male terms. In the Bible the Evil One is consistently referred to as *he,* whether the reference is to the serpent in the Garden of Eden, Satan as Adversary in Job, Lucifer and Beelzebub in the gospels, Jesus' tempter in the desert, or the dragon in Revelations. *Beelzebub,* incidentally, is often translated as *lord of the flies,* a term designating the demon as masculine. So masculine is the word *devil* that the female prefix is needed, as in *she-devil,* to make a feminine noun of it. The masculinization of evil is so unconsciously accepted that writers often attest to it even while attempting to deny it, as in this passage:

> From the very beginning, the Judeo-Christian tradition has linked women and evil. When second-century theologians struggled to explain the Devil's origins, they surmised that Satan and his various devils had once been angels.
>
> Gerzon 224

If the Judeo-Christian tradition has linked women and evil so closely, why is the writer using the masculine pronoun *his* to refer to Satan, the source of evil according to that tradition? Critics of sex-bias in religious language seldom notice or mention its masculinization of evil: of those objecting to *God the Father* as sexist, no one—to my knowledge—has suggested that designating Satan as the *Father of*

Lies is equally sexist. Few theologians talk about Satan and her legions.

The tendency to blame nearly everything on men has climaxed in recent times with the popularity of such terms as *patriarchy, patriarchal society,* and *male-dominated society.* More political than descriptive, these terms are rapidly becoming meaningless, used as all-purpose smear words to conjure up images of male oppressors and female victims. They are a linguistic sleight of hand which obscures the point that, as Mead has observed (299–300), societies are largely created by both sexes for both sexes. By using a swift reference to *patriarchal structures* or *patriarchal attitudes,* a writer can absolve females of all blame for society's flaws while fixing the onus solely on males. The give-away of this ploy can be detected when *patriarchy* and its related terms are never used in a positive or neutral context, but are always used to assign blame to males alone.

Wholesale denunciations of males as oppressors, exploiters, rapists, Nazis, and slave-drivers have become all too familiar during the past fifteen years. Too often the academic community, rather than opposing this sexism, has been encouraging it. All too many scholars and teachers have hopped on the male-bashing bandwagon to disseminate what John Gordon calls "the myth of the monstrous male." With increasing frequency, this academically fashionable sexism can also be heard echoing from our students. "A white upper-middle-class straight male should seriously consider another college," declares a midwestern college student in *The New York Times Selective Guide to Colleges.* "You [the white male] are the bane of the world. . . . Ten generations of social ills can and will be strapped upon your shoulders" (qtd. in Fiske 12). It would be comforting to dismiss this student's compound of misinformation, sexism, racism, and self-righteousness as an extreme example, but similar yahooisms go unchallenged almost everywhere in modern academia.

Surely it is time for men and women of good will to reject and protest such bigotry. For teachers and writers, the first task is to recognize and condemn forms of anti-male bias in language, whether they are used to exclude males from equal consideration with females, to reinforce restrictive aspects of the masculine gender role, or to stereotype males callously. For whether males are told that *fathers don't make good mothers,* that *real men don't cry,* or that *all men are rapists,* the results are potentially dangerous: like any other group, males can be subtly shaped into what society keeps telling them they are. In *Why Men Are the Way They Are* Warren Farrell puts the matter succinctly: "The more we make men the enemy, the more they will have to behave like the enemy" (357).

WORKS CITED

Bardwick, Judith. *In Transition: How Feminism, Sexual Liberation, and the Search for Self-Fulfillment Have Altered Our Lives.* New York: Holt, 1979.

Baring-Gould, William S., and Ceil Baring-Gould. *The Annotated Mother Goose: Nursery Rhymes Old and New, Arranged and Explained.* New York: Clarkson N. Potter, 1962.

Brownmiller, Susan. *Against Our Will: Men, Women and Rape.* New York: Simon, 1975.

Collier, Phyllis K. *How to Marry a Winner.* Englewood Cliffs, NJ: Prentice, 1982.

Dinnerstein, Dorothy. *The Mermaid and the Minotaur: Sexual Arrangements and Human Malaise.* New York: Harper, 1976.

Farrell, Warren. *Why Men Are the Way They Are: The Male-Female Dynamic.* New York: McGraw-Hill, 1986.

Fiske, Edward B. *The New York Times Selective Guide to Colleges:* New York: Times Books, 1982.

Gerzon, Mark. *A Choice of Heroes: The Changing Faces of American Manhood.* Boston: Houghton, 1982.

Glass, Andrew J. "President wants to unleash military power, but cannot." *Dayton Daily News* 18 June 1985: 1.

Goldberg, Herb. *The Hazards of Being Male: Surviving the Myth of Masculine Privilege.* 1976. New York: NAL, 1977.

———. *The New Male: From Self-Destruction to Self-Care.* 1979. New York: NAL, 1980.

Gordon, John. *The Myth of the Monstrous Male, and Other Feminist Fables.* New York: Playboy P, 1982.

Hartley, Ruth E. "Sex-Role Pressures and the Socialization of the Male Child." *The Forty-Nine Percent Majority: The Male Sex Role.* Ed. Deborah S. David and Robert Brannon. Reading, MA: Addison-Wesley, 1976. 235–44.

Hoch, Paul. *White Hero, Black Beast: Racism, Sexism and the Mask of Masculinity.* London: Pluto P, 1979.

"Indiana jury finds Brown guilty of murder, molesting." *Dayton Daily News* 18 May 1986: 7A.

Inglis, Ruth. *Sins of the Fathers: A Study of the Physical and Emotional Abuse of Children.* New York: St. Martin's, 1978.

Jennes, Gail. "All Men Are Rapists." *People* 20 Feb. 1978: 33–34.

Lehne, Gregory. "Homophobia Among Men." *The Forty-Nine Percent Majority: The Male Sex Role.* Ed. Deborah S. David and Robert Brannon. Reading, MA: Addison-Wesley, 1976. 66–88.

Levine, James A. *Who Will Raise the Children? New Options for Fathers (and Mothers).* Philadelphia: Lippincott, 1976.

Mead, Margaret. *Male and Female: A Study of the Sexes in a Changing World.* New York: Morrow, 1949, 1967.

Money, John, and Patricia Tucker. *Sexual Signatures: On Being a Man or a Woman.* Boston: Little, 1975.

Mougey, Kate. "An act of confiscation: Rape." *Kettering-Oakwood* [OH] *Times* 4 Feb. 1981: 1b.

" 'Nerd' day gets a boot after suicide." *Dayton Daily News* 24 Jan. 1986: 38.

Ong, Walter J. *Fighting for Life: Contest, Sexuality, and Consciousness.* Ithaca, New York: Cornell University Press, 1981.

O'Reilly, Jane, et al. "Wife-Beating: The Silent Crime." *Time* 5 Sept. 1983: 23–4, 26.

"Police: Print links Coleman, death." *Dayton Daily News* 31 Aug. 1984: 26.

Roman, Mel, and William Haddad, *The Disposable Parent: The Case for Joint Custody.* 1978. New York: Penguin, 1979.

Schulz, Muriel R. "Is the English Language Anybody's Enemy?" *Speaking of Words: A Language Reader.* Ed. James MacKillop and Donna Woolfolk Cross. 3rd ed. New York: Holt, 1986. 125–27.

Sorrels, Bobbye D. *The Nonsexist Communicator: Solving the Problems of Gender and Awkwardness in Modern English.* Englewood Cliffs, NJ: Prentice, 1983.

Straus, Murray A., Richard J. Gelles, and Suzanne K. Steinmetz. *Behind Closed Doors: Violence in the American Family.* 1980. Garden City, New York: Doubleday, 1981.

Theroux, Paul. "The Male Myth." *New York Times Magazine* 27 Nov. 1983: 116.

Discussing Issues and Themes

1. Define anti-male bias. Give five of August's examples, and five of your own. Are such examples as numerous as Miller and Swift's examples of sexist language are in "One Small Step for Genkind"?
2. When is anti-male bias likely to occur? Is it motivated by the same factors or misunderstandings that motivate anti-female bias?
3. List the three kinds of anti-male usage which August defines here. Do the same categories exist in anti-female usage? Give examples of both anti-male and anti-female language in each of the three categories.
4. In what ways does anti-male bias in our language strengthen the bias that occurs against minority groups such as women or homosexuals? How might this example support the argument that subtle degrees of bias in language can lead to a hierarchical division of social roles in the world?
5. Compare August's discussion of Biblical language with Miller and Swift's discussion of theological language. What kind of influence does each assume the church has played on language and social roles? In what ways do the two accounts differ? How do they concur?

Discussing Rhetoric and Style

1. August attacks the conventional dominant-passive model of male-female relationships to prove that men and women are engaged in a symbiotic partnership that depends on mutual acceptance and understanding. Are you satisfied with his argument? Does he prove his point? Outline the essay in order to grasp his method more clearly.
2. August's essay is structured similarly to a research paper. Which conventions of the research paper does August adopt; which does he avoid? Make a list, describing the merits of each and why August uses or doesn't use it.
3. How dated are August's sources? Are his examples still relevant?
4. Does August change, for you, the definition of the word "sexism"? Does he move it to a new category, or does he simply offer

a new dimension of it? How has your understanding of the word "sexism" changed after reading this essay?

5. How foolproof are August's arguments? Whether or not you agree with him, can you think of exceptions to any of his ideas? Does he ever anticipate such exceptions? Explain.

Ideas for Writing

1. Pick a passage from the Bible (the first or second Books of *Genesis,* for example, or one of St. Paul's letters, such as I or II *Corinthians),* and discuss the Biblical roots of anti-male prejudice. Do you agree that the Bible depicts "evil" as synonymous with "male"?

2. If women have been treated as "invisible" (as Miller and Swift argue), men, in August's view, have suffered the burden of visibility, being held responsible for a world full of problems. Write an essay discussing the merits and problems of invisibility and visibility.

Why No Honorifics? Newspapers Are Making a Ms. Stake

JOSEPH MEHAN

The use of honorifics is traditional: newspapers around the country used to report the facts of a case involving a Mr. John Doe, in which Miss Jones sat on the jury, and Judge Evans presided. But more often than not Evans now sits on the bench, while Jones hears evidence for and against Doe. Why have honorifics disappeared, and should they be reinstated? Joseph Mehan explores these questions in the following essay, which appeared around 1986 on the editorial page of The New York Times. *Dismissing the feminist objection to honorifics, Mehan urges the return of Mr., Miss, and Mrs., arguing that "newspapers should deal in facts, not promote social trends."*

I must have been out to lunch when momentous changes were taking place in American newspapers.

Almost universally, I read of Anderson addressing a meeting or Jones issuing a statement. Klein is described as a "chair," although I know him to be a bona fide human being.

What astounds me is how this all came about. The press prides itself on its prickly independence. Yet somehow, mysteriously, for the last few years it has been marching like lemmings to an off-stage, unseen drummer.

Who said all titles have to go? Who said no more Mr., Mrs., Miss, Dr., Judge and Bishop? Did the American Newspaper Publishers Association issue such a decree? Was there a national plebiscite?

Feminists, who prefer Ms., argue that Mrs. and Miss are blatantly discriminatory designations, publicly disclosing a woman's marital status while Mr. conceals that of a man.

I never thought that this information was negative, defamatory or shamelessly exploitative. I thought that these were facts and that papers dealt in facts.

If this feminist complaint is the mysterious drummer that sends all newspapers marching in lockstep, editors certainly have not taken much time to look hard at that argument.

To begin with, in the real world nobody uses a stark last-name-only format like newspapers do. Jones is Mr. Jones when we address him. In an introduction, Anderson is certainly Mr., Mrs. or Miss, as the case may be. Whoever heard, "Jones, this is Anderson"?

An editor critically examining the no-titles practice would have to acknowledge, too, that probably his own paper violates this general edict. Obituary columns of most newspapers say that "Mrs. Smith will be buried tomorrow" and that "Mr. Brown is survived by . . ."

Here, at last, the offensive secret can come out. Likewise, engagement or wedding columns carry the kinds of normal expressions everyone uses in daily life. "Miss Addlesby was married to Mr. Winter in the little chapel . . . ," not "Addlesby married Winter."

The same editor might have to admit that at these two milestones in life—marriage and death—American papers inconsistently find it acceptable to use the traditional, conventional titles they ban from their news columns.

In the rush to the new egalitarianism, even hard-earned or honored titles are jettisoned. Bishops, who are hardly examples of dubious sexual identity, are commonly referred to in print now by only their last names.

Likewise, doctors, lawyers and even judges suffer the same fate. Can you imagine a bailiff calling the court to order by shouting: "Hear ye, hear ye, court is now in session! Adams presiding! Everybody rise!" The judge would have apoplexy.

Taking our society as a whole, what have been some of the effects of title amputation? Have we created the sense of respect that is so desperately needed in our times? Hardly. In fact, the opposite seems to have occurred.

Leaders of minority communities especially complain that the newspaper practice of chopping out Mr., Mrs., Miss, Judge, Dr. and such religious titles as Father and Sister shocks young members of their communities who have been taught to respect and emulate just such people.

When the title amputation affects a black professional, so that

Dr. Andrews becomes Andrews or Professor Jenkins becomes Jenkins, the feeling is, as one man put it in a magazine interview, of being called "boy" again.

Has the no-honorifics practice added some sense of order or grace to a disordered and increasingly graceless society? Not according to letters from educators, social scientists and concerned parents sent to newspapers throughout the country.

Norman E. Isaacs, former president of the American Society of Newspaper Editors, commented on the reaction contained in such letters in a speech to editors: "We've stripped all civility from people in society by this nonsense." Incidentally, Mr. Isaacs reported in an interview later that editors swamped him after his speech, shaking his hand, patting his back and congratulating him.

The same thing happened to James M. Ragsdale, editor of The Standard-Times, when he wrote a column saying that his New Bedford, Mass., newspaper was going back to courtesy titles.

Mr. Ragsdale wrote: "We do this to restore and improve our tone of respect for individuals. . . . Rather than find equality by stripping away all courtesy titles, why not go the other way?" Letters from readers warmly endorsed the move.

An American editor looking freshly at the no-titles practice here might glance beyond our shores and see what other journalists are doing.

The Times of London, as you might expect, has its Mr., Mrs. and Miss, and other titles, too. (In fairness, so does The New York Times.) French and Japanese editors would never, never forget their honorifics.

Even the Russians use them. Soviet newspapers use Comrade, but Dr., Professor, Academician and General are all there, too. This from a press in a supposedly classless society!

As they teach in journalism schools, newspapers should deal in facts, not promote social trends.

Discussing Issues and Themes

1. What are honorifics? Do you ever use them, and do you expect others to?

2. On what grounds does Mehan dismiss the feminist objection to Mr., Miss, and Mrs.? Do you agree with his assessment of the feminist position? Explain in a few sentences.

3. What is Mehan's argument for honorifics? Where and when does he think they should be used?

4. Why do you think titles have disappeared? Is it because feminists object to them; or does the disappearance of such honorifics indicate a more complex change in the social mores of our culture?

Discussing Rhetoric and Style

1. Describe the effect of Mehan's deadpan opening. To what extent does Mehan's tone control your reactions? Do you find the piece funny?
2. Consider the length of Mehan's paragraphs. Should they be filled out more? Could any of them be combined into larger paragraphs? Explain, using as many examples from the essay as possible.
3. How effectively does Mehan present his examples? Does he manipulate them so they do more than illustrate a point? For instance, are they ever humorous? Sarcastic? Ironic? Do they ever serve to establish a particular ethical appeal? Do his examples give you an idea of what Mehan himself—or the persona he is trying to create—is like? Discuss, with a few brief references to the essay.
4. To what American assumptions is Mehan appealing when he says that "even the Russians use [honorifics]"? Are there any other attempts on his part to align himself with the audience's politics? What exactly does he imagine these politics to be?
5. Consider Mehan's use of understatement and hyperbole. For example, Mehan's opening sentence employs both of these figures: "I must have been out to lunch [understatement] when momentous changes were taking place in American newspapers [hyperbole]." How well does he play one technique off the other—does each seem more effective because of the presence of the other? Cite at least one example.

Ideas for Writing

1. Write a letter to Mehan in which you adopt the persona of a public figure—perhaps a famous feminist, such as Gloria Steinem, Alice Walker, or Simone de Beauvoir. What kinds of things would a feminist have to say to Mehan? Would she find him as irrelevant as he finds feminists to be?

2. Choose a linguistic trend in advertising or news reporting, and discuss the ways in which political interest groups promote it. Are popular conventions—such as honorifics—defined by popular culture, or are they dictated by the media and powerful political groups? Discuss these issues in a five-page paper.

Non-Gendered Language—Can It Work?

ANTHONY MAIMONE

Anthony Maimone, a student at Rutgers, discusses the resolution of the Douglass College Governing Association (DCGA) to ban the use of the word "freshman" from all college publications and to replace it instead with the non-gendered term "first-year student." Many students at Douglass, the all-women's college affiliate at Rutgers, had reported dissatisfaction with the use of the word freshman, because first-year students are no longer all male, as they once were. Although Maimone directly addresses the particular concerns of the DCGA, his essay goes on to consider the problem of gendered vs. non-gendered language in general and to point out many of the difficulties that might follow sweeping renovations of a language.

Female students of the Douglass College Governmental Association (DCGA) at Rutgers University have recently hoped to challenge institutionalized sexist language by replacing the word "freshman" with "first-year student." In doing so, the belief is that the "new" neutral label will catch on to other supposedly sexist terminology such as "mankind," "chairman," "manager," "women," or "mentor."

Can this work? Will people slowly adapt to the usage of non-gender-related words? First, let's imagine that it already happened; all administrators of Rutgers agreed to make a switch of some of the words mentioned above. So "first-year student" is now the norm, and so are the words "people-kind," "chairperson," and "womyn." Immediately, such an idea becomes increasingly silly, narrow-minded, and unnatural. I am reminded of the idea of burning books because some contemporaries find the old stuff to be unrealistically threatening.

Without a doubt, the "labeling" of certain words as sexist or discriminating to women automatically increases tensions between both men and women, which does not help in promoting equality between the sexes. If this should be the ultimate purpose of the DCGA, it must realize that posting "word changes" around campus or passing out pamphlets on the new language will in effect only create hostility between the sexes rather than hoping to establish a unified, equal relationship between man and woman, necessary to a peaceful democracy.

This by no means suggests that women should be blended into society along with men, but only illustrates that hampering with a non-negotiable concept such as "language-reincarnation" creates notions of inequality that are not actual. Why turn on the heat when the weather is cooling down? DCGA has made remarkable triumphs in publishing information on sexual harassment, date-rape, women victimization, and other related issues. No one is questioning the rights of women in regard to all of these areas because the unfairness to women is well understood by the majority who believes in protecting her equality. DCGA should focus on other areas that are similar and those that may not be so clear to the public of the rights women deserve; focusing the organization's attention on a superficial idea of reconstructing language is time-consuming and undeserving to women. The message received is that there are no other important issues in which women's rights may be enhanced if not brought on equal levels with men.

DCGA has unfortunately also failed in emphasizing the obvious by dramatically depicting the literal. In other words, by concentrating on root words that incorporate the word "man" or "men," DCGA has disregarded the obvious definition of the word as understood by most people on campus, if not across the country. For example, "human" distinguishes people from animals, not men from women. Furthermore, DCGA has neglected those possible sexist terms that don't incorporate the root word of "man" or "men" in them. For example, for me, the words "junior" and "senior" have male-related connotations. Men are the only sex to have "Jr." attached to their last names. And correspondingly, their fathers are frequently addressed by "senior." Should we just change everything to "first-year, second-year, third-year, or fourth-year students?"

Most importantly ignored by the DCGA is the right to free speech. Should students be prevented from saying words that they have been accustomed to legally say for most of their lives—which arouses another question of suspicion: how does DCGA or Rutgers for that matter plan to assure that the new language is being used? There is no big book that snaps the tongues of people by simply writing down the rules to be followed. How do we punish repeat offenders? Would the fifth Bill of Right, the right to protect oneself from self-incrimination keep people from talking on campus?

Discussing Issues and Themes

1. What issue does Maimone's essay address? Does this problem have larger implications? Explain.
2. What is Maimone's view about the issue? Do you agree with him? When does he make his view clear?
3. What does Maimone mean by "language-reincarnation"? What might the language become if the advocates of non-gendered language were to prevail?
4. Maimone suggests that the DCGA has missed the "obvious definition" of the word "freshman." What, if you follow the logic of his paragraph, would this definition entail?
5. Maimone implies that there are "more important issues in which women's rights may be enhanced" than the question of "freshman" versus "first-year student." What might some of these issues be? Do you agree with Maimone's logic?

Discussing Rhetoric and Style

1. What audience does Maimone address here? Is he addressing the DCGA? Or else whom?
2. Maimone compares the formulation of "non-gendered language" to "book burning." Why is this analogy effective? For example, what are our emotional associations with "book burning"?
3. Maimone makes several arguments against non-gendered language. He suggests that "the 'labeling' of certain words as sexist . . . automatically increases tensions between both men and women." Which of his arguments do you find most persuasive? Explain.
4. How would you characterize Maimone's voice? Does he sound like an authority? Is his appeal effective?

Ideas for Writing

1. Maimone's essay responds to an issue on his college campus. The author cites all the arguments he can, addressing the problem first from one perspective and then from another. Pick a topic that is current at your school, and write an essay in which you defend one side, using, as Maimone does, every reasonable argument you can think of.

2. Both Susan Jacoby and Anthony Maimone address the issue of semantics. Compare Jacoby's treatment of the word "feminism" with Maimone's response to the DCGA's resolution. In an essay, compare these writers' attitudes towards the uses of particular words.

CHAPTER 4

Race Is a Four-letter Word: But What Does It Mean?

"Race" is a word whose meaning has changed radically in the twentieth century, often with catastrophic results. Skin color, country of origin, supposed ancestors (or even *one* ancestor however remote)—these categories have been employed at some time to justify the enslavement or murder of millions of people. A word so flexible and dangerous as race requires careful scrutiny, and the essays in this section explore the term from several points of view.

Racial categories, however arbitrary or nonsensical, can seem all too real in everyday application, especially (it has often been argued) if everyday language supports them. The poet and author Langston Hughes invented a famous character, Jesse B. Simple, as a means to comment on a range of everyday habits in American speech. In "That Word 'Black,' " Hughes looks into the range of idioms in English that employ the term "black." He finds a clear tendency to oppose "black" and "white" so as to imply an invariable distinction of "bad" and "good." This dichotomy stems from the origins of the English language, whose early speakers were homogeneous by today's notions of race—though not at all by those of the originators. Still, when such language is used in twentieth-century America, the evaluative implications of the words "white" and "black" have to be faced.

The economist and social historian Thomas Sowell takes a different look at the current American categories of White and Black in "Pink and Brown People." Sowell describes some of the ways that racial thinking tends to polarize and oversimplify even the obvious possibilities for language of skin pigment and ancestry.

The positive associations of racial language make the subject of the next selection. "A Name That Reaches Back" focuses on the current debate over the construction "African American"; the author, Ellen Goodman, sees the term as a way of solving or avoiding some of the issues that concerned Langston Hughes. She concludes that "it is a fitting impulse to choose a name that looks backward in order to move forward."

In "If Black English Isn't a Language, Then Tell Me What Is," James Baldwin ascribes positive value to Black linguistic inventiveness. He traces the origins and purposes of what he and others call Black English. As a writer, Baldwin is particularly sensitive to the resources and possibilities of everyday speech as a means of expression whose implications extend well beyond the issues of name-calling raised in the first two selections.

Everyday speech for the young Richard Rodriguez meant not English in any sense, but Spanish. Bilingual education, like the use of Black English in the public schools, is a topic that has led to political policies addressing emotionally charged issues; but Rodriguez looks into the issue from a more private perspective. His bilingualism was not just a different set of names for the same things, but an evocation of home with all its personal and social resonances.

How racialism has used language against the people called "Indians" is the subject of the next essay. Haig Bosmajian explores the issue that began when Columbus mistakenly thought he had reached India and that the native population should therefore be called Indians.

Racial discrimination is an undeniable part of twentieth-century American life. But how are we to combat that injustice today? How much deference to the historically insulted is mere fairness, and how much leads to a hypocritical and self-serving license to badger innocent, well-meaning people? Robert R. Detlefson reports on these questions as they related to a program at Harvard University that claimed to work against racially prejudiced thinking and talking.

The essays in the section show race to be a category lending itself to constant redefinition. Categorizing people gives power to and implies superiority of the categorizer. Joshua Ozersky, a columnist for the Rutgers *Daily Targum,* makes fun of this process, pretending to have received a letter from a man who has reached the limits of racial thinking by the ingenious means of excluding *everyone* else from membership in his own race.

That Word "Black"

LANGSTON HUGHES

Born in Joplin, Missouri, Langston Hughes (1902–1967) was one of the most prolific writers and energetic figures in the Harlem Renaissance of the 1920s. He published ten volumes of poetry as well as histories, biographies, song lyrics, children's books, film scripts, and journalism. In 1943, Hughes invented one of his most enduring characters: Jesse B. Simple, a wryly humorous, streetwise working man from Harlem. In "That Word 'Black,'" an excerpt from Simple Takes a Wife *(1953), Simple turns his considerable eloquence to the question, "where do white folks get off calling everything bad black?"*

"This evening," said Simple, "I feel like talking about the word *black*."

"Nobody's stopping you, so go ahead. But what you really ought to have is a soap-box out on the corner of 126th and Lenox where the rest of the orators hang out."

"They expresses some good ideas on that corner," said Simple, "but for my ideas I do not need a crowd. Now, as I were saying, the word *black*, white folks have done used that word to mean something bad so often until now when the N.A.A.C.P. asks for civil rights for the black man, they think they must be bad. Looking back into history, I reckon it all started with a *black* cat meaning bad luck. Don't let one cross your path!

"Next, somebody got up a *black-list* on which you get if you don't vote right. Then when lodges come into being, the folks they didn't want in them got *black-balled*. If you kept a skeleton in your closet, you might get *black-mailed*. And everything bad was *black*. When it came down to the unlucky ball on the pool table, the eight-rock, they made it the *black* ball. So no wonder there ain't no equal rights for the *black* man."

"All you say is true about the odium attached to the word *black*,"

I said. "You've even forgotten a few. For example, during the war if you bought something under the table, illegally, they said you were trading on the *black* market. In Chicago, if you're a gangster, the *Black Hand-Society* may take you for a ride. And certainly if you don't behave yourself, your family will say you're a *black* sheep. Then if your mama burns a *black* candle to change the family luck, they call it *black* magic."

"My mama never did believe in voodoo so she did not burn no black candles," said Simple.

"If she had, that would have been a *black* mark against her."

"Stop talking about my mama. What I want to know is, where do white folks get off calling everything bad *black*? If it is a dark night, they say it's *black* as hell. If you are mean and evil, they say you got a *black* heart. I would like to change all that around and say that the people who Jim Crow me have got a *white* heart. People who sell dope to children have got a *white* mark against them. And all the white gamblers who were behind the basketball fix are the *white* sheep of the sports world. God knows there was few, if any, Negroes selling stuff on the black market during the war, so why didn't they call it the *white* market? No, they got to take me and my color and turn it into everything *bad*. According to white folk, black is bad.

"Wait till my day comes! In my language, bad will be *white*. Blackmail will be *white* mail. Black cats will be good luck, and *white* cats will be bad. If a *white* cat crosses your path, look out! I will take the black ball for the cue ball and let the *white* ball be the unlucky eight-rock. And on my blacklist—which will be a *white* list then—I will put everybody who ever Jim Crowed me from Rankin to Hitler, Talmadge to Malan, South Carolina to South Africa.

"I am black. When I look in the mirror, I see myself, daddy-o, but I am not ashamed. God made me. He did not make us no badder than the rest of the folks. The earth is black and all kinds of good things comes out of the earth. Trees and flowers and fruit and sweet potatoes and corn and all that keeps mens alive comes right up out of the earth—good old black earth. Coal is black and it warms your house and cooks your food. The night is black, which has a moon, and a million stars, and is beautiful. Sleep is black which gives you rest, so you wake up feeling good. I am black. I feel very good this evening.

"What is wrong with black?"

Discussing Ideas and Themes

1. What are some of the common uses of "black" that Hughes cites in the essay? Can you think of others?
2. What is the point of offering a list of the ways we use the word "black"? What issues does such usage bring up about race and language?
3. How does this essay try to bring a private language to public view? For example, the dialogue form of the essay allows the reader to feel that he or she is overhearing a private conversation. How else does Hughes create the illusion of privacy?
4. What positive "black" images does Simple suggest at the end of the essay? How are these images different from the others that precede them (besides the obvious fact that they are positive rather than negative)?

Discussing Rhetoric and Style

1. How do the slight grammatical irregularities in Simple's speech help to build a strong voice that is markedly different from the other (the first-person voice) in the essay? Are there other differences between the voices (diction, syntax, sentence variety, and so on)?
2. Hughes's long, often rambling lists of phrases are punctuated by comic moments. How do such moments add to your understanding of the essay?
3. Early in the essay, Simple's friend advises him that "what [he] really ought to have is a soap-box out on the corner of 126th and Lenox where the rest of the orators hang out." How is this essay "oratorical"? In what ways are Simple and his friend "orators"? Read the essay out loud—as an orator would—before answering.
4. Hughes describes the way we use a word and then offers an alternative to that usage. How does his treatment of "black" illustrate both the arbitrariness with which language may be used and its symbolic power?

Ideas for Writing

1. Pick a symbolically, politically, or morally loaded word, such as "white" or "right," and list the different ways we use it. Are common usage and idiom linked to any social uses of the word, as Hughes suggests here?

2. Compare Hughes's meditation on the word "black" with Hugh Rawson's discussion of euphemisms (in Chapter 2). Does Hughes's attempt to transform our understanding differ from Rawson's approach? Write an essay in which you discuss Hughes's essay either as an exploration of the possibilities of euphemism as Rawson describes them, or as a denial of the uses of euphemism.

Pink and Brown People

THOMAS SOWELL

Born in Gastonia, North Carolina in 1930, Thomas Sowell worked to pay his way through Harvard University, where he received his B.A. magna cum laude *in 1958, and later through Columbia for an M.A. and the University of Chicago, where he finished a Ph.D. in economics. Now a senior fellow at Stanford University's Hoover Institute, Sowell has led a distinguished life of teaching and public service in economics. In the following essay, he turns his attention to something other than the economy, expounding his ideas about "pink and brown people": "Race," he notes, "is not an area especially noted for accuracy—or for rationality or candor." Pitting common sense against "provincialism" and "reckless rhetoric," Sowell argues that issues of race are not as clear-cut as they often seem to be. The essay appeared in 1981 in* Pink and Brown People and Other Controversial Essays.

A man who says we should really "tell it like it is" refers to whites and blacks as "pink people" and "brown people." These jarring phrases are of course more accurate, but that may be why they are jarring. Race is not an area especially noted for accuracy—or for rationality or candor. More often it is an area of symbolism, stereotype, and euphemism. The plain truth sounds off-key and even suspicious. Gross exaggerations like *white* and *black* are more like the kind of polarization we are used to. Racial classifications have always been a problem, but in the United States such attempts at neat pigeonholing become a farce, in view of the facts of history.

Less than a fourth of the "black" population of the United States is of unmixed African ancestry. And a noted social historian estimates that tens of millions of whites have at least one black ancestor somewhere in generations past. Even in the old South, where "one drop of Negro blood" was supposed to make you socially black, the actual laws required some stated fraction of black ancestry, to avoid "embarrassing" some of the "best" white families.

What all this boils down to is a wide spectrum of racial mixtures with an arbitrary dividing line and boldly contrasting labels applied to people on either side of the line. The human desire for classification is not going to be defeated by any biological facts. Those who cannot swallow pseudobiology can turn to pseudohistory as the basis for classification. Unique cultural characteristics are now supposed to neatly divide the population.

In this more modern version, the ghetto today is a unique social phenomenon—a unique problem calling for a unique solution. Many of those who talk this way just happen to have this solution with them and will make it available for a suitable combination of money and power.

Ghettos today certainly differ from white middle-class neighborhoods. But past ghettos always differed from past middle-class neighborhoods, even when both were white. Indeed, the very word *ghetto* came historically from a white minority community of people, classified by the fact that they held religious services one day earlier than others. People will classify on any basis. With today's recreation-oriented weekends, religious classifications are often based on what service you *would have* attended.

American ghettos have always had crime, violence, overcrowding, filth, drunkenness, bad school teaching, and worse learning. Nor are blacks historically unique even in the degree of these things. Crime and violence were much worse in the nineteenth-century slums, which were almost all white. The murder rate in Boston in the middle of the nineteenth century was about three times what it was in the middle of the twentieth century. All the black riots of the 1960s put together did not kill half as many people as were killed in one white riot in 1863.

The meaning of the term *race riot* has been watered down in recent times to include general hell raising (and posing for television) in the hell-raisers' own neighborhood. In the nineteenth century it was much uglier. Thousands of members of one "race" invaded the neighborhood of another "race"—both, typically, European—to maim, murder, and burn. Today's disorders are not in the same league, whether measured in blood or buildings.

Squalor, dirt, disease? Historically, blacks are neither first nor last in any of these categories. There were far more immigrants packed into the slums (per room or per square mile) than is the case with blacks today—not to mention the ten thousand to thirty thousand children with no home at all in nineteenth-century New York.

They slept under bridges, huddled against buildings or wherever they could find some semblance of shelter from the elements.

Even in the area where many people get most emotional—educational and I.Q. test results—blacks are doing nothing that various European minorities did not do before them. As of about 1920, any number of European ethnic groups had I.Q.'s the same as or lower than the I.Q.'s of blacks today. As recently as the 1940s, there were schools on the Lower East Side of New York with academic performances lower than those of schools in Harlem.

Much of the paranoia that we talk ourselves into about race (and other things) is a result of provincialism about our own time as compared to other periods of history. Violence, poverty, and destroyed lives should never be accepted. But there is little chance of solving any problem unless we see it for what it is, not what it appears to be in the framework of reckless rhetoric.

Discussing Ideas and Themes

1. Why might someone who "tells it like it is" prefer the adjectives "pink" and "brown" to "white" and "black"?
3. Is Sowell successful in proving his thesis? Are you convinced, persuaded, or moved by his argument? Why or why not?
3. What example does Sowell offer to blur our distinction between who is white in this country and who is black? Where does he get his information?
4. How does Sowell's discussion of the origin of the word "ghetto" relate to and enhance his larger argument?
5. Do you agree with Sowell that "much of the paranoia that we talk ourselves into about race (and other things) is a result of provincialism about our own time as compared to other periods in history"?

Discussing Rhetoric and Style

1. Sowell claims that "the plain truth sounds off-key and even suspicious." Do you find his essay truthful? Off-key? Are you suspicious of it?
2. Does this essay ever fall into "reckless rhetoric"? Before answering, be sure to decide just what that phrase means, both to you and to Sowell.

3. What techniques does Sowell use to blur the line between white and black and between 19th-century ghettoes and today's? Why does his argument depend on these ambiguities?

4. Skim the essay to acquaint yourself with Sowell's use of the three-item list. How effective are they as rhetorical strategy? For instance, do you find them eloquent? Rhythmically satisfying? Or merely functional?

5. Sowell often marks a shift in tone by placing a word or phrase in quotation marks (for instance, "Less than one-fourth of the 'black' population. . . ." Can you hear a shift in tone? How is it different from the shift one might indicate by the use of parentheses or italics?

Ideas for Writing

1. Sowell points out that "black" and "white" are not quite the "plain truth" when it comes to people's color. Can you think of any other tendencies to use words that are not strictly appropriate? Compile a short list (for example: "plump," "morbidly obese," "slim") and then discuss why and when we do this.

2. Using Sowell's essay as a model, write a paper in which you compare some other era with today. Restrict yourself to one topic, for instance, "Politics in the 1960s versus Politics in the 1980s" or "Education in the Renaissance versus Education Today."

A Name That Reaches Back

ELLEN GOODMAN

Born in Newton, Massachusetts in 1941 and a graduate of Radcliffe College, Ellen Goodman is now a Boston-based syndicated columnist. She has won many awards for her distinguished columns, including a Pulitzer Prize and a Distinguished Writing Award for commentary. She has published several collections, including At Large *and* Keeping in Touch, *as well as* Turning Points, *a critical analysis of the feminist movement. In this reworking of a 1988 column, Goodman explores whether blacks should adopt the title of "African Americans"; she concludes that it is "a fitting impulse to choose a name that looks backward in order to move forward."*

. . . I cannot trace my roots very deep. I run out of names and places quickly.

Of my eight great-grandparents, only two were born in America. The others, whose names I do not know, came from all over Europe, mostly from towns that were German one year, Polish the next, Russian the third.

Some were kicked out of those towns, still others chose to emigrate. They came and married each other—sometimes against their families' wishes—and begat. They became Americans. To trace my ancestry back through even such a short history to one set of ancestors in one town in one country would mean cutting out the others the way Alex Haley did when he chose Kunta Kinte from his lexicon of forebears.

Like most third- and fourth-generation Americans, then, I am a genetic molting pot, the product of nationalities that spent centuries trying to murder each other.

If there is an ethnicity that makes any sense at all it has been expanded from a country to an entire continent. European American.

It is from this personal vantage point that I witness the movement of some of my countrymen and women to name themselves after a different mother continent: Africa.

Twenty years ago, the civil-rights leadership told its followers to drop the names that white Americans had given them. They were no longer colored, no longer Negro, but black.

Black and proud, black and powerful, black and beautiful.

Now there is an impulse to turn from a name that promoted unity on the basis of color to a name that promotes unity on the basis of origin. To turn from a title that describes people in contrast to others, whites, to a title that describes people in connection to their own ancestry. African American.

"We are not just former slaves living in the United States," says Ramona Edelin the head of the National Urban Coalition who raised the issue at a recent meeting of leaders, "We are African Americans."

"To be called African American has cultural integrity; it puts us in our proper historical context," says Jesse Jackson, speaking for himself and others who have urged the use of a title that until now has been mainly used by academics.

At first, as an American who regards her ties to the mother continent Europe with great distance, I regarded the phrase African American with great skepticism. After all, what is in a name? Does this one promise to be more precise? If black is a word used to describe a huge range of skin color that rarely resembles ebony, then African is a word that covers countries as different as Ethiopia and Kenya. It covers cultures as diverse as the Kikuyu and the Bakuba.

Does this name promise unity? How do you find unity identifying with Africans when Africans themselves, like Europeans and Asians, are often in deadly conflict with each other?

When the Americans in question may trace their strongest roots to the Caribbean, or may indeed trace much of their genetic heritage to Europe?

Does this name make some symbolic point? Trace back 100,000 years and all humans are descendants of a single African "Eve." Go forward far enough from the mother country to the mother continent and we are people of the mother earth.

But that line of reasoning is far too abstract, too starry-eyed. The question, it seems to me now, isn't whether this name change makes genetic or ethnic sense, but whether it makes emotional sense. And it does.

A change of name is a serious business. A name is identity, a handle on consciousness, a public and collective description of who you are. It may be especially important for those who still carry the surnames of slaveholders.

The name "black" emerged out of confrontational politics of the civil-rights movement. But now the toughest battles are not against segregation but against violence and drugs, the destruction of family and community and culture. Today among the leadership you hear less talk of rights and more of values.

In this context of change, African American sounds right.

It's a name that resonates of cultural history, a name that reflects the real desire to teach children that "I am Somebody." A name that reaches back past slavery and out past the limits of an embattled city block for that lesson.

"Who are we if we don't acknowledge our motherland?" asks Ramona Edelin. "We are really adrift if we are just former slaves." She adds, "When a child in a ghetto calls himself African American, immediately he's international. You've taken him from the ghetto and put him on the globe."

The black leadership of today has turned inward, toward internal healing, toward self-help. It is a fitting impulse to choose a name that looks backward in order to move forward.

Discussing Ideas and Themes

1. How does Goodman distinguish "genetic," "ethnic," and "emotional" reasons for taking a name? Why does she choose the last as the most reasonable?

2. What does Goodman decide about the title "African American"? Do you agree?

3. How does Goodman's position as a white American woman shape the essay? Would the essay have been radically different if written by an African American?

4. How is Goodman's identity as a "European American" related to her discussion of "African Americans"? How is the epithet "European American" different from "African American"? Or isn't it?

5. Compare this essay with Langston Hughes's "That Word 'Black'." What does each author say about the relationship between racial identity and language?

Discussing Rhetoric and Style

1. How is Goodman's style both personal and journalistic? For instance, whom does she imagine her audience to be?
2. By withholding her opinion until halfway through the essay, Goodman allows us to follow her thinking. Write a brief outline of the major steps in her argument.
3. Goodman asks many rhetorical questions. How do these questions contribute to her argument? Why does she ask questions rather than make the statements that the questions imply?
4. Both Goodman and Hughes write about black attempts to regain or maintain identity through the use of language. But while Hughes's essay imaginatively redeems a common word ("black") from abuse, Goodman's simply sanctions something it has no real power to deny. How does Goodman's chatty style help defuse the issue?

Ideas for Writing

1. Goodman defends the use of "African American" for what she calls "emotional" reasons. Write a brief essay that either defends or rejects the epithet for social reasons.
2. Develop a paper that compares and contrasts Goodman's essay to Thomas Sowell's "Pink and Brown People." How does each of these writers think about the problems of language and race?

If Black English Isn't a Language, Then Tell Me, What Is?

JAMES BALDWIN

An acclaimed writer of fiction, drama, and essays, James Baldwin (1924–1989) was born in Harlem. His major works include the novels Go Tell It On the Mountain *and* Giovanni's Room *as well as an autobiography,* Notes of a Native Son. *The following essay, which first appeared as a letter to the editor in* The New York Times *in 1979, was written amid popular controversy over whether black English is a language in its own right. As one can assume from the title of the piece, Baldwin certainly thinks that it is a language—one of "incredible music" and "sheer intelligence" which, he suggests, whites refuse to understand because of racial differences.*

The argument concerning the use, or the status, or the reality, of black English is rooted in American history and has absolutely nothing to do with the question the argument supposes itself to be posing. The argument has nothing to do with language itself but with the *role* of language. Language, incontestably, reveals the speaker. Language, also, far more dubiously, is meant to define the other—and, in this case, the other is refusing to be defined by a language that has never been able to recognize him.

People evolve a language in order to describe and thus control their circumstances, or in order not to be submerged by a reality that they cannot articulate. (And, if they cannot articulate it, they *are* submerged.) A Frenchman living in Paris speaks a subtly and crucially different language from that of the man living in Marseilles; neither sounds very much like a man living in Quebec; and they would all have great difficulty in apprehending what the man from Guadeloupe, or Martinique, is saying, to say nothing of the man from Senegal—although the "common" language of all these areas is French. But each has paid, and is paying, a different price for this "common" language, in which, as it turns out, they are not saying, and cannot be saying, the same things: They each have very different realities to articulate or control.

What joins all languages, and all men, is the necessity to confront life, in order, not inconceivably, to outwit death: The price for this is the acceptance, and achievement, of one's temporal identity. So that, for example, though it is not taught in the schools (and this has the potential of becoming a political issue) the south of France still clings to its ancient and musical Provençal, which resists being described as a "dialect." And much of the tension in the Basque countries, and in Wales, is due to the Basque and Welsh determination not to allow their languages to be destroyed. This determination also feeds the flames in Ireland for among the many indignities the Irish have been forced to undergo at English hands is the English contempt for their language.

It goes without saying, then, that language is also a political instrument, means, and proof of power. It is the most vivid and crucial key to identity: It reveals the private identity, and connects one with, or divorces one from, the larger public, or communal identity. There have been, and are, times, and places, when to speak a certain language could be dangerous, even fatal. Or, one may speak the same language, but in such a way that one's antecedents are revealed, or (one hopes) hidden. This is true in France, and is absolutely true in England: The range (and reign) of accents on that damp little island make England coherent for the English and totally incomprehensible for everyone else. To open your mouth in England is (if I may use black English) to "put your business in the street": You have confessed your parents, your youth, your school, your salary, your self-esteem, and, alas, your future.

Now, I do not know what white Americans would sound like if there had never been any black people in the United States, but they would not sound the way they sound. *Jazz,* for example, is a very specific sexual term, as in *jazz me baby,* but white people purified it into the Jazz Age. *Sock it to me,* which means, roughly, the same thing, has been adopted by Nathaniel Hawthorne's descendants with no qualms or hesitations at all, along with *let it all hang out* and *right on! Beat to his socks,* which was once the black's most total and despairing image of poverty, was transformed into a thing called the Beat Generation, which phenomenon was, largely, composed of *uptight,* middle-class white people, imitating poverty, trying to *get down,* to *get with it,* doing their *thing,* doing their despairing best to be *funky,* which we, the blacks, never dreamed of doing—we *were* funky, baby, like *funk* was going out of style.

Now, no one can eat his cake, and have it, too, and it is late in the day to attempt to penalize black people for having created a language that permits the nation its only glimpse of reality, a language without which the nation would be even more *whipped* than it is.

I say that this present skirmish is rooted in American history, and it is. Black English is the creation of the black diaspora. Blacks came to the United States chained to each other, but from different tribes: Neither could speak the other's language. If two black people, at that bitter hour of the world's history, had been able to speak to each other, the institution of chattel slavery could never have lasted as long as it did. Subsequently, the slave was given, under the eye, and the gun, of his master, Congo Square, and the Bible—or, in other words, and under these conditions, the slave began the formation of the black church, and it is within this unprecedented tabernacle that black English began to be formed. This was not, merely, as in the European example, the adoption of a foreign tongue, but an alchemy that transformed ancient elements into new language: *A language comes into existence by means of brutal necessity, and the rules of the language are dictated by what the language must convey.*

There was a moment, in time, and in this place, when my brother, or my mother, or my father, or my sister, had to convey to me, for example, the danger in which I was standing from the white man standing just behind me, and to convey this with a speed, and in a language, that the white man could not possibly understand, and that, indeed, he cannot understand, until today. He cannot afford to understand it. This understanding would reveal to him too much about himself, and smash that mirror before which he has been frozen for so long.

Now, if this passion, this skill, this (to quote Toni Morrison) "sheer intelligence," this incredible music, the mighty achievement of having brought a people utterly unknown to, or despised by "history"—to have brought this people to their present, troubled, troubling, and unassailable and unanswerable place—if this absolutely unprecedented journey does not indicate that black English is a language, I am curious to know what definition of language is to be trusted.

A people at the center of the Western world, and in the midst of so hostile a population, has not endured and transcended by means of what is patronizingly called a "dialect." We, the blacks, are in trouble, certainly, but we are not doomed, and we are not inarticulate because we are not compelled to defend a morality that we know to be a lie.

The brutal truth is that the bulk of the white people in America never had any interest in educating black people, except as this could serve white purposes. It is not the black child's language that is in question, it is not his language that is despised: It is his experience. A child cannot be taught by anyone who despises him, and a child cannot afford to be fooled. A child cannot be taught by anyone whose demand, essentially, is that the child repudiate his experience, and all that gives him sustenance, and enter a limbo in which he will no longer be black, and in which he knows that he can never become white. Black people have lost too many black children that way.

And, after all, finally, in a country with standards so untrustworthy, a country that makes heroes of so many criminal mediocrities, a country unable to face why so many of the nonwhite are in prison, or on the needle, or standing, futureless, in the streets—it may very well be that both the child, and his elder, have concluded that they have nothing whatever to learn from the people of a country that has managed to learn so little.

Discussing Ideas and Themes

1. How does Baldwin define language? How does black English constitute a language?
2. How, according to Baldwin's model, is language controlled by reality? What distinctions does he make between language and experience?
3. What does Baldwin say that "all languages, and all men" have in common? Do you agree?
4. How does Baldwin distinguish between dialect and language? Why does he consider black English a language rather than merely a dialect? What is the social significance of such a distinction—what is at stake for the status of black English here?
5. What are the roots of black English? How do these roots reinforce Baldwin's ideas about language and about race relations in this country?

Discussing Rhetoric and Style

1. This essay originally appeared as a letter to the editor in the *New York Times* and was available to a very wide audience. Does Baldwin's rhetorical attitude here suggest that he is inter-

ested in reaching a large audience of newspaper readers? Why or why not?

2. Whom does Baldwin see as his audience? How does this perception affect his choice of language?

3. Study Baldwin's sentences, particularly his use of commas. How do his sentences sound, with so many pauses in them? Do the commas emphasize certain words?

4. How does the language of Baldwin's essay differ from black English?

Ideas for Writing

1. Make a list of any bits of private communication you share with your family or friends ("inside" words or jokes—phrases that only your small group understands). Considering Baldwin's ideas about language, write an essay that describes when and why these private words might constitute a language of their own.

2. Write an essay that explores the similarities and differences between Baldwin and Orwell ("Politics and the English Language"). What would Baldwin think of Orwell's essay and vice versa?

Memoirs of a Bilingual Childhood

RICHARD RODRIGUEZ

Richard Rodriguez, born in 1944 to Mexican-American parents, quickly mastered English as his second language and eventually earned a Ph.D. in English Literature; as well, he received fellowships from the National Endowment for the Humanities and the Fulbright Foundation. His strong sympathy for disadvantaged Mexican-Americans caused him eventually to abandon academia and devote himself to writing and to various odd jobs. This essay, taken from his acclaimed autobiography, Hunger of Memory *(1982), discusses the differences between "private" and "public" languages and describes the loss that can accompany the transition from one to the other.*

I remember to start with that day in Sacramento—a California now nearly thirty years past—when I first entered a classroom, able to understand some fifty stray English words.

The third of four children, I had been preceded to a neighborhood Roman Catholic school by an older brother and sister. But neither of them had revealed very much about their classroom experiences. Each afternoon they returned, as they left in the morning, always together, speaking in Spanish as they climbed the five steps of the porch. And their mysterious books, wrapped in shopping-bag paper, remained on the table next to the door, closed firmly behind them.

An accident of geography sent me to a school where all my classmates were white, many the children of doctors and lawyers and business executives. All my classmates certainly must have been uneasy on that first day of school—as most children are uneasy—to find themselves apart from their families in the first institution of their lives. But I was astonished.

The nun said, in a friendly but oddly impersonal voice, "Boys and girls, this is Richard Rodriguez." (I heard her sound out: *Rich-heard Road-ree-guess.*) It was the first time I had heard anyone name me in English. "Richard," the nun repeated more slowly, writing my name down in her black leather book. Quickly I turned to see my mother's face dissolve in a watery blur behind the pebbled glass door.

Many years later there is something called bilingual education—a scheme proposed in the late 1960s by Hispanic-American social activists, later endorsed by a congressional vote. It is a program that seeks to permit non-English-speaking children, many from lower-class homes, to use their family language as the language of school. (Such is the goal its supporters announce.) I hear them and am forced to say no: It is not possible for a child—any child—ever to use his family's language in school. Not to understand this is to misunderstand the public uses of schooling and to trivialize the nature of intimate life—a family's "language."

Memory teaches me what I know of these matters; the boy reminds the adult. I was a bilingual child, a certain kind—socially disadvantaged—the son of working-class parents, both Mexican immigrants.

In the early years of my boyhood, my parents coped very well in America. My father had steady work. My mother managed at home. They were nobody's victims. Optimism and ambition led them to a house (our home) many blocks from the Mexican south side of town. We lived among *gringos* and only a block from the biggest, whitest houses. It never occurred to my parents that they couldn't live wherever they chose. Nor was the Sacramento of the fifties bent on teaching them a contrary lesson. My mother and father were more annoyed than intimidated by those two or three neighbors who tried initially to make us unwelcome. ("Keep your brats away from my sidewalk!") But despite all they achieved, perhaps because they had so much to achieve, any deep feeling of ease, the confidence of "belonging" in public was withheld from them both. They regarded the people at work, the faces in crowds, as very distant from us. They were the others, *los gringos*. That term was interchangeable in their speech with another, even more telling, *los americanos*.

I grew up in a house where the only regular guests were my relations. For one day, enormous families of relatives would visit and there would be so many people that the noise and the bodies would spill out to the backyard and front porch. Then, for weeks, no one came by. (It was usually a salesman who rang the doorbell.) Our house stood apart. A gaudy yellow in a row of white bungalows. We were the people with the noisy dog. The people who raised pigeons and chickens. We were the foreigners on the block. A few neighbors smiled and waved. We waved back. But no one in the family knew the names of the old couple who lived next door; until I was seven years old, I did not know the names of the kids who lived across the street.

In public, my father and mother spoke a hesitant, accented, not always grammatical English. And they would have to strain—their bodies tense—to catch the sense of what was rapidly said by *los gringos*. At home they spoke Spanish. The language of their Mexican past sounded in counterpoint to the English of public society. The words would come quickly, with ease. Conveyed through those sounds was the pleasing, soothing, consoling reminder of being at home.

During those years when I was first conscious of hearing, my mother and father addressed me only in Spanish; in Spanish I learned to reply. By contrast, English (*inglés*), rarely heard in the house, was the language I came to associate with *gringos*. I learned my first words of English overhearing my parents speak to strangers. At five years of age, I knew just enough English for my mother to trust me on errands to stores one block away. No more.

I was a listening child, careful to hear the very different sounds of Spanish and English. Wide-eyed with hearing, I'd listen to sounds more than words. First, there were English (*gringo*) sounds. So many words were still unknown that when the butcher or the lady at the drugstore said something to me, exotic polysyllabic sounds would bloom in the midst of their sentences. Often, the speech of people in public seemed to me very loud, booming with confidence. The man behind the counter would literally ask, "What can I do for you?" But by being so firm and so clear, the sound of his voice said that he was a *gringo*; he belonged in public society.

I would also hear then the high nasal notes of middle-class American speech. The air stirred with sound. Sometimes, even now, when I have been traveling abroad for several weeks, I will hear what I heard as a boy. In hotel lobbies or airports, in Turkey or Brazil, some Americans will pass, and suddenly I will hear it again—the high sound of American voices. For a few seconds I will hear it with pleasure, for it is now the sound of *my* society—a reminder of home. But inevitably—already on the flight headed for home—the sound fades with repetition. I will be unable to hear it anymore.

When I was a boy, things were different. The accent of *los gringos* was never pleasing nor was it hard to hear. Crowds at Safeway or at bus stops would be noisy with sound. And I would be forced to edge away from the chirping chatter above me.

I was unable to hear my own sounds, but I knew very well that I spoke English poorly. My words could not stretch far enough to form complete thoughts. And the words I did speak I didn't know well enough to make into distinct sounds. (Listeners would usually lower their heads, better to hear what I was trying to say.) But it was one thing for *me* to speak English with difficulty. It was more troubling for me to hear my parents speak in public: their high-whining vowels and guttural consonants; their sentences that got stuck with "eh" and "ah" sounds; the confused syntax; the hesitant rhythm of sounds so different from the way *gringos* spoke. I'd notice, moreover, that my parents' voices were softer than those of *gringos* we'd meet.

I am tempted now to say that none of this mattered. In adulthood I am embarrassed by childhood fears. And, in a way, it didn't matter very much that my parents could not speak English with ease. Their linguistic difficulties had no serious consequences. My mother and father made themselves understood at the county hospital clinic and at government offices. And yet, in another way, it mattered very much—it was unsettling to hear my parents struggle with English. Hearing them, I'd grow nervous, my clutching trust in their protection and power weakened.

There were many times like the night at a brightly lit gasoline station (a blaring white memory) when I stood uneasily, hearing my father. He was talking to a teenaged attendant. I do not recall what they were saying, but I cannot forget the sounds my father made as he spoke. At one point his words slid together to form one word—sounds as confused as the threads of blue and green oil in the puddle next to my shoes. His voice rushed through what he had left to say. And, toward the end, reached falsetto notes, appealing to his listener's understanding. I looked away to the lights of passing automobiles. I tried not to hear anymore. But I heard only too well the calm, easy tones in the attendant's reply. Shortly afterward, walking toward home with my father, I shivered when he put his hand on my shoulder. The very first chance that I got, I evaded his grasp and ran on ahead into the dark, skipping with feigned boyish exuberance.

But then there was Spanish. *Español:* my family's language. *Español:* the language that seemed to me a private language. I'd hear strangers on the radio and in the Mexican Catholic church across town speaking in Spanish, but I couldn't really believe that Spanish was a public language, like English. Spanish speakers, rather, seemed related to me, for I sensed that we shared—through our language—the experience of feeling apart from *los gringos.* It was thus a ghetto Spanish that I heard and I spoke. Like those whose lives are bound by a barrio, I was reminded by Spanish of my separateness from *los otros, los gringos* in power. But more intensely than for most barrio children—because I did not live in a barrio—Spanish seemed to me the language of home. (Most days it was only at home that I'd hear it.) It became the language of joyful return.

A family member would say something to me and I would feel myself specially recognized. My parents would say something to me and I would feel embraced by the sounds of their words. Those sounds said: *I am speaking with ease in Spanish. I am addressing you in words I never use with* los gringos. *I recognize you as someone special, close, like no one outside. You belong with us. In the family.*

(*Ricardo*.)

At the age of five, six, well past the time when most other children no longer easily notice the difference between sounds uttered at home and words spoken in public, I had a different experience. I lived in a world magically compounded of sounds. I remained a child longer than most; I lingered too long, poised at the edge of language—often frightened by the sounds of *los gringos,* delighted by the sounds of Spanish at home. I shared with my family a language that was startlingly different from that used in the great city around us.

For me there were none of the gradations between public and private society so normal to a maturing child. Outside the house was public society; inside the house was private. Just opening or closing the screen door behind me was an important experience. I'd rarely leave home all alone or without reluctance. Walking down the sidewalk, under the canopy of tall trees, I'd warily notice the—suddenly—silent neighborhood kids who stood warily watching me. Nervously, I'd arrive at the grocery store to hear there the sounds of the *gringo*—foreign to me—reminding me that in this world so big, I was a foreigner. But then I'd return. Walking back toward our house, climbing the steps from the sidewalk, when the front door was open in summer, I'd hear voices beyond the screen door talking in Spanish. For a second or two, I'd stay, linger there, listening. Smiling, I'd hear my mother call out, saying in Spanish (words): "Is that you, Richard?" All the while her sounds would assure me: *You are home now; come closer; inside. With us.*

"Sí," I'd reply.

Once more inside the house I would resume (assume) my place in the family. The sounds would dim, grow harder to hear. Once more at home, I would grow less aware of that fact. It required, however, no more than the blurt of the doorbell to alert me to listen to sounds all over again. The house would turn instantly still while my mother went to the door. I'd hear her hard English sounds. I'd wait to hear her voice return to soft-sounding Spanish, which assured me, as surely as did the clicking tongue of the lock on the door, that the stranger was gone.

Plainly, it is not healthy to hear such sounds so often. It is not healthy to distinguish public words from private sounds so easily. I remained cloistered by sounds, timid and shy in public, too dependent on voices at home. And yet it needs to be emphasized: I was an extremely happy child at home. I remember many nights when my father would come back from work, and I'd hear him call out to my mother in Spanish, sounding relieved. In Spanish, he'd sound light and free notes he never could manage in English. Some nights I'd jump up just at hearing his voice. With *mis hermanos* I would come running into the room where he was with my mother. Our laughing (so deep was the pleasure!) became screaming. Like others who know the pain of public alienation, we transformed the knowledge of our public separateness and made it consoling—the reminder of intimacy. Excited, we joined our voices in a celebration of sounds. *We are speaking now the way we never speak out in public. We are alone—together,* voices sounded, surrounded to tell me. Some nights, no one seemed willing to loosen the hold sounds had on us. At dinner, we invented new words. (Ours sounded Spanish, but made sense only to us.) We pieced together new words by taking, say, an English verb and giving it Spanish endings. My mother's instructions at bedtime would be lacquered with mock-urgent tones. Or a word like *sí* would become, in several notes, able to convey added measures of feeling. Tongues explored the edges of words, especially the fat vowels. And we happily sounded that military drum roll, the twirling roar of the Spanish *r*. Family language: my family's sounds. The voices of my parents and sisters and brother. Their voices insisting: *You belong here. We are family members. Related. Special to one another. Listen!* Voices singing and sighing, rising, straining, then surging, teeming with pleasure that burst syllables into fragments of laughter. At times it seemed there was steady quiet only when, from another room, the rustling whispers of my parents faded and I moved closer to sleep.

Discussing Ideas and Themes

1. What is the difference between private and public language? Does Rodriguez directly define his terms? If so, where?
2. How does language both threaten and reinforce Rodriguez's sense of family? How does he reconcile the good and the bad things about experience of private and public languages?
3. Rodriguez opens with a recollection. What significance do memory and forgetfulness have in the rest of the essay? How are they related to the way he hears his languages—both in childhood and in adult life? With this in mind, why is the sleepy ending of the essay so appropriate?
4. In what ways do Rodriguez's experiences of childhood—perceptions of home and school, of inside and outside worlds—

remind you of your own experience of childhood (whether you were bilingual or not)? Are the fears and anxieties and losses linked specifically to his situation as a bilingual child, or are they part of the universal experience of growing up?

Discussing Rhetoric and Style

1. Rodriguez has a talent for turning childhood conflicts into the primary governing patterns of his most successful prose—for instance, public vs. private, English vs. Spanish, hard vs. soft sounds, alienation vs. intimacy. Pick one of these conflicts and trace its development throughout the essay.
2. Rodriguez writes in the impressionistic prose of childhood nostalgia (impressionistic in the sense of including many impressions, details, and images). Can you find examples of this style? Try to emulate it in a few sentences of your own.
3. Rodriguez confides that he is still "embarrassed by childhood fears." How would you characterize this statement? Is it a rhetorical tactic designed to disarm a cynical audience, or merely a confessional moment? Why?
4. How vivid do you find Rodriguez's memories? What accounts for their effect on you—whether you find them vivid or not?
5. Rodriguez uses parenthetical remarks to shift to a personal, more "private" or intimate tone. Can you identify places within the essay that play along the spectrum of public to private? Look for one sentence that seems to you very public or formal (such as the discussion of the congressional bill on bilingual education) and another that sounds private and confidential. You will find that you will have to listen attentively to hear the differences.

Ideas for Writing

1. Both Rodriguez and Miriam Tucker ("Aunt Ethel") employ memory as a narrative opener, but Rodriguez's essay moves toward a different end from Tucker's, partially because it has very different motives. Discuss the difference in effect in a few pages.
2. Write a brief memoir of your own childhood, imitating Rodriguez's use of remembered conflict as the starting point for adult understanding. You might discuss female vs. male or black vs. white conflicts from childhood.

Defining the "American Indian"

A Case Study in the Language of Suppression

HAIG A. BOSMAJIAN

A professor of speech communication at the University of Washington in Seattle, Haig Bosmajian is the author of The Language of Oppression. *Here he discusses the consequences of language suppression on oppressed peoples. "One of the first important acts of an oppressor," he says, "is to redefine the oppressed victim he intends to jail or eradicate." Bosmajian then goes on to illustrate his point, using as his example the Native American, who was redefined legally, religiously, politically, and culturally, and who gained the right to vote only in 1948. The essay, first appeared in the journal* The Speech Teacher.

One of the first important acts of an oppressor is to redefine the oppressed victim he intends to jail or eradicate so that they will be looked upon as creatures warranting suppression and in some cases separation and annihilation. I say "creatures" because the redefinition usually implies a dehumanization of the individual. The Nazis redefined the Jews as "bacilli," "parasites," "disease," and "demon."[1] The language of white racism has for centuries attempted to "keep the nigger in his place."[2] Our sexist language has allowed men to define who and what a woman is.[3] The labels "traitors," "queers," "pinkos," "saboteurs," and "obscene degenerates" have all been used to attack students protesting the war in Vietnam and the economic and political injustices in this country.[4] One obviously does not listen to, much less talk to, traitors and outlaws, sensualists and queers. One only punishes them or, as Spiro Agnew suggested in one of his 1970 campaign speeches, indicates that there are some dissenters who should be separated "from our society with no more regret than we should feel over discarding rotten apples from a barrel."[5]

Through the use of the language of suppression the human animal can seemingly justify the unjustifiable, make palatable the unpalatable, and make decent the indecent. Just as our thoughts affect our language, so does our language affect our thoughts and eventually our action and behavior. As George Orwell observed in his famous essay "Politics and the English Language," our language becomes ugly and inaccurate because our thoughts are foolish and then "the slovenliness of our language makes it easier for us to have foolish thoughts." Orwell maintained that "the decadence of our language is probably curable" and that "silly words and expressions have often disappeared, not through any evolutionary process but owing to the conscious action of a minority."[6] This then is our task: to identify the decadence in our language, the silly words and expressions which have been used to justify oppression of varying degrees. . . .

A case study of this inhumane use of language and of the linguistic dehumanization process is provided in the manner in which the European invaders of the New World redefined the occupants of what is now called North America and the manner in which white Americans have perpetuated through language the suppression of the "Indians" into the twentieth century. This essay will focus on and examine (1) the natural-religious redefinition of the "Indians"; (2) the political-cultural redefinition of the "Indians"; and (3) the legal redefinition of the "Indians."

The "de-civilization," the dehumanization and redefinition of the Indian, began with the arrival of Columbus in the New World. The various peoples in the New World, even though the differences between them were as great as between Italians and Irish or Finns and Portuguese, were all dubbed "Indians," and then "American Indians."[7] Having renamed the inhabitants, the invaders then proceeded to enslave, torture, and kill them, justifying this inhumanity by defining these inhabitants as "savages" and "barbarians." The Europeans' plundering and killing of the Indians in the West Indies outraged a Spanish Dominican missionary, Bartolome de las Casas, who provided the following account of the conquest of the Arawaks and Caribs in his *Brief Relation of the Destruction of the Indies:*

> They [the Spaniards] came with their Horsemen well armed with Sword and Launce, making most cruel havocks and slaughters. . . . Overrunning Cities and Villages, where they spared no sex nor age; neither would their cruelty pity

> Women with childe, whose bellies they would rip up, taking out the Infant to hew it in pieces. . . . The children they would take by the feet and dash their innocent heads against the rocks, and when they were fallen into the water, with a strange and cruel derision they would call on them to swim. . . . They erected certain Gallowses . . . upon every one of which they would hang thirteen persons, blasphemously affirming that they did it in honor of our Redeemer and his Apostles, and then putting fire under them, they burnt the poor wretches alive. Those whom their pity did think to spare, they would send away with their hands cut off, and so hanging by the skin.[8]

After the arrival of the Spaniards, "whole Arawak villages disappeared through slavery, disease, and warfare, as well as by flight into the mountains. As a result, the native population of Haiti, for example, declined from an estimated 200,000 in 1492 to a mere 29,000 only twenty-two years later."[9]

The Spaniards were followed by the English who brought with them their ideas of their white supremacy. In his *The Indian Heritage in America,* Alvin M. Josephy, Jr., observes that "in the early years of the sixteenth century educated whites, steeped in the theological teaching of Europe, argued learnedly about whether or not Indians were humans with souls, whether they, too, derived from Adam and Eve (and were therefore sinful like the rest of mankind), or whether they were a previously subhuman species."[10] Uncivilized and satanic as the Indian may have been, according to the European invaders, he could be saved; but if he could not be saved then he would be destroyed. As Roy H. Pearce has put it, "Convinced thus of his divine right to Indian lands, the Puritan discovered in the Indians themselves evidence of a Satanic opposition to the very principle of divinity."[11] However, continues Pearce, the Indian "also was a man who had to be brought to the civilized responsibilities of Christian manhood, a wild man to be improved along with wild lands, a creature who had to be made into a Puritan if he was to be saved. Save him, and you saved one of Satan's victims. Destroy him, and you destroyed one of Satan's partisans."[12] Indians who resisted Puritan invasions of their lands were dubbed "heathens," the "heathen" definition and status in turn justifying the mass killing of Indians who refused to give up their lands to the white invaders: "when the Pequots resisted the migration of settlers into the Connecticut Valley in 1637, a party of Puritans surrounded the Pequot village and set fire to it. . . . Cotton Mather was grateful to the Lord that 'on this day we have sent six hundred heathen souls to hell.' "[13]

The European invaders, having defined themselves as culturally superior to the inhabitants they found in the New World, proceeded to their "manifest destiny" and subsequently to the massive killing of the "savages." "This sense of superiority over the Indians," write L. L. Knowles and K. Prewitt in *Institutional Racism in America,* "which was fostered by the religious ideology they carried to the new land, found its expression in the self-proclaimed mission to civilize and Christianize—a mission which was to find its ultimate expression in ideas of a 'manifest destiny' and a 'white man's burden.' "[14] But the Christianizing and "civilizing" process did not succeed and "thus began an extended process of genocide, giving rise to such aphorisms as 'The only good Indian is a dead Indian' . . . Since Indians were capable of reaching only the state of 'savage,' they should not be allowed to impede the forward (westward, to be exact) progress of white civilization. The Church quickly acquiesced in this redefinition of the situation."[15]

If the Indians were not defined as outright "savages" or "barbarians," they were labeled "natives," and as Arnold Toynbee has observed in Volume One of *A Study of History,* "when we Westerners call people 'Natives' we implicitly take the cultural colour out of our perceptions of them. We see them as trees walking, or as wild animals infesting the country in which we happen to come across them. In fact, we see them as part of the local flora and fauna, and not as men of like passions with ourselves; and, seeing them thus as something infrahuman, we feel entitled to treat them as though they did not possess ordinary human rights."[16] Once the Indian was labeled "native" by the white invaders, the latter had in effect established the basis for domesticating or exterminating the former.

In 1787, at the Constitutional Convention, it had to be decided what inhabitants of the total population in the newly formed United States should be counted in determining how many representatives each state would have in Congress. The Founding Fathers decided: "Representatives and direct taxes shall be apportioned among the several states . . . according to their respective numbers, which shall be determined by adding to the whole number of free persons, including those bound to service for a term of years, and excluding Indians not taxed, three fifths of all other persons." The enslaved black came out three fifths of a person and the Indian came out a nonentity.

When the Indians had been defined as "savages" with no future, the final result, as Pearce states, "was an image of the Indian out of society and out of history."[17] Once the Indians were successfully defined as governmental nonentities, no more justification was needed to drive them off their lands and to force them into migration and eventual death. In the nineteenth century, even the "civilized Indians" found themselves being systematically deprived of life and property. . . .

While the state and the church as institutions have defined the Indians into subjugation, there has been in operation the use of a suppressive language by society at large which has perpetuated the dehumanization of the Indian. Our language includes various phrases and words which relegate the Indian to an inferior status: "The only good Indian is a dead Indian"; "Give it back to the Indians"; "drunken Indians," "dumb Indians," and "Redskins." Writings and speeches include references to the "Indian problem" in the same manner that references have been made by white Americans to the "Negro problem" and by the Nazis to the "Jewish problem." There was no "Jewish problem" in Germany until the Nazis created the myth; there was no "Negro problem" until white Americans created the myth; similarly, the "Indian problem" has been created in such a way that the oppressed, not the oppressor, evolve as "the problem."

As the list of negative "racial characteristics" of the "Indian race" grew longer and longer over the years, the redefinition of the individual Indian became easier and easier. He was trapped by the racial definitions, stereotypes, and myths. No matter how intelligent, how "civilized" the Indian became, he or she was still an Indian. Even the one who managed to become a citizen (prior to 1924) could not discard his or her "Indian-ness" sufficiently to participate in white society. The language of the law was used to reinforce the redefinition of the oppressed into non-persons and this language of suppression, as law, became governmentally institutionalized, and in effect legitimatized. One of the most blatant examples of the use of the racial characteristic argument appears in an 1897 Minnesota Supreme Court decision dealing with the indictment of one Edward Wise for selling intoxicating liquors to an Indian who had severed all his relations with his tribe and had through the provision of the "Land in Severality Act" of February 8, 1887, become a citizen of the United States.[18] Wise was indicted for violating a statute which provided that "whosoever sells . . . any spiritous liquors or wines to any Indian in this state shall on conviction thereof be punished. . . ." In finding against Wise, the Minnesota Supreme Court emphasized the weaknesses of the "Indian race" and the fact that as a race Indians were not as "civilized" as the whites:

> . . . in view of the nature and manifest purpose of this statute and the well-known conditions which induce its enactment, there is no warrant for limiting it by excluding from its operation sales of intoxicating liquors to any person of Indian blood, even although he may have become a citizen of the United States, by compliance with the act of congress. The statute is a police regulation. It was enacted in view of the well-known social condition, habits, and tendencies of Indi-

> ans as a race. While there are doubtless notable individual exceptions to the rule, yet it is a well-known fact that Indians as a race are not as highly civilized as the whites; that they are less subject to moral restraint, more liable to acquire an inordinate appetite for intoxicating liquors, and also more liable to be dangerous to themselves and others when intoxicated.[19]

The Minnesota statute, said the Court, applied to and included "all Indians as a race, without reference to their political status. . . . The difference in condition between Indians as a race and the white race constituted a sufficient basis of classification."[20] Under the Court's reasoning, the individual Indian could not control his or her identity. Like it or not, the individual Indian was defined by the Court's language, by the "well-known fact" that "Indians as a race are not as highly civilized as whites," that Indians are "less subject to moral restraint." Like it or not, the individual Indian was identified in terms of the "characteristics" of the "Indians as a race," whether he or she had those characteristics or not, whether he or she was a citizen of the United States or not.

Twenty years later, Minnesota denied voting rights to Indians on the basis of their not being "civilized.". . .[21]

The state of Arizona, the state with the largest Indian population, until 1948 did not allow Indians the right to vote. Article 7 of Arizona's Constitution concerning the qualifications of voters placed the Indians in that state in the same category as traitors and felons, the same category as persons not of sound mind and the insane; Article 7 provided, in part: "No person under guardianship, *non compos mentis* or insane shall be qualified to vote in any election or shall any person convicted of treason or felony, be qualified to vote at any election unless restored to civil rights." In 1928, the Arizona Supreme Court decided in *Porter v. Hall* that Arizona Indians did not have the right to vote since they were within the specific provisions of Article 7 denying suffrage to "persons under guardianship";[22] the Arizona Supreme Court said that " . . . so long as the federal government insists that, notwithstanding their citizenship, their responsibility under our law differs from that of the ordinary citizen, and that they are, or may be, regulated by that government, by virtue of its guardianship, in any manner different from that which may be used in the regulation of white citizens, they are, within the meaning of our constitutional provision, 'persons under guardianship,' and not entitled to vote."[23] In defining the Indians of Arizona as it did in the above decision, the Arizona Supreme Court denied suffrage rights to the Indians even though four years earlier, on June 2, 1924, all non-citizen Indians born within the territorial limits of the United States were made citizens thereof by an Act of Congress. After devoting a paragraph to defining "insanity" and "*non compos mentis*," the Arizona Supreme Court followed with a definition and discussion of "persons under guardianship," the category into which the Indians were placed:

> Broadly speaking, persons under guardianship may be defined as those who, because of some peculiarity of status, defect of age, understanding or self-control, are considered incapable of managing their own affairs, and who therefore have some other person lawfully invested with the power and charged with the duty of taking care of their persons or managing their property, or both. It will be seen from the foregoing definitions that there is one common quality found in each: The person falling within any one of the classes is to some extent and for some reason considered by the law as incapable of managing his own affairs as a normal person, and needing some special care from the state.[24]

In 1948, however, the Porter decision was overruled in the case of *Harrison v. Laveen*,[25] thus allowing Indians in Arizona the right to vote. In the 1948 decision, the Supreme Court of Arizona stated that the designation of "persons under guardianship" as it appeared in Article 7 did not apply to Indians. As to the argument that the Indians generally fell into that group of people "incapable of managing their own affairs," the Court said in 1948 that "to ascribe to all Indians residing on reservations the quality of being 'incapable of handling their own affairs in an ordinary manner' would be a grave injustice, for amongst them are educated persons as fully capable of handling their affairs as their white neighbors."[26] Finally, four and a half centuries after Columbus "discovered" "America," almost all the descendants of the original occupants of this land were allowed by the descendants of the invaders to participate, through the vote, in effecting some control (however small) over their destiny in their own land. Almost all of the "red natives" of the land finally were recognized legally as being as fully capable of handling their affairs as "their white neighbors.". . .

NOTES

1. See Haig A. Bosmajian, "The Magic Word in Nazi Persuasion," *ETC.*, 23 (March 1966), 9–23; Werner Betz, "The National-Socialist Vocabulary," *The Third Reich* (London: Weidenfeld and Nicolson, 1955); Heinz Paechter, *Nazi-Deutsch* (New York: Frederick Ungar, 1944).
2. See Simon Podair, "Language and Prejudice," *Phylon Review*, 17 (1956), 390–394; Haig A. Bosmajian, "The Language of White Racism," *College English*, 31 (December 1969), 263–272.

3. See Haig A. Bosmajian, "The Language of Sexism," *ETC.*, 29 (September 1972), 305–313.
4. See Haig A. Bosmajian, "The Protest Generation and Its Critics." *Discourse: A Review of the Liberal Arts*, 9 (Autumn 1966), 464–469.
5. *The New York Times*, October 31, 1969, p. 25.
6. "Politics and the English Language," in C. Muscatine and M. Griffith. *The Borzoi College Reader*, 2nd ed. (New York: Alfred A. Knopf, 1971), p. 88.
7. Peter Farb, *Man's Rise to Civilization as Shown by the Indians of North America from Primeval Times to the Coming of the Industrial State* (New York: E. P. Dutton and Company, 1968), p. xx.
8. Alvin M. Josephy, Jr., *The Indian Heritage of America* (New York: Bantam Books, Inc., 1969), p. 286.
9. Farb, p. 243.
10. Josephy, p. 4.
11. Roy H. Pearce, *The Savages of America* (Baltimore: The Johns Hopkins Press, 1965), p. 21.
12. Pearce, pp. 21–22.
13. Farb, p. 247.
14. Louis L. Knowles and Kenneth Prewitt, eds., *Institutional Racism in America* (Englewood Cliffs, N.J.: Prentice-Hall, Inc., 1969), p. 7.
15. Knowles and Prewitt, p. 8.
16. *A Study of History* (London: Oxford University Press, 1935), I, p. 152. For further discussion of the connotation of "natives," see Volume II of *A Study of History*, pp. 574–580.
17. Pearce, p. 135.
18. *State v. Wise*, 72 N.W. 843 (1897).
19. *In re Liquor Election in Beltrami County*, 989.
20. *In re Liquor Election in Beltrami County*, 989.
21. *In re Liquor Election in Beltrami County*, 990.
22. *Porter v. Hall*, 271 P. 411 (1928).
23. *Porter v. Hall*, 419.
24. *Porter v. Hall*, 416.
25. *Harrison v. Laveen*, 196 P.2d 456 (1948).
26. *Harrison v. Laveen*, 463.

Discussing Ideas and Themes

1. What, according to Bosmajian, is one of the primary acts an oppressor initiates? Do you agree? Can you think of any examples other than Bosmajian's?
2. With a little help from Orwell, Bosmajian describes the interaction between thought and language. How does he relate them?
3. When did the Native American finally gain the right to vote? Why did it take so long? How was the old ruling overturned? Do you think that a legal redefinition ever marks the end of oppression?
4. How does Bosmajian's discussion of the early settlers "redefine" your sense of the American frontier? Does it replace any notions you might have had—for instance, the traditional vision of the first Thanksgiving?
5. Compare Bosmajian's notions of oppressive language to Dorothy Thompson's cry for anti-tolerance in "On Tolerance." Does Thompson ever redefine groups in the way Bosmajian warns against? Does Bosmajian tolerate groups in the way Thompson warns against?

Discussing Rhetoric and Style

1. How does Bosmajian's first paragraph prepare you for his characterization of men as "human animals" at the opening of the second paragraph? Are you ready for such a characterization at this point? Does it seem harsh or accurate or something else? Why or why not?
2. This is an essay about the uses and misuses of language and the morality of speaking a certain way. How would you characterize Bosmajian's use of language? For instance, is it socially responsible, vindictive, non-judgmental? Support your answer with quotations from the essay.
3. Why does Bosmajian call his essay a case study? Do you think his prime interest is the oppression of the Native American, or is it the general power of language to cause oppression?
4. Outline Bosmajian's argument. What is his thesis? How does he try to prove it? Does he succeed?

Ideas for Writing

1. Bosmajian argues: "There was no 'Jewish problem' in Germany until the Nazis created the myth; there was no 'Negro problem' until white Americans created the myth; similarly, the 'Indian problem' has been created in such a way that the oppressed, not the oppressor, emerges as the problem." Discuss the idea that the oppressor, not the oppressed, creates the problem in such situations. Do you agree?
2. Compile a brief case study (look for two or three newspaper articles from the period, and perhaps one article from a popular national periodical) on an example Bosmajian doesn't treat—for example, the oppression of blacks in America at any time, or of Jews, or of Japanese in America during World War II. Stay as close as you can to a stylistic analysis of the oppressor's language.

White Like Me

ROBERT R. DETLEFSON

In this essay, which appeared in the New Republic *in 1989, Robert Detlefson describes Harvard University's recent AWARE week program—a week-long series of workshops for those "Actively Working Against Racism and Ethnocentrism." According to Detlefson, the current trend of "racial sensitivity," while it may seem the sign of a new intellectual openmindedness, might actually jeopardize "academic freedoms"—the freedom, for instance, to speak and teach one's own ideas and opinions freely (even if they clash with popular conscience). Such endangered freedoms are, according to Detlefson, the real source of equality in American education, scholarship, and thought. Detlefson is currently a postdoctoral fellow in the Government department at Harvard University.*

"Professors should have less freedom of expression than writers and artists, because professors are supposed to be creating a better community."

"When delivering a lecture, one should be careful not to introduce any sort of thing that might hurt a group."

"Throwing tampons at the male, sexist dogs of Dartmouth was educational."

"These places might be the slickest form of genocide going."

Talk such as this is a sure sign that one is on the campus of a great university. Recently at Harvard I was part of an audience treated to these and other truisms. The occasion was a week-long program of panels and "workshops" collectively titled "AWARE"—an acronym standing for "Actively Working Against Racism and Ethnocentrism."

AWARE week was the brainchild of Dean Hilda Hernandez-Gravelle of Harvard's Office of Race Relations and Minority Affairs. (Dean Hernandez-Gravelle made a splash last fall by calling for a ban on '50s nostalgia parties because racism was rampant in America during that decade.) According to the "Workshop Evaluation Forms" that were distributed to the audience after each event, the goals of AWARE week were: "a) to address people's denial about racism; b) to engage people in trying to understand racism and to take responsibility to change it through action; c) to give people some new perspectives, ideals, and tools to use."

The week's events opened on Tuesday with an exercise in collective guilt. As keynote speaker, Professor John Dovidio, a research psychologist from Colgate University, delivered a speech titled "Racism Among the Well-Intentioned." That includes about everyone; according to Dovidio, 85 percent of white Americans harbor some form of subtle racism, while 15 percent are overt racists. He devoted most of his speech to reciting the results of clinical research that purports to show how even the most compassionate among us harbor "racist attitudes": we prefer the company of other white people, we are more likely to make positive assumptions about members of "our" group, etc. He even led the audience through a word-association exercise to show how racial bias is culturally ingrained:

DOVIDO: What do you think of when I say the word "black"?
AUDIENCE: Black magic! Witches! Devil's food cake!
DOVIDIO: And when I say "white"?
AUDIENCE: Snow White! Angel food cake!

Get the picture?

Dovidio was especially instructive when he spoke of his own culturally ingrained bias. He described an incident in which he was trying to locate a library book. Finally he narrowed his search to two specific aisles—the book was definitely in one of them. After some further searching he realized that he had been concentrating, for no immediately discernable reason, on just one of the two aisles. Why was he avoiding the other aisle? Then it dawned on him. At the end of the aisle in which he had concentrated his search was a white person seated at a study carrel; at the end of the other aisle—the one he had been subconsciously avoiding—was a black person seated at a study carrel.

There are surely few places in America that are more secular and cosmopolitan than Harvard, and yet I was struck by how closely the atmosphere surrounding Dovidio's keynote address had resembled a religious revival meeting. Instead of the doctrine of Original

Sin and the resultant inherent sinfulness of man—even the most pious of men—we had the clinically proven fact of pandemic racism, manifest even among the well-intentioned. Instead of a feverish evangelical preacher who mesmerizes audiences with lurid tales of his own moral transgressions, we had a professor of psychology who delivered his own stunning mea culpa. And like a religious congregation, Dovidio's flock consisted entirely of the already converted; when told of their manifest racism, they nodded in agreement. During the question period that followed the speech, no one rose to challenge his contention that we are all guilty of racism.

On Thursday a panel titled "Institutional Racism: What Price Are You Paying?" afforded an opportunity to learn about the practical consequences of racism at Harvard. One panelist, Wayne Dudley, a history professor at Fitchburg State College, saw institutional racism in the hiring and promotion of college faculty. In one specific case that he described, a black female Ph.D. was hired as an assistant professor. As a junior faculty member who was the only black in her department, she worked tirelessly to increase minority student enrollments, yet she was denied tenure because she had not published sufficiently in the scholarly journals. I waited for the smoking gun that would point to racism in this story, but instead Dudley proceeded to "Case No. 2."

That evening a film titled "Racism 101" was shown in one of the large lecture halls on campus. According to the AWARE calendar, the film would be followed by a discussion led by Gregory Ricks, identified as "Senior Fellow at the Campus Opportunity Outreach League." "Racism 101" is a documentary originally broadcast as part of the "Frontline" series on public television. It provides a fairly evenhanded examination of racial conflict at the University of Michigan, the University of Massachusetts—Amherst, and Dartmouth College. But the film was just a mundane prelude to the evening's main production, whose star was the irrepressible Ricks.

We had just seen him, larger than life, on the big screen; he had been a dean at Dartmouth during the contretemps there. As soon as the film ended, he moved to the front of the auditorium and modestly introduced himself to the racially mixed audience. "I'm not an expert, and I'm not a martyr—I'm just a brother like you, just struggling and trying to make it." Ricks didn't want to discuss the film. He had something else on his mind, and he delivered it in the form of a rhetorical question: "Are these schools [Harvard, Dartmouth, and other elite colleges] genocidal in nature?"—genocidal, that is, with respect to "blacks, feminists, and others trying to change the status quo?" He answered by telling of a black student whom he had counseled at Dartmouth. The student asked him if Dartmouth "had an agenda to take away his confidence." In high school, the student explained, he had had "visions of kicking the world's ass," but now, thanks to Dartmouth, he wasn't sure if he was up to it. Ricks, of course, confidently assured the student that Dartmouth had indeed conspired against him: "They have brought you in, turned you around, and fucked up your mind." The implication was that genocide of this sort was also being waged against the black students of Harvard. So much for an Ivy League education.

Ricks was warmed up now, and he concluded his remarks with a furious barrage of exhortations and admonitions: "Don't tolerate racist jokes!" "Don't tolerate any racist, sexist, homophobic discussions at the dining table, or anywhere else!" "Don't sleep with racist, sexist dogs just because they're cute!" "Throwing tampons at the male, sexist dogs of Dartmouth was educational!" "Create an environment that will force these institutions to do what is just; why do we have to have a fact-finding commission before we respond to student demands?" When he had finished, a young white woman in the audience said she had experienced "minority ethnocentrism"—in her dormitory, in the dining hall, in the classroom. "They don't want to know anything about me," she said. "How do you know?" Ricks shot back. The young woman sheepishly admitted that she may have overgeneralized. It was the only time all week that I heard an allegation of racial insensitivity challenged by an AWARE participant.

Friday's single event was a faculty panel convened to discuss "Racial Awareness, Sensitivities, and Academic Freedom." The issue the panelists would address—whether there are circumstances under which the demand for racial sensitivity in the academy compromises academic freedom—was a subject fit for more than abstract speculation at Harvard. Last year, in an incident that received wide publicity, three black undergraduates formally charged two eminent Harvard history professors with displaying racial insensitivity while teaching a course on "The Peopling of America"—citing, for example, their use of the term "American Indian" instead of "Native American."

It was against this backdrop that the panel of five distinguished Harvard professors—including three holders of endowed chairs—took up the matter of racial sensitivity and academic freedom. Professor of Science William Bossert was no stranger to racism, he told the audience. He had grown up in the Jim Crow South, and he knew it when he saw it; the racism that he had observed as a white Southerner had made a profound and lasting impression upon him. Professors, he declared, should "edit" potentially offensive material from their lectures unless it is undeniably relevant and necessary to the subject being taught. Karel Liem, a professor of ichthyology, was far less equivocal: in large lecture situations, he asserted, one should never "introduce any sort of thing that might hurt a group." "Modulating" was the name Liem gave to this practice of self-censorship. "The pain that racial insensitivity can create is more important than a professor's academic freedom," he declared. Two other panelists voiced their agreement. Barbara Johnson, a comparative literature professor, chimed in with her opinion that professors should have less freedom of expression than writers and artists, because professors are supposed to be creating a better community.

At this point the lone dissenting panelist was heard. Taking the position that professors should not shrink from the pursuit of truth for any reason—a position that hardly anyone within the academy would have questioned 20 years ago—Harvey Mansfield, a professor of government, rattled the audience by speaking not only in defense of free speech but in opposition to the very purpose of AWARE week. The kind of sensitivity that the AWARE organizers sought to instill in people would have the perverse effect of closing them off from ideas and experiences that might broaden their horizons and disabuse them of their prejudices, he said. In other words, hypersensitivity can promote parochialism and intolerance. Moreover, in addition to these "general disadvantages for learning," AWARE-style sensitivity also had "specific disadvantages for blacks." As an example, Mansfield cited the reception that greeted the Moynihan Report on the causes of poverty among blacks in the 1960s. Many black leaders were offended by the report's focus on the dissolution of the black family as a principal cause of poverty, and they reacted by vilifying Daniel Moynihan, the messenger who had brought the bad news. Today few doubt the validity of the Moynihan Report, yet in the 20 years since its release the destructive trends it described have only accelerated—in part, perhaps, because of the intransigence of those whose prejudices kept them from accepting a painful reality.

Nor was this all. The Moynihan phenomenon, Mansfield continued, was repeated a year ago right here at Harvard, as "black students wrongly accused two history professors of racial insensitivity. The charges were made irresponsibly, reported irresponsibly, and dealt with inadequately." Finally, Mansfield observed, AWARE-style sensitivity makes it difficult for blacks to make friends with whites, and vice versa. A sensitivity that takes the form of a never-ending harangue is hardly conducive to harmonious relations: "Charges of racism pull us apart." "The burden of my remarks," Mansfield concluded, "has been that people need to relax a little about racial insensitivity. . . . We should all tell a few more jokes." This was almost too much for the AWAREists to bear; Johnson, who was seated next to Mansfield on the panel, had by now lowered her head and buried her face in her hands. One of the black students who had brought the charges of insensitivity against the two history professors rose to denounce Mansfield. Mansfield wasn't qualified to speak in defense of the accused professors, she declared, because as "a white male over 40" he was incapable of judging the merits of a charge of racial insensitivity. This drew a big ovation.

After the discussion had concluded and the panelists had left the stage, a few knots of students remained in the auditorium, talking among themselves. As I came close to one group, I realized the students were talking about Mansfield. "What an asshole," said one woman. Her companions nodded. I asked her if she thought it had been a mistake to invite someone like Mansfield to be on an AWARE-week panel. "Not at all," she said brightly. "There are lots of professors here who feel the way he does. That's what we have to struggle against."

Saturday was the final day of AWARE week. Fred Jewett, dean of Harvard College, launched the day's festivities with a rhapsodic speech in which he praised the goals of AWARE week and challenged the audience to keep its spirit alive throughout the rest of the year. Many of the people who had served on earlier panels were back for one last fling. Among the speakers whom I listened to that day, one in particular stood out. He was Lawrence Watson, identified in the AWARE week calendar as "Assistant Dean for Academic Administration at the Graduate School of Design and the Co-Chairman of the Association of Black Faculty and Administrators." Watson was the moderator of a panel on "Classroom Sensitivity: The Experience of Teaching and Learning," and after reading a lengthy list of specific elements of "white privilege"—a litany that included, inter alia, white people's unique ability to purchase band-aids that match their skin tone—he offered the following assurance to minority students: "When you experience racial insensitivity in the classroom, whatever way you choose to deal with it is valid, provided you are willing to accept the consequences." And later, in the same vein: "Overreacting and being paranoid is the only way we can deal with this system. . . . Never think that you imagined it [racial insensitivity], because chances are that you didn't."

This is remarkable counsel for a responsible adult to give to impressionable youths in such a highly charged context. And it is almost unbelievable in its lack of empathy—"sensitivity," you might say—for innocent persons who are certain to be the targets of censorship and character assassination at the hands of a zealous squadron of self-styled thought police.

What will be the legacy of AWARE week? If I were a Harvard professor—particularly if I taught in the humanities or the social sciences—I would start to worry. The same administration that refused to defend two of the university's most distinguished professors against an onslaught of scurrilous attacks actively supported a program whose effect, whatever its stated intent, was to encourage more such attacks.

Presumably one of the reasons that students and their parents are willing to spend $19,000 a year on Harvard is to gain access to one of the world's best collections of scholarly minds. Yet now students may not be offered all that those minds have to give, because many professors will be cowed into submission by the forces of bigotry and intolerance that have been newly empowered by the purveyors of "sensitivity." Black students at Harvard will pay an additional price. At one of the AWARE events I attended I heard a black student say that he preferred to sit at the "black table" in the dining hall because he found whites "boring." "They don't want to contend with me on anything," he said. But who can blame them? What can one expect from a group of people who have been told incessantly that they are racist, and that they must be highly circumspect in their relations with blacks lest their racism reveal itself in the form of an offensive word or two? Moreover, to the extent that the charge of "racism" is repeatedly and gratuitously tossed about as it was during AWARE week, there is a danger that the evil of genuine racism will become trivialized and hence will be ignored.

Discussing Ideas and Themes

1. What does Detlefson see as the dangers inherent in programs such as Harvard's AWARE week? What examples of dangerous attitudes does he offer? What long-term effects does he project?
2. Detlefson opens his essay with several epigrams that he immediately labels truisms. Where else in the essay do you find truisms? How does this essay come to be about the dangerous power of such phrases? Consider, for instance, Detlefson's analogy of AWARE week to a series of religious revival meetings. Does Detlefson himself ever resort to truisms?
3. Who, according to Detlefson, are the "self-styled thought police"? Do you agree with this assessment?
4. What is Detlefson's final line on AWARE week? Do you detect any ambivalence in his argument? For instance, does his essay call for the reform or the abolishment of similar programs?
5. Why does Detlefson never use the phrase "reverse discrimination"? Is that what this essay is about? How would Detlefson characterize it?

Discussing Rhetoric and Style

1. Detlefson's choice of title conjures up associations for us before we ever hear any of his actual arguments. What is the tone of this phrase, and where does it originate? Do you hear a strong contrast between this title and the various titles of the AWARE week workshops he quotes throughout the essay? What is the effect of this contrast?
2. Detlefson makes an extended analogy between AWARE week and a "religious revival meeting." How appropriate do you find this analogy, and how much of its effectiveness can be attributed to Detlefson's prose style? You might want to find the passage in question and circle all the words relevant to the analogy and then rewrite the passage without these words. What does this exercise teach you about the power of analogy?
3. How does Detlefson go out of his way to assert his academic freedoms here? Why is a bold assertion of these freedoms rhetorically effective in this situation? Or isn't it? In answering, you might consider the identity of Detlefson's intended audience.
4. Detlefson writes, "This is remarkable counsel for a responsible adult to give to impressionable youths in such a highly charged context." How is this sentence itself highly charged? How does Detlefson's choice of adjectives shape tone and meaning here? Is the sentence a persuasive one?
5. Only in his final sentence does Detlefson overtly condemn racism. Why doesn't he come out more clearly as an anti-racist before this? Do you think this suspension tactic strengthens his argument or simply invites confusion about his stance on racial equality?

Ideas for Writing

1. Write a brief essay in response to an extreme scenario—one in which the "self-styled thought police" have free rein over your campus. You are free to choose your own side: you can pin the badge on a Detlefson supporter or on an AWARE week supporter; however, be sure to remember that you are writing a socially responsible satire, not a free-for-all piece of propaganda.
2. Do you think academic freedoms and racial sensitivity are necessarily at odds? Cite as many examples as you can from your own academic experiences.

STUDENT ESSAY

The Last American Racist

JOSH OZERSKY

During his undergraduate years at Rutgers University, Josh Ozersky wrote a biweekly column on current social and political issues for the Rutgers student newspaper, The Daily Targum. *This essay, which first appeared in the* Targum *in early 1989, explores with high satire (reminiscent of Samuel Johnson, one of Ozersky's favorites) what remains an important topic at Rutgers—racism. Deflating the issue by approaching it from a new viewpoint, Ozersky suggests that pure "racism" is a ridiculous proposition. Ozersky, known at Rutgers for his satirical, free-wheeling style, is currently enrolled in New York University's graduate journalism program.*

Mr. Ozersky, I have long been aware of your column, and consider you to be a very keen observer of human nature. For this reason, and so that the considerable number of young persons who read your work may be enlightened to my (I suspect) unique plight, I have taken it upon myself to write to you. I am the last American racist.

It is always with great rage and frustration that I observe various people posing as racists, on the glamorous soundstages of "Mort" and "Oprah." Recently, the former Grand Mystic Imperial Cyclops of the Ku Klux Klan, David Duke, was elected to the Louisiana House of Representatives. Asked about his racist views, this obsequious quisling recanted everything that he and his cowardly brethren had said about race. For the sake of political office, this man has compromised himself irrevocably, and I for my part (who only partially agreed with him before) can barely repress a rumplestiltskin fit of rage.

In like manner, the "skinheads" of the White People's Liberation

Front, the Caucasian Defense League, and other supposedly "racist" groups are simply mindless thugs, without any philosophy to speak of. As a group, they are harmless. But in any case, I wish to make clear that I am in no way one of their number.

I am alone, apart from any group or organization. Here, in my isolated motel room, I see myself as the sole guardian of that pure racism, polluted versions of which are mouthed by skinheads, recanted by Klansmen, hidden by employers, and denied by the sheepish, "reasonable" man and woman in the street. Everyone in this country is aware of the cultural differences and uneasy stratification that persists between black and white.

But for me, only the smallest part of the whole is represented by that vulgar struggle. Blacks were brought to this country largely as machinery, and the attitude taken towards them has not greatly changed, for economic reasons. I am the first to admit that. Nor do I charge that they are in any way inferior to white people; it is not my business to make value judgements. I am an organizer, a taxonomist, a subdivider of mankind: for it is only in the meticulous, orderly definition of divisions that meaning may be found. "Race" is mere shorthand; "class" or "subspecies," although less elegant, would fit my purpose equally.

As you may have guessed, Mr. Ozersky, my racial concerns are not limited to the black person, or the fiery citizen of the sands, nor the quiet Hindu, nor the cerebral sons and daughters of the orient. Such standard xenophobic fare is the province of bitter laborers and uncultivated bigots. Since the biological basis for any racial distinctions has long been shown to be specious humbug, I do not limit myself to such crude demarcation.

I see mankind as being almost infinitely subdivisible; not only foreigners and minorities, but any group of people, united by one observable feature, enter my ken stamped and classified. Capricorns, computer illiterates, men who look like Benny Hill, are all marked in my mind. Their refusal to accept my definitions is to be expected; this classifies them within the largest of my groupings, those persons who do not participate in my understanding. I expect that the readers of this letter will generally fall into this category.

Although I generally attempt to live as a purely rational being, without contaminating the orb of my intellect with passion, I am filled with despair and hatred when I consider the low esteem which my ideas should find within the discourse of most of the world. Glimmers and flashes of my pure taxophilia appear in the speech and thought of practically everyone; yet I am routinely abused, in absentia, by a race of people that seem to encompass me with their unanimous opprobrium.

I am confined to this motel by reason of paralysis; I sit helplessly in front of my television set, the hot plate will not shut off, and the desk clerk gives me no messages. In the midst of this squalor I ponder and classify. Were I able to move I should attempt to further the cause of racism by physical means; in my present state, I can only stand as the sole representative of a species of thoughtful observer.

I am, sir, yours,
(name and address withheld)

Discussing Ideas and Themes

1. Who is the speaker supposed to be? Why does he wait until the end of the essay to introduce himself and describe his situation? Are we supposed to like this speaker?
2. The speaker calls himself a "pure racist." What is his definition of the term? Does this kind of racist have anything to do with what we normally think of as racism?
3. The speaker confides that "as a group [the White People's Liberation Front and the like] are harmless." Are we meant to take this statement at face value? What does it tell you about the speaker and about the aims of the essayist (as opposed to the speaker)?
4. The speaker tells us that he is a "pure racist," but also that "it is not [his] business to make value judgments." Reconcile these two statements, if you can.

Discussing Rhetoric and Style

1. Why does Ozersky write this essay in the form of a reader's letter? Do you find that the letter restricts or broadens the scope of the essay? Why or why not?
2. What part does irony play in Ozersky's remodeling of the concept of racism? Do you find the essay socially responsible or simply frivolous?
3. How can you distinguish between the author and the speaker? Why is this distinction a crucial one to understanding and enjoying satire?
4. Characterize the speaker's voice in this essay. In what ways is this voice actually only a caricature? Why is such a caricature appropriate here?

5. How does Ozersky take apart and reassemble the concept of racism? How does he create an entire essay out of literalizing a single word?

Ideas for Writing

1. Write a letter in the persona of Josh Ozersky responding to "The Last American Racist" or a letter in your own voice to the editor of *The Daily Targum* (where Ozersky's column first appeared) either praising or criticizing the piece. Limit your letter to two typewritten pages.
2. Some readers might find this essay "racially insensitive" (see Robert Detlefson's "White Like Me") because it seems to make light of an urgent and dangerous social problem. Write an essay in which you either defend or attack Ozersky's right to play with the idea of racism.

CHAPTER 5

The Political and Social Power of Words

The essays in this chapter address the public power of language for good and ill. They connect many of the themes explored in earlier sections. In essays on gender and race we have already seen how language may function as a source and carrier of political, social, and professional powers that have favorable or unfavorable meaning for a given individual. We have seen how all groups outside the political and social mainstream receive derogatory names, and in turn make up derogatory names for those inside the power structure.

Derogatory language is strong language, and most people understand its implications quite clearly; but high-sounding words can also serve, more subtly, as sources of oppressive power. In his famous "Politics and the English Language" George Orwell makes this and other points about the connections between language and politics.

In the next selection, Dorothy Thompson, one of the most influential journalists of the first half of the century, takes on the issue of a particularly high-sounding word that still resonates very powerfully today. In "On Tolerance," written on the eve of World War II, Thompson argues that democracy risks its own destruction when it aspires to unlimited toleration as a self-evident and sacred goal. Should we tolerate the forces that assure us we will not ourselves be tolerated if they succeed? As the twentieth century—a time marked by massive human destruction and political intolerance—draws to a close, Thompson's essay still stimulates thought on issues that spring from the question of free speech.

Thompson tries to persuade her readers not to use "toleration" as what David Wilson in the next selection calls a "weasel word." Wilson sees these words as attempts to avoid confronting issues that need confronting. In "The Language of Debased Values," he discusses the importance of moral language to what is often called a value-free society and concludes that values are often cheapened by words that try to avoid facing the difficulties of taking *any* stand at all for fear someone might be offended.

Thomas Middleton brings the issue of language and social power closer to where most students live. While attending a college football game, he was shocked at the language used by students and wonders what sense of "class" in its educational and social meanings are implied by such linguistic behavior. The definition of acceptable language is an apt topic for debate, and Middleton's essay is a good starting point for discussion.

In his "Extra! Much of Europe Feels Blah," Gerald Nachman examines the use of the word "mood" by journalists and exposes the shaky basis on which political trends are assessed.

Student writer Catherine Barrier closes the section by taking on a more serious issue of political "language"—the constitutionality of flag burning.

Politics and the English Language

GEORGE ORWELL

George Orwell is the pen name for English writer Eric Blair (1903–1950) who was born in Bengal, India in 1903. Widely remembered for his novels Animal Farm *and* 1984, *Orwell is also a master of the essay. "Politics and the English Language," reprinted here from* Shooting An Elephant and Other Essays *(1946), is the most famous example of a form Orwell knew well and practiced often. Here, he discusses some of the chronic misuses of language and proposes that language abuses and political abuses go hand in hand.*

Most people who bother with the matter at all would admit that the English language is in a bad way, but it is generally assumed that we cannot by conscious action do anything about it. Our civilization is decadent and our language—so the argument runs—must inevitably share in the general collapse. It follows that any struggle against the abuse of language is a sentimental archaism, like preferring candles to electric light or hansom cabs to aeroplanes. Underneath this lies the half-conscious belief that language is a natural growth and not an instrument which we shape for our own purposes.

Now, it is clear that the decline of a language must ultimately have political and economic causes: it is not due simply to the bad influence of this or that individual writer. But an effect can become a cause, reinforcing the original cause and producing the same effect in an intensified form, and so on indefinitely. A man may take to drink because he feels himself to be a failure, and then fail all the more completely because he drinks. It is rather the same thing that is happening to the English language. It becomes ugly and inaccurate because our thoughts are foolish, but the slovenliness of our language makes it easier for us to have foolish thoughts. The point is that the process is reversible. Modern English, especially written English, is full of bad habits which spread by imitation and which can be avoided if one is willing to take the necessary trouble. If one gets rid of these habits one can think more clearly, and to think clearly is a necessary first step towards political regeneration: so that the fight against bad English is not frivolous and is not the exclusive concern of professional writers. I will come back to this presently, and I hope that by that time the meaning of what I have said here will have become clearer. Meanwhile, here are five specimens of the English language as it is now habitually written.

These five passages have not been picked out because they are especially bad—I could have quoted far worse if I had chosen—but because they illustrate various of the mental vices from which we now suffer. They are a little below the average, but are fairly representative samples. I number them so that I can refer back to them when necessary:

1. I am not, indeed, sure whether it is not true to say that the Milton who once seemed not unlike a seventeenth-century Shelley had not become, out of an experience ever more bitter in each year, more alien [*sic*] to the founder of that Jesuit sect which nothing could induce him to tolerate.

   Professor Harold Laski
   (Essay in *Freedom of Expression*)

2. Above all, we cannot play ducks and drakes with a native battery of idioms which prescribes such egregious collocations of vocables as the Basic *put up with* for *tolerate* or *put at a loss* for *bewilder*.

   Professor Lancelot Hogben (*Interglossa*)

3. On the one side we have the free personality: by definition it is not neurotic, for it has neither conflict nor dream. Its desires, such as they are, are transparent, for they are just what institutional approval keeps in the forefront of consciousness; another institutional pattern would alter their number and intensity; there is little in them that is natural, irreducible, or culturally dangerous. But *on the other side*, the social bond itself is nothing but the mutual reflection of these self-secure integrities. Recall the definition of love. Is not this the very picture of a small academic? Where is there a place in this hall of mirrors for either personality or fraternity?

   Essay on Psychology in *Politics* (New York)

4. All the "best people" from the gentlemen's clubs, and all the frantic fascist captains, united in common hatred of Socialism and bestial horror of the rising tide of the mass revolutionary movement, have turned to acts of provocation, to foul incendiarism, to medieval legends of poisoned wells, to legalize their own destruction of proletarian organizations, and rouse the agitated petty-bourgeoisie to chauvinistic fervor on behalf of the fight against the revolutionary way out of the crisis.

   Communist Pamphlet

5. If a new spirit *is* to be infused into this old country, there is one thorny and contentious reform which must be tackled, and that is the humanization and galvanization of the B.B.C. Timidity here will bespeak canker and atrophy of the soul. The heart of Britain may be sound and of strong beat, for instance, but the British lion's roar at present is like that of Bottom in Shakespeare's *Midsummer Night's Dream*—as gentle as any sucking dove. A virile new Britain cannot continue indefinitely to be traduced in the eyes or rather ears, of the world by the effete languors of Langham Place, brazenly masquerading as "standard English." When the voice of Britain is heard at nine o'clock, better far and infinitely less ludicrous to hear aitches honestly dropped than the present priggish, inflated, inhibited, school-ma'amish arch braying of blameless bashful mewing maidens!

   Letter in *Tribune*

Each of these passages has faults of its own, but, quite apart from avoidable ugliness, two qualities are common to all of them. The first is staleness of imagery; the other is lack of precision. The writer either has a meaning and cannot express it, or he inadvertently says something else, or he is almost indifferent as to whether his words mean anything or not. This mixture of vagueness and sheer incompetence is the most marked characteristic of modern English prose, and especially of any kind of political writing. As soon as certain topics are raised, the concrete melts into the abstract and no one seems able to think of turns of speech that are not hackneyed: prose consists less and less of *words* chosen for the sake of their meaning, and more and more of *phrases* tacked together like the sections of a prefabricated hen-house. I list below, with notes and examples, various of the tricks by means of which the work of prose-construction is habitually dodged:

DYING METAPHORS

A newly invented metaphor assists thought by evoking a visual image, while on the other hand a metaphor which is technically "dead" (e.g., *iron resolution*) has in effect reverted to being an ordinary word and can generally be used without loss of vividness. But in between these two classes there is a huge dump of worn-out metaphors which have lost all evocative power and are merely used because they save people the trouble of inventing phrases for themselves. Examples are: *Ring the changes on, take up the cudgels for, toe the line, ride roughshod over, stand shoulder to shoulder with, play into the hands of, no axe to grind, grist to the mill, fishing in troubled waters, on the order of the day, Achilles' heel, swan song, hotbed.* Many of these are used without knowledge of their meaning (what is a "rift," for instance?), and incompatible metaphors are frequently mixed, a sure sign that the writer is not interested in what he is saying. Some metaphors now current have been twisted out of their original meaning without those who use them even being aware of the fact. For example, *toe the line* is sometimes written *tow the line.* Another example is *the hammer and the anvil,* now always used with the implication that the anvil gets the worst of it. In real life it is always the anvil that breaks the hammer, never the other way about: a writer who stopped to think what he was saying would be aware of this, and would avoid perverting the original phrase.

OPERATORS OR VERBAL FALSE LIMBS

These save the trouble of picking out appropriate verbs and nouns, and at the same time pad each sentence with extra syllables which give it an appearance of symmetry. Characteristic phrases are *render inoperative, militate against, make contact with, be subjected to, give rise to, give grounds for, have the effect of, play a leading part (role) in, make itself felt, take effect, exhibit a tendency to, serve the purpose of,* etc., etc. The keynote is the elimination of simple verbs. Instead of being a single word, such as *break, stop, spoil, mend, kill,* a verb becomes *a phrase,* made up of a noun or adjective tacked on to some general-purpose verb such as *prove, serve, form, play, render.* In addition, the passive voice is wherever possible used in preference to the active, and noun constructions are used instead of gerunds (*by examination of* instead of *by examining*). The range of verbs is further cut down by means of the *-ize* and *de-* formations, and the banal statements are given an appearance of profundity by means of the *not un-* formation. Simple conjunctions and prepositions are replaced by such phrases as *with respect to, having regard to, the fact that, by dint of, in view of, in the interests of, on the hypothesis that;* and the ends of sentences are saved from anticlimax by such resounding commonplaces as *greatly to be desired, cannot be left out of account, a development to be expected in the near future, deserving of serious consideration, brought to a satisfactory conclusion,* and so on and so forth.

PRETENTIOUS DICTION

Words like *phenomenon, element, individual* (as noun), *objective, categorical, effective, virtual, basic, primary, promote, constitute, exhibit, exploit, utilize, eliminate, liquidate,* are used to dress up simple statements and give an air of scientific impartiality to biased judgments. Adjectives like *epoch-making, epic, historic, unforgettable, triumphant, age-old, inevitable, inexorable, veritable,* are used to dignify the sordid processes of international politics, while writing that aims at glorifying war usually takes on an archaic color, its characteristic words being: *realm, throne, chariot, mailed fist, trident, sword, shield, buckler, banner, jackboot, clarion.* Foreign words and expressions such as *cul de sac, ancien régime, deus ex machina, mutatis mutandis, status quo, gleichschaltung, weltanschauung,* are used to give an air of culture and elegance. Except for the useful abbreviations *i.e., e.g.,* and *etc.*, there is no real need for any of the hundreds of foreign phrases now current in English. Bad writers, and especially scientific, political and sociological writers, are nearly always haunted by the notion that Latin or Greek words are grander than Saxon ones, and unnecessary words like *expedite, ameliorate, predict, extraneous, deracinated, clandestine, subaqueous* and hundreds of others constantly gain ground from their Anglo-Saxon opposite numbers.[1] The jargon peculiar to Marxist writing (*hyena, hangman, cannibal, petty bourgeois, these gentry, lacquey, flunkey, mad dog, White Guard,* etc.) consists largely of words and phrases translated from Russian, German or French; but the normal way of coining a new word is to use a Latin or Greek root with the appropriate affix and, where necessary, the *-ize* formation. It is often easier to make up words of this kind (*deregionalize, impermissible, extramarital, nonfragmentary* and so

1 An interesting illustration of this is the way in which the English flower names which were in use till very recently are being ousted by Greek ones, *snapdragon* becoming *antirrhinum, forget-me-not* becoming *myosotis,* etc. It is hard to see any practical reason for this change of fashion: it is probably due to an instinctive turning-away from the more homely word and a vague feeling that the Greek word is scientific.

forth) than to think up the English words that will cover one's meaning. The result, in general, is an increase in slovenliness and vagueness.

MEANINGLESS WORDS

In certain kinds of writing, particularly in art criticism and literary criticism, it is normal to come across long passages which are almost completely lacking in meaning.[2] Words like *romantic, plastic, values, human, dead, sentimental, natural, vitality,* as used in art criticism, are strictly meaningless, in the sense that they not only do not point to any discoverable object, but are hardly ever expected to do so by the reader. When one critic writes, "The outstanding feature of Mr. X's work is its living quality," while another writes, "The immediately striking thing about Mr. X's work is its peculiar deadness," the reader accepts this as a simple difference of opinion. If words like *black* and *white* were involved, instead of the jargon words *dead* and *living,* he would see at once that language was being used in an improper way. Many political words are similarly abused. The word *Fascism* has now no meaning except in so far as it signifies "something not desirable." The words *democracy, socialism, freedom, patriotic, realistic, justice,* have each of them several different meanings which cannot be reconciled with one another. In the case of a word like *democracy,* not only is there no agreed definition, but the attempt to make one is resisted from all sides. It is almost universally felt that when we call a country democratic we are praising it: consequently the defenders of every kind of régime claim that it is a democracy, and fear that they might have to stop using the word if it were tied down to any one meaning. Words of this kind are often used in a consciously dishonest way. That is, the person who uses them has his own private definition, but allows his hearer to think he means something quite different. Statements like *Marshal Pétain was a true patriot, The Soviet Press is the freest in the world, The Catholic Church is opposed to persecution,* are almost always made with intent to deceive. Other words used in variable meanings, in most cases more or less dishonestly, are: *class, totalitarian, science, progressive, reactionary, bourgeois, equality.*

2 Example: "Comfort's catholicity of perception and image, strangely Whitmanesque in range, almost the exact opposite in aesthetic compulsion, continues to evoke that trembling atmospheric accumulative hinting at a cruel, an inexorably serene timelessness. . . . Wrey Gardiner scores by aiming at simple bull's-eyes with precision. Only they are not so simple, and through this contented sadness runs more than the surface bitter-sweet of resignation." (*Poetry Quarterly.*)

Now that I have made this catalogue of swindles and perversions, let me give another example of the kind of writing that they lead to. This time it must of its nature be an imaginary one. I am going to translate a passage of good English into modern English of the worst sort. Here is a well-known verse from *Ecclesiastes:*

> I returned and saw under the sun, that the race is not to the swift, nor the battle to the strong, neither yet bread to the wise, nor yet riches to men of understanding, nor yet favour to men of skill; but time and chance happeneth to them all.

Here it is in modern English:

> Objective consideration of contemporary phenomena compels the conclusion that success or failure in competitive activities exhibits no tendency to be commensurate with innate capacity, but that a considerable element of the unpredictable must invariably be taken into account.

This is a parody, but not a very gross one. Exhibit (3), above, for instance, contains several patches of the same kind of English. It will be seen that I have not made a full translation. The beginning and ending of the sentence follow the original meaning fairly closely, but in the middle the concrete illustrations—race, battle, bread—dissolve into the vague phrase "success or failure in competitive activities." This had to be so, because no modern writer of the kind I am discussing—no one capable of using phrases like "objective consideration of contemporary phenomena"—would ever tabulate his thoughts in that precise and detailed way. The whole tendency of modern prose is away from concreteness. Now analyze these two sentences a little more closely. The first contains forty-nine words but only sixty syllables, and all its words are those of everyday life. The second contains thirty-eight words of ninety syllables: eighteen of its words are from Latin roots, and one from Greek. The first sentence contains six vivid images, and only one phrase ("time and chance") that could be called vague. The second contains not a single fresh, arresting phrase, and in spite of its ninety syllables it gives only a shortened version of the meaning contained in the first. Yet without a doubt it is the second kind of sentence that is gaining ground in modern English. I do not want to exaggerate. This kind of writing is not yet universal, and outcrops of simplicity will occur here and there in the worst-written page. Still, if you or I were told to write a few lines on the uncertainty of human fortunes, we should probably come much nearer to my imaginary sentence than to the one from *Ecclesiastes.*

As I have tried to show, modern writing at its worst does not consist in picking out words for the sake of their meaning and inventing images in order to make the meaning clearer. It consists in gumming together long strips of words which have already been set in order by someone else, and making the results presentable by sheer humbug. The attraction of this way of writing is that it is easy. It is easier—even quicker, once you have the habit—to say *In my opinion it is not an unjustifiable assumption that* than to say *I think*. If you use ready-made phrases, you not only don't have to hunt about for words; you also don't have to bother with the rhythms of your sentences, since these phrases are generally so arranged as to be more or less euphonious. When you are composing in a hurry—when you are dictating to a stenographer, for instance, or making a public speech—it is natural to fall into a pretentious, Latinized style. Tags like *a consideration which we should do well to bear in mind* or *a conclusion to which all of us would readily assent* will save many a sentence from coming down with a bump. By using stale metaphors, similes and idioms, you save much mental effort, at the cost of leaving your meaning vague, not only for your reader but for yourself. This is the significance of mixed metaphors. The sole aim of a metaphor is to call up a visual image. When these images clash—as in *The Fascist octopus has sung its swan song, the jackboot is thrown into the melting pot*—it can be taken as certain that the writer is not seeing a mental image of the objects he is naming; in other words he is not really thinking. Look again at the examples I gave at the beginning of this essay. Professor Laski (1) uses five negatives in fifty-three words. One of these is superfluous, making nonsense of the whole passage, and in addition there is the slip *alien* for *akin*, making further nonsense, and several avoidable pieces of clumsiness which increase the general vagueness. Professor Hogben (2) plays ducks and drakes with a battery which is able to write prescriptions, and while, disapproving of the everyday phrase *put up with*, is unwilling to look *egregious* up in the dictionary and see what it means; (3), if one takes an uncharitable attitude towards it, is simply meaningless: probably one could work out its intended meaning by reading the whole of the article in which it occurs. In (4), the writer knows more or less what he wants to say, but an accumulation of stale phrases chokes him like tea leaves blocking a sink. In (5), words and meaning have almost parted company. People who write in this manner usually have a general emotional meaning—they dislike one thing and want to express solidarity with another—but they are not interested in the detail of what they are saying. A scrupulous writer, in every sentence that he writes, will ask himself at least four questions, thus: What am I trying to say? What words will express it? What image or idiom will make it clearer? Is this image fresh enough to have an effect? And he will probably ask himself two more: Could I put it more shortly? Have I said anything that is avoidably ugly? But you are not obliged to go to all this trouble. You can shirk it by simply throwing your mind open and letting the ready-made phrases come crowding in. They will construct your sentences for you—even think your thoughts for you, to a certain extent—and at need they will perform the important service of partially concealing your meaning even from yourself. It is at this point that the special connection between politics and the debasement of language becomes clear.

In our time it is broadly true that political writing is bad writing. Where it is not true, it will generally be found that the writer is some kind of rebel, expressing his private opinions and not a "party line." Orthodoxy, of whatever color, seems to demand a lifeless, imitative style. The political dialects to be found in pamphlets, leading articles, manifestos, White Papers and the speeches of undersecretaries do, of course, vary from party to party, but they are all alike in that one almost never finds in them a fresh, vivid, home-made turn of speech. When one watches some tired hack on the platform mechanically repeating the familiar phrases—*bestial atrocities, iron heel, bloodstained tyranny, free peoples of the world, stand shoulder to shoulder*—one often has a curious feeling that one is not watching a live human being but some kind of dummy: a feeling which suddenly becomes stronger at moments when the light catches the speaker's spectacles and turns them into blank discs which seem to have no eyes behind them. And this is not altogether fanciful. A speaker who uses that kind of phraseology has gone some distance towards turning himself into a machine. The appropriate noises are coming out of his larynx, but his brain is not involved as it would be if he were choosing his words for himself. If the speech he is making is one that he is accustomed to make over and over again, he may be almost unconscious of what he is saying, as one is when one utters the responses in church. And this reduced state of consciousness, if not indispensable, is at any rate favorable to political conformity.

In our time, political speech and writing are largely the defense of the indefensible. Things like the continuance of British rule in India, the Russian purges and deportations, the dropping of the atom bombs on Japan, can indeed be defended, but only by arguments which are too brutal for most people to face, and which do not square with the professed aims of political parties. Thus political language has to consist largely of euphemism, question-begging and sheer cloudy vagueness. Defenseless villages are bombarded from the air, the inhabitants driven out into the countryside, the cattle machine-gunned, the huts set on fire with incendiary bullets: this is called *pacification*. Millions of peasants are robbed of their farms and sent trudging along the roads with no more than they can carry: this is called *transfer of population* or *rectification of frontiers*. People are imprisoned for years without trial, or shot in the back of the neck or sent to die of scurvy in Arctic lumber camps: this is called *elimination of unreliable elements*. Such phraseology is needed if one wants to name things without calling up mental pictures of them. Consider for instance some comfortable English professor defending Russian totalitarianism. He cannot say outright, "I believe in killing off your opponents when you can get good results by doing so." Probably, therefore, he will say something like this:

> While freely conceding that the Soviet regime exhibits certain features which the humanitarian may be inclined to deplore, we must, I think, agree that a certain curtailment of the right to political opposition is an unavoidable concomitant of transitional periods, and that the rigors which the Russian people have been called upon to undergo have been amply justified in the sphere of concrete achievement.

The inflated style is itself a kind of euphemism. A mass of Latin words falls upon the facts like soft snow, blurring the outlines and covering up all the details. The great enemy of clear language is insincerity. When there is a gap between one's real and one's declared aims, one turns as it were instinctively to long words and exhausted idioms, like a cuttlefish squirting out ink. In our age there is no such thing as "keeping out of politics." All issues are political issues, and politics itself is a mass of lies, evasions, folly, hatred and schizophrenia. When the general atmosphere is bad, language must suffer. I should expect to find—this is a guess which I have not sufficient knowledge to verify—that the German, Russian and Italian languages have all deteriorated in the last ten to fifteen years, as a result of dictatorship.

But if thought corrupts language, language can also corrupt thought. A bad usage can spread by tradition and imitation, even among people who should and do know better. The debased language that I have been discussing is in some ways very convenient. Phrases like *a not unjustifiable assumption, leaves much to be desired, would serve no good purpose, a consideration which we should do well to bear in mind*, are a continuous temptation, a packet of aspirins always at one's elbow. Look back through this essay, and for certain you will find that I have again and again committed the very faults I am protesting against. By this morning's post I have received a pamphlet dealing with conditions in Germany. The author tells me that he "felt impelled" to write it. I open it at random, and here is almost the first sentence that I see: "[The Allies] have an opportunity not only of achieving a radical transformation of Germany's social and political structure in such a way as to avoid a nationalistic reaction in Germany itself, but at the same time of laying the foundations of a co-operative and unified Europe." You see, he "feels impelled" to write—feels, presumably, that he has something new to say—and yet his words, like cavalry horses answering the bugle, group themselves automatically into the familiar dreary pattern. This invasion of one's mind by ready-made phrases (*lay the foundations, achieve a radical transformation*) can only be prevented if one is constantly on guard against them, and every such phrase anaesthetizes a portion of one's brain.

I said earlier that the decadence of our language is probably curable. Those who deny this would argue, if they produced an argument at all, that language merely reflects existing social conditions, and that we cannot influence its development by any direct tinkering with words and constructions. As far as the general tone or spirit of a language goes, this may be true, but it is not true in detail. Silly words and expressions have often disappeared, not through any evolutionary process but owing to the conscious action of a minority. Two recent examples were *explore every avenue* and *leave no stone unturned,* which were killed by the jeers of a few journalists. There is a long list of flyblown metaphors which could similarly be got rid of if enough people would interest themselves in the job; and it should also be possible to laugh the *not un-* formation out of existence,[3] to reduce the amount of Latin and Greek in the average sentence, to drive out foreign phrases and strayed scientific words, and, in general, to make pretentiousness unfashionable. But all these are minor points. The defense of the English language implies more than this, and perhaps it is best to start by saying what it does *not* imply.

To begin with it has nothing to do with archaism, with the salvaging of obsolete words and turns of speech, or with the setting up of a "standard English" which must never be departed from. On the contrary, it is especially concerned with the scrapping of every word or idiom which has outworn its usefulness. It has nothing to do with correct grammar and syntax, which are of no importance so long as one makes one's meaning clear, or with the avoidance of Americanisms, or with having what is called a "good prose style." On the other hand it is not concerned with fake simplicity and the attempt to make

3 One can cure oneself of the *not un-* formation by memorizing this sentence: *A not unblack dog was chasing a not unsmall rabbit across a not ungreen field.*

written English colloquial. Nor does it even imply in every case preferring the Saxon word to the Latin one, though it does imply using the fewest and shortest words that will cover one's meaning. What is above all needed is to let the meaning choose the word, and not the other way about. In prose, the worst thing one can do with words is to surrender to them. When you think of a concrete object, you think wordlessly, and then, if you want to describe the thing you have been visualizing you probably hunt about till you find the exact words that seem to fit it. When you think of something abstract you are more inclined to use words from the start, and unless you make a conscious effort to prevent it, the existing dialect will come rushing in and do the job for you, at the expense of blurring or even changing your meaning. Probably it is better to put off using words as long as possible and get one's meaning as clear as one can through pictures or sensations. Afterwards one can choose—not simply *accept*—the phrases that will best cover the meaning, and then switch round and decide what impression one's words are likely to make on another person. This last effort of the mind cuts out all stale or mixed images, all prefabricated phrases, needless repetitions, and humbug and vagueness generally. But one can often be in doubt about the effect of a word or a phase, and one needs rules that one can rely on when instinct fails. I think the following rules will cover most cases:

1. Never use a metaphor, simile or other figure of speech which you are used to seeing in print.
2. Never use a long word where a short one will do.
3. If it is possible to cut a word out, always cut it out.
4. Never use the passive where you can use the active.
5. Never use a foreign phrase, a scientific word or a jargon word if you can think of an everyday English equivalent.
6. Break any of these rules sooner than say anything outright barbarous.

These rules sound elementary, and so they are, but they demand a deep change of attitude in anyone who has grown used to writing in the style now fashionable. One could keep all of them and still write bad English, but one could not write the kind of stuff that I quoted in those five specimens at the beginning of this article.

I have not here been considering the literary use of language, but merely language as an instrument for expressing and not for concealing or preventing thought. Stuart Chase and others have come near to claiming that all abstract words are meaningless, and have used this as a pretext for advocating a kind of political quietism. Since you don't know what Fascism is, how can you struggle against Fascism? One need not swallow such absurdities as this, but one ought to recognize that the present political chaos is connected with the decay of language, and that one can probably bring about some improvement by starting at the verbal end. If you simplify your English, you are freed from the worst follies of orthodoxy. You cannot speak any of the necessary dialects, and when you make a stupid remark its stupidity will be obvious, even to yourself. Political language—and with variations this is true of all political parties, from Conservatives to Anarchists—is designed to make lies sound truthful and murder respectable, and to give an appearance of solidity to pure wind. One cannot change this all in a moment, but one can at least change one's own habits, and from time to time one can even, if one jeers loudly enough, send some worn-out and useless phrase—some *jackboot, Achilles' heel, hotbed, melting pot, acid test, veritable inferno* or other lump of verbal refuse—into the dustbin where it belongs.

Discussing Ideas and Themes

1. Examine Orwell's argument that misuses of language promote political degeneration. Consider two or three of his examples—how do they strengthen his argument?
2. Orwell opens his essay by saying that "most people . . . would admit that the English language is in a bad way." Do you agree? Explain.
3. How does Orwell think we can improve our English usage?
4. Orwell makes a link between language and politics, as do many other writers. Review some of the essays you have already read, such as Langston Hughes's "That Word 'Black,' " John Simon's "Why Good English Is Good for You," or Miller and Swift's "One Small Step for Genkind." How does Orwell's analysis of the political ramifications of language differ from other treatments of the same topic?
5. Orwell concludes that "political language . . . is designed to make lies sound truthful and murder respectable, and to give an appearance of solidity to pure wind." Find some examples of this kind of rhetoric in contemporary political language. What "lies" are being made to "sound truthful" there?

Discussing Rhetoric and Style

1. Orwell devotes a section of his essay to his critique of "dying metaphors"—comparisons that no longer surprise or enlighten the audience because they have been repeated so often. Compare the metaphors that Orwell himself uses with the ones he criticizes.

2. Orwell offers us six rules for better writing. Why does he include the sixth rule? What does it add?

3. How is Orwell's essay organized? Why does he use headings? Do his divisions make the essay clearer? Explain.

4. Orwell offers four categories of language abuse: dying metaphors, operators or verbal false limbs, pretentious diction, and meaningless words. Which of these abuses do you think is the most pervasive in our language? Provide examples from your own observation.

Ideas for Writing

1. Write a short essay arguing that our language is in a "bad way" today. Cite current examples in your essay, as Orwell does in his. You might find these examples in a number of places: advertising copy, political speeches, newspapers, academic journals, and so on. You need not refer to Orwell, though you might want to.

2. Using Orwell's critiques as a model, pick an old essay of your own and analyze your prose. Note those moments where you succeed as well as those where you fail.

On Tolerance

DOROTHY THOMPSON

As a young woman, Dorothy Thompson (1893–1961) was active in the woman's suffrage movement. She began a highly successful career in journalism in the early 1920s, working as an American reporter in Europe. Thompson was an outspoken political commentator throughout her career and was perhaps best known for her syndicated, thrice-weekly column "On the Record," which promoted opposition to fascism before and during the Second World War. In "On Tolerance," written in 1939, Thompson argues from definition, exploring the roots of the term in order to persuade her audience that Communism and Nazism are "absolutely incompatible" with "order and civilization."

The open mind has been greatly praised, but somebody once said that an open mind was often a mind with nothing in it. It has also been said that "to understand all is to forgive all," but it is perhaps truer to say that to understand nothing is to forgive everything.

Every saw and every truism needs inspection. Words need periodic inspection. And one word that needs some reconsideration is the great word "tolerance." For it has been abused past recognition. From being a positive expression of respect for other people's rights, it has become a weasel word for the avoidance of responsibility.

The Latin root of the word "tolerance" refers to things that can be borne, endured, are supportable. The intrinsic meaning of "tolerance" is the capacity to sustain and endure, as of hardship. From this comes the inferential meaning of patience with the opinions and practices of those who differ. It is interesting that the word is used in connection with the coining of money and with machinery, to indicate the margin within which coins may deviate from the fixed standard, or the dimensions or parts of a machine from the norm.

But the word "tolerance" does not suggest that everything is supportable and that any amount of deviation is allowable. It suggests that one's principles and standards should be tempered with patience, and with readiness to subject them to modification, through practical or intellectual tests. But it does not suggest that one should have no principles or standards. In the contemporary world, I find that for many people this is, however, exactly what they mean by tolerance: a vapid openness to the condoning of anything. Tolerance carried to this conclusion is anarchy. It is not an instrument of civilization, but an instrument of barbarism.

We are not tolerant of diphtheria bacilli, tuberculosis germs, or cancer cells. We do not assert their right also to live and work. We know that they cannot continue to exist if the organism which they have entered, or in which they have grown, is also to continue to exist. Therefore we eradicate them with the greatest intolerance. We know that there is no way for noncancerous tissue to come to an agreement with cancerous tissue. There is no possible *modus vivendi* between them. Therefore, a cancer is eradicated.

But in our social and political life we seem to think that democracy is only a casual host for the entertainment of all conceivable viewpoints and organizations, including those whose clear intention is to destroy the host. Instead of allowing that margin, even a very wide margin, for variation which is the essence of tolerance, we entertain those in whom there is no speck of tolerance whatsoever for democracy itself, or for tolerance itself, and who seek to substitute for ordered popular government under law a regime of dictatorship and violence.

The margin of tolerance in a democracy, or in any other organized and civilized state ruled by law, stops when standards essential to the continuance of an orderly and civilized community are seriously menaced. It is impossible, for instance, to continue any sort of orderly, civilized, and legal community at all if the police powers are captured, by whatever legal methods, by gangsters, and then used to destroy the law, the courts, private property, all civilian immunities, and to kill people arbitrarily, without indictment or trial.

It is of not the slightest consequence, for instance, that the American Communist Party is a legal organization, that it pays lip service to democracy—and, indeed, calls itself democracy's agent—and that it does not seek to make its way by throwing bombs or by other acts of violence, but uses instead the legal methods of persuasion and organization, assisted by more dubious instruments of slander and intimidation. Its object is what is important, and its object is to destroy the law, and to substitute for law the absolute dictatorship of a party itself dictatorially ruled, and acting as the self-appointed agents of what they choose to delineate as the proletariat, or "working masses." This is demonstrably the object of the Communist Party. This is the actual form of organization that exists in Soviet Russia, and it is a form of organization that has been consistently praised and never denounced by any Communist Party leader—or by any one of them who has continued thereafter to hold his position. The American Communist Party is in alliance with the Communist Party of Russia. And, therefore, the American Communist Party is outside the bounds of possible tolerance by anyone who is not a Communist, for the achievement of its object is incompatible with the continuance of our existence as a civilized community ruled by law.

Exactly the same thing holds true for the German-American Bund and its kindred and supporting organizations. The legality of their methods does not obscure the fact that their object is to destroy the essential integrity of this country both as an independent power and as an organized commonwealth. If anyone doubts that, after what has happened in Central Europe, he is verging on feeble-mindedness. Their program is to deprive millions of our citizens of their citizenship rights and make them "subjects" of the rest of us. The pattern of society which is their model is the dictatorship of a gang, knowing no limitations of ethics or law, and ruling with total arbitrariness. As I write these lines, this regime, if you can call it a regime, is engaged on an international plunder expedition.

It is impossible to tolerate the absolutely incompatible. Tolerating then leads either to the destruction of order and civilization by capitulation, or to civil war. It cannot possibly lead anywhere else. You cannot make a "pact" with Communism or Nazism. They demand all or nothing; that is their nature. Therefore there is, in respect of them, no supportable plea for the rights of civil liberty. Al Capone could not appeal to civil liberties for the right openly to organize his gang, with the protection of the police. No state can tolerate that which is hostile to the very concept of the state as such.

In this country we can tolerate every political group, from the right to the left, Socialists and Bourbons, provided they are not acting as agents of foreign powers and do not have as their object the substitution of the legally ordered society by the rule of violence. To extend tolerance to such is to abdicate intelligence and prepare for the extermination of tolerance itself.

Discussing Ideas and Themes

1. How does Thompson use the word "tolerance," and how does her usage differ from standard definitions of tolerance?
2. Why does Thompson say, "It is not of the slightest consequence . . . that the American Communist Party is a legal organization"? Do you agree? Explain.
3. Although Thompson titles her essay "On Tolerance," it actually comes to advocate—even urge—*intolerance*. Why does the title not mention intolerance? What would be the effects of such a title?
4. "To extend tolerance to [enemies of the state] is to abdicate intelligence and prepare for the extermination of tolerance itself." Is this assertion necessarily true? Explain.

Discussing Rhetoric and Style

1. Thompson remarks that "it has . . . been said that 'to understand all is to forgive all,' but it is perhaps truer to say that to understand nothing is to forgive everything." How rhetorically effective is the switch from "all" to "nothing"?
2. Discuss Thompson's use of analogy. Although she clearly opposes Nazi ideology, her representation of an outsider as a disease that must be eradicated strikingly parallels analogies used by the Nazis in their "extermination" of the Jews during World War II. How can two such divergent viewpoints make use of a similar analogy?
3. Skim the essay for sentence types. What kinds of sentences (declarative, imperative, interrogative) does Thompson write? How are Thompson's sentences suitable to her attitude throughout the essay?
4. Thompson moves from apolitical contexts for tolerance—such as coinage, machinery, and disease—to "our social and political life." How does she achieve the transition?
5. Examine Thompson's discussion of the American Communist Party. How does she attempt to convince us that we should not tolerate this organization? Is her argument logical?

Ideas for Writing

1. Write a brief response to Thompson's essay. Try to find and use points she has not considered.

2. Pick a word (such as *freedom, democracy, education* or *industry*) that interests you as *tolerance* interests Thompson, and make a list of the different ways that word might be defined—even those ways you yourself might not agree with. Then, following Thompson's cue, write an essay on whatever word you have chosen.

The Language of Debased Values

DAVID B. WILSON

Born in Brooklyn in 1927, David B. Wilson is a journalist and popular columnist for the Boston Globe. *In this essay, written in 1988, Wilson discusses some of the ways that watered-down language, euphemism, and understatement dominate the media in a world which he feels is "value-free" and "relativistic." "What is happening here is pretty obvious," he tells us: We look for words that are "sufficiently anonymous and meaningless to avoid disturbing the mindless collectivity of the mass audience of what is mistakenly termed the communications age. . . . The bland really are leading the bland."*

Accepting her Oscar, Jodie Foster made the observation that the act of gang-rape or its toleration, the subject of a film in which she starred as the victim, was "unacceptable."

One morning last week, one of those undergraduate newscast voices on public radio quoted somebody from Exxon or the White House or some advocacy group to the effect that the oil spill in Prince William Sound was not "acceptable."

This is elitist, silly, pretentious language. Perhaps some awesome authority has empaneled a review board or appointed a censor in charge of defining acceptability, to determine just what is or is not "acceptable"; but I doubt it. Just because something is acceptable to me does not mean that it is to you nor should it be.

What is happening here is pretty obvious. In a value-free, relativistic society innocent of standards, no one is so courageous or gauche as to risk any positive, objective evaluation of conduct or phenomena.

So the fallback position is acceptability, a quality sufficiently anonymous and meaningless to avoid disturbing the mindless collectivity of the mass audience of what is mistakenly termed the communications age.

Who in this time of weasel words and weasel behavior would be so bold as to use the words “good” or “bad” or “right” or “wrong”? If there is neither black nor white but only shades of gray, who would risk insistence on absolutes? Moderation in all things, right? Don’t get caught out on a limb of absolute conviction.

Remember Barry Goldwater in 1964: “Extremism in the defense of liberty is no vice. And . . . moderation in the pursuit of justice is no virtue.”

Despite the fact that Bartlett’s cross-reference to this eloquent line traces its theme to the Revolutionary radical Thomas Paine and the abolitionist William Lloyd Garrison, poor Goldwater was pilloried as a right-wing threat to democracy for using it.

To say what you mean or mean what you say is dangerous in late 20th-Century America.

Clearly gang-rape is wrong, a vicious, wicked act of moral turpitude, public indecency, cruelty and felonious criminality punishable in Massachusetts by life imprisonment. To call it “unacceptable” is to trivialize it.

Certainly it is not “acceptable” for the master of an ocean-going tanker containing millions of dollars worth of crude oil to get drunk and leave his vessel in the charge of an uncertified officer who then allows it to rip its bottom out on the rocks outside a 10-mile-wide channel, thereby causing a world-class spill with Lord-knows-what consequences for marine life and the stockholders.

But it is also blatant, flagrant, gross negligence, willful, wanton and reckless misconduct, dereliction of duty and professional failure, irresponsible, inexcusable, contemptible and damnable stupidity; and to dismiss it as merely unacceptable is to demean both language and feeling.

Unacceptable is to wear brown shoes with a blue suit or eat meat with a fish fork or tip one’s host’s servants. Unacceptable is to request ketchup in a Thai restaurant.

People use a lot of other weasel words to avoid saying what they mean and meaning what they say. How about objectionable, irrelevant, premature, incompatible, inconsistent, improper, inappropriate, untimely, obsolete, meaningful? Add your own candidates.

But when the term righteous refers to the quality control of recreational narcotics, it’s hard to crank up much moral fervor.

In the value-free society, weasel-wording is in part the consequence of collective judgment. Because unacceptable does not really mean anything at all, it can be employed as moderately negative comment without much risk or disagreement from members of the committee. The bland really are leading the bland.

Discussing Ideas and Themes

1. How, according to Wilson, is language linked to national morality? What examples does he provide to support this view?
2. What is Wilson's thesis, and what does Jodie Foster have to do with it?
3. Wilson asserts that words such as "acceptable" and "unacceptable" "demean both language and feeling." How does he go about proving this claim?
4. What values does Wilson espouse? How does he embody them in his essay? Give one or two examples.
5. Wilson asserts that "acceptability" is "a quality sufficiently anonymous and meaningless to avoid the mindless collectivity of the mass audience." Do you agree with him? How is this statement related to his thesis?

Discussing Rhetoric and Style

1. Notice Wilson's adjectives. Might we say that his argument is *about* adjectives?
2. What persona does Wilson adopt? What is his audience?
3. Make a list of the examples Wilson uses to demonstrate his argument (for instance, Jodie Foster, the Exxon oil spill, Barry Goldwater). Are they effective? Why are some so current and some so old?
4. Consider Wilson's transitions between paragraphs. Circle them and then read the essay without them. How essential do you find them?

Ideas for Writing

1. Listen to the news for two or three nights, and make a list of the euphemisms and understatements that you hear. Then write a brief essay (or even a script for a news show) that satirizes the "language of debased values" that we hear from the media.
2. Compare Wilson's essay to Dorothy Thompson's "On Tolerance." What does each have to say about relativistic values and the dissipation of language?

Freshman Class?

THOMAS H. MIDDLETON

Thomas H. Middleton's essay, which first appeared in the "Language" column of the Saturday Review *in 1983, discusses the author's ambivalence about changes that occur when language taboos are violated by the young. Considering the gaps between the young and the old, between men and women, and between "sucks" and "heck," Middleton brings up some important issues about the impermanence of private language and the powers of public language.*

A few years ago, my wife and I were in Vermont on one of our soul-refreshing trips from Southern California back to our Eastern origins. We were with two friends, native Californians who, we had learned to our astonishment, had never experienced New York or New England. This was in early October, and the Vermont foliage was coming into its full autumnal splendor.

In Woodstock, we saw a poster announcing that Princeton and Dartmouth would be playing football in Hanover, New Hampshire, that coming Saturday. We decided to go.

The day of the game barely dawned at all: lowering skies, pregnant storm clouds, no sun. Nevertheless, we drove over to New Hampshire, buying foul-weather gear at an Army-Navy store on the way.

The gods were with us, and the sky cleared spectacularly, leaving a few drifting clouds for dramatic effect. It was the sort of great football day I remembered from my youth: chilly, breezy, with those glorious gold and russet leaves swirling all over the ground. Our friends were delighted, and so, of course, were we. Hanover was gorgeous, Dartmouth proved to be quintessentially Ivy League—a refreshingly far cry from the mammoth UCLA—and I was relishing the anticipated casual elegance of an Ivy League football afternoon.

We took our seats on the visitors' side of the stadium, appreciating the crisp air and the fresh faces of the young men and women. In my day, there were no female students at Dartmouth or Princeton; I'm glad they're finally there.

Then, as the Princeton team came romping out onto the field, a classic picture of exuberant amateurism, a large portion of the Dartmouth freshman class started shouting in chorus "Princeton sucks! Princeton sucks!"

It was a depressing moment. Here were these 17- and 18-year-old boys and girls, just embarking on their higher education, shouting what struck us as an obscenity.

Later, I talked to young people of the approximate age of those Dartmouth freshmen, and I asked them about expressions like "Princeton sucks." It turns out that *sucks* isn't an obscenity at all to the younger generation. "Princeton sucks" is just about the same as "Princeton stinks."

Words do, indeed, change their meanings and their flavors, and what was unprintable and unsayable a few years ago is printed and said with some regularity this year.

In 1980, a play by Bill C. Davis called *Mass Appeal* opened in New York. It involves a middle-aged priest and a young seminarian. The seminarian prepares a sermon, and the priest criticizes it, at first referring to it as a "kick-ass" sermon. That's a phrase that would have shocked at least some members of a New York audience thirty-five years ago. The priest later tells the young seminarian "Mark, your sermon sucks."

I guess *sucks* has indeed taken on the connotation of *stinks*. Still, "Princeton sucks!" is a lousy thing for a bunch of kids to yell at a football game, and if I'd heard a bunch of Princeton freshmen yelling "Dartmouth sucks!"—as I am now reasonably certain they might—I'd have been embarrassed and a bit angry.

Language changes, and words that were once considered to be ultimately taboo are now out in the open. Cultured young ladies now freely use language that, thirty years ago, a young man would have been ostracized for using, had he done so in mixed company. I am ambivalent about this sort of thing.

The acceptability of certain words and phrases is dependent in large part upon social mores, and social mores are, in turn, influenced to a great degree by words and phrases. Vast numbers of people sincerely believe that many of the problems of the modern world—the high divorce rate, illegitimate births, abortions, prostitution, and crime in the streets—can be pegged directly to the Berkeley "free-speech" movement of the Sixties. That was actually less of a free-speech movement than an insistence upon students' rights to scream obscenities at anyone they disagreed with, drowning out the offending speech.

Some sort of release of the power of obscenity was inevitable, especially given the enormous social pressures of the Sixties. In some ways, that release has been welcome.

Remember the Hollywood films made during and about World War II in which, with bullets whining and crashing, bombs screaming and exploding, death and pandemonium everywhere, our G.I. Joes said things like "Heck!" and "Darn!"? To those of us who were in the service or, indeed, to anyone who knew anything at all about human behavior, this sort of dialogue was not simply laughable, it was embarrassing. I for one was delighted to see some of those absurd taboos fall.

I'm sure freshman classes will continue to captivate us older people at times and to infuriate us at others, not least in their use of language. I pray fervently that they will very quickly learn richer aspersions than "Princeton (or anyone) sucks!" That's just too infra dig.

Discussing Ideas and Themes

1. Why does Middleton entitle the essay "Freshman Class?" Do you see a pun here? How do the meanings of the word *class* relate to the theme of "Language and Power"?
2. How does Middleton feel about the way certain words (such as "sucks") gradually change? Are his feelings explicit or implicit?
3. Does Middleton promote language taboos, or does he simply reject obscenity? What would he claim?
4. Consider Middleton's discussion of women's public language today versus men's private language in the past. Would you say that the relationship between men and women becomes a subtheme in this essay?

Discussing Rhetoric and Style

1. Compare Middleton's diction ("Vermont foliage," "autumnal splendor," "pregnant storm clouds," etc.) to that of the students ("Princeton sucks!"). Does the contrast strengthen Middleton's essay?
2. Go through the essay, and circle all words that come from Latin roots. If you're unsure whether a word comes from Latin, you

can always look it up in the dictionary; however, if you're short on time, polysyllabic words are generally a safe bet. What kind of voice do such words create, and how appropriate is that voice to Middleton's goal?

3. Why does Middleton introduce examples from popular movies? How does the movie screen differ from the football stands? Does Middleton ever acknowledge a difference?
4. How effective is Middleton as a storyteller? What techniques does he borrow from fiction to make his essay more interesting?
5. Middleton closes his essay with the phrase "infra dig." Were you prepared for this shift in tone and word choice? Whether or not you were, what effect did it have on you?

Ideas for Writing

1. Pick a mildly offensive word (one that wouldn't be used in "polite" society) that you commonly hear at school, on television, or at home, and write a few brief paragraphs either defending or rejecting its use. Keep in mind: different situations may dictate different standards of appropriateness.
2. Analyze some of the differences between the language of your generation and that of your parents' and teachers' (and presumably Thomas Middleton's) generation. Interview two people from the older generation for this project. How do new generations repossess old words or make up new words to express old ideas? Give some examples.

Extra! Much of Europe Feels Blah

GERALD NACHMAN

Born in Oakland, California in 1938, Gerald Nachman is a well-known humorist. His books include Playing House *and* Out on a Whim: Some Very Close Brushes with Life *(1983), from which "Much of Europe Feels Blah" is taken. In the essay, Nachman pokes fun at what he calls "mood reporting"—news that describes international moods rather than international events. Akin to Russell Baker's "New Age Babble" and William Safire's "Bizbuzz" (see Chapter 2), Nachman's essay also carries some of the serious implications pointed out in David Wilson's "Language of Debased Values": Wilson describes the dissipation of the media's attentiveness to language, and Nachman sees the media as the unabashed promoter of clichés and empty rhetoric.*

Easily the most envied job in journalism is that of mood reporter—the foreign correspondent who determines how vast multitudes of people feel at any given moment.

Recently, for instance, there was a lengthy analysis of "Germany's mood" ("a pervasive sense of deadlock and immobility, touching almost every aspect of national life"), which ran just in time for Ronald Reagan's meeting with the German Chancellor.

It permitted our President to greet the head of state, as he stepped off the plane, with a consoling embrace. "There, there, old man," Reagan told the Chancellor. "I'm sure that pervasive sense of deadlock and immobility will vanish in no time! You just wait—almost every aspect of your national life is sure to look rosier by morning."

A mood specialist continually roams about Europe and Asia,

stopping in world capitals long enough to take the nation's pulse and analyze its psyche, after which he writes a dispatch that begins: "The mood today in Belgrade is one of great calm, but there are undercurrents of unrest."

In Spain, he cables home: "The mood in Madrid now is one of unrest, but there are undercurrents of great calm." Or in Tokyo: "The mood here is one of calm unrest, with undercurrents of Spain."

Reporting on the mood abroad is nice work if you can get it, for it's hard to imagine an editor back home questioning your acute description of the state of mind of, say, Paraguay—although perhaps there are occasional conflicting views:

"Hello, McGuinness? This is Garbel on the foreign desk in New York. Look—you say here in this piece that the mood in Paraguay today is 'extreme anguish and fear, tempered by a faint glimmer of hope.' This doesn't jibe at all with a Reuters story that just came in and claims that the Paraguayans are 'happy as clams.' Now which is it?"

The problem in doing mood stories is that you must keep coming up with a hot new mood to satisfy the editors. You can't very well cable New York that there's been no noticeable shift in Israel's mood since Lebanon.

"Get off the dime, Perkins!" editors would yelp. "We can't go with this article on 'Israel Today' without a paragraph or two on the national mood. Get your butt out there and find me a mood—and we need it by eight o'clock tonight, no later!"

Today, there's a major industry devoted to plumbing the mood in America from hour to hour, and everywhere you turn you bump into it. In reviews of *Annie*, theater critics in 1977 remarked as how the musical "somehow caught the mood of the new Carter Administration, with its hope, optimism and openness."

Even veteran journalists were impressed by this refreshing twist in mood-divining. Nobody had ever thought to compare a Broadway show—let alone Little Orphan Annie—with government policy. Mood experts, though, are always on the lookout for anything to hitch their angles to, such as:

"The tall ships floating confidently down the East River on July 4 seemed to reflect the feeling in America of a new hand at the helm in Washington."

People who do nationwide mood stories at news magazines must first check with their bureaus to nail down the mood in Chicago, Atlanta, Seattle, etc., before reporting a major coast-to-coast mood. Luckily, the moods always dovetail nicely, otherwise, chaos might result at *Time* and *Newsweek*.

"Say, Fred, how's the mood down there in Dallas these days? I'm writing a cover story on 'America: A New Buoyancy.' Would you say it's pretty buoyant in the Dallas–Fort Worth area? Joe tells me that Miami is buoyant as hell, and I understand Boston was never perkier."

"Sorry, Pete. Texans here are grouchy as all get-out nowadays."

"Uh-oh. You wouldn't even want to say they're less grouchy than usual?"

"I really can't, Pete. It's not just here—the grouchiness is spreading as far west as Phoenix and even into parts of California."

"Hmm . . . Well, maybe I'll see if we can switch the angle slightly and do a cover on 'America: The New Grouchiness' . . ."

Discussing Issues and Themes

1. Nachman says that a "mood reporter" would "continually roam around Europe and Asia." Are any aspects of Nachman's fictional job description likely to be true of an actual reporter's job?
2. Nachman implies that mood reporting may have some political uses. For example, he says that an analysis of Germany's mood permitted Ronald Reagan to greet the German Chancellor "with a consoling embrace." Why does Nachman point this out? Whom or what is he satirizing here?
3. What are the main components of the moods that Nachman fabricates or quotes? For example, why would he want to hear about "the mood of the new Carter Administration"?
4. Why would Nachman want to satirize mood reporting? What other kinds of things might you expect to find out about from a newspaper or news magazine?

Discussing Rhetoric and Style

1. Nachman chooses to satirize the "mood" sections of the news by inventing a job. The mood reporter is more of an allegorical figure than a real one. What does the personification accomplish that a straightforward critique couldn't do?
2. What is the difference between the mood report in Nachman's title and the quotations that he uses? For example, how would you compare the phrase "feels blah" to the phrase "a pervasive sense of deadlock and immobility"? What do these comparisons tell you about the tone of Nachman's title?
3. Nachman uses a number of quotations in his essay, most of which are imagined. How effective is this technique?

4. How do the real quotations in his essay compare to the ones Nachman fabricates? Would you read the real quotations differently in another context?
5. What is the effect of the essay's final satiric dialogue? Nachman might have added some editorial comment after this bit of fantasy, but he doesn't; does that absence make the ending stronger or weaker? Explain.

Ideas for Writing

1. Nachman's satire depends on a tongue-in-cheek mixture of real quotations and imaginary scenarios and dialogues. Find another aspect of news reporting or advertising that you can ridicule, and write a brief essay using Nachman's tongue-in-cheek technique in which you poke gentle fun at it.
2. Nachman suggests that there is "a major industry devoted to plumbing the mood in America" today. He cites reviews of *Annie* as his example but also suggests that "everywhere you turn you bump into it." Write an essay in which you analyze mood reporting, citing examples from two different newspapers or magazines. How does the overall tone of a publication affect the way mood is described? Do you find this aspect of journalistic writing as ridiculous as Nachman evidently does? How do you feel?

The Supreme Court Rules Correctly

CATHERINE BARRIER

The June 21, 1989 Supreme Court ruling that flag-burning is constitutional under the First Amendment prompted Catherine Barrier's essay, "The Supreme Court Rules Correctly." The flag-burning issue inspires controversy because its symbolism offends our patriotism and national pride, yet is protected by the constitutional freedom of expression. Barrier adroitly sidesteps the pitfalls of emotionalism, instead defending the constitutionality of an action that she does not approve of. The essay was written in 1989 for a class assignment.

On June 21, the Supreme Court ruled flag-burning, as a political protest, constitutional under the First Amendment—except when accompanied by violence. Intense reaction followed this unpopular decision, a decision arrived at by a narrow 5–4 vote. The issue at hand: should this ruling be changed?

Chief Justice Rehnquist believes so. He advocates legislation against conduct considered evil or offensive to the majority of people. This reasoning makes emotions, not the Constitution, the standard for lawmaking.

President Bush sees the need for a separate Flag Amendment, but this is definitely not the answer. Such an amendment would put into question the legality of all self-expression protected under the First Amendment.

The Supreme Court ruling should stand unchallenged. "Old Glory" is but a symbol of freedom, not freedom itself. Burning the flag in no way damages the freedom the flag represents, just as burning a Christian cross (another signifier of freedom—from sin) would in no way make the Christian unfree.

Tolerance is necessary to maintain a free society. And if the lack of tolerance limits freedom, then reversing the Supreme Court decision would move us closer to the kind of rule found under the Inquisition, or Hitler. As Justice William J. Brennan wrote, "The government may not prohibit expression simply because it disagrees with its message."

Legislation alone is inadequate. The would-be flag-burner needs to be convinced that desecrating the flag is wrong—that it not only demoralizes our citizens, but degrades our international reputation.

Essentially, those who think legal action should be taken against flag-burners tend to react from their emotions, not from reason. The Supreme Court did not condone flag-burning; it only ruled it constitutionally legal. Flag-burning is definitely not desirable, but criminalizing it tampers with the freedom that each American holds so dear. As Americans, each of us should abhor such tampering.

Discussing Issues and Themes

1. In the first part of her essay, Barrier cites different opinions about the constitutionality of flag-burning. For example, she offers us Chief Justice Rehnquist's opinion in the second paragraph, and President Bush's in the third. What are her opinions about what Bush and Rehnquist believe?
2. Barrier tends to argue from broad, general premises; for example, she distills Rehnquist's argument by suggesting that "this reasoning makes emotions, not the Constitution, the standard for lawmaking." What other premises does Barrier base her argument on?
3. Does Barrier approve of flag-burning? Where does she make her position clear?
4. Why does Barrier think that "the Supreme Court ruling should stand unchallenged"? She states that "those who think legal action should be taken against flag-burners tend to react from their emotions"; what other arguments does she use to defend the Supreme Court's ruling?

Discussing Rhetoric and Style

1. Many essays open with citations of other authorities; Barrier opens with critiques of two authority figures, Bush and Rehnquist. Do you find Barrier persuasive?

2. Barrier generally avoids figures of speech in her essay; instead of anecdotes or metaphors, she relies on reason. How does Barrier's non-figurative style affect you?

3. Barrier makes very few analogies in her essay; her comparison of flag-burning with cross-burning is one. Does the scarcity of analogies highlight the ones she uses? Explain.

4. Near the end of her essay, Barrier addresses the reader, referring to "us" as "Americans." How does this identification reinforce her argument? Throughout her essay, Barrier criticizes "emotional" arguments; does her final reference to "Americans" constitute an emotional appeal?

Ideas for Writing

1. Pick another controversial issue (such as abortion or farm subsidies) and argue for one side. Using Barrier as your model, try to maintain a calm, reasonable tone throughout your paper and to argue from general premises.

2. Barrier makes an argument that is based on an implicit definition of "tolerance" and on an explicit condemnation of emotional grounds for argument. Dorothy Thompson, in "On Tolerance," makes an entirely different kind of argument, based on a different definition of the term. Compare these two writers' uses of the word "tolerance." What is each writer's ideological or political bias?

CHAPTER 6

Language and the Media: Public Speech and Private Meaning

The mass media have the whole country, perhaps the whole world, for an audience, and its language thus can be very influential indeed. In the essays that follow, the public speech of the media—newspapers, television, and comic books among them—is seen as an influence on as well as a reflection of private thinking. How much does what we hear and read affect our world view? How much do our views influence what we hear and read? The writers who try to answer these questions make some amusing as well as some alarming observations.

Journalist/novelist Tom Wolfe perceives a trend in the media toward what he calls "porno-violence." Using examples from avidly read publications such as *The National Enquirer*, Wolfe shows how their methods of arousing emotions have substituted violence for sex in both material and vocabulary.

The next selection gives us testimony from the other side. Journalist Simon Barber tells us what it is like actually to work for *The National Enquirer* and shows us some of the ways language is taken very seriously if not very intelligently in "The Boss Don't Like Swindle—Make It Robbery."

Francine Hardaway investigates an ostensibly more respectable use—the language of sports. She finds that its respectability is the basis for its misuse in other areas, as she tells us in "Foul Play: Sports Metaphors as Public Doublespeak."

George F. Will is repelled by another widespread misuse of language, one that results in what he labels "printed noise." Giving examples from the style of fast food menus, Will argues for resistance to a linguistic system that tries to require grown men to order ham and cheese sandwiches by asking for a "Yumbo."

Humorist David B. Wilson asks "Whatever Happened to Plain Old Weather?" He criticizes a simplemindedness that has become the obligatory style in the weather segments of the nightly news.

Bob Swift finds a brighter side to the language of the mass media, particularly in that found throughout the medium of popular fiction. Swift testifies to the origins of his love for reading in the excitements of what he is willing to call "trash." He believes the next generation can learn from experience: "If you want your kids to become omnivorous readers, let them read trash."

Student Dan Moran has taken Swift's advice and examines the great tradition of comic books. He concludes the section by taking the measure of the language of *Batman.*

Porno-violence

TOM WOLFE

Born in 1931, Tom Wolfe graduated from Yale with a Ph.D. and worked as a correspondent for the Washington Post *and then for the* New York Herald Tribune. *Today, Wolfe is a nationally recognized journalist and author whose books include* The Right Stuff, The Electric Kool-Aid Acid Test, *and most recently,* The Bonfire of the Vanities. *As does much of his work, the following essay, taken from* Mauve Gloves & Madmen, Clutter & Vine, *concerns itself with a pop-culture phenomenon: porno-violence, the technique of sensationalism that national newspaper reporters and even artists have adapted from tabloids such as* The National Enquirer. *According to Wolfe, porno-violence marks a distinct age of American and journalistic ethics.*

Keeps His Mom-in-law in Chains, meet *Kills Son and Feeds Corpse to Pigs.* Pleased to meet you. *Teenager Twists Off Corpse's Head . . . To Get Gold Teeth,* meet *Strangles Girl Friend, then Chops Her to Pieces.* Likewise, I'm sure. *Nurse's Aide Sees Fingers Chopped Off in Meat Grinder,* meet. . . .

In ten years of journalism I have covered more conventions than I care to remember. Podiatrists, theosophists, Professional Budget Finance dentists, oyster farmers, mathematicians, truckers, dry cleaners, stamp collectors, Esperantists, nudists and newspaper editors—I have seen them all, together, in vast assemblies, sloughing through the wall-to-wall of a thousand hotel lobbies (the nudists excepted) in their shimmering grey-metal suits and Nicey Short Collar white shirts with white Plasti-Coat name cards on their chests, and I have sat through their speeches and seminars (the nudists included) and attentively endured ear baths such as you wouldn't believe. And yet some of the truly instructive conventions of our times I seem to have missed altogether. One, for example, I only heard about from one of the many anonymous men who have labored in . . . a curious field. This was a convention of the stringers for *The National Enquirer.*

The Enquirer is a weekly newspaper that is probably known by sight to millions more than know it by name. In fact, no one who ever came face-to-face with *The Enquirer* on a newsstand in its wildest days is likely to have forgotten the sight: a tabloid with great inky shocks of type all over the front page saying something on the order of *Gouges Out Wife's Eyes to Make Her Ugly, Dad Hurls Hot Grease in Daughter's Face, Wife Commits Suicide After 2 Years of Poisoning Fails to Kill Husband. . . .*

The stories themselves were supplied largely by stringers, i.e., correspondents, from all over the country, the world, for that matter, mostly copy editors and reporters on local newspapers. Every so often they would come upon a story, usually via the police beat, that was so grotesque the local sheet would discard it or run it in a highly glossed form rather than offend or perplex its readers. The stringers would preserve them for *The Enquirer,* which always rewarded them well and respectfully.

In fact, one year *The Enquirer* convened and feted them at a hotel in Manhattan. It was a success in every way. The only awkward moment was at the outset when the stringers all pulled in. None of them knew each other. Their hosts got around the problem by introducing them by the stories they had supplied. The introductions, I am told, went like this:

"Harry, I want you to meet Frank here. Frank did that story, you remember that story, *Midget Murderer Throws Girl Off Cliff After She Refuses To Dance With Him.*"

"Pleased to meet you. That was some story."

"And Harry did the one about *I Spent Three Days Trapped at Bottom of Forty-foot-deep Mine Shaft and Was Saved by a Swarm of Flies.*"

"Likewise, I'm sure."

And *Midget Murderer Throws Girl Off Cliff* shakes hands with *I Spent Three Days Trapped at Bottom of Forty-foot-deep Mine Shaft,* and *Buries Her Baby Alive* shakes hands with *Boy, Twelve, Strangles Two-year-old Girl,* and *Kills Son and Feeds Corpse to Pigs* shakes hands with *He Strangles Old Woman and Smears Corpse with Syrup, Ketchup and Oatmeal* . . . and. . . .

. . . There was a great deal of esprit about the whole thing. These men were, in fact, the avant-garde of a new genre that since then has become institutionalized throughout the nation without anyone knowing its proper name. I speak of the new pornography, the pornography of violence.

Pornography comes from the Greek word *porne,* meaning harlot, and pornography is literally the depiction of the acts of harlots. In the new pornography, the theme is not sex. The new pornography depicts practitioners acting out another, murkier drive: people staving teeth in, ripping guts open, blowing brains out and getting even with all those bastards. . . .

The success of *The Enquirer* prompted many imitators to enter the field, *Midnight, The Star Chronicle, The National Insider, Inside News, The National Close-up, The National Tattler, The National Examiner.* A truly competitive free press evolved, and soon a reader could go to the newspaper of his choice for *Kill the Retarded! (Won't You Join My Movement?)* and *Unfaithful Wife? Burn Her Bed!, Harem Master's Mistress Chops Him with Machete, Babe Bites Off Boy's Tongue,* and *Cuts Buddy's Face to Pieces for Stealing His Business and Fiancée.*

And yet the last time I surveyed the Violence press, I noticed a curious thing. These pioneering journals seem to have pulled back. They seem to be regressing to what is by now the Redi-Mix staple of literate Americans, plain old lust-o-lech sex. *Ecstasy and Me (By Hedy Lamarr),* says *The National Enquirer. I Run A Sex Art Gallery,* says *The National Insider.* What has happened, I think, is something that has happened to avant-gardes in many fields, from William Morris and the Craftsmen to the Bauhaus group. Namely, their discoveries have been preempted by the Establishment and so thoroughly dissolved into the mainstream they no longer look original.

Robert Harrison, the former publisher of *Confidential,* and later publisher of the aforementioned *Inside News,* was perhaps the first person to see it coming. I was interviewing Harrison early in January of 1964 for a story in *Esquire* about six weeks after the assassination of President Kennedy, and we were in a cab in the West Fifties in Manhattan, at a stoplight, by a newsstand, and Harrison suddenly pointed at the newsstand and said, "Look at that. They're doing the same thing *The Enquirer* does."

There on the stand was a row of slick-paper, magazine-size publications, known in the trade as one-shots, with titles like *Four Days That Shook the World, Death of a President, An American Tragedy* or just *John Fitzgerald Kennedy (1921–1963).* "You want to know why people buy those things?" said Harrison. "People buy those things to see a man get his head blown off."

And, of course, he was right. Only now the publishers were in many cases the pillars of the American press. Invariably, these "special coverages" of the assassination bore introductions piously commemorating the fallen President, exhorting the American people to strength and unity in a time of crisis, urging greater vigilance and safeguards for the new President, and even raising the nice metaphysical question of collective guilt in "an age of violence."

In the three and a half years since then, of course, there has been an incessant replay, with every recoverable clinical detail, of those less than five seconds in which a man got his head blown off.

And throughout this deluge of words, pictures and film frames, I have been intrigued with one thing. The point of view, the vantage point, is almost never that of the victim, riding in the Presidential Lincoln Continental. What you get is . . . the view from Oswald's rifle. You can step right up here and look point-blank right through the very hairline cross in Lee Harvey Oswald's Optics Ordinance four-power Japanese telescopic sight and watch, frame by frame by frame by frame by frame, as that man there's head comes apart. Just a little History before your very eyes.

The television networks have schooled us in the view from Oswald's rifle and made it seem a normal pastime. The TV viewpoint is nearly always that of the man who is going to strike. The last time I watched *Gunsmoke,* which was not known as a very violent Western in TV terms, the action went like this: The Wellington agents and the stagecoach driver pull guns on the badlands gang leader's daughter and Kitty, the heart-of-gold saloonkeeper, and kidnap them. Then the badlands gang shoots two Wellington agents. Then they tie up five more and talk about shooting them. Then they desist because they might not be able to get a hotel room in the next town if the word got around. Then one badlands gang gunslinger attempts to rape Kitty while the gang leader's younger daughter looks on. Then Kitty resists, so he slugs her one in the jaw. Then the gang leader slugs him. Then the gang leader slugs Kitty. Then Kitty throws hot stew in a gang member's face and hits him over the back of the head with a revolver. Then he knocks her down with a rock. Then the gang sticks up a bank. Here comes the sheriff, Matt Dillon. He shoots a gang member and breaks it up. Then the gang leader shoots the guy who was guarding his daughter and the woman. Then the sheriff shoots the gang leader. The final exploding bullets signals The End.

It is not the accumulated slayings and bone-crushings that make this porno-violence, however. What makes it porno-violence is that in almost every case the camera angle, therefore the viewer, is with the gun, the fist, the rock. The pornography of violence has no point of view in the old sense that novels do. You do not live the action through the hero's eyes. You live with the aggressor, whoever he may be. One moment you are the hero. The next, you are the villain. No matter whose side you may be on consciously, you are in fact with the muscle, and it is you who disintegrate all comers, villains, lawmen, women, anybody. On the rare occasions in which the gun is emptied into the camera—i.e., into your face—the effect is so startling that the pornography of violence all but loses its fantasy charm. There are not nearly so many masochists as sadists among those little devils whispering into your ears.

In fact, sex—"sadomasochism"—is only a part of the pornography of violence. Violence is much more wrapped up, simply, with status. Violence is the simple, ultimate solution for problems of status competition, just as gambling is the simple, ultimate solution for economic competition. The old pornography was the fantasy of easy sexual delights in a world where sex was kept unavailable. The new pornography is the fantasy of easy triumph in a world where status competition has become so complicated and frustrating.

Already the old pornography is losing its kick because of overexposure. In the late Thirties, Nathanael West published his last and best-regarded novel, *The Day of the Locust,* and it was a terrible flop commercially, and his publisher said if he ever published another book about Hollywood it would "have to be *My Thirty-nine Ways of Making Love by Hedy Lamarr.*" *Ecstasy and Me* is not quite that . . . but maybe it is. I stopped counting. I know her account begins: "The men in my life have ranged from a classic case history of impotence, to a whip-brandishing sadist who enjoyed sex only after he tied my arms behind me with the sash of his robe. There was another man who took his pleasure with a girl in my own bed, while he thought I was asleep in it."

Yawns all around. The sin itself is wearing out. Pornography cannot exist without certified taboo to violate. And today Lust, like the rest of the Seven Deadly Sins—Pride, Sloth, Envy, Greed, Anger and Gluttony—is becoming a rather minor vice. The Seven Deadly Sins, after all, are only sins against the self. Theologically, the idea of Lust—well, the idea is that if you seduce some poor girl from Akron, it is not a sin because you are ruining her, but because you are wasting your time and your energies and damaging your own spirit. This goes back to the old work ethic, when the idea was to keep every able-bodied man's shoulder to the wheel. In an age of riches for all, the ethic becomes more nearly: Let him do anything he pleases, as long as he doesn't get in my way. And if he does get in my way, or even if he doesn't . . . well . . . we have *new* fantasies for that. *Put hair on the walls.*

Hair on the walls is the invisible subtitle of Truman Capote's book *In Cold Blood.* The book is neither a who-done-it nor a will-they-be-caught, since the answers to both questions are known from the outset. It does ask why-did-they-do-it, but the answer is soon as clear as it is going to be. Instead, the book's suspense is based largely on a totally new idea in detective stories: the promise of gory details, and the withholding of them until the end. Early in the game one of the two murderers, Dick, starts promising to put "plenty of hair on them-those walls" with a shotgun. So read on, gentle readers, and on and on; you are led up to the moment before the crime on page 60—yet the specifics, what happened, the gory details, are kept out of sight, in grisly dangle, until page 244.

But Dick and Perry, Capote's killers, are only a couple of lower-class bums. With James Bond the new pornography has already reached dead center, the bureaucratic middle class. The appeal of Bond has been explained as the appeal of the lone man who can solve enormously complicated, even world problems through his own bravery and initiative. But Bond is not a lone man at all, of course. He is not the Lone Ranger. He is much easier to identify than that. He is a salaried functionary in a bureaucracy. He is a sport, but a believable one; not a millionaire, but a bureaucrat on expense account. He is not even a high-level bureaucrat. He is an operative. This point is carefully and repeatedly made by having his superiors dress him down for violations of standard operating procedure. Bond, like the Lone Ranger, solves problems with guns and fists. When it is over, however, the Lone Ranger leaves a silver bullet. Bond, like the rest of us, fills out a report in triplicate.

Marshall McLuhan says we are in a period in which it will become harder and harder to stimulate lust through words and pictures—i.e., the old pornography. In an age of electronic circuitry, he says, people crave tactile, all-involving experiences. The same thing may very well happen to the new pornography of violence. Even such able craftsmen as Truman Capote, Ian Fleming, NBC and CBS may not suffice. Fortunately, there are historical models to rescue us from this frustration. In the latter days of the Roman Empire, the Emperor Commodus became jealous of the celebrity of the great gladiators. He took to the arena himself, with his sword, and began dispatching suitably screened cripples and hobbled fighters. Audience participation became so popular that soon various *illuminati* of the Commodus set, various boys and girls of the year, were out there, suited up, gaily cutting a sequence of dwarves and feebles down to short ribs. Ah, swinging generations, what new delights await?

Discussing Issues and Themes

1. How does Wolfe define porno-violence? What examples of it does he offer? Have you encountered it? If so, where do you find it?

2. If we find tabloid headlines less shocking than we used to, does our ennui indicate that there have been widespread changes in our national attitude? Do you think political factors are involved?

3. In what ways have tabloid techniques spread to other fields? Do you see these techniques on television, in national magazines, on the radio? Are the fine arts exempt—do novelists use these techniques? Painters? Movie directors?

4. How does Wolfe link tabloid techniques to pornography? What do the genres have in common? Where do they diverge? Do you agree with Wolfe's assessment? Explain.

Discussing Rhetoric and Style

1. Does the opening disorient you at all? That is, do you grasp Wolfe's intent (get the joke) right away? Does it make more sense later in the essay?
2. Why does Wolfe relate the plot of a *Gunsmoke* episode in such detail? What is the effect of this synopsis? Can you connect this effect with the stylistic or narrative technique he adopts? Explain, citing examples from the text.
3. How does the author use incomplete sentences to create a personal voice? Where is he most likely to use fragments—at the beginning of paragraphs, in the middle, or at the end? What effects do these fragments have on a reader?
4. Is there anything sensationalist about Wolfe's coverage of porno-violence? Why, for example, does he want to write about it? Does it fascinate him? Or is he a detached observer? Use examples from the essay to support your position.
5. Do you think Wolfe's essay appeals to a mainstream audience? If it does, explain why he avoids using "porno-violent" techniques to engage his readers' interests. If not, whom is he writing for?

Ideas for Writing

1. Write a parody porno-violence piece, and give an analysis of the kinds of stylistic gestures you adopted. For example, what kinds of sentences did you find yourself writing? How long were they? How varied was the vocabulary?
2. Choose any sensational event currently in the news and research it thoroughly and seriously. For example, you might look up Satanic cults, mass murderers, or child abusers. What statistics can you find on these topics, and how do they compare to the kind of information released about them in tabloids? Are these groups ever misrepresented? Develop your responses in an essay.

The Boss Don't Like Swindle, Make It Robbery

SIMON BARBER

Born in Britain, Simon Barber has written for numerous newspapers and magazines on both sides of the Atlantic, ranging from the National Enquirer *to the* Washington Journalism Review, *in which this essay first appeared. After the demise of the British-based magazine* NOW!, *for which he was the Washington correspondent, Barber briefly worked as articles editor for the* Enquirer, *an experience which prompted, if nothing else, the following article. In it, Barber scathingly critiques both the* Enquirer's *methods and products, suggesting that the commodity the* Enquirer *sells over the supermarket checkout counters is no better than "printed Valium."*

The genial Scot at the National Press Club bar in November painted a pleasing picture of *National Enquirer* opulence in the Florida sunshine. Winter enhanced his plausibility. My visions of having to invade Hollywood funeral parlors, sift through mountains of celebrity garbage or track Senator Kennedy to see whether he broke the speed limit on the George Washington Parkway were dispelled. "Mythology," he said. And if there was a touch of the hustler in his broad Glasgow accent, it was belied by the half-moon reading glasses, professional tweeds and Mont Blanc fountain pen.

The *Enquirer*'s recruiter found me at the vulnerable moment. My previous employer, a British newsweekly, had folded some months previously; the job hunt was going badly; I was broke. I could scarcely afford to go to the supermarket, much less scorn the drivel on its checkout counters. Sympathy for Carol Burnett, whose suit against the *Enquirer* I once cheered, had become a luxury.

He suggested I try my hand as articles editor. It started at a $1,000 a week, carried the responsibility of creating and running a network of reporters, and might, in the event of some really spectacular death or disaster, involve a little travel. Hopelessness, and the rakish idea of building a Smileyesque Circus dedicated to ferreting out the Untold, Amazing and Bizarre, were ample stimuli. I bit, and three days later I was on a prepaid flight to Florida.

The *Enquirer* resides in Lantana, one of those countless ribs of real estate whose primary function is to separate Palm Beach from Fort Lauderdale and I-95 from the Intracoastal Waterway. A bland tract of telegraph poles, tired palm trees and prefabrication, it is remarkable on two counts: it has a large population of Finns and coruscating soullessness.

In the midst of this refugee camp for the cold and old, wedged between a railway line and a crumbling sports facility, the *National Enquirer* makes its one stab at irony and keeps a low profile. Once the visitor has given up trying to figure out the Minoan-style bull's horns that mark the entrance, he is pleasantly surprised by the landscaping. The grounds are thick with hibiscus and other fragrant shrubs, each thoughtfully labelled with its botanical name. The building itself lives up to a more squalid expectation. No bastion of multimillion-dollar publishing this, instead a sleepy single-story sprawl that might serviceably house a small electronics factory. Like everything in Lantana, it exudes the grim quality of being *instant*.

It was perhaps my misfortune to be ushered into the presence of executive editor Mike Hoy at lunchtime. The editorial offices were all but empty, and conveyed, in an efficiently pastel way, a sense of innocent cheerfulness, like an outsized kindergarten. Indeed, one of the newsroom cubicles was stacked with exotic toys. I began to suspect that the people who worked here might be having fun.

Hoy, thirtyish, Australian and modelled on the lines of a hygienic rock star, encouraged this view by offering me a job, on a trial basis, within 15 minutes of our meeting, and by explaining why the company would not, as had once been its practice, rent a car for me. One of my more exuberant predecessors had driven an *Enquirer* Hertz into the Waterway.

Then he said something rather strange. "I want you to know that we really are looking for editors." Having been tracked down by a recruiter and flown in from Washington to be interviewed for such a slot, and having just been offered a month's trial at it, I thought this scarcely needed saying. That impermanence was an institution at the *Enquirer* did not occur to me, nor, as yet, did the connection between its desperation for new blood and whatever had possessed the predecessor to sink his car.

Every aspect of the *Enquirer*, from its management to what it prints, is governed by a surgically precise appreciation of human frailty. This is the great achievement of its owner and publisher, the splendidly named Generoso Pope, Jr., and evidently appreciated by six million supermarket purchasers a week. Pope's relationship with his employees approximates that between the God of the Old Testament and the Children of Israel minus forgiveness. His control is total and awe-inspiring, his ways mysterious, his retribution swift. When he deals with a man, he likes, to use his own very secular phrase, to "have him by the balls," and usually succeeds. Under Hoy's guidance, it was hoped I would quickly learn to divine his will.

Known simply as The Boss or GP, Pope dominates the waking thoughts, and more than a few sleeping ones as well, of all at the *Enquirer.* An authorized account, published in 1978 by the *Miami Herald,* describes Pope as "a tall man, built like a Bronx precinct captain." Fifty-four years have softened that image somewhat, except for the face. Said an editor, one of the few women in the *Enquirer*'s higher echelons, "There doesn't seem to be anything behind his eyes." The effect is a mask of staring malevolence, which does little to endear.

He is educated. A top of his class graduate in engineering from MIT, according to the authorized account, he served in the CIA's psychological warfare unit. Further glimpses of his life beyond the *Enquirer,* which he purchased in 1952, are virtually nonexistent. His father was the publisher of the New York Italian-language paper *Il Progresso.* Some see murkiness in the fact that since he moved the operation from New Jersey in 1971, Pope has never left south Florida. He says he hates to fly.

There is an eeriness about him enhanced by gun-toting plainclothes security men who haunt the premises, spot checks on reporters' telephone conversations, and the uniformed Lantana patrolman who escorts Pope to and from his car.

My first day should have taught me more, perhaps, than it did. My initial mistake was to turn up in coat and tie. Higher authority wore shirtsleeves and an increasingly familiar pair of pants, a style, admonished Hoy, that I would do well to emulate. I blundered again by trying to strike up a conversation. Apparently one did not talk to colleagues, be they only six feet away, except by internal telephone and with one's back turned. I needed coffee. "Put a top on it," someone hissed as I carried a cup to my desk. "The Boss don't like stains on his carpet." To atone, I worked through lunch, another miscalculation. "The Boss believes in lunch." Next day I ate, grateful for a temporary escape, only to be informed that I'd been seen leaving the office with the wrong people. My companions were said to be under some form of cloud and best avoided. Besides, what was I doing having lunch? I wondered whether Pope ever specified his desires before punishing those who transgressed them.

The arena in which this curious drama was to be played out might have been a newsroom in any large daily before the electronic age. Its open plan layout was symmetrical about a narrow avenue across which two rows of editors, about nine in all, numbers varied, were occasionally polite to one another. Behind them sat their secretaries, each busily pretending to callers that her boss worked in a private office. Next, pinched into lines of narrow, benchlike desks were 40 or so reporters, each owing allegiance and his job to a particular editor. Finally the writers, who are responsible for the *Enquirer*'s deathless prose and probably the happiest employees. Deemed creative by The Boss, they were left in peace. At the end of the central aisle, rather too close to where I had been stationed, was a series of glass cubicles. Pope had a grander sanctum elsewhere, but it was here he would come when he wished to make his presence felt. Assistants ensured that a pack of Kents and a lighter always awaited his arrival.

As a deracinated Englishman, I should have had some cause to feel at home. A surprising proportion of my new colleagues hailed from Britain and parts of its old empire. A buzz of familiar accents could be heard insinuating charm down various telephones. Having had some success in this department myself, I could imagine the interrogatees being thoroughly disarmed. To their cost.

Pope's predilection for what one American writer has called British Empire Journalists has little to do with the narcotic power of the speech patterns, however, but derives more from their tradition. American reporters tend to take a rather romantic view of their trade, see themselves as somehow in the public service. Their minds are burdened with scruple. Not so the British Empire Journalist. He can report, as in 1978 one imaginative correspondent for the *London Daily Mail* actually did, that President Carter was growing a beard to look more Lincolnesque, and receive a kudogram from his superiors. Rupert Murdoch ranks high in the Pope pantheon, and as publisher of the *Star*, constitutes Pope's most serious opposition.

My first impression was that my fellow editors all looked very ill: exchange their typewriters for oars and they would have made perfect (though, on $60,000 a year and up, very expensive) extras for the sea battle in *Ben Hur*.

Enquirer reporters had the furtive look of kicked and beaten Labrador Retrievers. Foot soldiers, they were at least insulated from The Boss by their editors, whose paranoia-induced savagery was the price of relative security. The reason I had been brought in from outside to be articles editor was that no reporter wanted to risk his neck or his $45,000 a year more than was strictly necessary. Now and then one or two were forcibly promoted—given the option of leaving or climbing—which regularly amounted to the same thing: climbers who failed at editor could expect to be fired, and the chances of making it were no better than those of a World War I subaltern on the Western Front.

One of the luckier ones was the young Englishman sitting to my left. Promoted some months previously, he had begun his career on a small provincial paper outside London, and had been lured to Florida by wealth and warmth. In an earlier age, he might have set out to make his fortune in some tropical outpost of Empire. He seemed to be doing all that was required of him; his file drawer was full of good stories in progress, yet there was an air of doom about him. Colleagues shied away, spoke of him with, of all things in this emotional charnel house, compassion. It turned out he was being executed, *Enquirer*-style.

First they cut his salary, then removed his reporters, forcing him to rely on stringers, finally demanded a massive increase in output. "This is the way Pope always does it," he said one evening towards the end. "They dig you a grave and say climb out if you can. You never can. The grave just gets deeper." Several days later his desk was empty. In this case the editor was allowed to reincarnate himself as a reporter. A rare privilege.

A reason would have been helpful, but my enquiries were about as fruitful as asking a priest to account plausibly for human suffering. The editor's defrocking could be ascribed to no particular commission or omission, it was just the way things worked around here. A sympathetic reporter noticed my puzzlement. "The Boss is a toy train freak," she explained. "I think he likes to see us as a vast toy train set. He throws switches, sets up obstructions, and races us off bridges just for the hell of seeing what happens."

In terms of how they are put together, there is essentially little difference between the *National Enquirer* and, say, *Time*. To the structuralist, anyway. Leads are developed and assigned, reporters and stringers turn in voluminous files, which are rigorously checked for accuracy, boiled down by writers into the house style, and finally, with luck, printed. There, however, the resemblance ends.

Appearances to the contrary, gungho fabulism is not the *Enquirer*'s line of business. Nor indeed is journalism, in any of the accepted senses of the word.

Bear in mind that the *Enquirer* is not designed primarily to inform, amuse, or even, really, to be read. It performs these functions, of course, but they are secondary. It exists to be consumed, much in the same way as premixed peanut butter and jelly. The idea is pretty simple. People enter the supermarket in a buying frame of mind, so let's give them one more brightly packaged object to shove into their shopping bags.

The editorial content addresses itself scientifically to the consuming mood, a condition frequently brought on by boredom, restlessness and unfocused dissatisfaction. The universe depicted is a bright, uncomplicated, unambiguous place where things either are (in this category we may include metempsychosis, UFOs and psychic fork-bending) or are not (unhappy endings, celibate celebrities, wise government). The buyer is told that he is basically good, that the rich and famous are basically miserable, and that the quality of life is improving immeasurably: cancer, obesity and arthritis can be cured.

In short the *Enquirer* is a kind of printed Valium, its editors little more than pharmacists, cutting each other's throats to combine and recombine a limited number of ingredients which Pope, the master chemist, has determined will have the desired effect. It is a mechanical and, the financial aspect apart, unrewarding task.

The process begins with the lead. Each editor is expected to submit 30 or so to The Boss every Friday, of which perhaps half a dozen may be approved. On the rest he scribbles the ubiquitous initials NG (No Good). The ideas come from reporters and stringers (all of whom receive up to $300 if their offering gets into print), other publications (there is always a race for the new *Omni, Cosmopolitan* and *Self*) and the imagination. Memorable specimens from the latter category include "The Junk Food Diet," "How Brooke Shields, Loni Anderson and Farrah Fawcett are Wrecking Your Marriage" and "Let's Get Accredited as a Salvation Army Fundraiser and Go Knocking on Celebrity Doors to See How Generous the Stars Are." A number of celebrity leads are preemptive. I myself proposed "Wedding Bells for Patti Reagan and Peter [Masada] Strauss." The Elizabeth Taylor-John Warner separation was in the works probably before they had even said their vows, and certainly for months before it occurred. At this very moment at least one editor is contemplating marriage between Robert Wagner, widower of Natalie Wood, and his television co-star Stephanie Powers.

Often, of course, celebrities do dramatic things that even the *Enquirer* cannot foresee, the deaths of Natalie Wood and William Holden for example. In these instances, leads are rushed through under the rubric of "Untold Story," the logic being that there will always be one. In the Wood case, which occurred a few weeks after I arrived, the editor involved went to extraordinary lengths to find something that the voluble Los Angeles coroner Thomas Noguchi had *not* said. What he came up with was the suggestion, ascribed to Top Doctors, that the actress, rather than drowning, had been asphyxiated by a potent mixture of drugs and alcohol. This on the basis of a well-stocked medicine cabinet and the alleged absence of froth on the victim's lips. What I heard of the interviews went as follows: "Doctor, if after consuming such and such a quantity of alcohol, a person were to take drugs x and y, what would be the result?"

Even the most grizzled veteran cannot second guess Pope's taste with any certainty. His notions of what constitutes a contemporary star are quixotic, but seem to derive from movies of the '50s and '60s (hence Sophia Loren, Princess Grace and, by association, her daughter Caroline) and the top ten Nielson-rated shows he happens to watch (not *60 Mintues*). Dudley Moore, of *10* and *Arthur* fame, fails to register on the grounds that he is, and I quote, "Not big enough." The currently lionized Tom Selleck (*Magnum, PI*), did not have the right stuff either, until Pope was persuaded to poll his favorite gauges of gut reaction, the secretaries.

There are, however, some totally predictable NG's, chief among them blacks, except when they practice voodoo, or are child comic Gary Coleman. I presented Hoy with a heart-warming story of a young New Orleans man who had survived a grain elevator explosion and 80 percent burns to become a multimillionaire (a surefire hit under the Rags to Riches category). He immediately asked me what color he was. Black. Kill it. Gays, on the other hand, may be beaten up at will. An outraged account of San Francisco's demographics was headlined "Sick! Sick! Sick!" The *Enquirer*, a self-styled Equal Opportunity Employer, has no minority employees.

Once an approved lead has pleased Story Control, a computer programmed to weed out duplicates, it is ready to be reported, and the ethical mayhem begins.

If celebrities are the potatoes of tabloid journalism, miraculous medicine is the meat. Unfortunately, the medical fraternity likes to be circumspect about describing its advances, and talks of percentages, hopes, possibilities, rarely of anything so definite as a cure. This is too gray for the *Enquirer* which does not recognize the subjunctive mood: a thing either is or it isn't. The trick, therefore, is to get the medical man, who in his right mind would never even talk to the *Enquirer*, to say things that would cost him his shingle if he tried to say them in the *New England Journal of Medicine*, and on tape. This is known in the trade as Burning Docs.

Technically, the reporter's path is strewn with regulations. Not only must his interviews be taped, but he has signed a waiver binding him to identify himself as working for the *Enquirer* and as using a recorder, thus excusing his employers when, as he must, he sidles past the law. If his editor wants him to get a doctor to say something, he is under considerably more pressure to produce than to be an upright citizen. Refusal to carry out an order is treated with military firmness.

There are many ways to ease on-the-record indiscretion from an interviewee, the most popular being the old 20 Questions ploy. The subject is stroked into a state of trust and then hit with a series of convoluted queries, to which he will answer, if the reporter is adroit enough, merely yes or no. These little words can be made to speak volumes. Critical readers may have wondered how it is that supposedly sophisticated professionals, when quoted in the *Enquirer*, always manage to clutter their remarks with an effusion of amazings, incredibles and fantastics.

This method is openly encouraged by Pope. In a memo distributed to all newcomers he commands bluntly: "Ask leading questions." Lest it be carried too far, reporters are then reminded, "Quotes should not only be appropriate but believable. A Japanese carpenter should not sound like Ernest Hemingway, or vice versa."

Add to this Pope's rather confining taste in vocabulary, and the results can be bizarre. Reporter Byron Lutz had worked hard to produce "The Biggest Swindle in U.S. History," a tale of a computer ripoff within the federal government. He had even persuaded a Justice Department official to agree that it was indeed "the biggest swindle," a questionable assertion by itself. Enter the Evaluator, a character whose task it is to condense finished files into single paragraphs for the benefit of Pope and the writers.

EVALUATOR: "This won't get through, Lutz. We don't use swindle."
LUTZ: "But that's what the guy at the Justice Department called it, it's on the tape."
EVAL.: "It's got to be robbery."
LUTZ: "But there's a difference."
EDITOR (INTERVENING): "He's right. Let's look it up in the dictionary."
EVAL.: "Hey, I don't care. The Boss don't like swindle make it robbery."
EDITOR (SNAPPING TO WHAT LOOKED SUSPICIOUSLY LIKE ATTENTION): "Get on it, Lutz, get your guy to say robbery. Now."

At least doctors and officials can be made to speak. Celebrities are less obliging with their reputations. To reveal the supposed drama of their lives the reporter must resort to an altogether higher order of guile. In compensation, he is required to offer less in the way of proof. Stars are public property, and consequently vulnerable to the First Amendment.

Much of the information on who is bedding whom, whose career is on the skids and who is currently being detoxified from what, emanates from the thriving gossip industry as a whole. I do not pretend to know how this works. Obviously, however, the *Enquirer* has to delve deeper to satisfy what the commercials call its readers' "Enquiring Minds."

What makes the reporter's mission particularly tough is that he is often covering not a set of circumstances his editor knows or believes to exist, but one that the editor *wishes* to have happen. A new TV series has emerged, perhaps, and The Boss wants an exciting story about its participants. Or an editor may conclude that there has been too striking an absence of Farrah Fawcett. A reconciliation with Lee Majors is needed to fill the gap. Thanks to a large array of "insiders," "friends" and "intimate sources," many of whom are in the *Enquirer*'s pay, such things can be arranged.

In some cases, a great deal of old-fashioned shoe-leather reporting does go on, though it has been known to get out of hand. The coffin photographs of Elvis Presley are not an isolated phenomenon. One reporter told me that while tracking the hometown life of a currently popular television actress, he stumbled onto the fact that she had had an abortion. Such was the pressure he was under, he lined up a neighborhood hoodlum to steal the records. Getting mixed signals from his editor, he thought better of it.

Celebrity romance stories are frequently the work of reporters whose main activity is to hang around fashionable watering holes. Maitre d's and waiters are also retained. Thus, the *Enquirer* often has a pair of eyes in place when an interesting couple appear in public for the first time, or have a violent quarrel.

Hollywood sex, in the *Enquirer,* is a formulaic affair. The starting assumption is that any physical contact represents romance. At the lower end of the scale, hand holding is described by "insiders," who do not have to be told the *Enquirer* style, as "they looked like a pair of teenagers in love." Any kiss less demure than a peck is evidence that the relationship has turned "hot and heavy."

Equally earnest is the *Enquirer*'s attitude towards the paranormal. Cranks are not tolerated, and anyone claiming to have been reborn, sighted UFOs or communicated with the beyond is subjected to hypnotic regression. This is considered sounder evidence than a lie detector because the latter has the unfortunate habit of being accurate.

The reigning exponent of what may be called the "Hey-Martha-Will-You-Get-A-Look-At-This" school is *Enquirer* super-stringer Henry Gris, a former UPI correspondent. His latest find is one "Dr.

Victor Azhazha," eminent Soviet scientist. Dr. Azhazha claimed, and there is an artist's conception complete with silhouetted Kremlin to back it up, that a mysterious shining cloud had drifted over Moscow one night causing great consternation. A friend of mine, stationed in Moscow for a well-known British daily, commented, "I didn't see this cloud, which was perhaps careless. It might have started World War III."

A cardinal rule of the information trade is that the more bald and unconvincing a story, the greater the machinery needed to lend it verisimilitude. The *Enquirer* is inordinately proud of its Research Department. A copy of a glowing account in *Editor & Publisher* that appeared in 1978 is compulsory reading for all arrivals.

E&P tells us that Research is staffed by probing professionals, headed by Ruth Annan, a 16-year veteran of *Time*. Her team includes "two medical specialists, two lawyers, a linguist who speaks four languages, a geographer, three with master's degrees in library science, one with a master's degree in educational psychology, and an author."

And yet it regularly lets through palpable inanities. The concept of a "4,000-year-old Stone Age statuette" does not bother it, for example, but this is a quibble. Most of what escapes the tireless fact-checkers is on a grander scale, even in cases where the facts can actually be checked.

Researchers are cunningly paid less than reporters whose work they scrutinize, and thus approach their task with the enthusiasm of inquisitors. That the *Enquirer* is published at all is not their fault.

I have no doubt that Research pursues Truth with genuine vigor, but it is hampered by one major defect: literalmindedness. If the tapes and copy jibe, and sources when contacted agree to what has been reported, the story must, however, reluctantly, be granted the imprimature of accuracy.

One disadvantage of Annan and her staff is that they clog up an already hopelessly slow system—lead time is usually three or four weeks—with haggling that, given the nature of the beast, is utterly unnecessary. On the upside, however, their mere existence enables reporters to tell a suspicious world that, yes, really, the *Enquirer* does strive after fact. As editor Paul Levy told *E&P*, "Today any reporter can say with justifiable pride that he works for the most accurate paper in the country."

Discussing Ideas and Themes

1. Why does Barber accept a job at the *National Enquirer?* What are his reservations about working there?
2. What are the power relationships among employees of the *National Enquirer?* Where does he fit into the power structure? As Barber sees it, what factors, aside from formal company rank or position, contribute to an employee's status?
3. Why is "editor" a dangerous position at the *National Enquirer?* Why would no reporter be willing to risk the job, even given a raise in pay?
4. How does the tabloid represent black and gay people? Why do you think the "lines" taken on these groups are different?
5. What degree of truth does Barber suggest the *National Enquirer* contains? How much truth, in general, do most newspapers contain? Why do some papers seem more credible than others? Explain.

Discussing Rhetoric and Style

1. How does Barber use description to denigrate the *National Enquirer?* For example, his description of the office tract implies a great deal about the paper's integrity. How do other descriptions work in the same way?
2. How does Barber use the first person to enhance his narrative? For example, he offers the readers his experiences in chronological order, creating some curiosity about what will happen next. In what other ways does the narrator get the reader involved?
3. Barber repeatedly uses hesitant constructions (look for the word "perhaps"). What are the rhetorical effects of these hesitations or qualifications? How do they affect the way a reader perceives his character?
4. How does Barber use metaphors to reinforce his argument and to create mood in this essay? For example, he calls the newsroom an "arena," invoking associations of conflict, theater, and victimization—we imagine an arena to be a place where someone gets fed to the lions. How do some of his other metaphors work?

Ideas for Writing

1. Analyze an article from a recent issue of the *National Enquirer* or a similar paper. Does it represent "the universe [to be] a bright, uncomplicated, unambiguous place where things either are or are not"? Is it, as Barber suggests, "printed Valium"? Pay close attention both to elements of style and to the subject and arrangement of the article you choose to analyze.
2. Compare three short articles from different publications: one from the *Enquirer*, one from a daily newspaper, and one from a popular magazine such as *Time* or *U.S. News & World Report*. Write a brief analysis of the three styles, and discuss what these styles reveal about whom they appeal to, and what their appeal might be.

Foul Play
Sports Metaphors as Public Doublespeak

FRANCINE HARDAWAY

Born in 1941, Francine Hardaway was educated at Syracuse University and now teaches at Rio Salada College in Arizona. A frequent contributor to scholarly journals, she has written several books on language, including Writing Through Reading, Doublespeak and Teaching, *and* Thinking into Writing. *In this essay, Hardaway examines the prevalence of sports metaphors in American business and politics, observing that these figures of speech are both ubiquitous and at the same time largely taken for granted. As Hardaway warns, sports references are "not merely ways of revealing our adolescent preoccupation with aggressiveness, with winning, with games, but also ways of perpetuating those concerns, of glorifying them, of passing them on unexamined to our children through our national culture." The essay appeared in the* Journal of the National Council of Teachers of English.

Nobody would argue the place of sports in American life; they are big business. And they are big business because they fit philosophically with the widely accepted American dream of open competition in a free market economy. Americans believe in competition, foster it, and encourage it. They live by its rules. No wonder the language of athletic competition has found its way as metaphor into every aspect of American life. If we are at a disadvantage, we say we've "got two strikes against us," things have "taken a bad bounce," or we're "on the ropes." If we are being aggressive, we "take the ball and run with it," "take the bull by the horns," "come out swinging," or "make a sweep." If the fates still conspire against us, we "take it on the chin," "throw in the towel," or "roll with the punches" until we're "saved by the bell."

It's worth taking some time to think about how these sports metaphors, so ubiquitous and so ignored until Watergate brought them to our attention, describe the quality of life in America.

The purpose of such metaphors is to explain unfamiliar or difficult concepts in terms of familiar images. But recently there have been some changes in our national self-concept and these changes are duly reflected in sports metaphors. We seem to have changed drastically from a society in which "it isn't whether you win or lose, but how you play the game," to one in which, to use Vince Lombardi's words, "winning isn't everything, it's the only thing." And our sports metaphors have changed with us. "The good fight" and "the old college try" have given way to the more sophisticated "game plans," "playcalling," and quarterbacking rhetoric of Vietnam and Watergate. Sports metaphors now often function as public doublespeak: language meant to manipulate its audience unconsciously. Analyzing sports doublespeak reveals some scary truths about how we Americans look at life. In John Mitchell's words, "when the going gets tough, the tough get going," and we turn out to be a society in which "nice guys finish last," and everybody wants to "be on the winning side."

The rhetoric of the playing field appears in advertising, business, and government. Let's take an obvious example first. President Ford, in publicizing his economic strategies when he first took office, devised the W.I.N. button. An offshoot of Ford's other unfortunate sports metaphor, the promise to "hold the line" on inflation, the W.I.N. button was meant to appeal by familiarity to the sports-minded American who will "get up for the game," and "tackle the job" if the coach just tells him what to do. Ford hoped that the "win" mentality was so strongly ingrained in America that the very word would alter attitudes and behavior.

With the W.I.N. button, Ford hoped to make use of a sports metaphor the way advertising does. He wanted to make the analogy from athletic success to success in other fields. We all expect to be manipulated by advertising, so it is no surprise to see professional athletes advertising hair tonic, shaving cream, even frozen pizza or panty hose. The doublespeak is implicit: use this product, and you will enjoy the same success as Frank Gifford, Arthur Ashe, Joe Namath. Associating the athlete with the product, however, makes another claim for the athlete: it extends his expertise beyond the playing field. Ad agencies hope we will take the advice of these "pros" about shaving cream, hair tonic, frozen pizza, or panty hose; after all, the pro wouldn't make a wrong choice about these products any more than he would throw the ball away at a crucial moment of the game. So the athlete is an expert, as well as a hero. His ability to "score" carries over into the financial and the sexual arenas as well; there is even a product named "Score."

Since it has been established by advertising that the athlete is both hero and expert, sports metaphors are used more subtly to sell products. In the MGB ad that reads "MGB. Think of it as a well-coordinated athlete," we can see how much athletic ability is admired. No longer do we compare the good athlete or the good team to a well-oiled machine: now we're comparing the machine to the good athlete. Like a well-conditioned athlete, you'll "score" in your MGB.

But advertising is an easy target for doublespeak analysis. More complex by far is the way sports metaphors function in business, where their analysis leads to crucial revelations about American ethics. Business has always been fond of the football analogy, as William H. Whyte, Jr. points out:

> No figure of speech is a tenth as seductive to the businessman. Just why this should be—baseball curiously is much less used—is generally explained by its adaptability to all sorts of situations. Furthermore, the football analogy is *satisfying*. It is bounded by two goal lines and is thus finite. There is always a solution. And that is what makes it so often treacherous.[1]

Business uses the team philosophy, says Whyte, to hedge on moral issues. By making analogies to sports, business convinces the outside world that its decisions aren't truly consequential: they are "games" executed by good "team players." The fact that dollars and human lives may also be involved is not included when the sports metaphor is used, for the sports metaphor imposes automatic limits on the way business activity is seen.

> The goal of sports activity is always unambiguous and non-controversial: participants do not come together to discuss or debate the ends for which the activity has been established, but rather take this end for granted and apply themselves in a single-minded fashion to the task of developing the most efficient means to achieve the predetermined, unchanging and non-controversial end: winning.[2]

So the sports metaphor precludes thought; it operates on unconscious and irrational levels, manipulating its users as well as its audiences. Perhaps its use in business, where the idea of competition in the free marketplace still carries moral force, has something to do with man's aggressive nature; what sports and business have in common that allows the sports metaphor to be drawn so often and so successfully by American businessmen is aggressiveness. Sports are an acceptable form of releasing aggressive impulses; if business uses the sports metaphor, isn't the aggressiveness of business automatically acceptable?

> . . . [the] same aggressive impulse which can lead to strife and violence also underlies man's urge to independence and achievement. Just as a child could not possibly grow up into an independent adult if it were not aggressive, so an adult must needs continue to express at least part of his aggressive potential if he is to maintain his own autonomy.[3]

No wonder the Duke of Wellington was able to observe that "the battle of Waterloo was won on the playing fields of Eton." The skills learned on the playing field by the child are translated into the battles of the adult.

But there is also a certain cynicism associated with the use of the sports metaphor by business:

> What happens to some guys is—well, I'll draw the analogy to sports again. Baseball has its hot players and the next year the hot players cool off, and what happens is that their salaries drop and they get optioned out to Toledo.[4]

In Jerry Della Femina's description of what happens to advertising men who don't produce, the sports metaphor obscures the human position of the advertising executive, the man who has a good year followed by a bad year and suddenly finds himself nursing an ulcer and out of a job. Like most sports metaphors, this one permits the reader to ignore the ethical implications of cut-throat competition among advertising agencies for top talent.

But business still isn't the "Big Game"—that's government. And, as we might now expect, the bigger the game, the more prevalent the sports metaphor as doublespeak. Watergate revealed the wholesale use of the sports lexicon by politicians, but Watergate was neither the beginning nor the end of the sports metaphor. As William Safire points out in his excellent book *The New Language of Politics*,[5] Shakespeare may have been the first to use the comparisons. King Henry V told his troops before Harfleur, "I see you stand like greyhounds in the slips, straining upon the start. The game's afoot; . . ." But Safire also notes that Shakespeare wasn't the last; the section on "Sports Metaphors" in *The New Language of Politics* is a wonderful compendium of quotations from past political greats beginning with Woodrow Wilson's "I have always in my own thought summed up individual liberty, and business liberty, and every other kind of liberty, in the phrase that is common in the sporting world, 'A free field and no favor,' " and stopping at JFK's "Politics is like football. If you see daylight, go through the hole."

Amusingly enough, politics doesn't content itself only with the football metaphor so favored by business. Instead, it inadvertently reveals its seamier side by the frequent use of the horse race analogy. There are front-runners and dark horses, long shots and shoo-ins. The winner takes the reins of government, while the loser is an also-ran who was "nosed out." Harry Truman said, "I am trying to do in politics what Citation has done in the horse races. I propose at the finish line on November 2 to come out ahead. . . ." It seems that in politics, more than in advertising or in business, the use of the sports metaphor reveals more than gamesmanship, competition, or vicarious aggression; it also reveals an affinity with gambling.

But Safire's compendium, while amusing and instructive, is pre-Watergate and he therefore views the sports metaphor as innocuous. He says,

> Sports metaphors relate closely to many people, which is why politicians spend the time to create them; at other times they are tossed off without thinking because they are already a part of the language. After a Kennedy aide appeared on Lawrence Spivak's television panel show *Meet the Press*, the President called to say "They never laid a glove on you." It is the classic remark of a trainer to a prize fighter who has been belted all over the ring. (pp. 421–22)

Since Watergate, we have become more attuned to the way sports metaphors are often used to make big decisions involving all our lives seem trivial and inconsequential.

> Nixon's "jocko' macho" talk (as Nicholas von Hoffman called it) was amply demonstrated; the limited supply of tough-guy metaphors, akin to verbal locker room swaggering or muscle-flexing *machismo* at the beach: . . . Years earlier, some critics

> had felt that Nixon's overt enthusiasm for spectator sports (shaking hands with athletes, telegrams and phone calls to coaches) was simply a calculated ploy ("a grandstand play") to win the favor of certain voters, to create the illusion that he was "just one of the guys." It was no illusion. Nixon was not the first politician to use the imagery of athletics . . . but the transcripts reveal that the traditional emphasis on "fair play," "following the rules," and "good sportsmanship" had been replaced by a "win at all costs" mentality.[6]

One need hardly comment further on what Watergate did to the language; its only good effect was to alert many Americans to the way language does both form and corrupt thinking. For that, we should probably be grateful.

Unfortunately, the effects of Watergate aren't longlasting. In the midst of the recent New York City financial crisis, the *Wall Street Journal*[7] carried the following story:

> After a seven-month game of political brinkmanship, the Ford administration has browbeaten New York City into "fiscal responsibility" and the city has pressured Washington into limited federal help.
>
> But the path to that outcome proved to be far different than either side had expected, and the ultimate results happier than either would have predicted just a short time ago. There seems to be no clear winner in the long struggle—just losers of varying degrees. . . .
>
> The reconstruction of these events leading up to the Wednesday statement discloses basic miscalculations by every player in the game. . . .
>
> The city's fiscal crisis, surfacing last May, rapidly developed into a high-level game of political chess—played out in Washington and New York and Albany, full of bluff and bombast, maneuver and surprise.

Only the name of the game has changed; the article goes on to discuss how New York's crisis developed into a standoff between Ford and the city, in which participants in the negotiations between New York and Washington felt that "it was hardball both ways, and nothing was spared." The "hardball season" of negotiations ran from September through November, when Ford and New York City finally reached a compromise.

This story illustrates very well the dangers of relying too heavily on sports metaphors. Here a genuine crisis has been reduced for readers to a game in which participants are trying to out-bluff and out-maneuver each other while New York and perhaps the rest of the nation await the consequences. And the crisis is portrayed as a strategy problem, rather than a human problem or a problem in responsible government.

What is the lesson to be learned from looking at our culture's continuing use of sports metaphors to render important situations innocuous in advertising, in business, and in government? If it is true, as Walker Gibson said to the NCTE[8] Convention in 1973, that "learning to read is learning to infer dramatic character from linguistic evidence," then examining the metaphors used in popular culture provides good insight into our character as a nation. And if it is also true, as Orwell remarked in *Politics and the English Language,* that "language can corrupt thought," then sports metaphors become not merely ways of revealing our adolescent preoccupation with aggressiveness, with winning, with games, but also ways of perpetuating those concerns, of glorifying them, of passing them on unexamined to our children through our national culture. It is at least worth a few minutes of our time to wrestle (there it is again) with the decision of whether we really want to see ourselves forever as a nation of team-players and sports fans.

NOTES

1. William H. Whyte, Jr., "The Language of Business," in *Technological and Professional Writing,* ed. Herman A. Estrin (New York: Harcourt, Brace & World, 1963), p. 83. In this part of the paper, I am indebted to an unpublished paper on "Sports Metaphors in Business" by John Driscoll.
2. Ike Balbus, "Politics as Sports: The Political Ascendancy of the Sports Metaphor in America," *Monthly Review,* March 1975, p. 30.
3. Anthony Stoor, *Human Aggression* (New York: Atheneum, 1970), p. 59.
4. Jerry Della Femina, *From Those Wonderful Folks Who Brought You Pearl Harbor* (New York: Simon & Schuster, 1971), p. 124.
5. New York: Random House, 1968, p. 421.
6. Hugh Rank, "Watergate and the Language," in *Language and Public Policy,* ed. Hugh Rank (Urbana, Ill.: NCTE, 1974), pp. 8–9.
7. November 28, 1975.
8. National Council of Teachers of English.

Discussing Ideas and Themes

1. What do sports and big business have in common? What, according to Hardaway, is particularly American about this relationship?
2. Hardaway asserts, "the rhetoric of the playing field appears in advertising, business, and government." Find an example for

each of these areas in her text. Can you think of another example in each of these categories?

3. How does Hardaway define doublespeak? What examples does she offer of it? Have you ever practiced or been the victim of it? Give examples.
4. What, according to Hardaway, did Watergate "do to the language"? Can national or historical events change the way we use and even think about words? Do you think Watergate did so? Explain.

Discussing Rhetoric and Style

1. What is the thesis of Hardaway's essay? Does she state it implicitly or explicitly? If implicitly, discuss how and when it is implied; if explicitly, cite the passage.
2. The essay opens with the assertion that "nobody would argue the place of sports in American life." What is the effect of opening an essay with such a proposition? Does Hardaway proceed to act as if no one will disagree with her? Does she really intend *not* to have to persuade her readers? Why then does she offer examples?
3. How far back does Hardaway trace the sports metaphor? Does she want to give us an historical context for her idea, and does she want to date it for us?
4. How effectively does Hardaway incorporate examples into the essay? Pick out two or three of Hardaway's examples. How do they enliven her style or support her argument—or both?
5. Does Hardaway use low or high diction in her essay? (Low diction is characterized by one- or two-syllable words and casual sounding phrases; high diction generally uses a larger number of polysyllabic words and sounds less casual.) What does her diction suggest about the audience she is writing for?

Ideas for Writing

1. Write a one- or two-page essay whose primary premise is a sports metaphor or analogy. For example, you might use as your thesis something like: "Going to college and working at the same time is like running an obstacle course on the drag-raceway to

hell." Whatever you choose, aim for originality. (For instance, try not to say that "marrying my girlfriend was like being on the rebound." We've all heard that before.) Fill out your essay with a sprinkling of nouns and verbs that refer to your metaphor.

2. Write an essay that explores the linguistic habits of sports reporters. Television sportscasters might be the most interesting group to concentrate on, but radio sportscasters, newspaper columnists, or sportswriters for magazines would be equally appropriate. Compare the linguistic styles of two or three reporters, citing specific examples.

Printed Noise

GEORGE F. WILL

Born in 1941, George F. Will received his Ph.D. from Princeton and has taught at the University of Michigan and at the University of Toronto. A syndicated columnist and the winner of the 1977 Pulitzer Prize for Distinguished Commentary, Will is now an editor for the National Review, *a conservative magazine of politics and culture, as well as a commentator for ABC News. "Cuteness" is the topic of Will's essay—the sickening cuteness that we see in phrases such as "Egg McMuffin," "Fribble," and "Yumbo." The prevalence of these slogans is what Will calls "printed noise"; we're so used to hearing them that we don't even notice when we use them ourselves. The essay first appeared in* Newsweek.

The flavor list at the local Baskin-Robbins ice cream shop is an anarchy of names like "Peanut Butter 'N Chocolate" and "Strawberry Rhubarb Sherbert." These are not the names of things that reasonable people consider consuming, but the names are admirably businesslike, briskly descriptive.

Unfortunately, my favorite delight (chocolate-coated vanilla flecked with nuts) bears the unutterable name "Hot Fudge Nutty Buddy," an example of the plague of cuteness in commerce. There are some things a gentleman simply will not do, and one is announce in public a desire for a "Nutty Buddy." So I usually settle for a plain vanilla cone.

I am not the only person suffering for immutable standards of propriety. The May [1978] issue of *Atlantic* contains an absorbing tale of lonely heroism at a Burger King. A gentleman requested a ham and cheese sandwich that the Burger King calls a Yumbo. The girl taking orders was bewildered.

"Oh," she eventually exclaimed, "you mean a Yumbo."

Gentleman: "The ham and cheese. Yes."

Girl, nettled: "It's called a Yumbo. Now, do you want a Yumbo or not?"

Gentleman, teeth clenched: "Yes, thank you, the ham and cheese."

Girl: "Look, I've got to have an order here. You're holding up the line. You want a Yumbo, don't you? You want a Yumbo!"

Whereupon the gentleman chose the straight and narrow path of virtue. He walked out rather than call a ham and cheese a Yumbo. His principles are anachronisms but his prejudices are impeccable, and he is on my short list of civilization's friends.

That list includes the Cambridge don who would not appear outdoors without a top hat, not even when routed by fire at 3 A.M., and who refused to read another line of Tennyson after he saw the poet put water in fine port. The list includes another don who, although devoutly Tory, voted Liberal during Gladstone's day because the duties of prime minister kept Gladstone too busy to declaim on Holy Scripture. And high on the list is the grammarian whose last words were: "I am about to—or I am going to—die: either expression is correct."

Gentle reader, can you imagine any of these magnificent persons asking a teenage girl for a "Yumbo"? Or uttering "Fishamajig" or "Egg McMuffin" or "Fribble" (that's a milk shake, sort of)?

At one point in the evolution of American taste, restaurants that were relentlessly fun, fun, fun were built to look like lemons or bananas. I am told that in Los Angeles there was the Toed Inn, a strange spelling for a strange place shaped like a giant toad. Customers entered through the mouth, like flies being swallowed.

But the mature nation has put away such childish things in favor of menus that are fun, fun, fun. Seafood is "From Neptune's Pantry" or "Denizens of the Briny Deep." And "Surf 'N Turf," which you might think is fish and horsemeat, actually is lobster and beef.

To be fair, there are practical considerations behind the asphyxiatingly cute names given hamburgers. Many hamburgers are made from portions of the cow that the cow had no reason to boast about. So sellers invent distracting names to give hamburgers cachet. Hence "Whoppers" and "Heroburgers."

But there is no excuse for Howard Johnson's menu. In a just society it would be a flogging offense to speak of "steerburgers," clams "fried to order" (which probably means they don't fry clams for you unless you order fried clams), a "natural cut" (what is an "unnatural" cut?) of sirloin, "oven-baked" meat loaf, chicken pot pie with "flaky crust," "golden croquettes," "grilled-in-butter Frankforts [sic]," "liver with smothered onions" (smothered by onions?), and a "hearty" Reuben sandwich.

America is marred by scores of Dew Drop Inns serving "crispy green" salads, "garden fresh" vegetables, "succulent" lamb, "savory" pork, "sizzling" steaks, and "creamy" or "tangy" coleslaw. I've nothing against Homeric adjectives ("wine-dark sea," "wing-footed Achilles") but isn't coleslaw just coleslaw? Americans hear the incessant roar of commerce without listening to it, and read the written roar without really noticing it. Who would notice if a menu proclaimed "creamy" steaks and "sizzling" coleslaw? Such verbal litter is to language as Muzak is to music. As advertising blather becomes the nation's normal idiom, language becomes printed noise.

Discussing Ideas and Themes

1. Will opens with a reference to "reasonable" people. Cite one or two of his examples of such people: what qualities make them reasonable? Do these qualities have anything to do with the use of reason, or not?
2. Will briefly digresses to discuss some of the odd-shaped restaurants of America's past. What does he think of these establishments? Do you think he would eat in a restaurant shaped like a giant toad?
3. Will objects to the "plague of cuteness in American commerce," but he doesn't define exactly what he means. How would you define cuteness, given his examples? Do you think that it is a prevalent quality in food advertising, or have other characteristics taken its place?
4. Will asserts that there is "no excuse" for the Howard Johnson's menu. What excuses might you come up with for this menu? Do you find this type of marketing as unpalatable as Will does?

Discussing Rhetoric and Style

1. The title of Will's essay is an oxymoron (a paradox compressed into two adjacent words): "print" cannot literally make "noise." What is the metaphor that informs this oxymoron? What are the connotations of the word noise, as opposed, for example, to sound? How do these connotations help make the essay's title make sense?
2. Early on, Will confesses that he likes a particular kind of ice cream, which makes him seem like a regular person—like us, he

eats ice cream and has a favorite flavor. He then asserts that he can't bring himself to order "Nutty Buddy." How does this technique help his credibility? What else does he do to establish his appeal?

3. How does Will use allusions and examples in this essay? For instance, what is the effect of following the example of the man who refused to order a "Yumbo" with the example of the Cambridge don? Explain.

4. One of Will's strategies is to suggest that there is a reason behind "the asphyxiatingly cute names given hamburgers." What is the logic of his argument here?

5. How do the examples that Will gives from menus in the last paragraph differ from Homeric adjectives, if at all? For example, what is the difference, really, between saying "wine-dark sea" and "sizzling steak"? Would one have to change the food adjectives much to make them more "Homeric"?

Ideas for Writing

1. Write an essay in defense of "printed noise." You should pick a position to write from—for example, you might want to write as if you were an owner of a McDonald's or a Burger King. Try to be as witty and clever as Will is, but in the opposite cause.

2. Write an analysis modeled after Will's of the advertising for some industry other than food—stereo equipment, for example, or automobiles. Use examples both of actual advertising and of what you consider to be the proper response to it. This should be a critique not so much of the products (though you may want to do that as part of your argument) but of the *language* with which they are marketed.

Whatever Happened to Plain Old Weather?

DAVID B. WILSON

David B. Wilson is a journalist and popular columnist for the Boston Globe *whose work often reflects a satirist's concern with the rise of popular conventions as well as the passing of traditional ones. The following essay, which appeared as one of Wilson's syndicated columns, laments the passing of old-fashioned, fact-based weather reports. An observation of various forecasting styles, the essay is itself stylized, balancing traditional argument with a snappy, slang-informed sense of humor.*

Once upon a time, a long time ago, before the tube began to make boobs of sensible people, there was something called the Weather Report.

It was heard at the end of hourly radio news programs and found ordinarily in the upper right-hand corner of the front page. It used to say things like: "Fair and warmer."

Dull.

But the old-fashioned Weather Report had its advantages. It didn't take long. It was terse and unequivocal, even if frequently wrong. You knew where to find it and what it was trying to say.

Meteorology, after all, is light entertainment masquerading as pseudo-science. At best, it ranks in credibility somewhere near astrology, phrenology and the analysis of entrails. Sensible people, even in this climate, consult wind and sky and go about their business without paying it too much attention.

Instead of the Weather Report, America now has The Weather,

which is quite another kettle of bouillabaisse, during which the "meteorologist" makes a point of not getting to the point.

It is trash news, pseudo-news, nonnews, glitzy junk, consisting largely of laborious flirtation between the female anchor and the weather person, who was hired because he is what high school sophomore girls used to call "cute."

North America lurches around the screen. Atmospheric ordeals afflict Utah and North Dakota. Radar and satellite photographs are supplemented with wiggly whatzits that snake across the continent.

If you manage to stay awake through all the grinning and giggling sparkling, you may be able to catch the forecast, which not infrequently consists of an admission that on the morrow there will, indeed, be some sort of weather.

All of which would be merely annoying were it not for the impact of The Weather on the rest of the news. The Weather is Gresham's Law news, cheap currency driving out dear.

The Weather is popular because weather is simple. There are only about six kinds: fair, cloudy, warmer, colder, rain and snow, plus a few subspecies. The audience is familiar with the subject. Weather does not perplex the dull of wit with big words or abstractions. By placing the forecast at the end of the copy, the producer teases his audience into paying attention not only to the fluff from Cut Bank, Mont., Bemidji, Minn., and Fitchburg, Mass., but also to the interlarded commercials.

Real news is expensive, requiring astute news directors, reporters who can talk and know what they're talking about, skilled camera crews, aircraft, vehicles and some familiarity with the community and its history. No such costly difficulties interfere with the production of The Weather.

The Weather is cheap. The hard data are furnished gratis by the government. The stage setting has a two-year life. Hoke up some visuals, prop a blow-dried yuppie up in front of them and your cost is his pay.

When great storms threaten or strike, two or three times a year, maybe, the weather becomes real news. Meanwhile, glittering sagas of moisture and sunshine must be concocted to fill the time between commercials. TV clearly is equal to the task.

Where is the broadcaster courageous enough to present brief, simple forecasts, introduced by an audio signature and delivered by a distinctive, anonymous voice, at the beginning and end of news programs? Such a policy would free up enough time to enrich a half-hour program with two or more additional hard news stories, add breadth and depth to lead pieces or permit a national and foreign summary of distinction.

Discussing Issues and Themes

1. Make a list of five differences that Wilson observes between the "old-fashioned Weather Report" and today's "Weather." Can you add some that he doesn't mention?
2. Why does Wilson prefer the old-fashioned Weather Report? Where does he explain his reasons? Cite the passage.
3. What, according to Wilson, is the difference between "the Weather" and "the real news." Do you agree?
4. Do you agree that "the Weather is popular because weather is simple"? What does such a statement imply about the audience for weather forecasts? About the author of this essay?
5. On what note does the essay end? Is the last paragraph conclusive, didactic, sarcastic? Does it reveal any purpose or thesis that had been previously unclear?

Discussing Rhetoric and Style

1. The essay makes use of various literary conventions—for instance, the fairy tale "once-upon-a-time" opening. Can you find any similar moments in the essay that draw on familiar forms or conventions? Do you recognize where the conventions originate?
2. Consider the first sentence of Wilson's essay. What two dictions does he mingle here? What is the effect of the mix of dictions—for instance, does it produce irony, sarcasm, light humor?
3. Wilson's prose slips easily into lists—for instance, "trash news, pseudo-news, nonnews, glitzy junk" or "astrology, phrenology, and the study of entrails." Consider the structure of one of these lists. Is it arranged climactically or anticlimactically, carefully or arbitrarily? Which item in the list is stressed? Is there a logical relationship among the items in the list?
4. Reread paragraph seven, considering Wilson's choice of verbs. Why does he use such frenetic words—"lurch," "afflict," and "snake"—to describe the weather? What connotations attach to each of these words? How useful are these associations? Explain.
5. Consider Wilson's style. How is it like or unlike the weather forecasts he describes? In answering, list some of the adjectives

Wilson uses to describe old and new forecasting styles. Which ones could be applied to this essay?

Ideas for Writing

1. Wilson's essay is set up as a simple comparison/contrast—it is a before-and-after, then-and-now piece. Write an essay that is similarly structured describing some particular aspect of life in high school and life in college, or what you looked like before a haircut and what you looked like after one. Whatever you choose, make it brief—one to two pages.
2. Wilson eulogizes an old ritual while deflating a newer one. Pick a comparison that can be similarly treated—old and new movies, traditional courtships and modern romance—and write an essay modeled on Wilson's. What difficulties do you have in balancing praise with irony?

On Reading Trash

BOB SWIFT

Born in North Carolina in 1929, Bob Swift has worked in the newspaper business in Florida most of his life. Once the editor of the Miami Herald's *"Home and Design" section as well as a columnist for* Newsweek *and an editor for the* Miami Beach Sun, *Swift now devotes his time to a nationally syndicated column, where the following essay appeared. Swift's concerns range from family matters to "life in general," as the following essay, with its surprising premise, illustrates.*

If you want kids to become omnivorous readers, let them read trash. That's my philosophy, and I speak from experience.

I don't disagree with The National Endowment for the Humanities, which says every high school graduate should have read 30 great works of literature, including the Bible, Plato, Shakespeare, Hawthorne, the Declaration of Independence, *Catcher in the Rye, Crime and Punishment* and *Moby Dick.*

It's a fine list. Kids should read them all, and more. But they'll be better readers if they start off on trash. Trash? What I mean is what some might call "popular" fiction. My theory is, if you get kids interested in reading books—no matter what sort—they will eventually go on to the grander literature all by themselves.

In the third grade I read my first novel, a mystic adventure set in India. I still recall the sheer excitement at discovering how much fun reading could be.

When we moved within walking distance of the public library a whole new world opened. In the library I found that wonder of wonders, the series. What a thrill, to find a favorite author had written a dozen or more other titles.

I read a series about frontiersmen, learning about Indian tribes, beef jerky and tepees. A Civil War series alternated young heroes from the Blue and the Gray, and I learned about Grant and Lee and the Rock of Chickamauga.

One summer, in Grandpa Barrow's attic, I discovered the Mother Lode, scores of dusty books detailing the adventures of Tom Swift, The Rover Boys, The Submarine Boys, The Motorcycle Boys and Bomba the Jungle Boy. It didn't matter that some were written in 1919; any book you haven't read is brand new.

Another summer I discovered Edgar Rice Burroughs. I swung through jungles with Tarzan, fought green Martians with John Carter, explored Pellucidar at the Earth's core, flew through the steamy air of Venus with Carson Napier. Then I came across Sax Rohmer and, for book after book, prowled opium dens with Nayland Smith, in pursuit of the insidious Fu Manchu.

In the seventh grade, I ran across Booth Tarkington's hilarious Penrod books and read them over and over.

My cousin went off to war in 1942 and gave me his pulp magazines. I became hooked on Doc Savage, The Shadow, G8 and His Battle Aces, The Spider, Amazing Stories. My folks wisely did not object to them as trash. I began to look in second-hand book shops for past issues, and found a Blue Book Magazine, with an adventure story by Talbot Mundy. It led me back to the library, for more of Mundy's Far East thrillers. From Mundy, my path led to A. Conan Doyle's *The Lost World,* Rudyard Kipling's *Kim,* Jules Verne, H. G. Wells and Jack London.

Before long I was whaling with Herman Melville, affixing scarlet letters with Hawthorne and descending into the maelstrom with Poe. In due course came Hemingway, Dos Passos, *Hamlet, The Odyssey, The Iliad, Crime and Punishment.* I had discovered "real" literature by following the trail of popular fiction.

When our kids were small, we read aloud to them from Doctor Dolittle and Winnie the Pooh. Soon they learned to read, and favored the "Frog and Toad" and "Freddie the Pig" series.

When the old Doc Savage and Conan the Barbarian pulps were reissued as paperbacks, I brought them home. The kids devoured them, sometimes hiding them behind textbooks at school, just as I had. They read my old Tarzan and Penrod books along with Nancy Drew and *The Black Stallion.*

Now they're big kids. Each kid's room is lined with bookshelves, on which are stacked, in an eclectic mix, Doc Savage, Plato, Louis L'Amour westerns, Thomas Mann, Gothic romances, Agatha Christie, Sartre, Edgar Allen Poe, science-fiction, Saul Bellow, Shakespeare, Pogo, Greek tragedies, Hemingway, Kipling, Tarzan, *Zen and the Art of Motorcycle Maintenance,* F. Scott Fitzgerald, Bomba the Jungle Boy, Nietzsche, *The Iliad,* Dr. Dolittle, Joseph Conrad, Fu Manchu, Hawthorne, Penrod, Dostoevsky, Ray Bradbury, Herman

Melville, Fitzgerald, Conan the Barbarian . . . more. Some great literature, some trash, but all good reading.

Discussing Ideas and Themes

1. How does Swift define trash? Would you use the same definition? Think of books you have read that might merit this appellation.
2. Swift suggests that "any book you haven't read is brand new." Do you, or people you know who read such stuff, think so? What, in your opinion, is today's most popular trash?
3. Swift lumps together several genres of written material—comic books, adventure stories, epic poetry. . . . In your experience, are most readers as omnivorous as he suggests he and his children were?
4. Does Swift value trash over great literature or great literature over trash? His essay suggests that he refuses to place a value judgment on one over the other, but do you find this to be true? Explain.
5. What model of education is Swift proposing here? What should the role of formal schooling be in such a model?

Discussing Rhetoric and Style

1. What is the effect of Swift's opening gambit? What response does he solicit with his first sentence? Explain.
2. How does Swift manipulate words like "philosophy" and "theory"? Does he sound like a philosopher or a theorist?
3. Most of Swift's essay is made up of lists of examples. How does he arrange these lists? What are the effects of his arrangement?
4. What is the logic behind Swift's paragraphing in this essay? What do the paragraphs separate? How does each new paragraph move the argument along?

Ideas for Writing

1. Write out several lists, either of reading materials or of some other collection, such as recordings of music or foods. Try

arranging these lists in different ways—grouping all the trash together, for example, or mixing up popular items and "high culture" items—and then pick one array and write a short essay that cites these lists to support an argument.

2. Write an essay based on your experience in which you describe and discuss the ways you read. Your essay should be part anecdote (telling your own experience) and part analysis (telling what it means or suggests). Does your experience support or contradict Swift's argument?

The Language of Batman

DANIEL MORAN

Dan Moran, a student at Rutgers University, may be a fan of Batman's, but he is also a critical observer of the technique and style of Batman *comics as they have evolved from the 1940s to the present. In "The Language of Batman," Moran fittingly pits Batman against the Joker, pointing out how one character acts as a foil to the other: "The Joker," he argues, "is the perfect archenemy for Batman because he is the Caped Crusader's opposite in so many different ways." Offering detailed discussions on the qualities of each character's voice—both alone and as it interacts with the other—Moran concludes that style is meaning for both Batman and the Joker: they are what they speak. The essay was written in 1989 especially for this book.*

A comic book hero is only as good as his villain. The Joker is the perfect archenemy for Batman because he is the Caped Crusader's opposite in so many different ways. Batman is a shadowy "Dark Knight," while the Joker's colorful costume guarantees him the center of attention. The Joker's face is fixed in a permanent grin while Batman rarely finds *anything* funny. Batman avoids publicity and strives to keep his identity secret; the Joker frequently announces his crimes to Batman and Gotham City beforehand. It is not only these immediately recognizable characteristics, however, which make the Joker so memorable and—like Iago—entertaining even in his most evil moments; it is also his means of expression that mark him as an enemy not only of Batman's values but of his language as well.

In his early years the persona of millionaire playboy Bruce Wayne carried over into Batman's speech, causing him to utter happy-go-lucky remarks each time he beat someone unconscious:

Batman vs. the Joker has him smashing a chair over a gunsel's head and saying, "Have a seat!"; and before punching the Joker for the very first time, he exclaims, "You may be the Joker, but I'm the King of Clubs."

It wasn't until the early 1970s, when comic books began taking themselves more seriously, that Batman's language adopted a weightier and more deadpan tone. Most of his speech was in the mode of narration, either narration of detective work or a mêlée in which he was able to think three seconds ahead of everybody else ("Three guards. The one in the middle comes after me. I decide to put him in a headlock while another one pulls out a knife. . . ." etc.) In the 1980s, with the publication of Frank Miller's brilliant *The Dark Knight Returns* series, Batman's speech has become more sparse and (unlike the Batman of the 1940s) stern:

> THUG WHOM BATMAN HAS JUST THROWN THROUGH WINDOW: No! Stay back! I got rights!
>
> BATMAN: You've got rights. Lots of rights. Sometimes I count them just to make myself feel crazy. But right now you've got a piece of glass shoved into a major artery in your arm. Right now you're bleeding to death. Right now I'm the only one who can get you to a hospital in time.

This is a far cry from when Batman punched a circus strongman and said, "You may have steel muscles, but I'm afraid you have a glass jaw!"

When nonviolently addressing the Joker, Batman tries to be rational and persuasive. Alan Moore's critically and commercially successful *The Killing Joke* begins with Batman visiting a person he thinks is the Joker in Arkham Asylum:

> Hello. I came to talk. I've been thinking lately. About you and me. About what's going to happen to us in the end. We're going to kill each other, aren't we? Perhaps you'll kill me. Perhaps I'll kill you. Perhaps sooner. Perhaps later. I just wanted to know that I'd made a genuine attempt to talk things over and avert that outcome. Just once.

Batman knows that the Joker is insane, not stupid, and tries to appeal to him as a "thinking man." The problem is that when Batman says things like, "We could work together. I could rehabilitate you" (44), the Joker responds with a joke whose punch line is, "What do you think I am—crazy?" (45).

Like Mercutio, the Joker loves to talk and often places as much emphasis on his oration as his crimes; like Mark Twain, he is always stretching jokes to their furthest limits. Once again, *The Killing Joke* provides an excellent example: after shooting Barbara Gordon, a librarian and daughter of Police Commissioner Gordon, through the stomach, causing her to crash through a glass table, the Joker tells her father:

> Please don't worry. It's a psychological complaint amongst ex-librarians. You see, she thinks she's a coffee table edition. . . . Mind you, I can't say much for the volume's condition. I mean, there's a hole in the jacket and the spine appears to be damaged. Frankly, she won't be walking off the shelves in that state of repair. In fact, the idea of her walking anywhere seems increasingly remote. But then, that's always a problem with softbacks. God, [raising a glass of champagne] these literary discussions are so dry. . . . (14)

This speech comes little by little as the Joker makes it up; one joke isn't enough for him, so he keeps rolling until he exhausts his supply. In Part IV of *A Death in the Family,* the Joker (now the Iranian Ambassador to the U.N.) makes a similar speech to the General Assembly, beginning with "I am proud to speak for the great Islamic Republic of Iran. That country's current leaders and I have a lot in common. Insanity and a great love of fish" (13). It seems natural that someone with the Joker's talent would get a job in politics.

The Joker is also fond of adapting clichés to suit his purposes. "If the police try to play against the Joker they had best be prepared to be dealt from the bottom of the deck!" he exclaims in *Batman vs. the Joker* (13). After giving an ex-gang member a cigar laced with nitroglycerin, he remarks, "Rest in pieces" (*The Joker's Five-Way Revenge,* 7). While trying to drive Commissioner Gordon insane, the Joker sings to him, "And if life should treat you bad,/Don't get ee-ee-even—get mad!" (*The Killing Joke,* 25). In *Dreadful Birthday, Dear Joker,* Robin screams, "Batman—no! You can't trust him," to which the Joker explains to Batman, "Out of the mouths of babes and all that" (13–14).

As long as the writers of DC Comics keep the Joker on the payroll, they will have to satisfy his insatiable appetite for oratorical competition. As he tells Batman in *Sign of the Joker,* "I want you to hear all my best lines!" (13). Fans of "The Clown Prince of Crime" can only hope that they all haven't been heard yet.

Discussing Issues and Themes

1. Why is the Joker the perfect villain for Batman? Cite several of Moran's reasons.
2. What is the difference between the Batman of early years and the later Batman? How does Moran illustrate the difference?
3. Near the end of his essay, Moran comments that "it seems natural that someone with the Joker's talent would get a job in politics." What does Moran imply about politics? Why would the Joker's talents be particularly suited to that arena?
4. Moran suggests that future editions of the *Batman* series will provide "oratorical competition" for the Joker. In what ways (according to Moran) is the Joker an "oratorical" character? Does he share traits with any of the great orators (for instance, Satan in *Paradise Lost* or Tennyson's Ulysses)?

Discussing Rhetoric and Style

1. Moran bases his essay on the topic of contrast: privacy vs. exhibitionism; humor vs. seriousness; the Joker's language vs. Batman's. Is this a valid model (from what you can tell from the examples)? Does Moran ever deviate from it?
2. Moran, setting up a contrast between Batman and the Joker, also sets up a comparison between the Joker and Iago and later between the Joker and Mercutio. How effective are these comparisons amid so many contrasts?
3. Consider Moran's rhetorical analysis of Batman's visit to the Joker in the asylum. Do you agree that Batman treats the Joker as a "thinking man"? For instance, do you find Batman's lines to be thoughtful and rational? Explain.
4. Moran's essay starts with one idea and ends with another. Paraphrase each idea, and then find the transition point in the essay.
5. Moran mixes a historical survey of comic books with his critical analysis of the relationship between Batman and the Joker. How do you respond to this technique? Can you hear a shift in voice? If so, where?

Ideas for Writing

1. Consider Moran's essay in light of Bob Swift's ("On Reading Trash"). Do you consider *Batman* comic books to be trash? And if so, does Moran's essay illustrate Swift's point?
2. Pick a favorite comic book or cartoon character—for example, Popeye or Snoopy, and do a stylistic analysis of that character's interaction with another character in the strip—say, Brutus or Charlie Brown. Can you base your analysis on contrasts such as Moran's?

CHAPTER 7

Language and Advertising

Whether willingly or not, most people spend a good deal of time listening to the language of advertisement. Advertising pervades the American environment today to a degree undreamt of before the growth of a mass economy coincided with the growth of a mass media. Advertising always has brought out strong sentiments from its audience. The essays in this section explore some of the issues that continue to evoke emotion.

Emotions in response to advertising are frequently negative; in "The Rhetoric of Democracy," however, historian Daniel Boorstin, a former Librarian of Congress, finds that the style of American advertising is deeply rooted in an American manner of speech traditionally associated with the "tall tale" of the western frontier. Boorstin explores how this and other aspects of our culture have become a part of American advertising style.

Carol Caldwell examines a particular tall tale in the next selection, "You Haven't Come a Long Way, Baby." Caldwell analyzes the techniques by which one advertising campaign has attempted to flatter the "advanced" views of its intended audience in order to advance sales of the cigarettes it promotes.

In "Teaching from the Classifieds," Andy Rooney takes a lighthearted view of the form that almost all advertising originally took. Rooney suggests that people can be taught to sharpen the skills needed to distinguish between what is meant and what is said in advertising by turning the classified columns into teaching tools.

Martin Esslin finds a more elevated tradition at work. In "Aristotle and the Advertisers," he discusses how when enormous financial pressures act on narrow sales opportunities, the brief commercial must fall back on the basic principles involved in creating audience interest. Many of these principles, as Esslin shows, were described long ago by Aristotle in his analysis of drama.

Advertisement has traditionally been regulated by "blue" laws, which seek on moral grounds to encourage or discourage certain language and the products described by that language. The recent promotion of condoms as a means of limiting the spread of AIDS has brought many traditional taboos into question. Television critic John Correy discusses the arguments pro and con in "The Question of Condom Ads."

Is nothing sacred to the advertising industry? Is nothing safe from commercial exploitation? May advertising use *anything* that it thinks will guarantee a momentary attention to its wares? Jon Wiener gives some sad answers to these questions in "Beatles Buy-Out."

The VCR is one of the latest forms through which advertisement is transmitted and a form that is itself advertised extensively. Student writer George Galuschak analyzes one example in "Fun Video," where he describes many of the techniques used by advertisers to transform pain and deprivation magically into pleasure and contentment—all for the price of a reel of tape.

The Rhetoric of Democracy

DANIEL J. BOORSTIN

A Librarian of Congress, Daniel Boorstin is a respected historian and the author of numerous books, including a Pulitzer Prize-winning history called The Americans. *The following essay, taken from his book,* Democracy and its Discontents, *suggests an essential link between advertising and American democracy: Boorstin writes, "advertising has been part of the mainstream of American civilization" even from its earliest days. "It has been one of the enticements to the settlement of this New World, it has been a producer of the peopling of the United States, and in its modern form, in its world-wide reach, it has been one of our most characteristic products."*

Advertising, of course, has been part of the mainstream of American civilization, although you might not know it if you read the most respectable surveys of American history. It has been one of the enticements to the settlement of this New World, it has been a producer of the peopling of the United States, and in its modern form, in its world-wide reach, it has been one of our most characteristic products.

Never was there a more outrageous or more unscrupulous or more ill-informed advertising campaign than that by which the promoters for the American colonies brought settlers here. Brochures published in England in the seventeenth century, some even earlier, were full of hopeful overstatements, half-truths, and downright lies, along with some facts which nowadays surely would be the basis for a restraining order from the Federal Trade Commission. Gold and silver, fountains of youth, plenty of fish, venison without limit, all these were promised, and of course some of them were found. It would be interesting to speculate on how long it might have taken to settle this continent if there had not been such promotion by enterprising advertisers. How has American civilization been shaped by the fact that there was a kind of natural selection here of those people who were willing to believe advertising?

Advertising has taken the lead in promising and exploiting the new. This was a new world, and one of the advertisements for it appears on the dollar bill on the Great Seal of the United States, which reads *novus ordo seclorum*, one of the most effective advertising slogans to come out of this country. "A new order of the centuries"—belief in novelty and in the desirability of opening novelty to everybody has been important in our lives throughout our history and especially in this century. Again and again advertising has been an agency for inducing Americans to try anything and everything—from the continent itself to a new brand of soap. As one of the more literate and poetic of the advertising copywriters, James Kenneth Frazier, a Cornell graduate, wrote in 1900 in "The Doctor's Lament":

> This lean M.D. is Dr. Brown
> Who fares but ill in Spotless Town.
> The town is so confounded clean,
> It is no wonder he is lean,
> He's lost all patients now, you know,
> Because they use *Sapolio*.

The same literary talent that once was used to retail Sapolio was later used to induce people to try the Edsel or the Mustang, to experiment with Lifebuoy or Body-All, to drink Pepsi-Cola or Royal Crown Cola, or to shave with a Trac II razor.

And as expansion and novelty have become essential to our economy, advertising has played an ever-larger role: in the settling of the continent, in the expansion of the economy, and in the building of an American standard of living. Advertising has expressed the optimism, the hyperbole, and the sense of community, the sense of reaching which has been so important a feature of our civilization.

Here I wish to explore the significance of advertising, not as a force in the economy or in shaping an American standard of living, but rather as a touchstone of the ways in which we Americans have learned about all sorts of things.

The problems of advertising are of course not peculiar to advertising, for they are just one aspect of the problems of democracy. They reflect the rise of what I have called Consumption Communities and Statistical Communities, and many of the special problems of advertising have arisen from our continuously energetic effort to give everybody everything.

If we consider democracy not just as a political system, but as a set of institutions which do aim to make everything available to everybody, it would not be an overstatement to describe advertising as the characteristic rhetoric of democracy. One of the tendencies of democracy, which Plato and other anti-democrats warned against a long time ago, was the danger that rhetoric would displace or at least overshadow epistemology; that is, *the temptation to allow the problem of persuasion to overshadow the problem of knowledge.* Democratic societies tend to become more concerned with what people believe than with what is true, to become more concerned with credibility than with truth. All these problems become accentuated in a large-scale democracy like ours, which possesses all the apparatus of modern industry. And the problems are accentuated still further by universal literacy, by instantaneous communication, and by the daily plague of words and images.

In the early days it was common for advertising men to define advertisements as a kind of news. The best admen, like the best journalists, were supposed to be those who were able to make their news the most interesting and readable. This was natural enough, since the verb to "advertise" originally meant, intransitively, to take note or to consider. For a person to "advertise" meant originally, in the fourteenth and fifteenth centuries, to reflect on something, to think about something. Then it came to mean, transitively, to call the attention of another to something, to give him notice, to notify, admonish, warn or inform in a formal or impressive manner. And then, by the sixteenth century, it came to mean: to give notice of anything, to make generally known. It was not until the late eighteenth century that the word "advertising" in English came to have a specifically "advertising" connotation as we might say today, and not until the late nineteenth century that it began to have a specifically commercial connotation. By 1879 someone was saying, "Don't advertise unless you have something worth advertising." But even into the present century, newspapers continue to call themselves by the title "Advertiser"—for example, the Boston *Daily Advertiser,* which was a newspaper of long tradition and one of the most dignified papers in Boston until William Randolph Hearst took it over in 1917. Newspapers carried "Advertiser" on their mastheads, not because they sold advertisements but because they brought news.

Now, the main role of advertising in American civilization came increasingly to be that of persuading and appealing rather than that of educating and informing. By 1921, for instance, one of the more popular textbooks, Blanchard's *Essentials of Advertising,* began: "Anything employed to influence people favorably is advertising. The mission of advertising is to persuade men and women to act in a way that will be of advantage to the advertiser." This development—in a country where a shared, a rising, and a democratized standard of living was the national pride and the national hallmark—meant that advertising had become the rhetoric of democracy.

What, then, were some of the main features of modern American advertising—if we consider it as a form of rhetoric? First, and perhaps most obvious, is *repetition*. It is hard for us to realize that the use of repetition in advertising is not an ancient device but a modern one, which actually did not come into common use in American journalism until just past the middle of the nineteenth century.

The development of what came to be called "iteration copy" was a result of a struggle by a courageous man of letters and advertising pioneer, Robert Bonner, who bought the old New York *Merchant's Ledger* in 1851 and turned it into a popular journal. He then had the temerity to try to change the ways of James Gordon Bennett, who of course was one of the most successful of the American newspaper pioneers, and who was both a sensationalist and at the same time an extremely stuffy man when it came to things that he did not consider to be news. Bonner was determined to use advertisements in Bennett's wide-circulating New York *Herald* to sell his own literary product, but he found it difficult to persuade Bennett to allow him to use any but agate type in his advertising. (Agate was the smallest type used by newspapers in that day, only barely legible to the naked eye.) Bennett would not allow advertisers to use larger type, nor would he allow them to use illustrations except stock cuts, because he thought it was undignified. He said, too, that to allow a variation in the format of ads would be undemocratic. He insisted that all advertisers use the same size type so that no one would be allowed to prevail over another simply by presenting his message in a larger, more clever, or more attention-getting form.

Finally Bonner managed to overcome Bennett's rigidity by leasing whole pages of the paper and using the tiny agate type to form larger letters across the top of the page. In this way he produced a message such as "Bring home the New York Ledger tonight." His were unimaginative messages, and when repeated all across the page they technically did not violate Bennett's agate rule. But they opened a new era and presaged a new freedom for advertisers in their use of the newspaper page. Iteration copy—the practice of presenting prosaic content in ingenious, repetitive form—became common, and nowadays of course is commonplace.

A second characteristic of American advertising which is not unrelated to this is the development of *an advertising style*. We have histories of most other kinds of style—including the style of many unread writers who are remembered today only because they have been forgotten—but we have very few accounts of the history of advertising style, which of course is one of the most important forms of our language and one of the most widely influential.

The development of advertising style was the convergence of several very respectable American traditions. One of these was the tradition of the "plain style," which the Puritans made so much of and which accounts for so much of the strength of the Puritan literature. The "plain style" was of course much influenced by the Bible and found its way into the rhetoric of American writers and speakers of great power like Abraham Lincoln. When advertising began to be self-conscious in the early years of this century, the pioneers urged copywriters not to be too clever, and especially not to be fancy. One of the pioneers of the advertising copywriters, John Powers, said, for example, "The commonplace is the proper level for writing in business; where the first virtue is plainness, 'fine writing' is not only intellectual, it is offensive." George P. Rowell, another advertising pioneer, said, "You must write your advertisement to catch damned fools—not college professors." He was a very tactful person. And he added, "And you'll catch just as many college professors as you will of any other sort." In the 1920s, when advertising was beginning to come into its own, Claude Hopkins, whose name is known to all in the trade, said, "Brilliant writing has no place in advertising. A unique style takes attention from the subject. Any apparent effort to sell creates corresponding resistance. . . . One should be natural and simple. His language should not be conspicuous. In fishing for buyers, as in fishing for bass, one should not reveal the hook." So there developed a characteristic advertising style in which plainness, the phrase that anyone could understand, was a distinguishing mark.

At the same time, the American advertising style drew on another, and what might seem an antithetic, tradition—the tradition of hyperbole and tall talk, the language of Davy Crockett and Mike Fink. While advertising could think of itself as 99.44 percent pure, it used the language of "Toronado" and "Cutlass." As I listen to the radio in Washington, I hear a celebration of heroic qualities which would make the characteristics of Mike Fink and Davy Crockett pale, only to discover at the end of the paean that what I have been hearing is a description of the Ford dealers in the District of Columbia neighborhood. And along with the folk tradition of hyperbole and tall talk comes the rhythm of folk music. We hear that Pepsi-Cola hits the spot, that it's for the young generation—and we hear other products celebrated in music which we cannot forget and sometimes don't want to remember.

There grew somehow out of all these contradictory tendencies—combining the commonsense language of the "plain style," and the fantasy language of "tall talk"—an advertising style. This characteristic way of talking about things was especially designed to reach and catch the millions. It created a whole new world of myth. A myth, the dictionary tells us, is a notion based more on tradition or convenience than on facts; it is a received ideal. Myth is not just fantasy and not just fact but exists in a limbo, in the world of the "Will to Believe," which William James has written about so eloquently and so perceptively. This is the world of the neither true nor false—of the statement that 60 percent of the physicians who expressed a choice said that our brand of aspirin would be more effective in curing a simple headache than any other leading brand.

That kind of statement exists in a penumbra. I would call this the "advertising penumbra." It is not untrue, and yet, in its connotation it is not exactly true.

Now, there is still another characteristic of advertising so obvious that we are inclined perhaps to overlook it. I call that *ubiquity.* Advertising abhors a vacuum and we discover new vacuums every day. The parable, of course, is the story of the man who thought of putting the advertisement on the other side of the cigarette package. Until then, that was wasted space and a society which aims at a democratic standard of living, at extending the benefits of consumption and all sorts of things and services to everybody, must miss no chances to reach people. The highway billboard and other outdoor advertising, bus and streetcar and subway advertising, and skywriting, radio and TV commercials—all these are of course obvious evidence that advertising abhors a vacuum.

We might reverse the old mousetrap slogan and say that anyone who can devise another place to put another mousetrap to catch a consumer will find people beating a path to his door. "Avoiding advertising will become a little harder next January," the *Wall Street Journal* reported on May 17, 1973, "when a Studio City, California, company launches a venture called StoreVision. Its product is a system of billboards that move on a track across supermarket ceilings. Some 650 supermarkets so far are set to have the system." All of which helps us to understand the observation attributed to a French man of letters during his recent visit to Times Square. "What a beautiful place, if only one could not read!" Everywhere is a place to be filled, as we discover in a recent *Publishers Weekly* description of one advertising program: "The $1.95 paperback edition of Dr. Thomas A. Harris' million-copy best-seller 'I'm O.K., You're O.K.' is in for full-scale promotion in July by its publisher, Avon Books. Plans range from bumper stickers to airplane streamers, from planes flying above Fire Island, the Hamptons and Malibu. In addition, the $100,000 promotion budget calls for 200,000 bookmarks, plus brochures, buttons, lipcards, floor and counter displays, and advertising in magazines and TV."

The ubiquity of advertising is of course just another effect of our uninhibited efforts to use all the media to get all sorts of information to everybody everywhere. Since the places to be filled are everywhere, the amount of advertising is not determined by the *needs* of advertising, but by the *opportunities* for advertising which become unlimited.

But the most effective advertising, in an energetic, novelty-ridden society like ours, tends to be "self-liquidating." To create a cliché you must offer something which everybody accepts. The most successful advertising therefore self-destructs because it becomes cliché. Examples of this are found in the tendency for copyrighted names of trademarks to enter the vernacular—for the proper names of products which have been made familiar by costly advertising to become common nouns, and so to apply to anybody's products. Kodak becomes a synonym for camera, Kleenex a synonym for facial tissue, when both begin with a small *k*, and Xerox (now, too, with a small x) is used to describe all processes of copying, and so on. These are prototypes of the problem. If you are successful enough, then you will defeat your purpose in the long run—by making the name and the message so familiar that people won't notice them, and then people will cease to distinguish your product from everybody else's.

In a sense, of course, as we will see, the whole of American civilization is an example. When this was a "new" world, if people succeeded in building a civilization here, the New World would survive and would reach the time—in our age—when it would cease to be new. And now we have the oldest written Constitution in use in the world. This is only a parable of which there are many more examples.

The advertising man who is successful in marketing any particular product, then—in our high-technology, well-to-do democratic society, which aims to get everything to everybody—is apt to be diluting the demand for his particular product in the very act of satisfying it. But luckily for him, he is at the very same time creating a fresh demand for his services as advertiser.

And as a consequence, there is yet another role which is assigned to American advertising. This is what I call "erasure." Insofar as advertising is competitive or innovation is widespread, erasure is required in order to persuade consumers that this year's model is superior to last year's. In fact, we consumers learn that we might be risking our lives if we go out on the highway with those very devices that were last year's lifesavers but without whatever special kind of brakes or wipers or seat belt is on this year's model. This is what I mean by "erasure"—and we see it on our advertising pages or our television screen every day. We read in the *New York Times* (May 20, 1973), for example, that "For the price of something small and ugly, you can drive something small and beautiful"—an advertisement for the Fiat 250 Spider. Or another, perhaps more subtle example is the advertisement for shirts under a picture of Oliver Drab: "Oliver Drab. A name to remember in fine designer shirts? No kidding. . . . Because you pay extra money for Oliver Drab. And for all the other superstars of the fashion world. Golden Vee [the name of the brand that is advertised] does not have a designer's label. But we do have designers. . . . By keeping their names *off* our label and simply saying Golden Vee, we can afford to sell our $7 to $12 shirts for just $7 to $12, which should make Golden Vee a name to remember. Golden Vee, you only pay for the shirt."

Having mentioned two special characteristics—the self-liquidating tendency and the need for erasure—which arise from the dynamism of the American economy, I would like to try to place advertising in a larger perspective. The special role of advertising in our life gives a clue to a pervasive oddity in American civilization. A leading feature of past cultures, as anthropologists have explained, is the tendency to distinguish between "high" culture and "low" culture—between the culture of the literate and the learned on the one hand and that of the populace on the other. In other words, between the language of literature and the language of the vernacular. Some of the most useful statements of this distinction have been made by social scientists at the University of Chicago—first by the late Robert Redfield in his several pioneering books on peasant society, and then by Milton Singer in his remarkable study of Indian civilization, *When a Great Tradition Modernizes* (1972). This distinction between the great tradition and the little tradition, between the high culture and the folk culture, has begun to become a commonplace of modern anthropology.

Some of the obvious features of advertising in modern America offer us an opportunity to note the significance or insignificance of that distinction for us. Elsewhere I have tried to point out some of the peculiarities of the American attitude toward the *high* culture. There is something distinctive about the place of thought in American life, which I think is not quite what it has been in certain Old World cultures.

But what about distinctive American attitudes to *popular* culture? What is our analogue to the folk culture of other peoples? Advertising gives us some clues—to a characteristically American democratic folk culture. Folk culture is a name for the culture which ordinary people everywhere lean on. It is not the writings of Dante and Chaucer and Shakespeare and Milton, the teachings of Machiavelli and Descartes, Locke or Marx. It is, rather, the pattern of slogans, local traditions, tales, songs, dances, and ditties. And of course holiday observances. Popular culture in other civilizations has been for the most part both an area of continuity with the past, a way in which people reach back into the past and out to their community, and at the same time an area of local variations. An area of individual and amateur expression in which a person has his own way of saying, or notes his mother's way of saying or singing, or his own way of dancing, his own view of folk wisdom and the cliché.

And here is an interesting point of contrast. In other societies outside the United States, it is the *high* culture that has generally been an area of centralized, organized control. In Western Europe, for example, universities and churches have tended to be closely allied to the government. The institutions of higher learning have had a relatively limited access to the people as a whole. This was inevitable, of course, in most parts of the world, because there were so few universities. In England, for example, there were only two universities until the early nineteenth century. And there was central control over the printed matter that was used in universities or in the liturgy. The government tended to be close to the high culture, and that was easy because the high culture itself was so centralized and because literacy was relatively limited.

In our society, however, we seem to have turned all of this around. Our high culture is one of the least centralized areas of our culture. And our universities express the atomistic, diffused, chaotic, and individualistic aspect of our life. We have in this country more than twenty-five hundred colleges and universities, institutions of so-called higher learning. We have a vast population in these institutions, somewhere over seven million students.

But when we turn to our popular culture, what do we find? We find that in our nation of Consumption Communities and emphasis on Gross National Product (GNP) and growth rates, advertising has become the heart of the folk culture and even its very prototype. And as we have seen, American advertising shows many characteristics of the folk culture of other societies: repetition, a plain style, hyperbole and tall talk, folk verse, and folk music. Folk culture, wherever it has flourished, has tended to thrive in a limbo between fact and fantasy, and of course, depending on the spoken word and the oral tradition, it spreads easily and tends to be ubiquitous. These are all familiar characteristics of folk culture and they are ways of describing our folk culture, but how do the expressions of our peculiar folk culture come to *us*?

They no longer sprout from the earth, from the village, from the farm, or even from the neighborhood or the city. They come to us primarily from enormous centralized self-consciously *creative* (an overused word, for the overuse of which advertising agencies are in no small part responsible) organizations. They come from advertising agencies, from networks of newspapers, radio, and television, from outdoor-advertising agencies, from the copywriters for ads in the largest-circulation magazines, and so on. These "creators" of folk culture—or pseudo-folk culture—aim at the widest intelligibility and charm and appeal.

But in the United States, we must recall, the advertising folk culture (like all advertising) is also confronted with the problems of self-liquidation and erasure. These are by-products of the expansive, energetic character of our economy. And they, too distinguish American folk culture from folk cultures elsewhere.

Our folk culture is distinguished from others by being discontinuous, ephemeral, and self-destructive. Where does this leave the common citizen? All of us are qualified to answer.

In our society, then, those who cannot lean on the world of learning, on the high culture of the classics, on the elaborated wisdom of the books, have a new problem. The University of Chicago, for example, in the 1930's and 1940's was the center of a quest for a "common discourse." The champions of that quest, which became a kind of crusade, believed that such a discourse could be found through familiarity with the classics of great literature—and especially of Western European literature. I think they were misled; such works were not, nor are they apt to become, the common discourse of our society. Most people, even in a democracy, and a rich democracy like ours, live in a world of popular culture, our special kind of popular culture.

The characteristic folk culture of our society is a creature of advertising, and in a sense it *is* advertising. But advertising, our own popular culture, is harder to make into a source of continuity than the received wisdom and commonsense slogans and catchy songs of the vivid vernacular. The popular culture of advertising attenuates and is always dissolving before our very eyes. Among the charms, challenges, and tribulations of modern life, we must count this peculiar fluidity, this ephemeral character of that very kind of culture on which other peoples have been able to lean, the kind of culture to which they have looked for the continuity of their traditions, for their ties with the past and with the future.

We are perhaps the first people in history to have a centrally organized mass-produced folk culture. Our kind of popular culture is here today and gone tomorrow—or the day after tomorrow. Or whenever the next semi-annual model appears. And insofar as folk culture becomes advertising, and advertising becomes centralized, it becomes a way of depriving people of their opportunities for individual and small-community expression. Our technology and our economy and our democratic ideals have all helped make that possible. Here we have a new test of the problem that is at least as old as Heraclitus—an everyday test of man's ability to find continuity in his experience. And here democratic man has a new opportunity to accommodate himself, if he can, to the unknown.

Discussing Issues and Themes

1. How is Boorstin's definition of advertising related to his definition of democracy? Which concept is the essay ultimately about? Explain.
2. Who coined the terms "Consumption Communities" and "Statistical Communities"? What exactly are they? Where do they originate? Why? Explain.
3. List some of the main features of American advertising. Why does Boorstin find these features of rhetorical interest? Do you agree with his classification? Explain your viewpoint with references to the text and to outside advertisements.
4. What does Boorstin have to say about popular culture? What effect does it have on the advertising business and vice versa? Does one define the other, or do they affect each other equally?

Discussing Rhetoric and Style

1. What is the relation of the title to the rest of the essay? Do you find the title appropriate?
2. Where does Boorstin state his thesis? What is it? Does he support it adequately?
3. Find Boorstin's definition of democracy. Has he altered the usual definition for his purposes? Do you think definition is central to his argument?
4. At one point Boorstin alludes to Heraclitus. Can you find other allusions in the essay? What are the advantages of writing an essay rich in allusions?

Ideas for Writing

1. Examine any advertisement, and apply Boorstin's criteria (repetition, style, ubiquity, and so on) to it. Does it follow his pattern? Does it have any features he didn't list?
2. Compare Boorstin's analysis of advertising rhetoric with George Orwell's critique of various political uses of the English language. How do these authors address similar topics? Where do their concerns and ideologies diverge?

You Haven't Come a Long Way, Baby
Women in Television Commercials

CAROL CALDWELL

Carol Caldwell is a freelance writer whose work on popular culture has appeared in national magazines such as Rolling Stone *and* Esquire. *In the following essay, she discusses some of the reasons why advertisers have had little motivation to rethink their ideas about women as consumers. Advertising, Caldwell notes, lags years behind the rest of the media in acknowledging the existence of a feminist audience and tends to represent traditional roles for both men and women. Based on scholarly research, experience in the business, and common sense, Caldwell's essay goes "a long way" in exposing the continuing stereotyping of women by American advertisers. The essay first appeared in* New Times.

It's the beginning of the age of television, and all around it's black and white. Millions of minuscule scan dots collide in electronic explosion to create Woman in her Immaculate Kitchen. She is Alpha, Omega, eternal and everlasting Mother Video, toasting and frying, cleansing and purifying, perfectly formed of fire and ice. Permanent-waved, magenta-lipped, demurely collared and cuffed, cone-shaped from her tightly cinched waist down through yards and yards of material that brush coquettishly midcalf, she is Betty Furness for Westinghouse; and you can be *sure* if it's Westinghouse.

The year is 1951. On the set of CBS-TV's *Studio One,* Furness has just captured the part to become America's first full-time product spokeswoman on television. Advertising execs at Westinghouse are taking a stab at having someone other than the host sell their product; they reason (and quite correctly) that Furness, with her Brearley School cool and her Broadway glamor, is a figure thousands of women will admire and listen to. During the audition Betty alters the script supplied by the casting director. Later, she tells *Time* magazine that she ad-libbed the refrigerator routine because "it was written like men think women talk!"

1952. While John Daly, Bill Henry, and Walter Cronkite monitor Ike and Adlai at the conventions, Betty Furness opens and shuts forty-nine refrigerators, demonstrates the finer points of forty-two television sets, twenty-three dishwashers and twelve ovens for a total of four-and-a-half hours of air time. General Eisenhower is on the air approximately an hour and twenty minutes; Mr. Stevenson, fifty minutes.

1956. Bright and blondeened, twenty-eight-year-old Julia Meade is the commercial spokeswoman for Lincoln on the *Ed Sullivan Show,* for Richard Hudnut hair products on *Your Hit Parade,* for *Life* magazine on John Daly's news show. She is pulling down a hundred thousand dollars a year, which moves *Time* to comment, "Julia (34-20-34) is one of a dozen or so young women on TV who find self-effacement enormously profitable." Howard Wilson, a vice-president of Kenyon & Eckhardt, Lincoln's ad agency, hired Julia for the spots with trepidation: a woman just couldn't be convincing about such things as high torque, turbo drive, and ball-joint suspensions. His fears, it turns out, were unfounded, and Meade becomes the perky prototype for a whole slew of carefully coiffed women selling cars—selling *anything*—by means other than their technical knowledge. And so Julia Meade begat Bess Myerson, who begat Anita Bryant, who begat Carmelita Pope, who begat Florence Henderson, each wholesome, flawless, clear of eye and enunciation, in short, sixty-second reminders of everything the American woman ought to be.

Times change, however, and eventually infant TV's ideal, untouchable dozen spokeswomen were replaced by hundreds of nameless actresses who portray "the little woman" in scenarios believed, by the agencies who create them, to be honest-to-God, middle-American, slice-of-life situations. As early as 1955, this new wave of commercial realism got a pat on the back by the industry's weekly trade paper, *Advertising Age.* Procter & Gamble had just come out with a revolutionary new way to sell soap on TV: "It is very difficult for a soap commercial to emerge from the mass of suds, with every known variant on the familiar theme of the woman holding up a box of "X" soap powder with a grisly smile pointing to a pile of clothes she has just washed. Cheer has come up with the unique approach of dramatizing an everyday washing problem from the poor woman's point of view with a sound-over technique of stream of consciousness."

That stream of consciousness flowed unchecked until Bill Free's famous National Airlines "Fly Me" faux pas in 1971. Women activists carried signs, stormed Free's and National's offices, read proclamations, and permeated the media with protest. Free talks of this trying and critical time with a humor and stoicism that comes from a six-year perspective, and from no longer handling the account. "The women's movement was identifying itself—and our 'Fly Me' campaign was an opportunity for a public platform. We were deluged with letters and calls. I even got an absurd letter from one of the leaders of the movement (who must go unnamed) demanding that I surely planned the sexual innuendo in the word 'fly'—she meant as in men's trouser pants." He paused. "The ad community continues to demean women, far more subtly than in our campaign."

There are some easy hints at why this is so: Of the seventy-five thousand people currently employed in advertising, only 16.7 percent are women in other than clerical positions—not exactly an overwhelming voice. And, while advertising executives often live in the suburbs of large cities, they just as often tend to have a low regard for anyone who isn't an urbanite. As one New York agency executive quipped, "All I really know about the Middle America I sell to everyday is that it's the place I fly over to get to L.A."

But these notations still don't answer the question: Why have advertisers, who make their living keeping up with trends, been so slow to get on board with the women's revolution? Where was everybody the recent night David Brinkley closed the book on America's traditional homelife structure, citing the fact that a mere seven percent of our nation's homes still maintained the time-honored tradition of the everyday housewife. Mom has officially flown the coop just about everywhere, except on TV in the commercials.

At a roundtable on women's advertising sponsored by the agency trade publication *Madison Avenue*, Harriet Rex, a vice-president at J. Walter Thompson, had this comment to make: "There's always been a lag between what is and what the ad business has codified as what 'is.' " And Rena Bartos, a senior VP at the same agency, said, "Advertising may be a mirror of society but somehow the image in that mirror is a little out of focus. It plays back a 1950s reflection in a 1970s world."

Madison Avenue's "little woman" is hardly new, and only partially improved. When feminists cite advertising that is "acceptable," it's invariably print ads. This isn't surprising, since magazine ads are prepared for specific subscribers whose personal backgrounds and attitudes have been carefully documented by the publication and noted by the agency. Television, on the other hand, commands a much larger and subsequently less definable audience.

So it is left to the advertisers and their agencies to define who television's consuming woman might be and what type of commercial she might like. The reward is compelling: Americans heap a total $9.2 billion every year into the coffers of the nation's top three TV advertisers—Procter & Gamble, Bristol-Myers, and General Foods. Still, the women portrayed aren't always to the customers' liking, and last year agitated viewers marched en masse outside P&G headquarters in Cincinnati, suggesting in rather unladylike terms what to do with Mr. Whipple and his grocery store groupies. Inside, P&G stockholders took little heed, voting down a suggestion that their commercial portrayal of women be reconsidered.

Others in the business did listen. When the National Organization for Women sent all major advertising agencies a position paper on the role of women in commercials, no one was surprised that most of the commercials on the air didn't jibe with the NOW requirements. Several agencies, fearing intervention by the Federal Trade Commission, prodded their own regulatory outfit to consider the matter. The National Advertising Review Board formed a panel, including Patricia Carbine, publisher of *Ms.*; Joyce Synder, coordinator of the task force on the image of women for NOW; the vice-presidents of broadcast standards for ABC and NBC; and a number of officers of sponsoring companies. A twenty-one page directive came out in 1975, in which the panel made a number of suggestions concerning ways in which advertisers could improve their portrayal of women. Here's what came out in the wash: "Advertising must be regarded as one of the forces molding society," the study asserted. "Those who protest that advertising merely reflects society must reckon with the criticism that much of the current reflection of women in advertising is out of date." Before airing a commercial, the panel urged advertisers to run down the NARB checklist, which included the following points:

- Are sexual stereotypes perpetuated in my ads? Do they portray women as weak, silly and over-emotional?
- Are the women portrayed in my ads stupid?
- Do my ads portray women as ecstatically happy over household cleanliness or deeply depressed because of their failure to achieve near-perfection in household tasks?
- Do my ads show women as fearful of not being attractive, of not being able to keep their husbands or lovers, fearful of in-law disapproval?
- Does my copy promise unrealistic psychological rewards for using the product?

Well now, does it? With these self-regulatory commandments in mind, I spent four weeks in front of daytime TV, logging current household product commercials and trying to determine just where women stand in the advertising scheme of things. During that time, Iris dickered with Rachel and Mac's teetering marriage, Beth died, Stacy miscarried, and Jennifer killed John's wife so they could finally be together.

Now a word from our sponsors.

Ring around the collar lives. After eight long years, the little woman is still exposing hubby and the kids to this awful embarrassment. It can strike virtually anywhere—in taxis, at ballgames, even on vacation doing the limbo. Our lady of the laundry is always guilty, always lucky to have a next-door neighbor who knows about Wisk, the washday miracle, and always back in hubby's good, but wary, graces by the happy ending. The Wisk woman faces the same unspoken commercial threat that the Geritol woman faces: "My wife, I think I'll keep her . . ." *if* she keeps in line.

Jim Jordan is president of Batten, Barton, Durstine and Osborn Advertising. Eight years ago, in a fit of cosmic inspiration, he came up with "ring around the collar" for his agency's client, Lever Bros. Since then, Jordan has run check-out-counter surveys on his commercials, asking shoppers who were purchasing Wisk, "You must be buying this product because you like the commercials." The reply he got was always the same: "Why no! I hate those commercials; but why should I hold that against the product?"

Jim Jordan echoes advertising's premier axiom: "The purpose of the commercial is not the aesthetic pleasure of the viewer—it's to sell the product." And Wisk is selling like gangbusters. He doesn't believe "ring around the collar" commercials show women in an embarrassing light; and to assume that, he says, "would be giving commercials more credit than they deserve."

Perhaps. And perhaps his "ring around the collar" campaign is getting more credit than it deserves for selling Wisk. Take any commercial with a simple message, repeat it again and again, and the product, if it's good, will sell, even if the spot is mindless and annoying. It's fixing the name of the product in the consumer's mind with a quick, catchy phrase that's important.

The household slice-of-life commercial is one of the classic offenders of the NARB checklist. (Are sexual stereotypes perpetuated? You'd best believe it. Are the women portrayed stupid? And how.) Crisco's current campaign is a flawless example of this much-imitated genre, which has been developed and designed by Procter & Gamble. In it various long-suffering husbands and condescending neighbors are put through the heartache of greasy, gobby chicken and fries, all because some unthinking corner-cutter spent "a few pennies less" on that mainstay of American cookery, lard. These pound-foolish little women cause their loved ones to live through "disasters" and "catastrophes." At the cue word "catastrophe," our video crumples into wavy electronic spasms and thrusts us back to the scene of the crime: to that excruciating point in the Bicentennial picnic or the backyard cookout when Dad has to wrinkle his upper lip and take Mom aside for a little set-to about her greasy chicken. The moral, delivered by an unseen pedantic male announcer, is plain: "Ladies who've learned—buy Crisco."

These examples are, sad to say, still very much the rule for women's portrayals in thirty- and sixty-second spots. They occur with alarming regularity during the daytime hours, when stations may sell up to sixteen commercial minutes an hour. (The nighttime rate is a mere eight minutes, 40 seconds per hour.) Now, you are probably not the average American who spends some six hours a day in front of the old boob tube (which, when the maximum number of commercials per hour is computed, means over an hour and a half of product propaganda). And you probably are quite sure that commercials have absolutely no effect on you. Maybe they don't. But a shaken agency copywriter told me the first word his child spoke was "McDonald's," and I've stood in a grocery store line and watched while a mother, tired of her child's tears, lets him wander off and return—not with a candy bar, but with a roll of Charmin. Make no mistake about it: the cumulative effects of commercials are awesome. As the NARB study argues: "An endless procession of commercials on the same theme, all showing women using household products in the home, raises very strong implications that women have no other interests except laundry, dishes, waxing floors, and fighting dirt in any form. . . . Seeing a great many such advertisements in succession reinforces the traditional stereotype that a "woman's place is *only* in the home."

There have, in the past few years, been commercials that break the homebody mold. The Fantastik spray commercial, "I'm married to a man, not a house" (which, incidentally was written and produced by men), has reaped much praised, as has L'Oreal's "I'm worth it" campaign. "Ten years ago, it would have been, 'John thinks I'm worth it,' " says Lenore Hershey, editor of *Ladies' Home Journal*. *Ms*' Pat Carbine thinks United Airlines is flying right when they address women executives, "You're the boss." She also likes the Campbell's soup "working wife" commercial, in which a man scurries around the kitchen, preparing soup for his woman, but adds, "I'm afraid they took the easy route and resorted to total role reversal—making her look good at the expense of the man."

Indeed, Lois Wyse of Wyse Advertising fears that advertisers are not only failing to talk to today's women, but they're missing men as well. The reason for this, as she sees it, is research—the extensive demographic studies done on who buys what product. Last winter Wyse told *Madison Avenue*, "About twenty years ago we were all little Ozzies and Harriets to all the people who do research, and now their idea of contemporizing is to make the Ozzies into Harriets and the Harriets into Ozzies."

Marketing research, with its charts and graphs and scientific jargon, has increased in importance over the last ten years or so, while creativity, the keystone to the Alka-Seltzer, Volkswagen, and Benson & Hedges campaigns of the sixties, has taken the backseat. Ask anybody in advertising why commercials still show the little woman bumbling around in a fearful daze, and you'll find the answer is always the same: "Because our research tells us it is so." Agencies devote hundreds of thousands of dollars to find out who's buying their client's stuff and why. And it's not just Mom up there on the charts and graphs. Marketing researchers dissect and analyze the buying habits, educational and income levels of every member of the family. They even know what we do with our leisure time, and how much God we've got.

This subjective form of research is amorphously titled life-style research, explained by the respected *Journal of Marketing* in the following brave-new-world lingo: "Life-style data—activities, interests, opinions—have proved their importance as a means of *duplicating* the consumer for the marketing researcher. . . ." And more: "Life-style attempts to answer questions like: What do women think about the job of housekeeping? Do they see themselves as homebodies or swingers? Life-style provides definitions like 'housewife role haters,' 'old-fashioned homebodies' and 'active affluent urbanites.' "

But life-style research is still in its infancy and very, very expensive. The trendiest and most attainable form of research going is called focus-group research, the grassroots movement of advertising research. From lairs of hidden cameras and tape-recording devices, agency and client-types, despite the experts' warnings that focus-group samples are far too small to be projected on a national scale, eke out a vision of their consumer that almost invariably fits just the stereotype they had in mind in the first place, and proceed to advertise accordingly.

The theory, quite simply, is to get inside women's heads in order to get inside their pocketbooks. From Satellite Beach to Spokane, fact-finding specialists are retained at grand sums to commune with the natives and document their particular buying habits. For instance:

The canned-meat industry's advertising wasn't paying off in the Southeast. Focus-group researchers were called in and groups of eight women were randomly selected from Memphis neighborhoods. The women fit the product's buyer profile—in this case, all came from families with middle to lower-middle incomes. Each woman was paid ten dollars. On an assigned day each focus group would meet for a two-hour session at the suburban home of the researcher's field representative—a woman who was a veteran of several similar exercises. As the women took their seats around the dining room table, loosening up with coffee and homemade cake, the client and agency folk sat, out of sight, in the rumpus room, carefully scanning the meeting on closed-circuit monitors. This is what they heard:

MODERATOR: Do any of you ever buy canned meats?

VOICES: Oh yes. Yeah. Uh, huh.

MODERATOR: When do you buy them?

ANN: Well, my husband went to New Orleans, so I bought a lot of canned goods. The children enjoy them.

LOU: Well, I bought Vienna sausage the other day 'cause the Giant had a special on it—seventy-nine cents a can—it's usually a dollar nine, a dollar nineteen. You could only get four at a time, so I went back twice that week.

MODERATOR: Do you buy these for particular members of the family?

NORMA: If they didn't like it, I wouldn't buy it.

DELORES: Melvin loves the hot dog chili. And the baby—you can just stick a Vienna sausage in her hand and she'll go 'round happy all day.

MODERATOR: Do you read the labels on canned meats?

VOICES: Oh sure. Yes.

NORMA: The children read the labels first and called my attention to it. When I saw it had things like intestines and things like that, I didn't want to buy potted meat any more.

LOU: Fats, tissues, organs. If you read the labels on this stuff—when they say hearts. . . . I don't know. I don't like hearts.

VIRGINIA: Well, psychologically you're not geared to it.

ALMA: They could lie on the label a little bit. Just don't tell us so much. (Laugh.) It would taste pretty good, but . . . yeah. I'd rather not know.

MODERATOR: What do you think ought to be on the labels?

ANNE: I think you ought to know about the chemicals.

NORMA: I love to read calories on the side of a can.

DELORES: I wonder what all's in those preservatives?

IDA: The side of this Hormel can here says that this meat is made by the same company that makes Dial soap. Says Armour-Dial.

NORMA: At least you think it's clean.

DELORES: Some preservatives do taste like soap. . . .

IDA: I wouldn't be eating that stuff with them chemicals.

ANN: Well, if you worry about that, you're going to starve to death.

VIRGINIA: You'd never eat in a restaurant if you ever got back in the kitchen.

MODERATOR: Would you buy a product because of the advertising?

VOICES: No. No. Maybe.

IDA: My children love that Libby's—the one, "Libby's, Libby's, Libby's. . . ."

NORMA: Now, if there's young kids that go to the grocery store with you, everytime they'll pick up something. . . . "Libby's, Libby's, Libby's."

DELORES: Every time I see Hormel chili . . . I think about them people out at a fireside by the beach eating that chili. One of them is playing a guitar and they start singing.

VIRGINIA: Armour has a cute hot dog commercial, that's where they're all marching around, weenies, ketchup and mustard. . . .

IDA: Yeah. That's cute.

MODERATOR: Do any of you ever buy Spam?

IDA: What's Spam?

ANNE: It's chopped something. Or pressed.

LOU: It's beaver board.

MODERATOR: Beaver what?

Most researchers claim that their studies are only as good as the people who interpret them. The interpreters are usually the agency and clients who—many advertising executives will admit, but only off the record—read their own product concerns into the comments of the panelists. Quite often, complaints about daytime commercials ("They're awful!" "Ridiculous!" "Laughable!") are brushed aside. "You can formulate breakthrough approaches in order to reach this new woman," Joan Rothberg, a senior VP at Ted Bates, told *Madison Avenue*, "and yet the traditional 'Ring Around the Collar' approach wins out in terms of creating awareness and motivating people to buy the product."

One of the final research tests a commercial can go through

after it's been created and storyboarded is the Burke test. One day up at my old agency, the creative director, a writer, and an art director came blazing through the halls with hats and horns, announcing at 120 decibels, "We Burked twenty-nine! We Burked twenty-nine!" Now this may sound to you as it did to me that day, as if these people were talking in tongues. What having "Burked twenty-nine" actually means is the percentage the commercial scored in recall after one viewing by a large audience. The average number of the Burke scale for the particular product my friends were testing was twenty-five—so you can understand the celebration.

Because the agencies and their clients accept Burke scores as valid, the scores become a powerful factor in what types of commercials will run. It's no accident that the Burke company is located in Cincinnati, since Cincinnati is the birthplace of Crest, Crisco, Comet, Charmin, Cheer, Bonus, Bounce, Bounty, Bold, Lava, Lilt, Pampers, Prell, Downy, Dash, and Duz—in other words, Cincinnati is the home of the King Kong of Household Cleanliness, Procter & Gamble. From high atop magnificent offices, P&G executives control daytime television and a goodly portion of prime time, too. They are the top-dollar spender on TV, having put out $260 million last year alone in commercial time bought. They produce and have editorial control over five of the biggest soap operas on TV: *As the World Turns, Another World, Edge of Night, Guiding Light,* and *Search for Tomorrow,* which reach some forty million women every day.

Procter & Gamble is the most blatant offender in perpetuating "the little woman" commercial stereotype. Because of its monopoly on both media and marketplace (it pulls in $3.6 billion every year) and because its research is the most expensive and extensive, P&G is the recognized leader and arbiter of format and content in household product commercials—where P&G goes, others will follow.

This does not spur innovation. In one P&G agency, the creative people have two formulae they use for "concepting" a commercial: regular slice-of-life (problem in the home, solution with the wonderful product) or what the agency guy calls "two C's in a K." The "K" stands for kitchen; the "C" is a four-letter word.

Once a commercial is written, tested, and approved by the client, it's got to be cast and shot. I asked Barbara Claman to talk about what agency people and their clients ask for when they're casting housewife roles. She should know: Barbara's built up one of the largest commercial casting agencies in the country. The day we talked all hell was breaking loose outside her office door. Scores of women and children had come to try out for a McDonald's commercial.

I wondered if agencies ever called for a P&G-type housewife for their commercials.

"Absolutely. She should be blond—or, if brunette, not too brunette. Pretty, but not too pretty. Midwestern in speech, middle-class looking, gentile. If they want to use blacks, they want *waspy* blacks."

"What about P&G-type husbands?"

"Same thing," Claman said. "But you'll find that the husband is getting to play the asshole more and more in American commercials."

"But do you see a change occurring? A trend in women's portrayals away from the traditional P&G type?"

"A little. I think they'd like to be a little more real. They're realizing, very slowly, that the working woman has a lot of money."

"What if they want a Rosie, a Madge or a Cora—one of the Eric Hoffer working-class philosopher-queens?"

Barbara laughed. "They'll say, 'Let's cast a ballsy one.' "

"Are you offended by the roles they want to put women in? Do you try to change their thinking on this?"

"I'm totally offended. I'm tired of seeing women hysterical over dirt spots on their glasses. I get lady producers in here all the time. We've tried to change their minds about the roles. You see how successful we've been."

Jane Green is another casting director in New York. She tells of a friend who was auditioning for a P&G spot in which the agency's creative people were trying to break out of the housewife mold. They'd called interesting faces—real people who wore real clothes. A couple of hours passed and the P&G client was obviously agitated. He turned to the agency producer: "What are you people trying to pull over on me? The woman in this commercial needs to be *my* wife, in *my* bathroom in Cincinnati—not some hip little chickie. Whom do you think we're selling to?"

One wonders. Recently an agency producer asked me and my cat Rayette to be in a kitty litter commercial. I arrived wearing blue jeans and a shirt, my usual at-home ensemble. The art director, who was wearing jeans himself, wasn't pleased: "Where is your shirtwaist? I told the producer I wanted a *housewife* look in this commercial." I tried to explain that most women—housewives and otherwise—had left those McMullans and Villagers back at the Tri Delt house in '66. The shoot was postponed until we found something that looked more housewifey.

Some commercial trends have passed: The damsel in distress has, for the time being, retreated to her tower. (Remember the thundering White Knight? The mystical, spotless Man from Glad? Virile, barrel-chested Mr. Clean?) But others remain, the most blatantly offensive, perhaps, being those commercials using women as sex objects to entice the consumer into buying the product. Most agency people aren't allowed to comment on the scheme of things in such commercials (one slip of the tongue and that multimillion-dollar account might choose another, more circumspect agency). But Dwight Davis, VP and creative director on the Ford dealers' account with J. Walter Thompson in Detroit, says it's no secret Detroit is still the national stronghold of selling with sex. Why? The male is still the decision maker in car buying ("Our research tells us it is so"); and the auto is still an extension of the American male libido. So we've got Catherine Deneuve hawking Lincoln-Mercurys. She circles the car in her long, slinky gown and slips inside to fondle the plush interior. Catherine signs off, sprawled across the hood of the car, with a seductive grrrrr. She is, as Davis describes the phenomenon, the car advertisers' "garnish on the salad."

Commercials like this, and the little woman slice-of-life, are caricatures of themselves. That's precisely why Carol Burnett and the people at *Saturday Night Live* have so much fun with them. Even the new wave of women's commercials isn't spared. In a spoof Anne Beatts wrote for *Saturday Night,* a middle-class Mom, dressed not in a shirtwaist but a polyester pantsuit, rushes into the kitchen, crashing through a café-curtained dutch door. She starts to have a heart-to-heart with the camera: "I'm a nuclear physicist and Commissioner of Consumer Affairs." She starts to put her groceries away.

"In my spare time, I do needlepoint, read, sculpt, take riding lessons, and brush up on my knowledge of current events. Thursday's my day at the day-care center, and then there's my work with the deaf; but I still have time left over to do all my own baking and practice my backhand, even though I'm on call twenty-four hours a day as a legal aid lawyer in Family Court. . . ." Our New-Wave Mom is still running on, all the time very carefully folding the grocery bags and stuffing them into a cabinet where literally hundreds of other carefully folded bags are stacked incredibly neatly, when the omniscient announcer comes in:

"How does Ellen Sherman, Cleveland housewife, do it all? She's smart! She takes Speed. Yes, Speed—the tiny blue diet pill you don't have to be overweight to need."

If the "average" woman is true to her portrayal in commercials, we've got a pretty bitter pill to swallow. But you know, we all know, commercials don't portray real life. Nice Movies' Dick Clark, who's done spots for Coca-Cola, Toyota, and Glade, points out, most commercials are "formula answers to advertising questions—bad rip-offs of someone else's bad commercials." They are bad rip-offs of their viewers too. But, someday, some bright young advertising prodigy will begin a whole new trend of commercials that don't talk down, don't demean or debase, and still sell soap or toothpaste or cars like crazy. And then everyone will be doing it. Double your money back, guaranteed.

Why am I so sure? Because, as Brinkley so neatly points out, only seven percent of our homes have the traditional resident Mom. Because there are more women doctors, engineers, copywriters, jockeys, linesmen, you name it, than ever before. Because women are becoming more selective in their buying habits. Because, quite simply, research tells me it is so.

Discussing Issues and Themes

1. About a third of the way through her essay, Caldwell reprints the National Advertising Review Board's checklist for sexism in advertising. Compare today's television ads with the checklist—have things changed much since 1975, when the checklist was made up? Caldwell suggests not. Do you agree with her?
2. What, exactly, is "life-style research"? What factors does it take into consideration and how is it different from "focus-group research"?
3. Although Caldwell concedes that the "ring around the collar" campaign has worked well for Wisk, she doesn't think the content of the ad is responsible. How does she think advertising works, based on this example? Do you agree with her?
4. What does it mean to "Burke twenty-nine"? Who is nominally responsible for the Burke scale? Ultimately?
5. What kinds of commercial messages does Caldwell think will come on the air in the future? What do you think that "research" tells her about women and the next trend in advertising? Do you think her prediction is probable, or do you think it is just wishful thinking?

Discussing Rhetoric and Style

1. How does Caldwell represent Bill Free, who was responsible for the "Fly Me" National Airline campaign? Does she make his character seem sympathetic or not? Why does she present him to us the way she does? Explain.
2. How does Caldwell represent herself in this essay? Her thesis is a feminist one, but she seems to be very careful not to step on any toes—or egos. Does she handle her emotionally loaded topic inoffensively? Explain.
3. Why does Caldwell reprint the minutes of a focus-group re-

search meeting? What effect does this format have on the rest of her essay?

4. What is the effect of quoting the phrase "two C's in a K" toward the end of the essay? Is the unspoken obscenity distressing or shocking, and, if so, are you more upset at the author for including the phrase or at the advertising people who use it? How does the implied obscenity reinforce Caldwell's thesis?

5. Why does Caldwell retell the *Saturday Night* spoof on advertising at the end of the essay? Caldwell has avoided the rhetorical tool of ridicule, so easily applied to her subject matter, and when she does use it she chooses to quote rather than invent the joke. Why does she include ridicule at this point, and why in a voice other than her own?

Ideas for Writing

1. Take a look at advertisements in another medium than television—for example, magazines or roadside billboards. What stereotypes do you find there? Write a brief essay analyzing *one* advertisement of your choice for negative stereotypes about race, gender, or both.

2. Write a paper on the rhetoric of advertising in which you discuss audience, appeal, and advertising techniques. Compare two or three specific ads, from the same medium or from different ones. Concentrate on specific details when you make your argument, using Caldwell's essay as your model.

Teaching from the Classifieds

ANDY ROONEY

Born in 1919 in Albany, New York, Andy Rooney is a widely syndicated columnist best known for his brief commentaries on CBS's successful news documentary 60 Minutes. *In the following piece, taken from his collection* And More by Andy Rooney *(1982), he turns his critical wit to the very ordinary topic of classified advertising, mildly satirizing the language of newspaper ads while at the same time discussing some dinosaur words—such as "creampuff" and "whippersnapper"—that have passed out of advertising lingo. In the tradition of Swift's "Modest Proposal," he goes on to sketch an outlandish plan for educating America's children about practical usage: Teach them the classifieds.*

Everyone says kids aren't being taught to read and write the way they used to be taught. Maybe the trouble is that they *are* still being taught the way they always have been. The trouble may be that our schools aren't being practical enough. Children still read Shakespeare, Dickens and Ralph Waldo Emerson as their writing role models. If they're going to be successful in our world, maybe young students ought to study more practical examples of English usage.

A course based on the classified advertising section of any newspaper would provide lots of examples of how we actually use the English language in practical situations. A study of the classifieds would also give students the same kind of mind-expanding exercise that translating from French into English gives them now.

One semester could be devoted to studying and translating the Houses for Sale section of the classifieds, and a second semester could be spent studying the Automobiles listings.

I have just made a comprehensive review of the classified pages of twenty newspapers. The single most frequently used word in the car ads is "loaded." I was surprised at this finding, because the last time I looked at classified ads for autos the most frequently used word was "creampuff." I don't see "creampuff" at all anymore. This would be a good lesson for children. Like so many words in our language—words like "whippersnapper," "humdinger," "dreamy," "soused" and "pickled"—"creampuff" served its purpose for a while as a linguistic fad and then disappeared into the never-never land of lost expressions.

The word "loaded" is a good example of how complex the English language can be, and kids might as well understand that at the beginning. Only recently the word was most used not to describe a secondhand car, but as a synonym for "soused" or "pickled." Now "loaded" is a synonym for "many extras," "custom features" and "fully equipped."

Studying the classifieds would help prepare children for the real world, because they'd learn that things are not always what they seem. Here, for instance, are a few translations for phrases from the automobile section:

Phrase	*Means*
Asking $3,500	Will take $2,700
$3,500 or best offer	Glad to get $2,500
Good station car	Don't try to go far in it
Runs good	Runs
Runs excellent	Runs
Runs well	Runs
Body needs work	Body rotted out
1981 model only 1100 miles	A lemon
Mint condition	Still some paint on it

Here are a few translations children might be taught from the housing ads:

Phrase	*Means*
Owner willing to sacrifice	For sale
Transferred, must sell	For sale
Wooded area	Tree in front of house
Heavily wooded area	Two trees in front of house
Landscaped	Has a bush on the lawn
Beautifully landscaped	Two bushes out front and one on the side

Cozy, intimate	A really small house
Secluded	Out in the boondocks
30 minutes from downtown	Out beyond the boondocks
$2\frac{1}{2}$ baths	Includes the birdbath out back
Wall-to-wall carpeting	House has no real flooring

That's the homework for tonight, children.

Discussing Issues and Themes

1. In his opening paragraph, Rooney suggests that Shakespeare, Dickens, and Emerson may not be the best writing models for today's students. Do you think he means this to be taken seriously, and, if so, do you think he's right?
2. Rooney says certain words have fallen by the wayside in our language. Can you think of other advertising words, from the classifieds or from magazines or television, that were used all the time just a little while ago, but that you never hear anymore?
3. What does "loaded" mean, according to Rooney? Is his translation of "loaded" like the other translations he offers in the two lists at the end of the essay? What does he say, for example, about "body needs work" and "wall-to-wall carpeting"?
4. Rooney seems to contradict himself in his second paragraph, saying first that the classifieds "would provide lots of examples of how we actually use the English language" and then declaring that "a study of the classifieds would also give students the same kind of mind-expanding exercise that translating from French into English gives them now." Is Rooney suggesting that the classifieds use language we are very familiar with, or that they use language we would be less likely to know (like French)? How do you reconcile these two statements?

Discussing Rhetoric and Style

1. What kind of audience is Rooney writing for? For example, do you think Rooney would rather read this essay at a PTA meeting in his hometown or to a little gathering of college buddies? Who do you think would be more sympathetic?

2. Why does Rooney open his essay the way he does? Is the essay really about the way today's children are taught to read and write? How does the first paragraph get your attention, and what is its tone?

3. What kind of diction does Rooney use in his essay? What are the effects of such locutions as "a comprehensive review" and "mind-expanding exercise," for instance?

4. Why does Rooney end his essay with two lists of "translations"? How and why do these lists change the tone of the piece?

5. Rooney stresses the idea of teaching "practical" English throughout the essay. How do his various repetitions of this concept, from the first paragraph to the closing line, communicate the essay's ironic message about classified ads?

Ideas for Writing

1. Compare Rooney to Swift ("On Reading Trash"). Both make suggestions about what children should read, but in what ways are the two pieces different?

2. Rooney says that he has made a "comprehensive review of the classified sections of twenty newspapers," but his findings would seem to indicate that classified ads always use the same language, no matter what paper they are in. Check this out for yourself: Find two or three newspapers that cater to widely different audiences (perhaps the *New York Times*, *USA Today*, and the *National Enquirer*) and compare their classified ads on one subject—for example, Help Wanted or Personals or Pets. Do you find any differences in the language between these newspapers? Write a short essay describing your investigation and results.

Aristotle and the Advertisers

MARTIN ESSLIN

Born in Hungary in 1918, Martin Esslin has studied and taught all over the world—from his early days as a student at the University of Vienna to his present position as professor of drama at Stanford University in California. In addition to his career in teaching, Esslin has also worked extensively in broadcasting in England and Europe as well as writing prolifically on topics and figures connected to modern drama. His works include books on Pinter, Brecht, and Beckett, as well as the famous The Theatre of the Absurd. *The following essay poses a connection between traditional dramatic conventions and television commercials. It appeared in 1979 in the* Kenyon Review, *of which Esslin is the drama editor.*

We have all seen it a hundred times, and in dozens of variations: that short sequence of images in which a husband expresses disappointment and distress at his wife's inability to provide him with a decent cup of coffee and seems inclined to seek a better tasting potion outside the home, perhaps even on the bosom of another lady; the anxious consultation, which ensues, between the wife and her mother or an experienced and trusted friend, who counsels the use of another brand of coffee; and finally the idyllic tableau of the husband astonished and surprised by the excellence of his wife's new coffee, demanding a second—or even a third!—cup of the miraculously effective product.

A television commercial. And, doubtless, it includes elements of drama. . . . Yet: is it not too short, too trivial, too contemptible altogether to deserve serious consideration? That seems the generally accepted opinion. But in an age when through the newly discovered technologies of mechanical reproduction and dissemination drama has become one of the chief instruments of human expression, communication, and, indeed, thought, all uses of the dramatic form surely deserve study. If the television commercial could be shown to be drama, it would be among the most ubiquitous and the most influential of its forms and hence deserve the attention of the serious critics and theoreticians of that art, most of whom paradoxically still seem to be spellbound by types of drama (such as tragedy) which are hallowed by age and tradition, though practically extinct today. And, surely, in a civilization in which drama, through the mass media, has become an omnipresent, all-pervasive, continuously available, and unending stream of entertainment for the vast majority of individuals in the so-called developed world, a comprehensive theory, morphology, and typology of drama is urgently needed. Such a theory would have to take cognizance of the fact that the bulk of drama today is to be found not on the stage but in the mechanized mass media, the cinema, television, and, in most civilized countries, radio; that both on the stage and in the mass media drama exists in a multitude of new forms which might even deserve to be considered genres unknown to Aristotle—from mime to musicals, from police serials to science fiction, from Westerns to soap opera, from improvisational theatre to happenings—and that among all these the television commercial might well be both unprecedented and highly significant.

The coffee commercial cited above, albeit a mere thirty to fifty seconds in length, certainly exhibits attributes of drama. Yet to what extent is it typical of the television commercial in general? Not all TV commercials use plot, character, and spoken dialogue to the same extent. Nevertheless, I think it can be shown that most, if not all, TV commercials are essentially dramatic, because basically they use mimetic action to produce a semblance of real life, and the basic ingredients of drama—character and a story line—are present in the great majority of them, either manifestly or by implication.

Take another frequently occurring type: a beautiful girl who tells us that her hair used to be lifeless and stringy, while now, as she proudly displays, it is radiantly vital and fluffy. Is this not just a bare announcement, flat and undramatic? I should argue that, in fact, there is drama in it, implied in the clearly fictitious character who is telling us her story. What captures our interest and imagination is the radiant girl, and what she tells us is an event which marked a turning point in her life. Before she discovered the miraculous new shampoo she was destined to live in obscurity and neglect, but now she has become beautiful and radiant with bliss. Are we not, therefore, here in the presence of that traditional form of drama in which a seemingly static display of character and atmosphere evokes highly charged, decisive events of the past that are now implicit in the present—the type of drama, in fact, of which Ibsen's *Ghosts* is a frequently cited specimen?

What, though, if the lady in question is a well-known show business or sporting personality and hence a *real* rather than a fictitious character? Do we not then enter the realm of reality rather than fictional drama? I feel that there are very strong grounds for arguing the opposite: for film stars, pop singers, and even famous sporting personalities project not their real selves but a carefully tailored fictional image. There has always, throughout the history of drama, been the great actor who essentially displayed no more than a single, continuous personality rather than a series of differing characters (witness the Harlequins and other permanent character types of the commedia dell'arte, great melodrama performers like Frédéric Lemaître, great comics like Chaplin, Buster Keaton, Laurel and Hardy, or the Marx Brothers, or indeed great film stars like Marilyn Monroe or John Wayne—to name but a very few). Such actors do not enact parts so much as lend their highly wrought and artistically crafted fictitious personality to a succession of roles that exist merely to display that splendid artifact. Hence if Bob Hope or John Wayne appear as spokesmen for banking institutions, or Karl Malden as the advocate of a credit card, no one is seriously asked to believe that they are informing us of their real experience with these institutions; we all know that they are speaking a preestablished, carefully polished text which, however brief it may be, has been composed by a team of highly skilled professional writers and that they are merely lending them the charisma of their long-established—and fictional—urbanity, sturdiness, or sincerity.

There remains, admittedly, a residue of nondramatic TV commercials: those which are no more than newspaper advertisements displaying a text and a symbol, with a voice merely reading it out to the less literate members of the audience; and those in which the local car or carpet salesman more or less successfully tries to reel off a folksy appeal to his customers. But these commercials tend to be the local stations' fill-up material. The bulk of the major, nationally shown commercials are profoundly dramatic and exhibit, in their own peculiar way, in minimal length and maximum compression, the basic characteristics of the dramatic mode of expression in a state of particular purity—precisely because here it approaches the point of zero extension, as though the TV commercial were a kind of differential calculus of the aesthetics of drama.

Let us return to our initial example: the coffee playlet. Its three-beat basic structure can be found again and again. In the first beat the exposition is made and the problem posed. Always disaster threatens: persistent headaches endanger the love relationship or success at work of the heroine or hero (or for headaches read constipation, body odor, uncomfortable sanitary pads, ill-fitting dentures, hemorrhoids, lost credit cards, inefficient detergents which bring disgrace on the housewife). In the second beat a wise friend or confidant suggests a solution. And this invariably culminates in a moment of insight, of conversion, in fact the classical anagnorisis that leads to dianoia and thus to the peripeteia, the turning point of the action. The third beat shows the happy conclusion to what was a potentially tragic situation. For it is always and invariably the hero's or heroine's ultimate happiness that is at stake: his health or job or domestic peace. In most cases there is even the equivalent of the chorus of ancient tragedy in the form of an unseen voice, or indeed, a choral song, summing up the moral lesson of the action and generalizing it into a universally applicable principle. And this is, almost invariably, accompanied by a visual epiphany of the product's symbol, container, trademark or logo—in other words the allegorical or symbolic representation of the beneficent power that has brought about the fortunate outcome and averted the ultimate disaster; the close analogy to the *deus ex machina* of classical tragedy is inescapable.

All this is compressed into a span of from thirty to fifty seconds. Moreover such a mini-drama contains distinctly drawn characters, who while representing easily recognizable human types (as so many characters of traditional drama) are yet individualized in subtle ways, through the personalities of the actors portraying them, the way they are dressed, the way they speak. The setting of the action, however briefly it may be glimpsed, also greatly contributes to the solidity of characterization: the tasteful furnishings of the home, not too opulent, but neat, tidy, and pretty enough to evoke admiring sympathy and empathy; the suburban scene visible through the living room or kitchen window, the breakfast table that bears witness to the housewifely skills of the heroine—and all subtly underlined by mood music rising to a dramatic climax at the moment of anagnorisis and swelling to a triumphant coda at the fortunate conclusion of the action. Of all the art forms only drama can communicate such an immense amount of information on so many levels simultaneously within the span of a few seconds. That all this has to be taken in instantaneously, moreover, ensures that most of the impact will be subliminal—tremendously suggestive while hardly ever rising to the level of full consciousness. It is this which explains the great effectiveness of the TV commercial and the inevitability of its increasing employment of dramatic techniques. Drama does not simply translate the abstract idea into concrete terms. It literally incarnates the abstract message by bringing it to life in a human personality and a human situation.

Thus it activates powerful subconscious drives and the deep animal magnetisms which dominate the lives of men and women who are always interested in and attracted by other human beings, their looks, their charm, their mystery.

"A message translated into terms of personality"—that, certainly, is one of the focal points around which TV commercials turn: the housewife, attractive but anonymous, who appears in such a commercial, exudes all the hidden attraction and interest she can command. Each of these mini-playlets stands by itself. Each is analogous to a complete play in conventional drama. It can be shown repeatedly, and can have a long run. But then the characters in it are spent. There is another form, however, even more characteristic of television drama—the serial. The series of plays featuring a recurring set of characters is the most successful dramatic format of television. No wonder, then, that the TV commercial mini-drama also resorts to the recurring personality, be he or she fictional; real-life synthetic, like the film stars or sporting heroes mentioned above; or allegorical, like the sweet little lady who embodies the spirit of relief from stomach acids and miraculously appears with her pills to bring comfort to a succession of truck drivers, longshoremen, or crane operators suffering from upset tummies.

The free interchangeability of real and fictional experts in this context once again underlines the essentially fictitious character even of the "real" people involved and shows clearly that we are dealing with a form of drama. The kindly pharmacist who recommends the headache powder, the thoughtful bespectacled doctor who recounts the successes of a toothpaste, the crusty small-town lady grocer who praises her coffee beans with the air of experience based on decades of wise counseling are manifestly actors, carefully type-cast; yet their authority is not a whit less weighty than that of the rare actual experts who may occasionally appear. The actor on the stage who plays Faust or Hamlet does not, after all, have to be as wise as the one or as noble as the other: it suffices that he can *appear* as wise or as noble. And the same is true of the dramatized advertisement: since illusion is the essence of drama, the illusion of authority is far more valuable in the dramatized commercial than any real authority. The fact that an actor like Robert Young has established himself as a medical character in an evening series enables him to exude redoubled authority when he appears in a long series of commercials as a doctor recommending caffeine-free coffee. It need not even be mentioned any longer that he is playing a doctor. Everybody recognizes him as a doctor while also remaining completely aware that he is an actor. . . . (It is Genêt, among modern playwrights, who has recognized the role of illusion as a source of authority in our society. His play *The Balcony* deals with precisely that subject: the insignificant people who have merely assumed the trappings of Bishop, Judge, or General in that house of illusions, the brothel, can, in the hour of need, be used to convince the masses that those authorities are still present. Many TV commercials are, in fact, mini-versions of *The Balcony*.)

The creation of authority figures—in a world where they are conspicuously absent in reality—can thus be seen as one of the essential features, and endeavors, of the TV commercial. That these authority figures are essentially creations of fiction gives us another important indication as to the nature of the drama we are dealing with: for these authority figures, whether fictional or not, are perceived as real in a higher sense. Fictions, however, which embody the essential, lived reality of a culture and society, will readily be recognized as falling within the strict definition of *myth*. The TV commercial, no less than Greek tragedy, deals with the myths at the basis of a culture.

This allows us to see the authority figures that populate the world of the TV commercial as analogous to the characters of a mythical universe: they form an ascending series that starts with the wise confidant who imparts to the heroine the secret of better coffee (a Ulysses or Nestor) and leads via the all-knowing initiate (pharmacist, grocer, doctor, or crusty father figure—corresponding to a Tiresias, a Calchas, or the priestess of the Delphic oracle) into the realm of the great film stars and sporting personalities who are not less but even more mythical in their nature, being the true models for the emulation of the society, the incarnation of its ideals of success and the good life, and immensely rich and powerful to boot. The very fact that a bank, a cosmetics firm, or a manufacturer of breakfast foods has been able to buy their services is proof of that corporation's immense wealth and influence. These great figures—Bob Hope, John Wayne, John Travolta, Farrah Fawcett-Majors—on the one hand lend their charisma to the businesses with whom they have become identified, and on the other they prove the power and effectiveness of those concerns. In exactly the same way, a priest derives prestige from the greatness of the deity he serves, while at the same time proving his own potency by his ability to command the effective delivery of the benefits his deity provides to the community. The great personalities of the TV commercial universe can thus be seen as the demigods and mythical heroes of our society, conferring the blessings of their archetypal fictional personality image upon the products they endorse and through them upon mankind in general, so that John Wayne becomes, as it were, the Hercules, Bob Hope the Ulysses, John Travolta the Dionysos, and Farrah Fawcett-Majors the Aphrodite of our contemporary Pantheon. Their presence in the TV commercial underlines its basic character as ritual drama (however debased it may appear in comparison to that of earlier civilizations).

From these still partially realistic demigods the next step up the ladder of authority figures is only logical: we now enter the realm of the wholly allegorical characters, either still invested with human form, like the aforementioned Mother Tums, a spirit assuming human shape to help humans as Athene does when she appears as a shepherd or Wotan as the Wanderer; or openly supernatural: the talking salad that longs to be eaten with a certain salad dressing; the syrup bottle that sings the praises of its contents; the little man of dough who incarnates the power of baking powder; the tiny pink and naked figure who projects the living image of the softness of a toilet tissue; or the animated figures of the triumphant knights (drawing on the imagery of St. George and the Dragon) who fight, resplendent in shining armor, endless but ever victorious battles against the demons of disease, dirt, or engine corrosion—a nasty crew of ugly devils with leering, malicious faces and corrosive voices.

The superhuman is closely akin to the merely extra-human: the talking and dancing animals who appear in the commercials for dog and cat foods are clearly denizens of a realm of the miraculous and thus also ingredients of myth; so, in a sense, are the objects that merely lure us by their lusciousness and magnetic beauty: the car lit up by flashes of lightning which symbolize its great power, the steaks and pizzas that visibly melt in the mouth. They, too, are like those trees and flowers of mythical forests which lure the traveler ever deeper into their thickets, because they are more splendid, more colorful, more magnetic than any object could ever be in real life.

Into this category, by extension, also fall the enlarged versions of the symbolic representation of products and corporations: those soft drink bottles the size of the Eiffel tower, those trademarks which suddenly assume gigantic three-dimensional shape so that they tower above the landscape and the people inhabiting it like mountain ranges, the long lines of dominoes that collapse in an immense chain reaction to form the logotype of a company. Here the drama of character has been reduced to a minimum and we are at the other end of the spectrum of theatrical expression, the one contained in the word itself—*theatron*—pure spectacle, the dominant element being the production of memorable images.

Like all drama, the TV commercial can be comprehended as lying between the two extremes of a spectrum: at one end the drama of character and at the other the drama of pure image. In traditional drama one extreme might be exemplified by the psychological drama-of-character of playwrights like Molière, Racine, Ibsen, or Chekhov; the other extreme by the drama of pure image like Ionesco's *Amedée*,

Beckett's *Happy Days* or *Not I.* On a slightly less ambitious plane, these extremes are represented by the French bedroom comedy and the Broadway spectacular. At one extreme ideas and concepts are translated into personality, at the other the abstract idea itself is being made visible—and audible.

It is significant, in this context, that the more abstract the imagery of the TV commercial becomes the more extensively it relies on music: around the giant soft drink bottle revolves a chorus of dancing singers; the mountain range of a trademark is surrounded by a choir of devoted singing worshippers. The higher the degree of abstraction and pure symbolism, the nearer the spectacle approaches ritual forms. If the Eucharist can be seen as ritual drama combining a high degree of abstraction in the visual sphere with an equally powerful element of music, this type of TV commercial approaches a secular act of worship: often, literally, a dance around the golden calf.

Between the extremes which represent the purest forms at the two ends of the spectrum are ranged, of course, innumerable combinations of both main elements. The character-based mini-drama of the coffee playlet includes important subliminal visual ingredients, and the crowd singing around the super-lifesize symbol contains an immense amount of instantaneous characterization as the faces of the singers come into focus when the camera sweeps over them: they will always be representative of the maximum number of different types—men, women, children, blacks, Asians, the young and the old—and their pleasant appearance will emphasize the desirable effects of being a worshipper of that particular product.

The reliance on character and image as against the two other main ingredients of drama—plot and dialogue—is clearly the consequence of the TV commercial's ineluctable need for brevity. Both character and image are instantly perceived on a multitude of levels, while dialogue and plot—even the simple plot of the coffee-playlet—require time and a certain amount of concentration. Yet the verbal element can never be entirely dispensed with. Still, all possible ways of making it stick in the memory must be employed: foremost among these is the jingle which combines an easily memorized, rhymed, verbal component with a melody, which, if it fulfills its purpose, will fix the words in the brain with compulsive power. Equally important is the spoken catchphrase, which, always emanating from a memorable personality and authority figure, can be briefer than the jingle and will achieve a growing impact by being repeated over and over until the audience is actually conditioned to complete it automatically whenever they see the character or hear the first syllable spoken.

Brecht, the great theoretician of the didactic play (*Lehrstueck*), was the first to emphasize the need for drama to be "quotable" and to convey its message by easily remembered and reproduced phrases, gestures, and images. His idea that the gist of each scene should be summed up in one memorable *Grundgestus* (a basic, gestural, and visual as well as verbal, instantly reproducible—quotable—compound of sound, vision, and gesture) has found its ideal fulfillment in the dramaturgy of the TV commercial. And no wonder: Brecht was a fervent adherent of behaviorist psychology and the TV commercial is the only form of drama which owes its actual practice to the systematic and scientifically controlled application of the findings of precisely that school of psychological thought. Compared with the TV commercial, Brecht's own effort to create a type of drama which could effectively influence human behavior and contribute to the shaping of society must appear as highly amateurish fumbling. Brecht wanted to turn drama into a powerful tool of social engineering. In that sense the TV commercial, paradoxically and ironically, is the very culmination and triumphant realization of his ideas.

From the point of view of its *form* the range of TV commercial drama can thus be seen as very large indeed: it extends from the chamber play to the grand spectacular musical; from the realistic to the utmost bounds of the allegorical, fantastical, and abstract. It is in the nature of things that as regards content its scope should be far more restricted. The main theme of this mini-species of drama—and I hope that by now the claim that it constitutes such will appear justified—is the attainment of happiness through the use or consumption of specific goods or services. The outcome (with the exception of a few noncommercial commercials, that is, public service commercials warning against the dangers of alcoholism or reckless driving) is always a happy one. But, as I suggested above, there is always an implied element of tragedy. For the absence of the advertised product or service is always seen as fatal to the attainment of peace of mind, well-being, or successful human relationships. The basic genre of TV commercial drama thus seems to be that of melodrama in which a potentially tragic situation is resolved by a last minute miraculous intervention from above. It may seem surprising that there is a relative scarcity of comedy in the world of the TV commercial. Occasionally comedy appears in the form of a witty catchphrase or a mini-drama concentrating on a faintly comic character, like that fisherman who urges his companions to abandon their breakfast cereal lest they miss the best hour for fishing, and who, when induced to taste the cereal, is so overwhelmed by its excellence that he forgets about the fishing altogether. But comedy requires concentration and a certain time span for its development and is thus less instantly perceivable than the simpler melodramatic situation, or the implied tragedy in the mere sight of a character who has already escaped disaster and can merely inform us of his new-found happiness, thus leaving the tragic situation wholly implicit in the past. The worshippers dancing around the gigantic symbol of the product clearly also belong in this category: they have reached a state of ecstatic happiness through the consumption of the drink, the use of the lipstick concerned, and their hymnic incantations show us the degree of tragic misfortune they have thus avoided or escaped. There is even an implication of tragedy in the straight exhortation uttered by one of the tutelary demigods simply to use the product or service in question. For the failure to obey the precepts uttered by mythic deities must inevitably have tragic results. Nonfulfillment of such commandments involves a grave risk of disaster.

And always, behind the action, there hovers the power that can bring it to its satisfactory conclusion, made manifest through its symbol, praised and hymned by unseen voices in prose or verse, speech or song. There can be no doubt about it: the TV commercial, exactly as the oldest known types of theatre, is essentially a religious form of drama which shows us human beings as living in a world controlled by a multitude of powerful forces that shape our lives. We have free will, we can choose whether we follow their precepts or not, but woe betide those who make the wrong choice!

The moral universe, therefore, portrayed in what I for one regard as the most widespread and influential art form of our time, is essentially that of a polytheistic religion. It is a world dominated by a sheer numberless pantheon of powerful forces, which literally reside in every article of use or consumption, in every institution of daily life. If the winds and waters, the trees and brooks of ancient Greece were inhabited by a vast host of nymphs, dryads, satyrs, and other local and specific deities, so is the universe of the TV commercial. The polytheism that confronts us here is thus a fairly primitive one, closely akin to animistic and fetishistic beliefs.

We may not be conscious of it, but this *is* the religion by which most of us actually live, whatever our more consciously and explicitly held beliefs and religious persuasions may be. This is the actual religion that is being absorbed by our children from almost the day of their birth.

And no wonder—if Marshall McLuhan is right, as he surely is, that in the age of the mass media we have turned away from a civilization based on reading, linear rational thought, and chains of logical reasoning; if we have reverted to a nonverbal mode of perception, based on the simultaneous ingestion of subliminally perceived visual and aural images; if the abolition of space has made us live again in the electronic equivalent of the tribal settlement expanded into a global village—then the reversion to a form of animism is merely logical. Nor should we forget that the rational culture of the Gutenberg Galaxy never extended beyond the very narrow confines of an educated minority elite and that the vast majority of mankind, even in the developed countries, and even after the introduction of universal education and literacy, remained on a fairly primitive level of intellectual development. The limits of the rational culture are shown only too clearly in the reliance on pictorial material and highly simplified texts by the popular press that grew up in the period between the spread of literacy and the onset of the electronic mass media. Even the Christianity of more primitive people, relying as it did on a multitude of saints, each specializing in a particular field of rescue, was basically animistic. And so was—and is—the literalism of fundamentalist forms of puritan protestantism.

Television has not created this state of affairs, it has merely made it more visible. For here the operation of the market has, probably for the first time in human history, led to a vast scientific effort to establish, by intensive psychological research, the real reactions, and hence also the implicit mechanisms of belief, displayed by the overwhelming majority of the population. The TV commercial has evolved to its present dramaturgy through a process of empirical research, a constant dialectic of trial and error. Indeed, it would be wrong to blame the individuals who control and operate the advertising industry as wicked manipulators of mass psychology. Ultimately the dramaturgy and content of the TV commercial universe is the outcrop of the fantasies and implied beliefs of those masses themselves; it is they who create the scenarios of the commercials through the continuous feedback of reactions between the makers of the artifacts concerned and the viewers' responses.

It would be wholly erroneous to assume that the populations of countries without TV commercials exist on a higher level of implied religious beliefs. In the countries of the Communist world, for example, where commercials do not exist, the experience of the rulers with the techniques of political persuasion has led to the evolution of a propaganda which, in all details, replicates the universe of the TV commercials. There too the reliance is on incantation, short memorable catchphrases endlessly repeated, the instant visual imagery of symbols and personality portraits (like the icons of Marx, Engels, and other demigods carried in processions; the red flags, the hammer-and-sickle symbolism) and a whole gamut of similarly structured devices that carry the hallmark of a wholly analogous primitive animism and fetishism. It is surely highly significant that a sophisticated philosophical system like Marxism should have had to be translated into the terms of a tribal religion in order to reach and influence the behavior of the mass populations of countries under the domination of parties which were originally, in a dim past, actuated by intellectuals who were able to comprehend such a complex philosophy. It is equally significant that citizens of those counties that are deprived of all commercials except political ones become literally mesmerized and addicted to the Western type of TV commercials when they have a chance to see them. There is a vast, unexpressed, subconscious yearning in these people, not only for the consumer goods concerned but also for the hidden forces and the miraculous action of the spirits inhabiting them.

In the light of the above considerations it appears that not only must the TV commercial be regarded as a species of drama but that, indeed, it comes very close to the most basic forms of the theatre, near its very roots. For the connection between myth and its manifestation and collective incarnation in dramatized ritual has always been recognized as being both close and organic. The myth of a society is collectively experienced in its dramatic rituals. And the TV commercial, it seems to me, is the ritual manifestation of the basic myth of our society and as such not only its most ubiquitous but also its most significant form of folk drama.

What conclusions are we to draw from that insight (if it were granted that it amounts to one)? Can we manipulate the subconscious psyche of the population by trying to raise the level of commercials? Or should we ban them altogether?

Surely the collective subconscious that tends to operate on the level of animistic imagery cannot be transformed by any short-term measures, however drastic. For here we are dealing with the deepest levels of human nature itself that can change only on a secular time-scale—the time-scale of evolutionary progress itself. Nor would the banning of TV commercials contribute anything to such a type of change.

What we can do, however, is to become aware of the fact that we are here in the presence of a phenomenon that is by no means contemptible or unimportant, but, on the contrary, basic to an understanding of the true nature of our civilization and its problems. Awareness of subconscious urges is, in itself, a first step towards liberation or at least control. Education and the systematic cultivation of rational and conscious modes of perception and thought might, over the long run, change the reaction of audiences who have grown more sophisticated and thus raise the visual and conceptual level of this form of folk-drama. A recognition of the impact of such a powerful ritual force and its myths on children should lead to efforts to build an ability to deal with it into the educational process itself. That, at present, is almost wholly neglected.

And a recognition of the true nature of the phenomenon might also lead to a more rational regulation of its application. In those countries where the frequency of use of TV commercials and their positioning in breaks between programs rather than within them is fairly strictly regulated (Germany, Britain, Scandinavia, for instance), TV commercials have lost none of their efficacy and impact but have become less all-pervasive, thus allowing alternative forms of drama—on a higher intellectual, artistic, and moral level—to exercise a counterbalancing impact. Higher forms of drama, which require greater length to develop more individualized character, more rationally devised story lines, more complex and profound imagery might, ultimately, produce a feedback into the world of the commercial. Once the commercial has ceased to be—as it is at present—the best produced, most lavishly financed, technically most perfect ingredient of the whole television package, once it has to compete with material that is more intelligent and more accomplished, it might well raise its own level of intelligence and rationality.

These, admittedly, may be no more than pious hopes, whistling in the dark. Of one thing, however, I am certain: awareness, consciousness, the ability to see a phenomenon for what it is must be an important first step towards solving any problem. Hence the neglect of the truly popular forms of drama—of which the TV commercial is the most obvious and most blatant example—by the serious critics and theoreticians of that immensely important form of human expression seems highly regrettable. The TV commercial—and all the other forms of dramatic mass entertainment and mass manipulation—not only deserve serious study; a theory of drama that neglects them seems to me elitist, pretentious, and out of touch with the reality of its subject matter.

Discussing Ideas and Themes

1. Esslin suggests that the television commercial can be considered as a new form of drama. What are the elements of drama that he perceives in the television commercial? Would you agree that commercials are drama?

2. What does Esslin mean when he says that television commercials display the "basic characteristics of the dramatic mode of expression in a state of particular purity"? In particular, what makes television commercials "pure" drama to Esslin?

3. Esslin suggests that commercials represent "easily recognizable

human types." Scan through his examples of commercials—what are the "types" in these advertisements? To what extent do you think these types exist in the world outside advertising?

4. What are the myths that television commercials deal with, according to Esslin? Do you agree that these commercials exploit modern cultural myths?

5. Esslin suggests a general absence of comedy in television commercials. Do you agree? What, in your experience, has been the general trend in advertising—comic or tragic? Support your response with examples.

Discussing Rhetoric and Style

1. How does Esslin use allusions in this essay? For example, what effect obtains when he compares a shampoo commercial to Ibsen's *Ghosts*?

2. What is the effect of Esslin's high diction in this essay? What does his diction tell the reader about his argument and his attitude toward his argument? Is Esslin's argument ironic?

3. Esslin suggests that one type of commercial uses the argument from authority (dentist, doctor, pharmacist, . . .) What are other rhetorical arguments that television commercials regularly use?

4. How does Esslin arrange his argument so that he finally ends up commenting, not so much on television commercials, but on the "myths," "religion," and "collective subconscious" of our culture? How does he justify his sweeping conclusions?

Ideas for Writing

1. Esslin uses the example of the coffee commercial to illustrate the drama of television commercials. How might a feminist reader (say, Carol Caldwell) read this advertisement differently? In a short paper, try to analyze Esslin's examples from Caldwell's perspective.

2. Discuss the ways that our culture is reflected and influenced by a medium other than television commercials—for example, video games or song lyrics. Try to stay close to Esslin's model, using examples and defining characteristics of your subject, but you don't necessarily need to come to conclusions like Esslin's.

The Question of Condom Ads

JOHN CORRY

John Corry reports for The New York Times, *writing frequently on popular culture and the performing arts. His interests range from the television and entertainment industries to news and advertising. In the following piece, which appeared in the* Times *in 1987, Corry delves into a topic of some moral ambiguity: "Should television carry advertisements for condoms?" An explosive topic, fueled by the national fear of AIDS, the question of condom ads might ultimately place advertising in the perhaps inappropriate role of public educator.*

Should television carry advertisements for condoms? The question is part of a growing debate. In a recent speech in Washington, Dr. Otis R. Bowen, the Secretary of Health and Human Services, said that a worldwide AIDS epidemic in the next 10 years would be more devastating than the Black Plague. Meanwhile, there are heated discussions over sex education. Virtually everyone agrees that something is wrong; there is still no unanimity on how to handle the problem. The discussion centers on AIDS, but worries about other sexually transmitted diseases, teenage pregnancies and matters of religion and morality arise, too. Inevitably, television is drawn into the discussion. It is seen, as always, as both a cause and a cure for the problem. Television, its critics say, merchandises easy sex and encourages promiscuity; if television presents advertisements for contraceptives, some also say, it could help repair the damage.

At the moment, the networks are balking. Condom commercials are seen as a breach of morality and good taste; viewers will be offended. Nonetheless, local stations in Indianapolis, San Francisco, Detroit and Washington have broken ranks. In a statement, Thomas B. Cookerly, the president of WJLA in Washington, an ABC affiliate, cited the threat from AIDS. "As broadcasters," he said, "we have a responsibility to our community to disseminate information to help slow the progress of this deadly disease through news reports, public-service announcements and now through select condom advertisements which meet our high copy-acceptance standards."

If you have ambivalent feelings about this, you should. In the real world of television, high copy-acceptance standards have a way of melting down. At the same time, news stories have said that the stations that are considering or already have accepted condom advertising will show the advertising only at night; presumably, children will be sleeping. This isn't quite correct, of course; children make up a large part of the night-time audience. Moreover, condom advertising, although apparently shown in response to the peril of AIDS, will ignore a critical issue. AIDS, or acquired immune deficiency syndrome, is not a homosexual disease, although the overwhelming majority of its victims are male homosexuals; they are most at risk.

It is unlikely, however, that condom advertisements will face up to this. The most daring television station will not show two males hugging one another or even holding hands. Nonetheless, this critic guesses, if a large enough number of local stations accept condom advertisements, eventually the networks will accept them, too. Advertising agencies, in fact, are anticipating this and are preparing trial commercials. One expects that the commercials will show a young man and woman walking on a beach or gazing into a sunset. We will be struck by their fresh good looks. Then, in a voice-over, we will hear about responsibility and commitment. The emphasis will be on the need for mature and thoughtful behavior.

Obviously, this will not mean abstinence; there are no commercial possibilities in selling that. No matter how mightily agencies and stations may strive for good taste and the high moral ground, it's difficult to see how the advertisements can avoid suggesting that abstinence is out of date, and that contraceptives allow for more attractive possibilities. This isn't necessarily true. Abstinence, or at least a monogamous relationship, is still the best way to avoid a sexually transmitted disease.

But the real world intrudes here. Dr. Bowen, who is hardly a crank, said that at least 270,000 cases of AIDS were expected in the United States in the next five years, and that the worldwide death toll could reach the millions in a decade. Meanwhile, there is scarcely a social scientist or serious student of our cities who has not worried about unwanted pregnancies and their relationship to the cycle of poverty, despair and crumbling family structure. Abstinence and monogamous relationships may indeed be the answer. The problem is, they are not exactly universally pursued.

Therefore, the condom advertisements; the real world demands that something be done. The advertisements will not solve all our problems, and invariably some will be offensive. There are commercials as well as programs that are offensive now; they trivialize serious subjects. On the other hand, condom advertisements may do some good, and the risks they present to the social fabric may be worth taking. This critic believes they are. It is just possible the advertisements could save lives. It is also just possible they could help to legitimatize the idea that sex is a serious matter. Thoughtfully done, they would at least be a step toward countering the commercials and programs that relentlessly indicate that sex, practiced only for fun, has no responsibilities attached.

The matter, I suspect, is mostly a question of time. Some magazines and newspapers, among them *The New York Times*, have now said they will accept advertising for condoms. The British Government has sponsored a television warning about AIDS. The warning, shown on American news broadcasts, presented a crumbling mountain; then the word AIDS was chiseled into a tombstone of black rock. "If you ignore AIDS, it could be the death of you," a voice said. "So don't die of ignorance."

The warning was meant to draw attention to a leaflet about AIDS that the British Government was mailing to the country's 23 million households. Presumably, it did draw attention; the television warning became a subject of national debate. At the same time, it did look a little goofy. One had the feeling the people who produced it were hesitant about taking on a real issue. As the Rt. Rev. Hugh Montefiore, the Bishop of Birmingham, said about the crumbling mountain in a news story, "Whatever sexual intercourse is, it is not like that." Advertisements for condoms, in these hazardous times, seem to be a good deal more to the point.

Discussing Issues and Themes

1. Make a list of three reasons why television should carry condom advertisements and three reasons why it shouldn't. Which list is more persuasive? Why?

2. Do you think television has greatly influenced your perceptions about sexuality and gender? Do you think it is a positive, a negative, or a fairly neutral influence?

3. In what ways is television both "a cause and a cure" for problems such as sexually transmitted disease and teenage pregnancy? Refer to the essay in your answer.

4. How would you explain a condom ad to a young child? Do you support or oppose the practice of explaining AIDS and other sex-related topics to youngsters? Would nationally televised condom ads force you to reconsider?

Discussing Rhetoric and Style

1. Consider the first paragraph of the essay. What is its function in the overall structure? How is it related to the final two paragraphs?
2. Is this essay based on factual evidence? Is Corry an unbiased reporter? Why or why not?
3. How central is AIDS to Corry's argument? How often does he use the term? Is it necessary to emphasize the disease so strongly?
4. Corry remarks that some "commercials as well as programs . . . are offensive now; they trivialize serious subjects." Is trivialization necessarily offensive?
5. Study Corry's writing style. How does he clarify his points? Does he make use of repetition? Strong transitions? Precise diction? Figurative language? Choose any one of these techniques and describe its use here in full.

Ideas for Writing

1. Look at either a box of condoms or an advertisement in a magazine, and then write an essay about how condom companies are representing their products. How are condoms being marketed? To what audience is the sales pitch directed?
2. Write an essay in which you explore some of the ways that the media has controlled public opinion about the AIDS epidemic. In researching the topic, you should consider at least three articles, dating from the late 1970s, when the disease was first detected, to the present. For instance, you might first consider the various names that the disease has been called and then discuss why those names have gradually changed.

Beatles Buy-Out

JON WIENER

Jon Wiener is a professor of history at the University of California. He has written extensively on popular culture—particularly the rock culture—for numerous national magazines. In addition, he has written a biography called Come Together: John Lennon in His Time. *"Beatles Buy-Out," which first appeared in the* New Republic, *traces the history of the Beatles' song "Revolution"—the sound now heard across the nation in advertisements for Nike shoes. Granting the commercial basis of music—the buying and selling, for instance, of stock and copyrights—Wiener nonetheless concludes that promotional ads sometimes unethically distort the larger context of a song.*

There is a revolution afoot, according to the Nike shoe company—a revolution in sneakers, heralded by a $7 million TV ad campaign featuring the Beatles song "Revolution." It's the first time that Capitol Records has licensed an original Beatles record for use in a TV commercial. The 30-second ads, done in a black-and-white documentary style, feature ordinary jocks intercut with sports superstars such as basketball player Michael Jordan and tennis champion John McEnroe, while John Lennon sings, "You say you want a revolution." The new sneakers cost $75 a pair.

Beatles fans are outraged. Chris Morris, the *L.A. Reader*'s rock critic, says: "When 'Revolution' came out in 1968 I was getting teargassed in the streets of Madison. That song is part of the sound track of my political life. It bugs the hell out of me that it has been turned into a shoe ad." Morris is right that the Beatles' purpose was not to sell shoes. But the story is a bit more complicated.

The 1968 song *criticized* young revolutionaries for having "minds that hate." Lennon's lyrics told the 1960s left to "count me out." They attacked kids for "carrying pictures of Chairman Mao." The

New Left was shocked when the song first appeared. *Ramparts* called it a "betrayal," and the *New Left Review* denounced it as "a lamentable petty bourgeois cry of fear."

"Revolution" was John Lennon's comment on May '68. It was recorded two weeks after student riots in Paris brought France to the brink of revolution. The song wasn't released until August. By that time, a thousand club-swinging New York City cops had driven Columbia University students from occupied campus buildings. In Chicago Hubert Humphrey had been "nominated in a sea of blood," as Theodore White put it. The Rolling Stones released "Street Fighting Man," in which Mick Jagger sang about the time being right for revolution; the record was banned from the airwaves in Chicago and Berkeley. Then the new Beatles single came out, addressing the kids in the streets: "You say you want a revolution. . . ."

The underground press responded immediately. The Berkeley *Barb* wrote with typical excess, " 'Revolution' sounds like the hawk plank adopted in the Chicago convention of the Democratic Death Party." John Landau, writing for Liberation News Service, agreed: "Hubert Humphrey couldn't have said it better," he wrote. Robert Christgau write in the *Village Voice,* "It is puritanical to expect musicians, or anyone else, to hew to the proper line. But it is reasonable to request that they not go out of their way to oppose it. Lennon has, and it takes much of the pleasure out of their music for me." *Ramparts* objected in particular to the line "You know it's gonna be all right": "It isn't," the magazine declared. "You *know* it's *not* gonna be all right."

But the song was irresistible, raucous hard rock. The music contained a message of its own, a message of excitement and freedom, which worked against the "sterility and repression in the lyrics," according to Greil Marcus, at the time a writer for the San Francisco *Express-Times.* "The music doesn't say 'cool it' or 'don't fight the cops,' " Marcus wrote.

There was a second version of the song, released on the White Album two months after the single. The single version had been produced the way Paul McCartney wanted it; the album version was done John's way—slower, so that the words could be understood better. And there was one significant change in the words: after he sang, "When you talk about destruction/Don't you know that you can count me out," he added "in." I put in both because I wasn't sure," he explained. Nike uses the first version in the ad.

Not everyone on the left attacked "Revolution." The SDS newspaper at Cornell declared that Lennon rightly rejected radicals with "minds that hate," and that the increasing violence of the left needed to be criticized. Then there was the issue of the "shoo-be-do-wahs" with which Paul and George answered John's "You know it's gonna be—" on the album version. Michael Wood addressed that problem in *Commonweal.* The Beatles are not fools, he argued; they know it's absurd to say "it's gonna be all right." The "shoo-be-do-wahs" suggested "they mean that statements about whether it is or it isn't are all part of that political crap they dislike so much."

The far right also took up the question of "Revolution." William Buckley paid mocking tribute to its message in his syndicated column, and was promptly attacked by the John Birch Society. "The Beatles are simply telling the Maoists that Fabian gradualism is working, and that the Maoists might blow it all by getting the public excited before things are ready for 'revolution'—'it's gonna be all right.' " The Birch Society concluded that " 'Revolution' takes the Moscow line against Trotskyites and the Progressive Labor Party, based on Lenin's *Left-Wing Extremism: An Infantile Disorder.*" (The actual title of Lenin's treatise was: *Left-Wing Communism, An Infantile Disorder.*)

Lennon and McCartney gave up ownership of their songs in the late '60s when their financial advisers told them they could reduce their tax payments (they were in Britain's 90 percent bracket) by forming a corporation called Northern Songs that would own their copyrights, and selling stock to the public. In 1969 Sir Lew Grade's entertainment conglomerate ATV Music offered seven times the original offering price of the Northern Songs stock in a takeover bid. Lennon and McCartney were feuding at the time and unable to organize a successful counteroffer. When the Northern Songs management and shareholders accepted Sir Lew's offer in September 1969, Lennon was outraged and inconsolable. Told that his massive capital gain would allow him to make his children secure—or, in the words of the poet, "Baby you're a rich man now"—Lennon replied, "I have no desire to create another fucking aristocracy." Grade in turn sold ATV in 1981 to an Australian tycoon with too many names: Robert Holmes a Court.

Enter Michael Jackson, whose 1982 *Thriller* album sold more than 30 million copies, making it the most successful album in the history of the world. After working with McCartney on the monster hit "Say, Say, Say," he told his lawyer. "I want to buy some copyrights, like Paul." "He only wanted songs that meant a lot to him," Robert Hilburn explained in the *Los Angeles Times,* so he bought Dion's "Runaround Sue" and "The Wanderer" but passed on Kris Kristofferson's "Help Me Make It Through the Night." But what he really wanted was the Beatles. Jackson appeared in person at the negotiations in London, wearing a colorful Sgt. Pepper outfit. That "brightened everyone's mood," Hilburn reports, and Holmes a Court agreed to sell—for $47.5 million. After agreeing to license the words and music of "Revolution" to Nike, Jackson persuaded Capitol Records, owner of the rights to the Beatles' recordings, to license the original record.

The "Revolution" ad is the most outrageous example of a familiar aspect of pop culture in the later Age of Reagan. Lou Reed, a rock hero loved for his rejection of everything soft and safe in the pop world, recently licensed his signature song, "Walk on the Wild Side," for a motor scooter ad. The Shirelles' captivating "Dedicated to the One I Love" (it peaked at No. 3 in 1961) is now used to suggest that if you are dedicated, you should serve bran flakes to the one you love. Johnny Nash's stirring "I Can See Clearly Now," one of the first reggae hits (No. 1 in 1972), sells—oh no—window cleaner. "Revolution" isn't even the first Beatles song to be licensed. John Lennon's "Help," a declaration of his unhappiness as a superstar, became a Mercury ad in 1985. But a sound-alike band sang the song. And Michael Jackson does Pepsi commercials.

"Mack the Knife," once sung by Lotte Lenya in "The Threepenny Opera," lyrics by Bertolt Brecht, music by Kurt Weill, has been turned into a McDonald's commercial: "It's Mac Tonight." Frank Sinatra licensed his original recording of "The Best Is Yet to Come" to Chrysler. Ringo Starr, meanwhile, is the first Beatle to appear in person endorsing a product—a pathetic ad for a wine cooler.

A few rockers have had the integrity to refuse to license their music. Notable among them are John Cougar Mellencamp, Bob Seger, and Joan Jett. Chrissie Hynde of the Pretenders has a song on their new album *Get Close* attacking Michael Jackson and others who have endorsed products, in which she asks, "How much did you get for your soul?" Bruce Springsteen has been offered the most to sell out, and he has refused. The admen, however, have taken revenge, expropriating Springsteen's style and attitude and reducing them to a formula for a variety of commercials. After The Boss turned down Lee Iacocca's offer to use "Born in the USA" to sell Plymouth Mini-Vans, the company ran a rip-off TV ad with the theme "Born in America." (As Dave Marsh points out in his new book on Springsteen, *Glory Days,* the car is assembled in Canada.)

What's next? "Give Peace a Chance" selling Star Wars? "Happiness is a Warm Gun" licensed to the National Rifle Association? "All You Need Is Love" as the *contras'* theme song? Yoko Ono says she's confident Michael Jackson would "say 'no' to any misuse of the songs." He's turned down dozens of offers before accepting Nike. And neither Ono nor McCartney objected to Jackson's licensing of "Revolution" for the Nike ad. "John's songs should not be part of a cult of glorified martyrdom," Ono argues. "They should be enjoyed by kids today. This ad is a way to communicate John's song to them, to make it part of their lives instead of a relic of the distant past." She argues also that there is nothing objectionable about Nike shoes: "Sports shoes are part of fitness consciousness that is actually better for your body than some of the things we were doing in the '60s."

Maybe there's no reason to object to turning some pop songs into commercials—they didn't say anything in particular, and were written to make money in the first place. Does anyone care that the Fifth Dimension's "Up, Up, and Away" (No. 7 in 1967) has become a TWA commercial? But the "Revolution" ad is different. The song had a meaning that Nike is destroying.

A spokesman for Michael Jackson says that he plans to make 40 other Beatles songs available for commercial exploitation.

Discussing Issues and Themes

1. Is Wiener for or against the Nike ad? How can you tell?
2. What, according to Wiener, is the difference between a song and a commercial? Why is the use of one in the other inappropriate? Do you agree?
3. Who owns the rights to the Beatles' songs, and how did he get them? Were you surprised by the big-business aspect of popular music, which Wiener presents here? Does he present the business as a mostly '80s phenomenon?
4. What, according to Wiener, are the earmarks of "the Age of Reagan." Does he explain this phrase explicitly, or do we understand the remark by inference? Where does he contrast "the Age of Reagan" with the 1960s?
5. The essay strongly contrasts "the soundtrack of [one's] political life" with a shoe ad, but materially these two things are the same thing—a song named "Revolution." How does the newer context—the commercial—change the song? Does the commercial trivialize the song? Does the song inspire the commercial?

Discussing Rhetoric and Style

1. What is the pun in Wiener's first sentence? Does he repeat this joke anywhere else?
2. What is the relationship of the last sentence in Wiener's first paragraph to the rest of that paragraph? Is there any logic in the relationship? What transitions might Wiener have used to make

the sentence fit in more smoothly, and, more importantly, why does he choose to omit such a transition?

3. How does Wiener portray the various celebrities in the essay—for instance, John Lennon, Michael Jackson, Yoko Ono, Ringo Starr? Who gets the most favorable treatment? Against whom does he seem most angry, and is his anger biased? Cite evidence from the essay in answering.
4. What is the effect of the final paragraph? Why do you think Wiener chose to make it a single sentence? Is it powerful?

Ideas for Writing

1. Take a song of your choice and read the lyrics, analyzing the logic, the argument, and the narrative of the song. Do you find that the lyrics seem to contradict the "sound" of the song? Are you surprised by what the song is really about? Explain.
2. Should rock-and-roll lyrics be used to sell things? Outline a careful argument considering both sides of the issue and forming a conclusion.

Fun Video

GEORGE GALUSCHAK

A writer of both prose fiction and poetry, George Galuschak is a senior studying literature and writing at Rutgers University. The following essay, written for a class assignment, takes a wry look at the advertising strategies behind the rhetoric of weight loss: From Jane Fonda to Richard Simmons, Galuschak notes, all exercise gurus are out to convince their audience of one thing—that exercise is fun. But is this conclusion sound? According to Galuschak, the logic may be faulty, but the net profit is sound.

Exercise fun? Well, yes, according to Richard Simmons. His brand new "Sweatin' to the Oldies" videotape makes these guarantees—"Have FUN while you exercise . . . and melt away ALL those extra pounds and inches with my No. 1 selling aerobic videotape." Ahh, aerobics. The word brings Jane Fonda to mind. That, and fat ladies trying to touch their toes.

In fact, one of the things that makes this ad interesting is the strong presence of fat ladies throughout. We see pictures of certain fatties, and then they reappear magically reduced; these pictures produce miracles in the minds of middle-aged, overweight housewives (the theoretical audience) by eliminating all in-between stages and any hint of work. Exercise isn't work, it's fun. To prove this we hear all about the video's group of fun-loving people (led by Mr. Fun himself, Richard Simmons) dancing ecstatically to great oldies such as "Great Balls of Fire" (and 9 others); songs that the wistful housewife grew up to. Exercise in this tape is likened to a party. A painless party, for the ad boasts—"no stress on ankles, joints, or lower back."

The real strength of any ad lies in its ability to effectively exploit its targeted audience; what this ad does is pretty much standard fare. However, it does have one stroke of genius. We are told that the tape features Richard Simmons and “real people” (we are guaranteed that), and also that many of these people are overweight (the group picture provided in the ad shows no overly obese men, but two huge women). Thus we don't have to watch a bunch of thin people effortlessly prance and caper—we get to see fat people puff and lumber about. Just like you and me.

Discussing Ideas and Themes

1. According to Galuschak, Richard Simmons's videotape promises a combination of “fun” and weight loss. Do you think this promise is typical of advertising aimed at people who want to reduce, or do you think other kinds of appeals are more common? Give examples.
2. At the end of his opening paragraph, Galuschak offers up two images associated with the word “aerobics”: “Jane Fonda” and “fat ladies.” Why, do you think, are both of these images feminine? Are aerobics a feminine preoccupation in our culture?
3. Galuschak's paper identifies at least two advertising tricks used by this advertisement. One trick is to represent exercise as “fun.” What is the other trick, and why does Galuschak think it will work?
4. What, according to Galuschak's essay, is the target audience for Simmons's ad? At what time of day would you guess this ad would run?

Discussing Rhetoric and Style

1. Galuschak opens with a rhetorical question. What is the effect of this opening on his reader?
2. How does Galuschak use vivid imagery to enhance his prose? For example, what is the effect of his image of “fat ladies trying to touch their toes” at the end of the first paragraph? What other images are particularly effective?
3. Galuschak lets us know that he thinks Richard Simmons's advertisement misrepresents “exercise.” For example, he says that Simmons's “pictures produce miracles in the *minds* of middle-aged, overweight housewives.” Where else does Galuschak's opinion show through?

4. The tone of this essay is casual, but a close look reveals that this relaxed tone is achieved only through Galuschak's careful use of language. Consider, for example, some of the verbs in the essay: "prance and caper," or "puff and lumber about." What other ways can you see that Galuschak's essay is carefully crafted?
5. How does Galuschak's last line change the tone of his essay? The line makes an appeal that includes us—the readers—in its admission of "fat." Are there any other such appeals in the essay?

Ideas for Writing

1. Write a brief essay in which you imitate Galuschak's style, while exploring another subject. Try to stay close to Galuschak's syntax, using, as he does, sentence fragments, parentheses, and quotations.
2. Carol Caldwell's essay, "You Haven't Come a Long Way, Baby," makes a feminist critique of today's advertising. Reread Caldwell's essay, and write a paper in which you apply her reasoning to the advertisement Galuschak describes.

CHAPTER 8

Language and Literature: The Best That Has Been Thought and Said

"Literature" has traditionally been a word that honors the highest uses of language whether in verse or prose. Until recently, most formal education in the West has been devoted to the study of the language and literature of Greece and Rome. The use of classical studies as the common denominator in education has been supplanted by the study of the language and literature of one's own country in most educational curriculums around the world. But why is this so? Of what use can such studies be to an educated man or woman in a modern world? The essays in this section provide some tentative answers to these questions and demonstrate literary merits of their own.

The chapter opens with "Education by Poetry," by Robert Frost, a teacher of literature as well as one of the best-known and most widely read modern American poets. Frost argues that the kind of attention to language fostered by literature—and especially by poetry—makes the very essence of mental activity and assumes an importance far beyond that of recreation. Poetry can educate us for life in general, Frost says.

The poet and novelist Vladimir Nabokov spent a good deal of his life educating people about great literature—he describes his method in "Good Readers and Good Writers." Nabokov argues that in addition to the eye and the brain, other sensory systems—the tiny hairs on the back of the neck, for example—come into play when reading is properly done.

Reuben Brower's approach to reading complements Nabokov's. Brower argues that literature is best appreciated by going slow, by "Reading in Slow Motion." Only by paying close attention to a book will a reader get out of the literary experience all that has gone into its creation.

Literary style is treated in a more carefree manner in the next two selections. In "Exercises in Style," Raymond Queneau shows the relation of style to content and suggests how various are the experiences available to a so-called single event when that event is expressed through language.

Frank Sullivan sees literature—especially as it appears in book reviews—as having a life of its own, independent of any particular book. Although his gentle mockery of the jargon of reviews was written a half century ago, a comparison of the language satirized to that still appearing in today's journals and newspapers can lead to a strange new appreciation of the timelessness of literary criticism.

Martin Gardner looks at one of America's best-known poems in "The Harvard Man Who Put the Ease in Casey's Manner." In giving us the history of this memorable and enduring use of language, Gardner also gives us an insight into the ways that literary language can become so powerful that its author can be forgotten.

To end the chapter, student writer Kimberly Mitchell examines another famous—even notorious—work of American literature in "The Language of *Lolita*." In her careful attention to the way the novel's language operates, Mitchell pays the best kind of tribute to the style she analyzes.

Education by Poetry

ROBERT FROST

As a young adult Robert Frost (1874–1963) worked at several jobs—newspaper editor, farmer, school teacher—and could not find a publisher for his poetry until 1913, when he travelled to England and published A Boy's Will. *After establishing himself as a serious poet abroad, he returned to the United States, bought a farm and settled down, working from time to time as professor of English or poet-in-residence at Michigan State University, Amherst College, and other schools. Although he got off to a slow start, Frost went on to publish a dozen critically acclaimed volumes of poetry. Considered to be the unofficial poet laureate of the United States, he was perhaps the most widely known American poet of the century, receiving five Pulitzer Prizes for poetry and serving under President Kennedy as a diplomat to foreign countries. In the following essay, which was delivered in 1930 as a speech before the Amherst College Alumni Council, Frost suggests that all thinking—not merely poetic thinking—is grounded in metaphor, but he concludes that the poet's attempt to "say matter in terms of spirit" is the highest form of thought. The essay, perhaps his most famous, was printed in 1966 in* The Selected Prose of Robert Frost.

I am going to urge nothing in my talk. I am not an advocate. I am going to consider a matter, and commit a description. And I am going to describe other colleges than Amherst. Or, rather say all that is good can be taken as about Amherst; all that is bad will be about other colleges.

I know whole colleges where all American poetry is barred—whole colleges. I know whole colleges where all contemporary poetry is barred.

I once heard of a minister who turned his daughter—his poetry-writing daughter—out on the street to earn a living, because he said there should be no more books written; God wrote one book, and that was enough. (My friend George Russell "Æ" has read no literature, he protests, since just before Chaucer.)

That all seems sufficiently safe, and you can say one thing for it. It takes the onus off the poetry of having to be used to teach children anything. It comes pretty hard on poetry, I sometimes think—what it has to bear in the teaching process.

Then I know whole colleges where, though they let in older poetry, they manage to bar all that is poetical in it by treating it as something other than poetry. It is not so hard to do that. Their reason I have often hunted for. It may be that these people act from a kind of modesty. Who are professors that they should attempt to deal with a thing as high and as fine as poetry? Who are *they*? There is a certain manly modesty in that.

That is the best general way of settling the problem; treat all poetry as if it were something else than poetry, as if it were syntax, language, science. Then you can even come down into the American and into the contemporary without any special risk.

There is another reason they have, and that is that they are, first and foremost in life, markers. They have the marking problem to consider. Now, I stand here a teacher of many years' experience and I have never complained of having had to mark. I had rather mark anyone for anything—for his looks, carriage, his ideas, his correctness, his exactness, anything you please,—I would rather give him a mark in terms of letters, A, B, C, D, than have to use adjectives on him. We are all being marked by each other all the time, classified, ranked, put in our place, and I see no escape from that. I am no sentimentalist. You have got to mark, and you have got to mark, first of all, for accuracy, for correctness. But if I am going to give a mark, that is the least part of my marking. The hard part is the part beyond that, the part where the adventure begins.

One other way to rid the curriculum of the poetry nuisance has been considered. More merciful than the others it would neither abolish nor denature the poetry, but only turn it out to disport itself, with the plays and games—in no wise discredited, though given no credit for. Any one who liked to teach poetically could take his subject, whether English, Latin, Greek or French, out into the nowhere along with the poetry. One side of a sharp line would be left to the rigorous and righteous; the other side would be assigned to the flowery where they would know what could be expected of them. Grade marks where more easily given, of course, in the courses concentrating on correctness and exactness as the only forms of honesty recognized by plain people; a general indefinite mark of X in the courses that scatter brains over taste and opinion. On inquiry I have found no teacher willing to take position on either side of the line, either among the rigors or among the flowers. No one is willing to admit that his discipline is not partly in exactness. No one is willing to admit that his discipline is not partly in taste and enthusiasm.

How shall a man go through college without having been marked for taste and judgment? What will become of him? What will his end be? He will have to take continuation courses for college graduates. He will have to go to night schools. They are having night schools now, you know, for college graduates. Why? Because they have not been educated enough to find their way around in contemporary literature. They don't know what they may safely like in the libraries and galleries. They don't know how to judge an editorial when they see one. They don't know how to judge a political campaign. They don't know when they are being fooled by a metaphor, an analogy, a parable. And metaphor is, of course, what we are talking about. Education by poetry is education by metaphor.

Suppose we stop short of imagination, initiative, enthusiasm, inspiration and originality—dread words. Suppose we don't mark in such things at all. There are still two minimal things, that we have got to take care of, taste and judgment. Americans are supposed to have more judgment than taste, but taste is there to be dealt with. That is what poetry, the only art in the colleges of arts, is there for. I for my part would not be afraid to go in for enthusiasm. There is the enthusiasm like a blinding light, or the enthusiasm of the deafening shout, the crude enthusiasm that you get uneducated by poetry, outside of poetry. It is exemplified in what I might call "sunset raving." You look westward toward the sunset, or if you get up early enough, eastward toward the sunrise, and you rave. It is oh's and ah's with you and no more.

But the enthusiasm I mean is taken through the prism of the intellect and spread on the screen in a color, all the way from hyperbole at one end—or overstatement, at one end—to understatement at the other end. It is a long strip of dark lines and many colors. Such enthusiasm is one object of all teaching in poetry. I heard wonderful things said about Virgil yesterday, and many of them seemed to me crude enthusiasm, more like a deafening shout, many of them. But one speech had range, something of overstatement, something of statement, and something of understatement. It had all the colors of an enthusiasm passed through an idea.

I would be willing to throw away everything else but that: enthusiasm tamed by metaphor. Let me rest the case there. Enthusiasm tamed to metaphor, tamed to that much of it. I do not think anybody ever knows the discreet use of metaphor, his own and other people's, the discreet handling of metaphor, unless he has been properly educated in poetry.

Poetry begins in trivial metaphors, pretty metaphors, "grace" metaphors, and goes on to the profoundest thinking that we have. Poetry provides the one permissible way of saying one thing and meaning another. People say, "Why don't you say what you mean?" We never do that, do we, being all of us too much poets. We like to talk in parables and in hints and in indirections—whether from diffidence or some other instinct.

I have wanted in late years to go further and further in making metaphor the whole of thinking. I find some one now and then to agree with me that all thinking, except mathematical thinking, is metaphorical, or all thinking except scientific thinking. The mathematical might be difficult for me to bring in, but the scientific is easy enough.

Once on a time all the Greeks were busy telling each other what the All was—or was like unto. All was three elements, air, earth, and water (we once thought it was ninety elements; now we think it is only one). All was substance, said another. All was change, said a third. But best and most fruitful was Pythagoras' comparison of the universe with number. Number of what? Number of feet, pounds, and seconds was the answer, and we had science and all that has followed in science. The metaphor has held and held, breaking down only when it came to the spiritual and psychological or the out of the way places of the physical.

The other day we had a visitor here, a noted scientist, whose latest word to the world has been that the more accurately you know where a thing is, the less accurately you are able to state how fast it is moving. You can see why that would be so, without going back to Zeno's problem of the arrow's flight. In carrying numbers into the realm of space and at the same time into the realm of time you are mixing metaphors, that is all, and you are in trouble. They won't mix. The two don't go together.

Let's take two or three more of the metaphors now in use to live by. I have just spoken of one of the new ones, a charming mixed metaphor right in the realm of higher mathematics and higher physics: that the more accurately you state where a thing is, the less accurately you will be able to tell how fast it is moving. And, of course, everything is moving. Everything is an event now. Another metaphor. A thing, they say, is an event. Do you believe it is? Not quite. I believe it is almost an event. But I like the comparison of a thing with an event.

I notice another from the same quarter. "In the neighborhood of matter space is something like curved." Isn't that a good one! It seems to me that that is simply and utterly charming—to say that space is something like curved in the neighborhood of matter. "Something like."

Another amusing one is from—what is the book?—I can't say it now; but here is the metaphor. Its aim is to restore you to your ideas of free will. It wants to give you back your freedom of will. All right, here it is on a platter. You know that you can't tell by name what persons in a certain class will be dead ten years after graduation, but you can tell actuarially how many will be dead. Now, just so this scientist says of the particles of matter flying at a screen, striking a screen; you can't tell what individual particles will come, but you can say in general that a certain number will strike in a given time. It shows, you see, that the individual particle can come freely. I asked Bohr about that particularly, and he said, "Yes, it is so. It can come when it wills and as it wills; and the action of the individual particle is unpredictable. But it is not so of the action of the mass. There you can predict." He says, "That gives the individual atom its freedom, but the mass its necessity."

Another metaphor that has interested us in our time and has done all our thinking for us is the metaphor of evolution. Never mind going into the Latin word. The metaphor is simply the metaphor of the growing plant or of the growing thing. And somebody very brilliantly, quite a while ago, said that the whole universe, the whole of everything, was like unto a growing thing. That is all. I know the metaphor will break down at some point, but it has not failed everywhere. It is a very brilliant metaphor, I acknowledge, though I myself get too tired of the kind of essay that talks about the evolution of candy, we will say, or the evolution of elevators—the evolution of this, that, and the other. Everything is evolution. I emancipate myself by simply saying that I didn't get up the metaphor and so am not much interested in it.

What I am pointing out is that unless you are at home in the metaphor, unless you have had your proper poetical education in the metaphor, you are not safe anywhere. Because you are not at ease with figurative values: you don't know the metaphor in its strength and its weakness. You don't know how far you may expect to ride it and when it may break down with you. You are not safe in science; you are not safe in history. In history, for instance—to show that [it] is the same in history as elsewhere—I heard somebody say yesterday that Aeneas was to be likened unto (those words, "likened unto"!) George Washington. He was that type of national hero, the middle-class man, not thinking of being a hero at all, bent on building the future, bent on his children, his descendants. A good metaphor, as far as it goes, and you must know how far. And then he added that Odysseus should be likened unto Theodore Roosevelt. I don't think that is so good. Someone visiting Gibbon at the point of death, said he was the same Gibbon as of old, still at his parallels.

Take the way we have been led into our present position morally, the world over. It is by a sort of metaphorical gradient. There is a kind of thinking—to speak metaphorically—there is a kind of thinking you might say was endemic in the brothel. It is always there. And every now and then in some mysterious way it becomes epidemic in the world. And how does it do so? By using all the good words that virtue has invented to maintain virtue. It uses honesty, first,—frankness, sincerity—those words; picks them up, uses them. "In the name of honesty, let us see what we are." You know. And then it picks up the word joy. "Let us in the name of joy, which is the enemy of our ancestors, the Puritans . . . Let us in the name of joy, which is the enemy of the kill-joy Puritan . . ." You see. "Let us," and so on. And then, "In the name of health . . ." Health is another good word. And that is the metaphor Freudianism trades on, mental health. And the first thing we know, it has us all in up to the top knot. I suppose we may blame the artists a good deal, because they are great people to spread by metaphor. The stage too—the stage is always a good intermediary between the two worlds, the under and the upper—if I may say so without personal prejudice to the stage.

In all this I have only been saying that the devil can quote Scripture, which simply means that the good words you have lying around the devil can use for his purposes as well as anybody else. Never mind about my morality. I am not here to urge anything. I don't care whether the world is good or bad—not on any particular day.

Let me ask you to watch a metaphor breaking down here before you.

Somebody said to me a little while ago, "It is easy enough for me to think of the universe as a machine, as a mechanism."

I said, "You mean the universe is like a machine?"

He said, "No, I think it is one . . . Well, it is like . . ."

"I think you mean the universe is like a machine."

"All right. Let it go at that."

I asked him, "Did you ever see a machine without a pedal for the foot, or a lever for the hand, or a button for the finger?"

He said, "No—no."

I said, "All right. Is the universe like that?"

And he said, "No. I mean it is like a machine, only . . ."

". . . it is different from a machine," I said.

He wanted to go just that far with that metaphor and no further. And so do we all. All metaphor breaks down somewhere. That is the beauty of it. It is touch and go with the metaphor, and until you have lived with it long enough you don't know when it is going. You don't know how much you can get out of it and when it will cease to yield. It is a very living thing. It is as life itself.

I have heard this ever since I can remember, and ever since I have taught: the teacher must teach the pupil to think. I saw a teacher once going around in a great school and snapping pupils' heads with thumb and finger and saying, "Think." That was when thinking was becoming the fashion. The fashion hasn't yet quite gone out.

We still ask boys in college to think, as in the nineties, but we seldom tell them what thinking means; we seldom tell them it is just putting this and that together; it is just saying one thing in terms of another. To tell them is to set their feet on the first rung of a ladder the top of which sticks through the sky.

Greatest of all attempts to say one thing in terms of another is the philosophical attempt to say matter in terms of spirit, or spirit in terms of matter, to make the final unity. That is the greatest attempt that ever failed. We stop just short there. But it is the height of poetry, the height of all thinking, the height of all poetic thinking, that attempt to say matter in terms of spirit and spirit in terms of matter. It is wrong to call anybody a materialist simply because he tries to say spirit in terms of matter, as if that were a sin. Materialism is not the attempt to say all in terms of matter. The only materialist—be he poet, teacher, scientist, politician, or statesman—is the man who gets lost in his material without a gathering metaphor to throw it into shape and order. He is the lost soul.

We ask people to think, and we don't show them what thinking is. Somebody says we don't need to show them how to think; bye and bye they will think. We will give them the forms of sentences and, if they have any ideas, then they will know how to write them. But that is preposterous. All there is to writing is having ideas. To learn to write is to learn to have ideas.

The first little metaphor . . . Take some of the trivial ones. I would rather have trivial ones of my own to live by than the big ones of other people.

I remember a boy saying, "He is the kind of person that wounds with his shield." That may be a slender one, of course. It goes a good way in character description. It has poetic grace. "He is the kind that wounds with his shield."

The shield reminds me—just to linger a minute—the shield reminds me of the inverted shield spoken of in one of the books of the "Odyssey," the book that tells about the longest swim on record. I forget how long it lasted—several days, was it?—but at last as Odysseus came near the coast of Phaeacia, he saw it on the horizon "like an inverted shield."

There is a better metaphor in the same book. In the end Odysseus comes ashore and crawls up the beach to spend the night under a double olive tree, and it says, as in a lonely farmhouse where it is hard to get fire—I am not quoting exactly—where it is hard to start the fire again if it goes out, they cover the seeds of fire with ashes to preserve it for the night, so Odysseus covered himself with the leaves around him and went to sleep. There you have something that gives you character, something of Odysseus himself. "Seeds of fire."

So Odysseus covered the seeds of fire in himself. You get the greatness of his nature.

But these are slighter metaphors than the ones we live by. They have their charm, their passing charm. They are as it were the first steps toward the great thoughts, grave thoughts, thoughts lasting to the end.

The metaphor whose manage we are best taught in poetry—that is all there is of thinking. It may not seem far for the mind to go but it is the mind's furthest. The richest accumulation of the ages is the noble metaphors we have rolled up.

I want to add one thing more that the experience of poetry is to anyone who comes close to poetry. There are two ways of coming close to poetry. One is by writing poetry. And some people think I want people to write poetry, but I don't; that is, I don't necessarily. I only want people to write poetry if they want to write poetry. I have never encouraged anybody to write poetry that did not want to write it, and I have not always encouraged those who did want to write it. That ought to be one's own funeral. It is a hard, hard life, as they say.

(I have just been to a city in the West, a city full of poets, a city they have made safe for poets. The whole city is so lovely that you do not have to write it up to make it poetry; it is ready-made for you. But, I don't know—the poetry written in that city might not seem like poetry if read outside of the city. It would be like the jokes made when you were drunk; you have to get drunk again to appreciate them.)

But as I say, there is another way to come close to poetry, fortunately, and that is in the reading of it, not as linguistics, not as history, not as anything but poetry. It is one of the hard things for a teacher to know how close a man has come in reading poetry. How do I know whether a man has come close to Keats in reading Keats? It is hard for me to know. I have lived with some boys a whole year over some of the poets and I have not felt sure whether they have come near what it was all about. One remark sometimes told me. One remark was their mark for the year; had to be—it was all I got that told me what I wanted to know. And that is enough, if it was the right remark, if it came close enough. I think a man might make twenty fool remarks if he made one good one some time in the year. His mark would depend on that good remark.

The closeness—everything depends on the closeness with which you come, and you ought to be marked for the closeness, for nothing else. And that will have to be estimated by chance remarks, not by question and answer. It is only by accident that you know some day how near a person has come.

The person who gets close enough to poetry, he is going to know more about the word *belief* than anybody else knows, even in religion nowadays. There are two or three places where we know belief outside of religion. One of them is at the age of fifteen to twenty, in our self-belief. A young man knows more about himself than he is able to prove to anyone. He has no knowledge that anybody else will accept as knowledge. In his foreknowledge he has something that is going to believe itself into fulfillment, into acceptance.

There is another belief like that, the belief in someone else, a relationship of two that is going to be believed into fulfillment. That is what we are talking about in our novels, the belief of love. And the disillusionment that the novels are full of is simply the disillusionment from disappointment in that belief. That belief can fail, of course.

Then there is a literary belief. Every time a poem is written, every time a short story is written, it is written not by cunning, but by belief. The beauty, the something, the little charm of the thing to be, is more felt than known. There is a common jest, one that always annoys me, on the writers, that they write the last end first, and then work up to it; that they lay a train toward one sentence that they think is pretty nice and have all fixed up to set like a trap to close with. No, it should not be that way at all. No one who has ever come close to the arts has failed to see the difference between things written that way, with cunning and device, and the kind that are believed into existence, that begin in something more felt than known. This you can realize quite as well—not quite as well, perhaps, but nearly as well—in reading as you can in writing. I would undertake to separate short stories on that principle; stories that have been believed into existence and stories that have been cunningly devised. And I could separate the poems still more easily.

Now I think—I happen to think—that those three beliefs that I speak of, the self-belief, the love-belief, and the art-belief, are all closely related to the God-belief, that the belief in God is a relationship you enter into with Him to bring about the future.

There is a national belief like that, too. One feels it. I have been where I came near getting up and walking out on the people who thought that they had to talk against nations, against nationalism, in order to curry favor with internationalism. Their metaphors are all mixed up. They think that because a Frenchman and an American and an Englishman can all sit down on the same platform and receive honors together, it must be that there is no such thing as nations. That kind of bad thinking springs from a source we all know. I should want to say to anyone like that: "Look! First I want to be a person. And I want you to be a person, and then we can be as interpersonal as you please. We can pull each other's noses—do all sorts of things. But, first of all, you have got to have the personality. First of all, you have got to have the nations and then they can be as international as they please with each other."

I should like to use another metaphor on them. I want my palette, if I am a painter, I want my palette on my thumb or on my chair, all clean, pure, separate colors. Then I will do the mixing on the canvas. The canvas is where the work of art is, where we make the conquest. But we want the nations all separate, pure, distinct, things as separate as we can make them; and then in our thoughts, in our arts, and so on, we can do what we please about it.

But I go back. There are four beliefs that I know more about from having lived with poetry. One is the personal belief, which is a knowledge that you don't want to tell other people about because you cannot prove that you know. You are saying nothing about it till you see. The love belief, just the same, has that same shyness. It knows it cannot tell; only the outcome can tell. And the national belief we enter into socially with each other, all together, party of the first part, party of the second part, we enter into that to bring the future of the country. We cannot tell some people what it is we believe, partly, because they are too stupid to understand and partly because we are too proudly vague to explain. And anyway it has got to be fulfilled, and we are not talking until we know more, until we have something to show. And then the literary one in every work of art, not of cunning and craft, mind you, but of real art; that believing the thing into existence, saying as you go more than you even hoped you were going to be able to say, and coming with surprise to an end that you foreknew only with some sort of emotion. And then finally the relationship we enter into with God to believe the future in—to believe the hereafter in.

Discussing Ideas and Themes

1. In the very beginning of his essay, Frost says, "I know whole colleges where all American poetry is barred." What might be the problem such colleges would have with poetry? Why does Frost think poetry is risky?

2. What does Frost think a student should and shouldn't be graded for? For example, he doesn't think students should be marked for merely knowing facts about a poet or a poem, but how and where does Frost explain this?

3. How does Frost tie scientific thinking with thinking by metaphor? What does he mean by "metaphor" when he uses it as a term for thinking, and what examples from science does he use to support his argument? Can you think of more examples from science that either support or refute Frost's idea?

4. How does Frost integrate social and political issues into this essay? For example, how does his discussion of the metaphor of "evolution" set up his later discussion of words like "honesty" and "health"?

5. According to Frost, what are the two ways that one can "come close to poetry"? What does he mean by the word "close"? One meaning might be that one gets close by reading with "enthusiasm passed through metaphor"—what are some other meanings?

Discussing Rhetoric and Style

1. Frost opens his essay by assuring the reader that he is "going to urge nothing," that he is "not an advocate." How does this rhetorical gambit work—do you, for even a moment, believe that he's telling you the truth here?

2. How does Frost develop the metaphor of safety and risk in relation to poetry? For example, how does his discussion of marking return to the issue of safety? How has this metaphor been extended by the end of the essay, and to what effect?

3. What is Frost's tone in this essay? How does he come across as a speaker, as a person? Be sure to base your ideas on specific observations about diction and syntax.

4. Describe the logic of this essay. Can you identify Frost's major premises, his methods of arguing, his conclusions? There *is* an argument here, but Frost has disguised it. How does he do this?

Ideas for Writing

1. Look up a poem of Frost's and write a brief essay that analyzes that poem using his theory of poetry. Frost argues that poets attempt to "say matter in terms of spirit or spirit in terms of matter"; does the poem you have chosen try to do either of these things, as far as you can tell? Does Frost's metaphor break down at some point within the poem?

2. Frost suggests that all metaphors break down at some point. Compose two metaphors of your own, or borrow two from somewhere or someone else (as Frost borrows from science, for example) and write an essay in which you discuss how these metaphors function and explain where and how they break down.

Good Readers and Good Writers

VLADIMIR NABOKOV

Vladimir Nabokov (1890–1977) once described himself as an "American writer born in Russia and educated in England, where I studied French literature before spending fifteen years in Germany." The author of poems, short stories, plays, novels, and literary criticism, Nabokov was also an avid butterfly hunter, teaching and lecturing in the humanities at Cornell and Wellesley. "Good Readers and Good Writers," one of a collection of lectures in Lectures on Literature *explores the ways in which great writers create fictional worlds through the powerful exercise of their imagination.*

"How to Be a Good Reader" or "Kindness to Authors"—something of that sort might serve to provide a subtitle for these various discussions of various authors, for my plan is to deal lovingly, in loving and lingering detail, with several European masterpieces. A hundred years ago, Flaubert in a letter to his mistress made the following remark: *Comme l'on serait savant si l'on connaissait bien seulement cinq à six livres:* "What a scholar one might be if one knew well only some half a dozen books."

In reading, one should notice and fondle details. There is nothing wrong about the moonshine of generalization when it comes *after* the sunny trifles of the book have been lovingly collected. If one begins with a ready-made generalization, one begins at the wrong end and travels away from the book before one has started to understand it. Nothing is more boring or more unfair to the author than starting to read, say, *Madame Bovary,* with the preconceived notion that it is a denunciation of the bourgeoisie. We should always remember that the work of art is invariably the creation of a new world, so that the first thing we should do is to study that new world as closely as possible, approaching it as something brand new, having no obvious connection with the worlds we already know. When this new world has been closely studied, then and only then let us examine its links with other worlds, other branches of knowledge.

Another question: Can we expect to glean information about places and times from a novel? Can anybody be so naive as to think he or she can learn anything about the past from those buxom best-sellers that are hawked around by book clubs under the heading of historical novels? But what about the masterpieces? Can we rely on Jane Austen's picture of landowning England with baronets and landscaped grounds when all she knew was a clergyman's parlor? And *Bleak House,* that fantastic romance within a fantastic London, can we call it a study of London a hundred years ago? Certainly not. And the same holds for other such novels in this series. The truth is that great novels are great fairy tales—and the novels in this series are supreme fairy tales.

Time and space, the colors of the seasons, the movements of muscles and minds, all these are for writers of genius (as far as we can guess and I trust we guess right), not traditional notions which may be borrowed from the circulating library of public truths but a series of unique surprises which master artists have learned to express in their own unique way. To minor authors is left the ornamentation of the commonplace: these do not bother about any reinventing of the world; they merely try to squeeze the best they can out of a given order of things, out of traditional patterns of fiction. The various combinations these minor authors are able to produce within these set limits may be quite amusing in a mild ephemeral way because minor readers like to recognize their own ideas in a pleasing disguise. But the real writer, the fellow who sends planets spinning and models a man asleep and eagerly tampers with the sleeper's rib, that kind of author has no given values at his disposal: he must create them himself. The art of writing is a very futile business if it does not imply first of all the art of seeing the world as the potentiality of fiction. The material of this world may be real enough (as far as reality goes) but does not exist at all as an accepted entirety: it is chaos, and to this chaos the author says "go!" allowing the world to flicker and to fuse. It is now recombined in its very atoms, not merely in its visible and superficial parts. The writer is the first man to map it and to name the natural objects it contains. Those berries there are edible. That speckled creature that bolted across my path might be tamed. That lake between those trees will be called Lake Opal or, more artistically, Dishwater Lake. That mist is a mountain—and that mountain must be conquered. Up a trackless slope climbs the master artist, and at the top, on a windy ridge, whom do you think he meets? The panting and happy reader, and there they spontaneously embrace and are linked forever if the book lasts forever.

One evening at a remote provincial college through which I happened to be jogging on a protracted lecture tour, I suggested a little quiz—ten definitions of a reader, and from these ten the students had to choose four definitions that would combine to make a good reader. I have mislaid the list, but as far as I remember the definitions went something like this. Select four answers to the question what should a reader be to be a good reader:

1. The reader should belong to a book club.
2. The reader should identify himself or herself with the hero or heroine.
3. The reader should concentrate on the social-economic angle.
4. The reader should prefer a story with action and dialogue to one with none.
5. The reader should have seen the book in a movie.
6. The reader should be a budding author.
7. The reader should have imagination.
8. The reader should have memory.
9. The reader should have a dictionary.
10. The reader should have some artistic sense.

The students leaned heavily on emotional identification, action, and the social-economic or historical angle. Of course, as you have guessed, the good reader is one who has imagination, memory, a dictionary, and some artistic sense—which sense I propose to develop in myself and in others whenever I have the chance.

Incidentally, I use the word *reader* very loosely. Curiously enough, one cannot *read* a book: one can only reread it. A good reader, a major reader, an active and creative reader is a rereader. And I shall tell you why. When we read a book for the first time the very process of laboriously moving our eyes from left to right, line after line, page after page, this complicated physical work upon the book, the very process of learning in terms of space and time what the book is about, this stands between us and artistic appreciation. When we look at a painting we do not have to move our eyes in a special way even if, as in a book, the picture contains elements of depth and development. The element of time does not really enter in a first contact with a painting. In reading a book, we must have time to acquaint ourselves with it. We have no physical organ (as we have the eye in regard to a painting) that takes in the whole picture and then can enjoy its details. But at a second, or third, or fourth reading we do, in a sense, behave towards a book as we do towards a painting. However, let us not confuse the physical eye, that monstrous masterpiece of evolution, with the mind, an even more monstrous achievement. A book, no matter what it is—a work of fiction or a work of science (the boundary line between the two is not as clear as is generally believed)—a book of fiction appeals first of all to the mind. The mind, the brain, the top of the tingling spine, is, or should be, the only instrument used upon a book.

Now, this being so, we should ponder the question how does the mind work when the sullen reader is confronted by the sunny book. First, the sullen mood melts away, and for better or worse the reader enters into the spirit of the game. The effort to begin a book, especially if it is praised by people whom the young reader secretly deems to be too old-fashioned or too serious, this effort is often difficult to make; but once it is made, rewards are various and abundant. Since the master artist used his imagination in creating his book, it is natural and fair that the consumer of a book should use his imagination too.

There are, however, at least two varieties of imagination in the reader's case. So let us see which one of the two is the right one to use in reading a book. First, there is the comparatively lowly kind which turns for support to the simple emotions and is of a definitely personal nature. (There are various subvarieties here, in this first section of emotional reading.) A situation in a book is intensely felt because it reminds us of something that happened to us or to someone we know or knew. Or, again, a reader treasures a book mainly because it evokes a country, a landscape, a mode of living which he nostalgically recalls as part of his own past. Or, and this is the worst thing a reader can do, he identifies himself with a character in the book. This lowly variety is not the kind of imagination I would like readers to use.

So what is the authentic instrument to be used by the reader? It is impersonal imagination and artistic delight. What should be established, I think, is an artistic harmonious balance between the reader's mind and the author's mind. We ought to remain a little aloof and take pleasure in this aloofness while at the same time we keenly enjoy—passionately enjoy, enjoy with tears and shivers—the inner weave of a given masterpiece. To be quite objective in these matters is of course impossible. Everything that is worthwhile is to some extent subjective. For instance, you sitting there may be merely my dream, and I may be your nightmare. But what I mean is that the reader must know when and where to curb his imagination and this he does by trying to get clear the specific world the author places at his disposal. We must see things and hear things, we must visualize the rooms, the clothes, the manners of an author's people. The color of Fanny Price's eyes in *Mansfield Park* and the furnishing of her cold little room are important.

We all have different temperaments, and I can tell you right now that the best temperament for a reader to have, or to develop, is a combination of the artistic and the scientific one. The enthusiastic artist alone is apt to be too subjective in his attitude towards a book, and so a scientific coolness of judgment will temper the intuitive heat. If, however, a would-be reader is utterly devoid of passion and patience—of an artist's passion and a scientist's patience—he will hardly enjoy great literature.

Literature was born not the day when a boy crying wolf, wolf came running out of the Neanderthal valley with a big gray wolf at his heels: literature was born on the day when a boy came crying wolf, wolf and there was no wolf behind him. That the poor little fellow because he lied too often was finally eaten up by a real beast is quite incidental. But here is what is important. Between the wolf in the tall grass and the wolf in the tall story there is a shimmering go-between. That go-between, that prism, is the art of literature.

Literature is invention. Fiction is fiction. To call a story a true story is an insult to both art and truth. Every great writer is a great deceiver, but so is that arch-cheat Nature. Nature always deceives. From the simple deception of propagation to the prodigiously sophisticated illusion of protective colors in butterflies or birds, there is in Nature a marvelous system of spells and wiles. The writer of fiction only follows Nature's lead.

Going back for a moment to our wolf-crying woodland little woolly fellow, we may put it this way: the magic of art was in the shadow of the wolf that he deliberately invented, his dream of the wolf; then the story of his tricks made a good story. When he perished at last, the story told about him acquired a good lesson in the dark around the camp fire. But he was the little magician. He was the inventor.

There are three points of view from which a writer can be considered: he may be considered as a storyteller, as a teacher, and as an enchanter. A major writer combines these three—storyteller, teacher, enchanter—but it is the enchanter in him that predominates and makes him a major writer.

To the storyteller we turn for entertainment, for mental excitement of the simplest kind, for emotional participation, for the pleasure of traveling in some remote region in space or time. A slightly different though not necessarily higher mind looks for the teacher in the writer. Propagandist, moralist, prophet—this is the rising sequence. We may go to the teacher not only for moral education but also for direct knowledge, for simple facts. Alas, I have known people whose purpose in reading the French and Russian novelists was to learn something about life in gay Paree or in sad Russia. Finally, and above all, a great writer is always a great enchanter, and it is here that we come to the really exciting part when we try to grasp the individual magic of his genius and to study the style, the imagery, the pattern of his novels or poems.

The three facets of the great writer—magic, story, lesson—are prone to blend in one impression of unified and unique radiance, since the magic of art may be present in the very bones of the story, in the very marrow of thought. There are masterpieces of dry, limpid, organized thought which provoke in us an artistic quiver quite as strongly as a novel like *Mansfield Park* does or as any rich flow of Dickensian sensual imagery. It seems to me that a good formula to test the quality of a novel is, in the long run, a merging of the precision of poetry and the intuition of science. In order to bask in that magic a wise reader reads the book of genius not with his heart, not so much with his brain, but with his spine. It is there that occurs the telltale tingle even though we must keep a little aloof, a little detached when reading. Then with a pleasure which is both sensual and intellectual we shall watch the artist build his castle of cards and watch the castle of cards become a castle of beautiful steel and glass.

Discussing Ideas and Themes

1. Nabokov says that "great novels are great fairy tales," citing work by Jane Austen, Dickens, and others for his examples. Do you agree with him? Can you think of any literary examples to support your position?

2. Why does Nabokov suggest that "Dishwater Lake" is a "more artistic" name than "Lake Opal"? Do you think most readers would agree with him?

3. What are the two kinds of imagination that Nabokov suggests a reader might have? Which does he prefer? Can you make any comparisons with Frost's "Education by Poetry"?

4. How does Nabokov link the story of the boy who cried wolf with the idea of the writer as prophet? What is the relation of the reader to the three possible functions of the writer, and is it related to the actions or attitudes of the villagers who listened to the boy? Or does the metaphor break down here?

Discussing Rhetoric and Style

1. What metaphor for reading is implied in the opening paragraph? How does Nabokov reinforce and develop it throughout the essay, and what effect does the metaphor have on the reader?
2. How does the logic of Nabokov's argument about "minor" writers versus "real" writers work? How does he set it up and develop it? What kind of argument is it? What other essayists have used the same kind of argument?
3. What are the effects of Nabokov's list of qualities of readers? For example, whom do you identify with more—Nabokov or his students?
4. How does Nabokov use adjectives (for example, "speckled" and "limpid") in the essay? Are they the adjectives you might expect?
5. What is Nabokov's main appeal to the reader? Is it to the reader's mind (logical), to emotions (emotional), or to beliefs (ethical)? Are you persuaded more by Nabokov's argument or by his style?

Ideas for Writing

1. In the last section of his essay, Nabokov begins with a fable (The Boy Who Cried Wolf) and makes an analogy from this fable to support his idea about writers. Write an imitation of Nabokov's last few paragraphs, using his structure to make a different argument based on a different fable—for example, The Tortoise and the Hare.
2. Write a response to Nabokov in which you (tactfully) take issue with one of the points of his argument (for example, you might disagree with him about artists not representing reality). Try to be careful—Nabokov, the reader you must imagine for your essay, is smart—and try to combine sound argument with vivid, interesting prose, just as Nabokov himself does.

Reading in Slow Motion

REUBEN BROWER

Born in Lanesboro, Pennsylvania, Reuben Brower (1908–1975) lived a life of distinguished scholarship, graduating from Amherst College summa cum laude *in 1930 and later attending Harvard, Oxford, and Cambridge Universities. He went on to become a fellow at Harvard, receiving numerous awards and fellowships and publishing books and essays on figures such as Pope, Shakespeare, Dryden, Austen, and Frost. In "Reading in Slow Motion," excerpted from* Reading for Life *(1959), Brower proposes that we need not to read more quickly, but more slowly and more thoroughly. In doing so, he offers us a course plan for "Literature X," a class that would embody his theories on writing and reading.*

The Question put to me at a conference on undergraduate education, "How shall we encourage and influence the lifetime reading habit?" brought to mind the words of Solon that Croesus recalled on the funeral pyre: "I shall not call you fortunate until I learn that the end of your life was happy too." Call no student a lifetime reader until . . . No teacher can be quite sure that he has a lifetime habit of reading, and if asked whether his students have acquired it or formed good reading habits, he will probably feel most uneasy about making an answer. But assuming that we could see each student's life as a whole, *sub specie æternitatis,* we should have to ask the further question: What reading habit are we evaluating? In the age of the New Stupid (a term Aldous Huxley once used for the age of mass literacy), nearly everyone has a reading habit of some sort. Everyone runs through the morning newspaper or *Time* and *Life* strictly as a matter of daily or weekly routine. Each social group has its "great readers," a term of admiration used to cover a wide range of activities that have little more than the printed page in common. There is, for example, reading as anodyne, and reading as extended daydream. There is reading as pursuit of fact or of useful technical knowhow, and reading that may or may not be useful, when we are interested solely in understanding a theory or a point of view. Still more remote from immediate usefulness comes reading as active amusement, a game demanding the highest alertness and the finest degree of sensibility, "judgment ever awake and steady self-possession with enthusiasm and feeling profound or vehement." Reading at this level—to borrow Coleridgean terms a second time—"brings the whole soul of man into activity." Coleridge was speaking of the poet and the power of imagination, but his words describe very well the way we read when we enter into, or rather engage in, experiences of imaginative literature. I say "amusement," not "pleasure," to stress the play of mind, the play of the whole being, that reading of this sort calls for. I am hardly suggesting that literary experience is not a "good," that it is not in some indirect and profound way morally valuable. But if it is to do us any good, it must be fun. The first line of a poem by D. H. Lawrence offers an appropriate motto for teachers and students of literature:

> If it's never any fun, don't do it!

Active "amusement" is the reading habit I am concerned with here and more especially with the role played by the teacher of literature in encouraging students to acquire it. I prefer to speak of the "teacher of literature," not the "humanities," because that noble term has become so debased in current usage, and because teachers of texts in humanities courses are or should be teachers of literature. The teacher of Plato or Hobbes or Hume is not only interpreting a system but an expression, an expression that uses many resources of language and uses them in ways that profoundly influence how we take the writer's radical meaning. We cannot subtract from our interpretations the effect of Platonic comedy or of Hobbesian metaphor or of Hume's dispassionate irony. But it remains true that the teacher of literature in the conventional sense has a special interest in encouraging students to respond actively to all the uses of language, from the barely referential to the rhythmic. He is always more or less consciously urging his students to make themselves readers of imagination.

How will the teacher go about reaching this noble aim? By a method that might be described as "slow motion," by slowing down the process of reading to observe what is happening, in order to attend very closely to the words, their uses, and their meanings. Since poetry is literature in its essential and purest form—the mode of writing in which we find at the same time the most varied uses of language and the highest degree of order—the first aim of the teacher of literature will be to make his students better readers of poetry. He will try by every means in his power to bring out the complete and agile response to words that is demanded by a good poem.

But in order not to create a wrong impression, a word needs to be said here about method, a term liable to please some and displease others for equally bad reasons. There is certainly no single sacred technique for teaching reading at the level I have in mind. In teaching literature—unlike science, one may suppose—no holds are barred, providing they work and providing that the injury to the work and to the student does not exceed the limits of humanity. The most distinctive feature of the kind of literature course I am about to describe is that the teacher does have some "holds," some ways of reading that he is willing to demonstrate and that his students can imitate. In this respect "Literature X," as I shall call it, differs from the old-time appreciation course in which the teacher mounted the platform and sang a rhapsody which he alone was capable of understanding and which the student memorized, with the usual inaccuracies, for the coming examination.

But why a course in slow reading? The parent who has a son or daughter in college may well feel confused, since almost certainly he has at least one child with a reading difficulty, the most common complaint being that the child cannot read fast enough. As the parent himself watches the mounting lists of important books, and as he scans the rivers of print in the daily paper, he may well feel that like Alice and the Red Queen, he and his children are going faster and faster but getting nowhere.

The difficulties of parent and child point to conditions that have led to the introduction of how-to-read courses in our colleges and universities. We might note first the sheer mass of printed material to which we are exposed—not to mention the flood of words and images pouring through radio and television. If by temperament or principle we resist the distracting appeals of the press and other media, we must nevertheless read a great deal as we run if we are to perform our tasks as citizens and wage earners. Add to such facts the changes in family life that have altered reading habits of both parents and children. Memorization of Bible texts and poetry is hardly common in school or home, and the family reading circle where books were read aloud and slowly, has all but disappeared even from the idyllic backwaters of academic communities. Yet many if not all of the writers of the past, from Homer to novelists like Jane Austen and Dickens, have assumed reading aloud and a relatively slow rate of intellectual digestion. Literature of the first order calls for lively reading; we must almost act it out as if we were taking parts in a play. As the average high school student reads more and more with less and less wholeness of attention, he may become positively incapacitated for reading the classics of his own or any literature. Incidentally, the parent of the slow reader should take heart: his child may not be stupid, but more than ordinarily sensitive to words. He may in fact have the makings of a poet.

Another change in precollege education is almost certainly connected with the decline in the ability to read literature of the first quality, a change that points also to profound changes in the literary public of the past century and a half. Until thirty or forty years ago a high proportion of students of literature in our liberal arts colleges had received a considerable training in Latin or Greek. If we move back to the much smaller reading publics of the seventeenth and eighteenth centuries, the audiences for whom much of our greatest literature was written, the relative number of readers trained in the classics becomes much higher. The principal method of teaching the ancient languages, translation into English or from English into Latin or Greek, may have had disadvantages compared with the direct method of today, but as a basic preparation for the study of literature it can hardly be surpassed. It may be doubted whether learning of a foreign language can take place without some translation, at least into what experts in linguistics call the "meta-language" of the learner. To translate from Latin and Greek demanded close attention to the printed word, and since the ideas being communicated and the linguistic and literary forms through which they were expressed were often quite unlike those in English, translation compelled the closest scrutiny of meanings and forms of expression in both the ancient and the modern language. Although the old-time classicist may not always have been successful as a teacher of literature, he cannot often be accused of lacking rigor. His students had to spend a good many hours in school and college reading some pieces of literature very attentively. One purpose of a course in slow reading is to offer a larger number of present-day undergraduates an equivalent for the older classical training in interpretation of texts.

It might be noted that Coleridge, who harshly criticized the practice of Latin versemaking in English schools, paid the highest tribute to that "severe master, the Reverend James Bowyer":

> At the same time that we were studying the Greek tragic poets, he made us read Shakespeare and Milton as lessons: and they were the lessons too, which required the most time and trouble to *bring up*, so as to escape his censure. I learned from him, that poetry, even that of the loftiest and, seemingly, that of the wildest odes, had a logic of its own, as severe as that of science; and more difficult, because more subtle, more complex, and dependent on more and more fugitive causes. In the truly great poets, he would say, there is a reason assignable

> not only for every word, but for the position of every word; and I well remember that, availing himself of the synonymes to the Homer of Didymus, he made us attempt to show, with regard to each, why it would not have answered the same purpose; and wherein consisted the peculiar fitness of the word in the original text.
>
> In our own English compositions (at least for the last three years of our school education) he showed no mercy to phrase, metaphor, or image, unsupported by a sound sense, or where the same sense might have been conveyed with equal force and dignity in plainer words. *Lute, harp,* and *lyre, Muse, Muses,* and *inspirations, Pegasus, Parnassus,* and *Hippocrene* were all an abomination to him. In fancy I can almost hear him now, exclaiming: "Harp? Harp? Lyre? Pen and ink, boy, you mean! Muse, boy, Muse? Your nurse's daughter, you mean! Pierian spring? Oh aye! the cloister-pump, I suppose!"

The Reverend James Bowyer and not Coleridge, it appears, was the original New Critic, which is to say that much New Criticism is old criticism writ large. Bowyer's example suggests another important point to which I shall return: that teaching of reading is necessarily teaching of writing. The student cannot show his teacher or himself that he has had an important and relevant literary experience except in writing or in speaking that is as disciplined as good writing.

To teach reading or any other subject in the style of the Reverend Bowyer demands an attitude toward the job that is obvious but easily overlooked in our larger universities, where increasing numbers of students often impose mass production methods. The most important requirement for teaching an undergraduate course—beyond belief in what one is doing—is to keep this question in mind: What is happening to the student? Other questions soon follow: What do I want him to do and how can I get him to do it? Planning and teaching from this point of view makes the difference between a course that engages the student and one that merely displays the teacher. The perfect model for the teacher of literature as for the teacher of science is Agassiz, who would come into the laboratory, pour out a basket of bones before the student, and leave him alone to sort them out. We learn that after this introduction to the "material" of the course, Agassiz limited his teaching to infrequent visits, when he checked on the learner's progress by an occasional nod or shake of the head to say "That's right!" or "No, not that!" The great thing in teaching is to get the basket of bones before the student and get him to sorting them for himself as soon as possible. What we must avoid at all costs is sorting out all the bones in advance. Agassiz' principle is of great importance in the teaching of literature, where far too often we present the undergraduate with the end products of literary scholarship without being sure he has read or has the capacity of reading the works we are interpreting.

If we are interested in fostering a habit of reading well, we must set up our introductory courses on a principle very different from that underlying the older survey or the now more fashionable history-of-ideas course. We are not handing the student a body of knowledge, so much "material"—the history of the Romantic Movement or an anatomy of the concepts labeled "Romanticism"—however useful such knowledge may be at a later stage in literary education. Our aim rather is to get the student in a position where he can learn for himself. If we succeed, we have reason to believe that he may acquire a lifetime habit of learning independently. The teacher who is working toward this noble end will always be working *with* the student, not *for* him or *over* him. Whitehead used to say that the student should feel he is present while the teacher is thinking, present at an occasion when thought is in process. Those who knew Whitehead in the classroom will know what he meant and why he never seemed to be lecturing, even before a class of a hundred or two hundred students. His listeners never knew exactly where he was coming out. Not knowing where one is coming out is an essential part of the experience of thinking.

To get the student to a point where he can learn for himself requires therefore a redefinition of a "lecture." It asks the teacher to share his ignorance with his students as well as his knowledge. Or if professors shrink from admitting less than omniscience, it calls for at least a Socratic simulation of ignorance. What is wanted is the "nonlecture," to borrow e. e. cummings's happy term, an action performed by the teacher but clearly directed to the next performance of the student. The ideal nonlecturer is setting a job for the student and showing him how he would go about doing it. If he is not in fact setting a job, he will clearly indicate a relevant kind of job to be done. A proper job means setting a question and offering a way, not a formula, for answering it. Student and teacher must clearly understand that a course in interpretation is a course in "right answering," not a course in "right answers."

Let me now attempt to describe Literature X, a course in slow reading that aims to meet the general requirements I have been outlining and that is designed also to meet the needs of young readers in our colleges and universities. I have said that we want students to increase their power of engaging in imaginative experience, and we assume—this was implied by our earlier reference to Coleridge—that a work of literature offers us an experience through words that is different from average, everyday experience. It is different in its mysterious wholeness, in the number of elements embraced and in the variety and closeness of their relationship. When Othello, just before Desdemona's death, says, "Put out the light, and then put out the light," we feel not only the horror of his intention but also a remarkable concentration of much that has gone on before: the moving history of the relations between the lovers and between them and Iago, the echoed presence of earlier moments of "lightness" and "darkness."

We all agree that such experiences in literature are wonderful, but what can a teacher do to guide a student to discover them? He will of course start from his own excitement, and he will do everything he can to infect his students with it: he will try to express in other words what Othello and the audience are experiencing; he will read the passage aloud or get a student to do it; he will exhort and entreat. But finally he cannot hand over his feelings to his students; he cannot force them to be more sensitive than they are. What can he do that the students may also do and that they can imitate when they read another scene or another play? He can do a great deal if he remembers that while he and his students do not have a common nervous system, they do have the same printed page and they share some knowledge of the English language. He will therefore direct their attention to the words, to what they mean and to their connection with other words and meanings. In considering the "put out the light" speech from *Othello,* the teacher may begin by asking what the words mean in terms of stage business. He may then call for a paraphrase: for "put out the light" someone may offer "bring darkness," or "put an end to." The class can next be asked to connect this expression with others used elsewhere in the play. Someone may recall Othello's earlier line associating Desdemona with darkness and death: ". . . when I love thee not,/ Chaos is come again." The reader can now begin to appreciate the poignancy and the irony of Othello's picturing his action as "putting out the light." So by directing attention to words, their meanings, and relationships, the teacher may put his students in a position where they too will feel the pity and terror of this moment in the play.

We might describe Literature X as a "mutual demonstration society," the work of the course being carried on mainly through student-teacher explorations of the kind I have been attempting to illustrate. For the students the most important and most strenuous demonstrations will be the exercises that they write on their own after being suitably prepared by the teacher. *Othello* may serve as an example once more. After several classes of reading aloud and exploring connections in the earlier acts of the play, an exercise will be set on a speech or scene from the last act. The students now have an opportunity to show whether they can practice independently the sort of interpretation they have been attempting in class. To guide them, they will be given an exercise sheet with a very carefully planned series of questions. Beginning with queries on words and phrases, the exercise goes on to ask about relationships of various kinds, and it concludes with a question demanding a generalization about the work as a whole or about a type of literature or experience. An exercise on *Othello* might finally call for a statement about the nature of Othello's tragedy and for a tentative definition of "tragic" as used in Shakespearean drama. But the words "tragic" or "tragedy" will not necessarily appear in the directions; rather, the students will be impelled to talk about these concepts because they are relevant. In the class on the exercise papers the student and his teacher will be admirably prepared to consider what is meant by tragic literature and experience. These discussions of the exercises should be among the most valuable classes in the course. Here the student can learn by comparing where he succeeded or failed as an interpreter, and frequently he may have the pleasure of finding that he has taught his teacher something, an event that can give satisfaction to both parties and that can take place more often in a course where the student is an active participant, not a passive member of an audience.

Literature X as a whole will consist of a series of these exercise waves, with some more terrifying than others, the seventh and last coming when the students are given two or more weeks without classes in which to read new material—poems, plays, or novels—with no teacher to guide them.

The course will not begin with Shakespeare, although Shakespeare is the necessary measure of imaginative experience and of the capacity to engage in it. We shall begin rather with the smaller model of the short poem, because as I have said it offers literary experience in its purest form. By beginning with poems we can be reasonably sure that the student learns early to distinguish between life and literature and not to be unduly distracted by questions of biography and history or by social and psychological problems of the type raised so often by the novel. Most important, the student will learn at the outset to deal with *wholes*, since within the limits of a class hour or a brief paper he can arrive at an interpretation of a whole literary expression. Poems may come to stand in his mind as Platonic forms of true and complete literary experience.

Beginning with poems has another advantage if students are to learn the value of attending closely to language and if they are to see the satisfactions that come from alert and accurate reading. In the small world of a sonnet, a reader can see how a single word may cause a shift in the equilibrium of feeling in the whole poem. So when Shakespeare says:

> For thy sweet love remember'd such wealth brings
> That then I scorn to change my state with kings.

"state" carries connotations of Elizabethan *state,* and as a result the speaker's voice takes on a tone of grandeur, a somewhat stagey grandeur that reminds us of gestures in a play. But the word "state" would hardly impart that quality without the reference to "kings." This fairly simple example brings home the importance in interpretation of considering the context. A course in interpretation is a course in definition by context, in seeing how words are given rich and precise meaning through their interrelations with other words. The student who acquires this habit of definition will be a better reader of philosophy or law or any other type of specialized discourse, and he may learn something about the art of writing, of how to control context in order to express oneself.

Reading poems also offers one of the best ways of lifting the student from adolescent to adult appreciation of literature. The adult reader realizes that reading a work of literature is at once a solitary and a social act. In reading we are alone, but we are also among the company of readers assumed by the poem or play or novel. The poem is more than a personal message, it invites us to move out of ourselves, to get into an "act," to be another self in a fictive drama. The sonnet of Shakespeare we have just quoted seems to call for a very simple identification of the actual reader with the imagined speaker,

> When in disgrace with fortune and men's eyes
> I all alone beweep my outcast state . . .

(Many will recall their own youthful readings of the poem.) Yet even this simple if not sentimental sonnet asks something more of us in the end; it asks us to take on the demonstrative air of the theatrical lover, to protest in language we would never actually use in our most romantic moments.

In Literature X we shall start by reading poems, and start with no apparent method or at least with method well concealed. We begin, as Frost says, with delight, to end in wisdom. "What is it *like,*" we say rather crudely, "to read this poem?" "With what feeling are we left at its close?" "What sort of person is speaking?" "What is he *like,* and where does he reveal himself most clearly?" "In what line or phrase?" We may then ask if there is a key phrase or word in the poem, and we can begin to introduce the notion of the poem as a structure, as an ordered experience built up through various kinds of meaning controlled in turn by various uses of language.

Remembering our questions about the speaker, we first direct attention to dramatic uses of language, to the ways in which the words create a character speaking in a certain role. We may ask, for example, who is speaking in Keats's sonnet on Chapman's *Homer.* An alert student may point out that he is a traveler (many do not see this), and that he uses idioms with a medieval coloring: "realms," "goodly," "bards in fealty," "demesne." But the speaker does not continue to talk in this vein:

> Till I heard Chapman speak out loud and bold.

He has changed, and the drama moves into a second act. We hear a voice that is powerful and young, the voice of the New World discoverer and the Renaissance astronomer. We now point out to our young reader (if he is still listening) that the poem is indeed an "act." The poet is speaking *as if* he were a traveler-explorer, and the whole poem is built on a metaphor. So, while reading many poems, we may introduce a few basic notions of literary design and some useful critical terms. But our emphasis will always be on the term as a tool, as a device for calling attention to the poem and how it is made. In time we can turn to study of the poem as an experience of ordered sounds, but not, we hasten to add, of sounds divorced from sense. Our aim in talking about rhythmic pattern, as in considering dramatic and metaphorical design, is to show how the poem "works" and what it expresses. We see, for example, that as Keats's sonnet moves from the medieval to the modern speaker, and as the metaphor also shifts, the rhythm changes from the "broken" couplets and inversions of the octave to the long and steady sweep of the sestet. The whole sonnet in its beautiful interaction of parts gives us the sense of discovery and release into a new world of literary and aesthetic experience.

Following a period of reading poems, the course will move ahead to a play by Shakespeare so that students can see at once that the way in which they have read poems works also for a poetic drama and that there are some basic similarities between the structure of these different types of literature. They may see, for example, that the man speaking in a poem corresponds to the character in a play, that Shakespeare has his large metaphors just as Keats has his smaller ones.

From drama we go to the reading of a novel, often via short stories. The short story like the poem gives us literary experience in microcosm and makes it easier to see analogies between fiction and poetry, to see that a tale by Hawthorne is the unfolding of a single metaphorical vision, or that the narrator in a story by Joyce controls our sense of being within the child's world, exiled from adult society. The novel, especially as we have it in its classic nineteenth century form in Dickens or George Eliot, demands a very different reading from a Shakespearean drama, but by putting the same question to both genres their likeness and their unlikeness can be defined, and the exact quality of a particular work can be discovered. The student will find, for example, that the "marshes" and "mists" of *Great Expectations* are nearer to the fixed symbols of allegory than to the fluid metaphors of Shakespeare. But he can also see that in a novel as in a poem the narrative voice is of immense importance. Comparison of the opening scene in the film of *Great Expectations* with Dickens's telling shows that when the sanely humorous, entertaining voice of Dickens is removed, we are left with images of pure nightmare. The major themes of *Great Expectations,* guilt and innocence, justice and injustice, are not un-Shakespearean, but we can hardly read the novel without an awareness that unlike *King Lear* and *Macbeth* and like most novels, the imaginative world of *Great Expectations* has a date. Jaggers is an awesome symbol of the link between criminality and legal justice, but he also embodies a sharp criticism of the actual court and prison world of mid-nineteenth century England.

Reading a novel forcibly reminds us that literature is embedded in history, that the meaning of the work in itself changes when we view it in relation to other works and to the social situation in which it first appeared. Literature X will move on in its later phases to some experiments in historical interpretation, "historical" being used here to include the relation of a work to its time, especially to more or less contemporary works, and to literary tradition. If we return to *Othello* or *Coriolanus* after reading the *Iliad* and after gaining some familiarity with the heroic tradition in Renaissance epic and drama, we find that both plays are clearer and richer in their meaning. We see in *Coriolanus* what happens when an Achilles enters the Roman forum: the simple absolutes of the hero, the code that makes Coriolanus prefer a "noble life before a long" one, bring confusion in a civil society. The teacher of our ideal course will not merely lay a comparison of this sort before his students, he will try to get them into a position where they can make the comparison for themselves. He will use all the ingenuity he can muster to devise assignments in which the student can practice thinking historically about works of literature.

In a year in which the class has made some study of the hero in Homer and in the Renaissance, a project might be focused on Fielding's *Tom Jones.* While the students are reading the novel outside class (it takes time!), they would study with their teacher readings useful for interpreting the novel in relation to the heroic tradition and to the climate of moral opinion in the eighteenth century. They could observe in Dryden's *Mac Flecknoe* the shift from the Renaissance "heroick" to the mock-heroic, and in *The Rape of the Lock,* they could see how allusions to the ancient heroic world are used to satirize eighteenth century high society while giving the world of the poem splendor and moral seriousness. After comparing the mock-heroic in Pope and Fielding, they might attempt a definition of the hero in *Tom*

Jones. By skillful prodding (in an exercise) they could be led to see that Fielding has created a new type of hero, a youth who is at once ridiculous and charmingly "good-natured," that although he finally gains a modicum of "prudence," he wins his way largely through "benevolence" and "goodness of heart."

As a final step in this experiment, there might be a series of readings in Chesterfield, Hume, and Dr. Johnson, all concerned with social "goodness," and more especially with "prudence" and "benevolence." The students would then be asked to define and place the moral attitudes expressed in *Tom Jones*, through comparing them with similar attitudes expressed in these eighteenth century moralists. By projects of this type undergraduates could be given some practice—at an elementary level—in writing intellectual history. At the same time their earlier practice in interpretation would protect them from reducing the experience of the novel to the abstracted idea. But they would also begin to see that a purely literary judgment is finally impossible, that we are impelled to move back from literature to life. Dr. Johnson's famous comparison of Fielding and Richardson might be used to show that "liking" or "disliking" a novel is an act of moral evaluation. At the end of Literature X, by returning to poetry we could make the point that a choice between poems is a choice between lives.

You may be asking by now what the connection is between our ideal course and the lifetime reading habits of undergraduates. I should reply that Literature X attempts to influence future reading habits by keeping to the principle of student activity. No test or exercise or final examination asks the student to "give back" the "material" of the course. On the contrary, each stage of the work is planned with a view to how the student reads the *next* work, whether poem or play or novel. At the end of the first half of the course the student is sent off to read and interpret on his own another play of Shakespeare and another novel. He is given leading questions that impel him to do likewise "differently." An appropriate midyear examination in the course might consist of a sight poem to interpret and an essay-exercise on a longer work read outside class. The test for the second half-year (whether an examination or a long essay) would ordinarily be based on a set of texts to be used in interpreting a work in the manner of the project on *Tom Jones*.

But the teacher of a course in slow reading will always be haunted by the question once asked by a colleague of mine: "Our students learn *how* to read, but *do* they read?" Do they, for example, ever read an author, read every one of his books they can lay their hands on, with an urge to know the writer's work as a whole? Can we do anything in our ideal course to stimulate this most valuable habit?

Some modest experiments can be made, I believe, and with some assurance of success. A model can be set by reading generously in a single poet, preferably a contemporary, such as Frost, Yeats, or Eliot. Or the teacher can give the class a start by reading a few poems in each of a number of writers, and then send the students off to read one of the poets independently. After some weeks they might write an essay "On Reading So-and-So." The essay must have a point (surprisingly few students know what a point is) supported by deft and apt interpretation of particular poems. The novel, the most important form for habitual readers in this generation, presents a problem, since we can hardly read all or even several novels of the same writer within the limits of an introductory course. But two novels and some stories by a single writer may rouse some readers to go ahead on their own, and sometimes the discovery that a difficult writer—James or Joyce—is understandable and rewarding or that an old-fashioned writer—Fielding or Jane Austen—is amusing, will start a student along the right path. The best way to influence later habits is the natural way: recommending without system books we have read with pleasure and without ulterior motives. Students recognize the difference between love and duty, and they will respond to genuine enthusiasm and avoid books that they "ought to" read or—and this is the lowest of all academic appeals—that "fill a gap" in preparing for general examinations or graduate school placement tests.

If we turn our attention from lifetime reading habits to the larger educational influence of courses in slow reading, we can note some possible correlations between classroom and later performances. In this connection we should recall the value for close reading of practice in equally close writing. The student who looks at poems as carefully as we have suggested will understand that poetry begins in grammar and that to express a just appreciation of a poem demands fine control of grammar on the part of the appreciator. But to help the student make such discoveries calls for guidance in small classes or at least careful criticism of written exercises. Good writing is an art not amenable to mass production methods.

Attentive criticism of written work is almost certainly of much more value for teaching good reading and writing than the usual discussions or section meetings. The value of a discussion meeting does not depend primarily on size, as many assume, but on the planning that precedes the meeting and the direction of the conversation to a defined goal. In our course in slow reading the discussion is not an addendum, but the culminating act toward which the teacher's demonstration and the student's exercise have been directed. Under these conditions student and teacher are fully prepared to say something meaningful to each other, since they have before them well-defined questions to pursue and alternative expressed answers to compare and judge.

But discussion of this type need not be vocal. The student can carry it on internally during a lecture, if the lecture is an exercise in how to ask and answer a question of interpretation. The indispensable requirement for an active course in literature is not "sections," but some form of independent performance for an attentive critical audience of one. Here is where large-scale production methods break down, and limitations in size are necessary. Very few readers can handle more than twenty to twenty-five papers of the type I have been describing and maintain the necessary vigilance and the power of viewing them as individual performances. A reader can handle them in the usual fashion—grade them and add a complimentary or devastating comment—but he cannot give them critical attention at a high level. The student who is to rise to the kind of reading and writing called for in our ideal course must feel that he has a responsible reader, one who addresses himself to this essay and to this mind. The most valuable discussion a teacher can give is a comment surely directed to an individual written performance. Here we have the ideal section: two actors engaged in a Socratic dialogue. A teacher who is not bewildered and dulled by reading too many papers on the same topic will be able to judge the student's present achievement in relation to what he has done in the past. He can also help him keep track of his development and show him where he is going, and when he has failed, show him how to build on an earlier successful performance. Again Coleridge's Reverend Bowyer may serve as a guide:

> . . . there was one custom of our master's, which I cannot pass over in silence, because I think it imitable and worthy of imitation. He would often permit our exercises, under some pretext of want of time, to accumulate, till each had four or five to be looked over. Then placing the whole number abreast on his desk, he would ask the writer, why this or that sentence might not have found as appropriate a place under this or that other thesis: and if no satisfying answer could be returned, and two faults of the same kind were found in one exercise, the irrevocable verdict followed, the exercise was torn up, and another on the same subject to be produced, in addition to the tasks of the day. The reader will, I trust, excuse this tribute of recollection to a man, whose severities, even now, not seldom furnish the dreams, by which the blind fancy would fain interpret to the mind the painful sensations of distempered sleep; but neither lessen nor dim the sense of my moral and intellectual obligations.

The marker of an English paper, as Coleridge realized though with "painful sensations," is a very important person indeed; he becomes the higher literary conscience, the intellectual guardian angel of his students.

It is evident that education in literature of this kind must be personal, and expensive, though scarcely more expensive than education in the sciences. Let us have at least as generous a supply of readers and conference rooms as we have of laboratory assistants and laboratories. The Humanities cannot flourish with *humanitas*. A protest is in order against the inhumanity of the Humanities when in some of our larger institutions the study of Great Books is reduced to display lectures before audiences of five and six hundred, and when the individual performance is measured by machine-graded examinations.

The teaching of great literary texts in Humanities courses has also had other if less depressing results which the teacher of literature should note if he is to fulfill his proper educational role. Because many works are taught in translation and taught often by staffs including many non-specialists in language and literature, and because the texts are often presented in some broad historical framework, a work of imaginative literature tends to be treated either as a document for studying the history of ideas or as a text for illustrating and enforcing desirable moral and social attitudes. Though neither of these approaches is in itself harmful or inappropriate to a university, it may involve serious losses, especially in courses in which many students are reading for the first time—or for the first time at an adult level—masterpieces of European literature. There is a danger, which is increased by the large amounts of reading assigned in Great Books courses, that rich and special experiences will be too readily reduced to crude examples of a historic idea or a moral principle. Though the reductions may be necessary and useful for certain purposes, we must not let students make them too soon or too easily, not if we are seriously concerned with lifetime habits of reading. The undergraduate who masters the trick too early and too well may in the process suffer real damage. He may have acquired the dubious art of reading carelessly, of making the reduction *before reading*, and he may have lowered rather than increased his capacity for responding precisely to a particular work and for making fine discriminations between works.

Hence the special function of the teacher of literature, which is not to be confused with that of the historian or the moral philosopher. The teacher of literature in a Humanities course must feel he has betrayed a trust if he has not given the lay reader what he is best qualified to give: training in the literary disciplines of reading and writing.

It is pertinent to recall the historic definition of the Humanities as it stands in the *Oxford English Dictionary:* "Learning or literature concerned with human culture, as grammar, rhetoric, poetry, and especially the ancient Latin and Greek classics." I suspect that some of the more enthusiastic general educators may be surprised by the words that follow "human culture": "as grammar, rhetoric, poetry . . ." (The order of items in the list is instructive, too.) The disciplines named are the ones that the teacher of literature has a special responsibility to impart. He is, like Horace's poet, a guardian of the language who shows (as Pope translates it) "no mercy to an empty line." His prime object is to maintain fineness of response to words, and his students rightly assume that he will be adept in discovering and illustrating refinements in writing whether in a great book or a student essay. This guardianship, once performed by teachers of the ancient Latin and Greek classics, now falls to the teachers of English and other modern literatures. Why is this so? Because they are committed to the principle that the study of letters is inseparable from the study of language.

Study of literature based on this principle can hardly be carried on in a course based mainly on texts in translation. Translations have their place in a course in interpretation, but only as ancillary to the main business of close reading in the original. The finer distinctions, the finer relationships which we are training our students to discover and make are almost invariably dulled or lost in the process of translation. We want the student to acquire the habit of recognizing and making such distinctions in his *own* language, and we can hardly teach him to do it if the examples before him are relatively crude. Whitehead once remarked when discussing Plato's cosmology, "After all, the translators of Plato have had B+ philosophic minds." With rare exceptions the translators of literature have had literary minds of similar quality. There are of course the handful of translations that are masterpieces, such as Pope's *Iliad,* North's *Plutarch,* and Dryden's *Aeneis,* texts that can bear the close study necessary for literary education. Ironically enough, these are the very translations avoided in most Great Books courses.

In speaking of the necessity for close attention to language, I am not forgetting that teachers of literature are also teachers of human culture and that they are therefore guardians of important values. But they do not set out to teach these values, although they inevitably impart them by the way they talk and act in the presence of works of literature. But they are especially concerned with another task, with teaching ways of discovering and experiencing values expressed through literary objects. The most precious thing they can give their students is some increase of power, some help however humble in getting into Shakespeare or Dr. Johnson or Joyce.

We may hope that a student who has learned how to get into these writers will go back for further experiences after he has left the classroom and the university. That he surely will we cannot say. Even if he does not return to Shakespeare or Johnson, the experiences in the classroom almost certainly have their value and their effect in determining the quality of his later reading. One play well read with a good teacher and well digested in a reflective essay may serve as a touchstone of what literary experience can be. But finally, our belief that students' habits of reading are permanently affected is Platonic. The model for most cultural education is to be found in the third book of the *Republic:*

> . . . our young men, dwelling as it were in a healthy region, may receive benefit from all things about them; the influence that emanates from works of beauty may waft itself to eye or ear like a breeze that brings health from wholesome places, and so from earliest childhood insensibly guide them to likeness, to friendship, to harmony with beautiful reason.

In the effort to realize this Platonic vision in a modern university the undergraduate library plays its part by surrounding our youth with fair works of literature through which they may come into "harmony with beautiful reason." No one knows how born readers are produced, but we can put books in their way and in the way of the less happily born in the hope that proximity will have its effect as it does in the formation of more mundane habits. Of one thing I am convinced: that a born reader on a library staff can have a tremendous effect on young readers who come his way. I remember with gratitude two librarians of that description, one in school and one in college, who led us to read books we might never have looked into by sharing their love for what they had read. If I were to found a library dedicated to influencing the reading habit, I should place a half-dozen of these enthusiasts at strategic points to ensnare wandering students. They would not necessarily be trained librarians, and they would surely waste students' time and occasionally disturb their colleagues, but like great authors they would create an ever-widening circle of readers. Mere teachers of literature could hardly hope to compete with them, and might in time quietly disappear from the academic scene.

Discussing Ideas and Themes

1. What does Brower mean by a "lifetime reading habit"? Does he really define his term for us? Drawing from your own experience, speculate on what such a habit might entail.
2. What does Brower think a teacher of literature should do for students? For example, what does Brower mean when he suggests that students should be encouraged to "respond actively" to "rhythmic" uses of language? Most importantly, what does he mean by "slow reading"?
3. Brower suggests that our methods of teaching fail to teach students to read thoroughly. Do you agree? Be sure to take his argument into account while you are thinking of yours.
4. What does Brower suggest to "get the student to the point where he can learn for himself"? For example, what does he mean when he says the student must "sort" the "basket of bones" for himself? Can you think of any problem with Brower's theory?
5. Brower quotes Plato in the last paragraph of his essay. How might you paraphrase the "Platonic vision" set forth in this passage? For example, what might "beautiful reason" mean to Brower, and what influences does he think literature should have on students' minds?

Discussing Rhetoric and Style

1. Brower alludes to several classical or literary figures—for example, "the words of Solon that Croesus recalled." How do these allusions work? What effects do they have on the reader?
2. Brower argues that the best texts for teaching students to read imaginatively, in the Coleridgean sense, are poems. How does he get to this conclusion? What are his premises, and how does he make his argument persuasive?
3. How does Brower use a long quotation of Coleridge to bolster his argument? Does this quotation have the same kind of rhetorical effect that his earlier allusions had, or does it do something different?
4. How does Brower establish his authority in this essay? Look for specific examples—for example, "pity and terror" are terms from Aristotle to describe the effect tragedy has on an audience,

but they are also words that arouse emotions, and Brower uses both these factors in establishing his voice.

Ideas for Writing

1. Brower carefully outlines his ideas for a literature course, "Literature X." Write a short essay, based on your own experience, responding to Brower's proposal. Try to respond directly to his ideas, as well as including particular examples from your own educational experience.
2. Both Brower and Frost (in "Education by Poetry") make suggestions about good teaching. How do their ideas compare? Write an essay comparing and contrasting their thinking. Which author do you think is more persuasive, and why?

Exercises in Style

RAYMOND QUENEAU

Raymond Queneau's Exercises in Style, *from which the following pieces are excerpted, first appeared in English in 1958. The book, translated from the French by Barbara Wright, mimics dozens of different styles—from the passive to the abusive, the retrograde to the astonomical. Exploring the vagaries of both casual talk and literary conventions, Queneau shows the reader that the ways a single incident can be represented may be close to inexhaustible.*

NOTATION

In the S bus, in the rush hour. A chap of about 26, felt hat with a cord instead of a ribbon, neck too long, as if someone's been having a tug-of-war with it. People getting off. The chap in question gets annoyed with one of the men standing next to him. He accuses him of jostling him every time anyone goes past. A snivelling tone which is meant to be aggressive. When he sees a vacant seat he throws himself on to it.

Two hours later, I meet him in the Cour de Rome, in front of the Gare Saint-Lazare. He's with a friend who's saying: "You ought to get an extra button put on your overcoat." He shows him where (at the lapels) and why.

DOUBLE ENTRY

Towards the middle of the day and at midday I happened to be on and got on to the platform and the balcony at the back of an S-line and of a Contrescarpe-Champerret bus and passenger transport vehicle which was packed and to all intents and purposes full. I saw and noticed a young man and an old adolescent who was rather ridiculous and pretty grotesque; thin neck and skinny windpipe, string and cord round his hat and tile. After a scrimmage and scuffle he says and states in a lachrymose and snivelling voice and tone that his neighbour and fellow-traveller is deliberately trying and doing his utmost to push him and obtrude himself on him every time anyone gets off and makes an exit. This having been declared and having spoken he rushes headlong and wends his way towards a vacant and a free place and seat.

Two hours after and a hundred and twenty minutes later, I meet him and see him again in the Cour de Rome and in front of the Gare Saint-Lazare. He is with and in the company of a friend and pal who is advising and urging him to have a button and vegetable ivory disc added and sewn on to his overcoat and mantle.

LITOTES

Some of us were travelling together. A young man, who didn't look very intelligent, spoke to the man next to him for a few moments, then he went and sat down. Two hours later I met him again; he was with a friend and was talking about clothes.

METAPHORICALLY

In the centre of the day, tossed among the shoal of travelling sardines in a coleopter with a big white carapace, a chicken with a long, featherless neck suddenly harangued one, a peace-abiding one, of their number, and its parlance, moist with protest, was unfolded upon the airs. Then, attracted by a void, the fledgling precipitated itself thereunto.

In a bleak, urban desert, I saw it again that selfsame day, drinking the cup of humiliation offered by a lowly button.

RETROGRADE

You ought to put another button on your overcoat, his friend told him. I met him in the middle of the Cour de Rome, after having left him rushing avidly towards a seat. He had just protested against being pushed by another passenger who, he said, was jostling him every time anyone got off. This scraggy young man was the wearer of a ridiculous hat. This took place on the platform of an S bus which was full that particular midday.

SURPRISES

How tightly packed in we were on that bus platform! And how stupid and ridiculous that young man looked! And what was he doing? Well, if he wasn't actually trying to pick a quarrel with a chap who—so he claimed! the young fop! kept on pushing him! And then he didn't find anything better to do than to rush off and grab a seat which had become free! Instead of leaving it for a lady!

Two hours after, guess whom I met in front of the Gare Saint-Lazare! The same fancy-pants! Being given some sartorial advice! By a friend!

You'd never believe it!

DREAM

I had the impression that everything was misty and nacreous around me, with multifarious and indistinct apparitions, amongst whom however was one figure that stood out fairly clearly which was that of a young man whose too-long neck in itself seemed to proclaim the character at once cowardly and quarrelsome of the individual. The ribbon of his hat had been replaced by a piece of plaited string. Later he was having an argument with a person whom I couldn't see and then, as if suddenly afraid, he threw himself into the shadow of a corridor.

HESITATION

I don't really know where it happened . . . in a church, a dustbin, a charnel-house? A bus, perhaps? There were . . . but what were there, though? Eggs, carpets, radishes? Skeletons? Yes, but with their flesh still round them, and alive. I think that's how it was. People in a bus. But one (or two?) of them was making himself conspicuous, I don't really know in what way. For his megalomania? For his adiposity? For his melancholy? Rather . . . more precisely . . . for his youth, which was embellished by a long . . . nose? chin? thumb? no: neck, and by a strange, strange, strange hat. He started to quarrel, yes, that's right.

PRECISION

In a bus of the S-line, 10 metres long, 3 wide, 6 high, at 3 km. 600 m. from its starting point, loaded with 48 people, at 12:17 P.M., a person of the masculine sex aged 27 years 3 months and 8 days, 1 m. 72 cm. tall and weighing 65 kg. and wearing a hat 35 cm. in height round the crown of which was a ribbon 60 cm. long, interpellated a man aged 48 years 4 months and 3 days, 1 m. 68 cm. tall and weighing 77 kg., by means of 14 words whose enunciation lasted 5 seconds and which alluded to some involuntary displacements of from 15 to 20 mm. Then he went and sat down about 1 m. 10 cm. away.

57 minutes later he was 10 metres away from the suburban entrance to the Gare Saint-Lazare and was walking up and down over a distance of 30 m. with a friend aged 28, 1 m. 70 cm. tall and weighing 71 kg. who advised him in 15 words to move by 5 cm. in the direction of the zenith a button which was 3 cm. in diameter.

THE SUBJECTIVE SIDE

I was not displeased with my attire this day. I was inaugurating a new, rather sprightly hat, and an overcoat of which I thought most highly. Met *X* in front of the Gare Saint-Lazare who tried to spoil my pleasure by trying to prove that this overcoat is cut too low at the lapels and that I ought to have an extra button on it. At least he didn't dare attack my headgear.

A bit earlier I had roundly told off a vulgar type who was purposely ill-treating me every time anyone went by getting off or on. This happened in one of those unspeakably foul omnibi which fill up with hoi polloi precisely at those times when I have to consent to use them.

ANOTHER SUBJECTIVITY

Next to me on the bus platform today there was one of those half-baked young fellows, you don't find so many of them these days, thank God, otherwise I should end up by killing one. This particular one, a brat of something like 26 or 30, irritated me particularly not so much because of his great long featherless-turkey's neck as because of the nature of the ribbon round his hat, a ribbon which wasn't much more than a sort of maroon-coloured string. Dirty beast! He absolutely disgusted me! As there were a lot of people in our bus at that hour I took advantage of all the pushing and shoving there is every time anyone gets on or off to dig him in the ribs with my elbow. In the end he took to his heels, the milksop, before I could make up my mind to tread on his dogs to teach him a lesson. I could also have told him, just to annoy him, that he needed another button on his overcoat which was cut too low at the lapels.

PASSIVE

It was midday. The bus was being got into by passengers. They were being squashed together. A hat was being worn on the head of young gentleman, which hat was encircled by a plait and not by a ribbon. A long neck was one of the characteristics of the young gentleman. The man standing next to him was being grumbled at by the latter because of the jostling which was being inflicted on him by him. As soon as a vacant seat was espied by the young gentleman it was made the object of his precipitate movements and it became sat down upon.

The young gentleman was later seen by me in front of the Gare Saint-Lazare. He was clothed in an overcoat and was having a remark made to him by a friend who happened to be there to the effect that it was necessary to have an extra button put on it.

ABUSIVE

After a stinking wait in the vile sun I finally got into a filthy bus where a bunch of bastards were squashed together. The most bastardly of these bastards was a pustulous creature with a ridiculously long windpipe who was sporting a grotesque hat with a cord instead of a ribbon. This pretentious puppy started to create because an old bastard was pounding his plates with senile fury, but he soon climbed down and made off in the direction of an empty seat that was still damp with the sweat of the buttocks of its previous occupant.

Two hours later, my unlucky day, I came upon the same bastard holding forth with another bastard in front of that nauseating monument they call the Gare Saint-Lazare. They were yammering about a button. Whether he has his furuncle raised or lowered, I said to myself, he'll still be just as lousy, the dirty bastard.

GASTRONOMICAL

After slowly roasting in the browned butter of the sun I finally managed to get into a pistachio bus which was crawling with customers as an overripe cheese crawls with maggots. Having paid my fare, I noticed among all these noodles a poor fish with a neck as long as a stick of celery and a loaf surmounted by a ridiculous donkey's dinner. This unsavoury character started to beef because a chap was pounding the joints of his cheeses to pulp. But when he found that he had bitten off more than he could chew, he quailed like a lily-livered dunghill-cock and bolted off to stew in his own juice.

Discussing Ideas and Themes

1. The "button" incident gets retold in many ways here. Do you think this incident has a basic meaning (such as that it is humiliating), or does the meaning of the incident change in different passages?
2. Quenneau includes two "subjective" accounts of the incident. Why do you think he chooses to do this? How do these two accounts differ?
3. Which of these passages do you think is the most clever? Which one is most appealing? If these are not the same, why not?
4. Some of Quenneau's rewrites of his narrative seem to be more literary than others—they employ literary conventions or their style evokes literary personalities. "Notation," for example, does not seem very literary, but "The Subjective Side" does. Among the other passages, which ones do you perceive as literary and which ones use fewer literary conventions? Why do the "literary" ones seem so?

Discussing Rhetoric and Style

1. What are the most consistent characteristics of Quenneau's basic story? What remains more or less the same about the story no matter how Quenneau retells it?
2. In the "metaphorically" told version of the story, Quenneau represents the bus passenger as a "chicken." What is the effect of this metaphor? That is, how do Quenneau's choices of vehicles, throughout this paragraph, create tone, and what tone do they create?
3. How docs Quenneau create the disjunctive quality of the "dream" version of the story? What elements of the basic narra-

tive seem to have changed? Would this version of the narrative be as effective if it were told first, before we had read any of the other versions?

4. How does Quenneau use shifts in diction to establish different speakers and illustrate different figures of speech? In which passages has he chosen to use high diction, and in which low diction, and why? For example, how would the effect be altered if you substituted "blurry" for "nacreous" and "many" for "multifarious" in the first section of the "dream" paragraph?

5. In several of the passages, Quenneau uses the first person. All of these passages represent very different personalities (for example, one is labeled "abusive"), but what particular elements of style create these different appeals? What kinds of diction, for example, do the different narrators use?

Ideas for Writing

1. Both Quenneau and George Orwell, in "Politics and the English Language," rewrite passages to emphasize the effects of style. What do you think Orwell would make of Quenneau's accomplishments here? Where would Quenneau's uses of language stand on Orwell's scale of political integrity? Write a brief paper in which you defend or condemn Quenneau's writing according to what you perceive as Orwell's ethics.

2. Pick or make up a brief anecdote, and tell it in the ways—or, rather, remake it using the figures—that Quenneau does. Be sure to choose an uncomplicated narrative: one, like Quenneau's basic story, that comprises only a couple of actions.

The Cliché Expert Testifies as a Literary Critic

FRANK SULLIVAN

Frank Sullivan (1892–1975) was born in Saratoga Springs, New York, was educated at Cornell, and later served as an infantryman in World War I. After the war, he moved to New York and began a career in journalism, writing for three different newspapers and finally settling with the New York World. *A humorist whose creations range from the ancient Aunt Sarah Gallup to the superficial Mr. Arbuthnot (whose testimony you will hear in the following essay), Sullivan was a favorite at the* New Yorker, *where "The Cliché Expert" first appeared in 1937. In addition to his magazine and newspaper work, Sullivan published several collections of his essays on his own, including* The Life and Times of Martha Hepplethwaite, Broccoli and Old Lace, Sullivan at Bay, *and* The Night the Old Nostalgia Burned Down.

Q. Mr. Arbuthnot, you are an expert in the use of the cliché as applied to literary criticism?
A. I am told that I am, Mr. Sullivan.
Q. We shall soon find out. What is this subject, marked Exhibit A?
A. That is a book.
Q. Good. What kind of book is it?
A. It is a minor classic.
Q. And what kind of document is it?
A. It is a valuable human document.
Q. Very good, Mr. Arbuthnot. Please continue.

A. It is a book in which the results of painstaking—or scholarly—research are embodied, and it should appeal to a wide public. This reviewer could not put it down.
Q. Why not?
A. Because of its penetrating insight. It is a sincere and moving study of family life against the background of a small cathedral town. It is also a vivid and faithful portrayal.
Q. How written?
A. Written with sympathy, pathos, and kindly humor. It throws a clear light on a little understood subject and is well worth reading.
Q. How is it illustrated?
A. Profusely. It is original in conception, devoid of sentimentality, highly informative, consistently witty, and rich in color. You should place it on your library list.
Q. Why?
A. Because it strikes a new note in fiction. Mystery and suspense crowd its pages. The author has blended fact and fiction and the result is an authentic drama of social revolution, a definite contribution to proletarian literature.
Q. Told with a wealth of what?
A. Told with a wealth of detail.
Q. And how portrayed?
A. Realistically portrayed, in staccato prose. For sheer brilliance of style there has been nothing like it since *Moby Dick*. Rarely does a narrative move at such a fast pace.
Q. What is it a shrewd comment on?
A. The contemporary scene. It marks a red-letter day in current literature. It is capital entertainment.
Q. What pervades it?
A. A faint tinge of irony.
Q. And how is it translated?
A. Ably. It is a penetrating study in abnormal psychology, and unlike most scientific words it is written in language understandable to the layman. It belongs in the front rank of modern picaresque literature. Ideology.
Q. I beg your pardon?
A. I said ideology. Also catharsis.
Q. What about them?
A. Well, they have to come in somewhere.
Q. I see. Now, to return to the minor classic, Mr. Arbuthnot. Would you call it a subtle and arresting piece of work?

A. Certainly I would. Why do you suppose I'm an expert in the use of the cliché? I'd also call it an honest attempt to depict, a remarkable first novel, a veritable triumph, a genuine contribution, a thrilling saga of life in frontier days, and the most impressive study of degeneration since Zola. It bids fair to go down as one of the great biographies of all time, including *Moby Dick*. In short, it has unusual merit.

Q. How does it augur?

A. It augurs well for the future of the author.

Q. And how does it bid?

A. It bids fair to become a best-seller.

Q. And how does it end?

A. It ends upon a distinct note of despair. It is a work of art.

Q. I'm glad you liked it, Mr. Arbuthnot.

A. Who said I liked it?

Q. Didn't you?

A. Certainly not.

Q. Why not?

A. Because it is, one fears, mawkishly sentimental and, one regrets, faintly pretentious. Curiously enough, it does not carry conviction. Strangely enough, it lacks depth. Oddly enough, the dénouement is weak. It is to be regretted that the title is rather misleading and it need hardly be pointed out that the book as a whole lacks cohesion and form. I am very much afraid, one regrets, that it falls definitely into the escapist school of fiction. And of course, like all first novels, it is autobiographical.

Q. I'm glad you told me. I won't buy it.

A. Ah, but in spite of its faults it contains much of real value. It kept me awake till three. In the opinion of the present reviewer it would be the long-awaited great American novel except for one serious defect.

Q. What is that?

A. It lacks an index.

Q. Mr. Arbuthnot, it is easy to see that you have earned your spurs in the field of literary criticism. So much for the book. Now, observe this object I hold here in my hand, marked Exhibit B. What is it?

A. That. *That* is an *author*.

Q. Whose are those italics, Mr. Arbuthnot?

A. The italics are mine.

Q. What kind of author is this?

A. A promising young author who should be watched.
Q. What kind of novels does he write?
A. Powerful first novels.
Q. What kind of storyteller is he?
A. He's a born storyteller.
Q. What kind of satirist is he?
A. A satirist of the first order.
Q. Tell us more about this interesting creature.
A. Well, he cannot be lightly dismissed. He is undoubtedly to be reckoned with, one feels, as a definite force. He is in the front rank of the younger writers.
Q. Why?
A. Because his work plainly shows the influence of Joyce, Hemingway, Huxley, Proust, Gertrude Stein, Auden, Eliot, and Virginia Woolf. Here is an authentic talent from which we may expect great things.
Q. So what do you do?
A. So I hail him. And I acclaim him. He has a keen ear for the spoken word. He also has a flair. He sets out to tell. He deals with themes, or handles them. He recaptures moods. His execution is brilliant, his insight is poetic, his restraint is admirable, and he has a sense of values. There is something almost uncanny in his ability to look into men's souls. And he paints a vivid word picture and works on a vast canvas.
Q. How?
A. With consummate artistry. He writes with commendable frankness.
Q. Using what kind of style?
A. Using a limpid prose style. He has a real freshness of approach that stamps him as an artist in the true sense of the word. He culls his material and his niche in the hall of literary fame seems secure.
Q. I'm glad you like him, Mr. Arbuthnot.
A. But I don't.
Q. No? Why not?
A. Because his talent is plainly superficial and ephemeral. He has an unfortunate habit of allowing his personality to obtrude. His book is badly documented and not the least of his many irritating mannerisms is his addiction to inexcusable typographical errors. His book is full of clichés and he does not make his characters live and feel and breathe. And he writes with one eye on Hollywood.

Q. You mean to tell me that a cad like that has the audacity to call himself an author?

A. Well now, don't be too hard on him. Although he decidedly does not justify his early promise it is as yet too early to evaluate his work. Want to know about the plot?

Q. Yes, indeed. What about the plot?

A. It is well rounded and fully developed. But it is marred by structural weaknesses.

Q. What kind of structural weaknesses?

A. Inherent structural weaknesses. It is motivated, of course. And its threads are cunningly woven into a harmonious texture by the deft hand of a skilled literary craftsman.

Q. Just one thing more, Mr. Arbuthnot. How many kinds of readers are there?

A. Three—casual, general, and gentle.

Q. Mr. Arbuthnot, I think that is all. I can't thank you enough for having come here today to help us out.

A. It has been a pleasure—a vivid, fascinating, significant, vigorous, timely, gracious, breath-taking, mature, adequate, nostalgic, unforgettable, gripping, articulate, engrossing, poignant, and adult pleasure to be of service to you, Mr. Sullivan. Good day, sir.

Discussing Ideas and Themes

1. Who is the cliché expert in this dialogue? How can you tell? Does the other person (the non-expert) also seem familiar with clichés or not?

2. What are the kinds of clichéd reviews Sullivan makes his expert illustrate here? The first kind, for example, involves Exhibit A.

3. What is the "one serious defect" of the "minor classic"? Would you consider this to be a major fault in a novel? What does Arbuthnot's stress on this one defect reveal about the quality of his judgments?

4. Do you think, judging from book reviews you have read elsewhere, that this is a good representation of book review style? Compare the information that Mr. Arbuthnot imparts with what you normally learn from a review. Is it about the same or very different?

Discussing Rhetoric and Style

1. Does Sullivan ever define "cliché"? How does he let us know what clichés are during the progress of the dialogue?
2. Why is this essay written as a dialogue? What are the effects of this format?
3. What are the roles of the questioner in this piece? How does the tone of the questioner shift between the "whys" and "why nots" of the first few exchanges to the "what" and "how" questions that immediately follow?
4. What are the effects of the shift from shorter to longer responses from Arbuthnot as the essay develops? Do these longer responses give us a greater insight into the responder (Arbuthnot), or into the nature of clichés?
5. How do we recognize this to be an ironic essay? How does Sullivan keep our interest up within his rather limited format?

Ideas for Writing

1. Write a short dialogue that illustrates a group of clichés (but *not* the clichés of literary criticism) and imitates Sullivan's use of dialogue. Try to make your effort entertaining, ironic, and fast-moving, at the same time exposing the misuse of language in whatever field you pick.
2. Read the book reviews in several magazines or newspapers and pick one or two you think either sound a great deal like Mr. Arbuthnot's reviews or not much like them at all. Write an essay in which you discuss the use of clichés in the book reviews you have selected, comparing them with the kinds of clichés that Sullivan illustrates in his ironic dialogue.

The Harvard Man Who Put the Ease in Casey's Manner

MARTIN GARDNER

Born in Tulsa, Oklahoma, in 1914, Martin Gardner was educated at the University of Chicago and worked for many years as a writer in the Mathematical Games Department at Scientific American. *Although Gardner specializes in math, he has written many kinds of essays and books, ranging from the philosophical to the literary to the scientific; his titles include* The Annotated Casey at the Bat, In the Name of Science, The Wizard of Oz and Who He Was, The Annotated Alice, *and* Mathematics, Magic, and Mystery. *A lover of both baseball and trivia, Gardner poses, in this essay, a question that not many of us can answer: Who wrote "Casey at the Bat," and how can a poem so enduring have been written by a man so completely forgotten? In answering these questions, Gardner both redeems Ernest Lawrence Thayer from obscurity and celebrates what is to him an American symbol—Casey's glorious failure at the bat. The essay appeared in* Edge of Awareness: Twenty-five Contemporary Essays.

A sly way to start an argument in a saloon is to quote "Casey at the Bat." It is so well known that hardly anyone knows it—but almost everyone, especially in saloons along toward closing time, is convinced he does. Not the whole thing, maybe, but certainly enough to lay down the law about it. If you really know the poem, and have paced your drinks wisely, you can win any number of bets. What was the score, for instance, when Casey came to bat? ("The score stood four to two with but one inning more to play.") What players were on base and how did they get there? (Look it up, why don't you?) Who—

and this is the one to rock the boilermaker literati back on their barstools—who wrote "Casey at the Bat?"

The name may be on the tip of everyone's tongue, but it's nice to be the one to blurt it out. The author of "Casey" was Ernest Lawrence Thayer, son of Edward Davis Thayer, a wealthy New England textile manufacturer. Ernest was born in Lawrence, Mass. on August 14, 1863. By the time he entered Harvard the family had moved to Worcester, where the elder Thayer ran one of his several woolen mills. At Harvard young Thayer made a brilliant record as a major in philosophy. The great William James was his teacher and friend. Thayer belonged to the Hasty Pudding Club. He was a member of the exclusive Fly Club and Delta Kappa Epsilon fraternity. He edited the college's humor magazine, the Harvard *Lampoon*. His best friend, Samuel E. Winslow (later a Congressman from Massachusetts), was captain of the senior baseball team. During his last year at Harvard, Thayer never missed a game.

Another friend of Thayer's college years was the business manager of the *Lampoon*, William Randolph Hearst. In 1885, when Thayer was graduated *magna cum laude*—he was Phi Beta Kappa and the Ivy orator of his class—Hearst was unceremoniously booted out of Harvard Yard. (He had a habit of playing practical jokes that no one in the faculty thought funny; for example, sending chamber pots to professors, their names inscribed thereon.) Hearst's father had recently bought the ailing *San Francisco Examiner*. Now that young Will was in want of something to occupy his time, the elder Hearst turned the paper over to him.

Thayer, in the meantime, after wandering around Europe with no particular goal, had settled in Paris to brush up on his French. Would he consider, Hearst cabled him, returning to the U.S. to write a humor column for the *Examiner*'s Sunday supplement? To the great annoyance of his father, who expected him to take over American Woolen Mills someday, Thayer agreed.

Thayer's Sunday column, under the by-line of "Phin" (at Harvard his friends had called him Phinney), began in 1886. Every other Sunday he tossed into the column a comic ballad that he dashed off in a few hours. These ballads started in the fall of 1887 and continued for several months. Then ill health forced Thayer to return to Worcester. For a while he continued sending ballads to the *Examiner*. The last of them was "Casey." It ran on June 3, 1888, page 4, column 4, sandwiched between editorials on the left and a weekly column by Ambrose Bierce on the right.

No one paid much attention to the poem. Baseball fans in San Francisco chuckled over it and a few eastern papers reprinted it, but it probably would have been quickly forgotten had it not been for a sequence of improbable events. In New York City, a young comedian and bass singer, DeWolf Hopper, was appearing in a comic opera at Wallack's theater. One evening (the exact date is a matter of controversy; it was probably late in 1888 or sometime in 1889) the New York Giants and the Chicago White Stockings were invited to the show as guests of the management. What could he do on stage, Hopper asked himself, for the special benefit of these men? I have just the thing, said Archibald Clavering Gunter, a novelist and friend. He took from his pocket a ragged newspaper clipping that he had cut from the *Examiner* on a recent trip to San Francisco. It was "Casey."

This poem, insisted Gunter, is great. Why not memorize it and deliver it on stage? Hopper recited it in the middle of the second act, with the Giants in boxes on one side of the theater, the White Stockings in boxes on the other.

Hopper made the recitation a permanent part of his repertoire. It became his most famous bit. Wherever he went, whatever the show in which he was appearing, there were always curtain shouts for "Casey." By his own count, he recited it more than 10,000 times, experimenting with hundreds of slight variations in emphasis and gesture to keep his mind from wandering. It took him exactly five minutes and forty seconds to deliver the poem.

All over the U.S. newspapers and magazines began to reprint it. No one knew who Phin was. Editors either dropped the name altogether or substituted their own or a fictitious one. Stanzas were lost. Lines got botched by printers or rewritten by editors who fancied themselves able to improve the original. Scarcely two printings of the poem were the same. In one early reprinting (by *The Sporting Times*, July 29, 1888) Mudville was changed to Boston and Casey's name to Kelly in honor of Mike (King) Kelly, a famous Boston star, about whom the popular song "Slide, Kelly, Slide" had been written.

From time to time various Caseys who played baseball in the late 1800s claimed to have been the inspiration for the ballad, but Thayer emphatically denied that he had had any ballplayer in mind for any of the men mentioned in his ballad. When the *Syracuse Post-Standard* wrote to ask him about this, he replied with a letter that is reprinted in full in Lee Allen's entertaining book on baseball, *The Hot Stove League* (1955):

> The verses owe their existence to my enthusiasm for college baseball, not as a player, but as a fan [Thayer wrote]. The poem has no basis in fact. The only Casey actually involved, I am sure about him, was not a ballplayer. He was a big, dour Irish lad of my high school days. While in high school, I composed and printed myself a very tiny sheet, less than two inches by three. In one issue, I ventured to gag, as we say, this Casey boy. He didn't like it and he told me so, and, as he discoursed, his big, clenched, red hands were white at the knuckles. This

> Casey's name never again appeared in the *Monohippic Gazette*. But I suspect the incident, many years after, suggested the title for the poem. It was a taunt thrown to the winds. God grant he never catches me.

By 1900 almost everyone in America knew the poem but hardly anyone knew who wrote it. Hopper himself did not discover the author's identity until about five years after he began reciting it. One evening, having delivered the poem in a Worcester theater, he received a note inviting him to a local club to meet "Casey's" author. "Over the details of wassail that followed," Hopper wrote later, "I will draw a veil of charity." He did disclose, however, that the club members had persuaded Thayer himself to stand up and recite "Casey." It was, Hopper declared, the worst delivery of the poem he had ever heard. "In a sweet dulcet whisper he [Thayer] implored Casey to murder the umpire, and gave this cry of animal rage all the emphasis of a caterpillar."

Thayer remained in Worcester for many years, doing his best to please his father by managing one of the family mills. He kept quietly to himself, studying philosophy in his spare hours and reading classical literature, a gracious, charming, modest man, soft-spoken, slight of build, a bit hard of hearing and with only the lowest opinion of his own verse. He dashed off a few more comic ballads in 1896, for Hearst's *New York Journal*, but he never considered them worth collecting in a book.

> During my brief acquaintance with the *Examiner*, [Thayer once wrote] I put out large quantities of nonsense, both prose and verse, sounding the whole newspaper gamut from advertisements to editorials. In general quality "Casey" (at least to my judgment) is neither better nor worse than much of the other stuff. Its persistent vogue is simply unaccountable, and it would be hard to say, all things considered, if it has given me more pleasure than annoyance. The constant wrangling about authorship, from which I have tried to keep aloof, has certainly filled me with disgust.

Throughout his life, he refused to discuss payments for reprintings of "Casey." "All I ask is never to be reminded of it again," he told one publisher. "Make it anything you wish."

Never happy in the family mills, Thayer finally quit working for them altogether. After a few years of travel abroad he retired in 1912 to Santa Barbara, Calif. The following year—he was then fifty—he married Mrs. Rosalind Buel Hammett, a widow from St. Louis. They had no children.

Thayer remained in Santa Barbara until his death in 1940.

"Casey" has had many imitations, sequels and parodies. Two silent motion pictures were based on Thayer's poem. The first, in 1916, starred Hopper himself as the mighty Casey. Thayer is said to have refused to appear in a short introductory scene. A second *Casey at the Bat* was released in 1927, with Wallace Beery in the leading role. (I can still recall Beery, bat in one hand and beer mug in the other, whacking the ball so hard that an outfielder has to mount a horse to retrieve it.) More recently, an animated short by Walt Disney featured the voice of Jerry Colonna reciting the ballad.

Several flimsy paperback editions of the poem, with illustrations, came out around the turn of the century. A. C. McClurg published a more substantial edition in 1912 with pictures by Dan Sayre Groesbeck. In 1964 Prentice-Hall brought out a hard-cover "Casey," profusely illustrated by Paul Frame; that same year Franklin Watts issued another, with art by Leonard Everett Fisher and a short introduction by Casey Stengel. The poem has also been illustrated innumerable times for newspaper and magazine appearances. The variant readings—including revisions by Thayer himself—might well make a thesis for a graduate student desperate for a subject.

How can one explain "Casey's" undying popularity? It is not great poetry. It was written carelessly. Parts of it are certainly doggerel. Yet it is almost impossible to read it several times without memorizing whole chunks, and there are lines so perfectly expressed, given the poem's intent, that one cannot imagine a word changed for the better. The late T. S. Eliot admired the ballad so much that he even wrote a parody about a cat, "Growl-tiger's Last Stand," in which many of Thayer's lines are echoed.

The poem's secret can be found, of all places, in the autobiography of George Santayana, another famous Harvard philosopher. Santayana was one of Thayer's associate editors on the *Lampoon*. "The man who gave the tone to the *Lampoon* at that time," Santayana writes, "was Ernest Thayer. . . . He seemed a man apart, his wit was not so much jocular as Mercutio-like, curious and whimsical, as if he saw the broken edges of things that appear whole. There was some obscurity in his play with words, and a feeling (which I shared) that the absurd side of things is pathetic. Probably nothing in his later performance may bear out what I have just said of him, because American life was then becoming unfavorable to idiosyncrasies of any sort, and the current smoothed and rounded out all the odd pebbles."

But Santayana was wrong. One thing *did* bear this out, and that was "Casey." It is precisely the blend of absurd and tragic that lies at the heart of Thayer's poem. Casey is the giant of baseball who, at his moment of greatest possible triumph, strikes out. A pathetic figure, yet comic because of the supreme arrogance and confidence with which he approached the plate: "There was ease in Casey's manner." It is the shock of contrast between the enormous buildup and the final fizzle that produces the poem's explosion point. The story of Casey has become an American myth because Casey is the incomparable symbol of the great and glorious poop-out.

One might argue that Thayer, with his extraordinary beginning at Harvard, his friendship with James and Santayana, his lifelong immersion in philosophy and the great books, was himself something of a Casey. In later years his friends were constantly urging him to write, but he would always shake his head and reply, "I have nothing to say." Not until just before his death, at the age of seventy-seven, did he make an attempt to put some serious thoughts on paper. By then it was too late. "*Now* I have something to say," he said, "and I am too weak to say it."

But posterity's judgments are hard to anticipate. Thayer's writing career was no strikeout. He swatted one magnificent, eternal home run—"Casey"—and as long as baseball is played on this old earth, on Mudville, the air will be shattered over and over again by the force of Casey's blow.

CASEY AT THE BAT

It looked extremely rocky for the Mudville nine that day;
The score stood two to four, with but one inning left to play.
So, when Cooney died at second, and Burrows did the same,
A pallor wreathed the features of the patrons of the game.

A straggling few got up to go, leaving there the rest,
With that hope which springs eternal within the human
    breast.
For they thought: "If only Casey could get a whack at that,"
They'd put even money now, with Casey at the bat.

But Flynn preceded Casey, and likewise so did Blake,
And the former was a pudd'n, and the latter was a fake.
So on that stricken multitude a deathlike silence sat;
For there seemed but little chance of Casey's getting to the bat.

But Flynn let drive a "single," to the wonderment of all.
And the much-despisèd Blakey "tore the cover off the ball."

And when the dust had lifted, and they saw what had
occurred,
There was Blakey safe at second, and Flynn a-huggin' third.

Then from the gladdened multitude went up a joyous yell—
It rumbled in the mountaintops, it rattled in the dell;
It struck upon the hillside and rebounded on the flat;
For Casey, mighty Casey, was advancing to the bat.

There was ease in Casey's manner as he stepped into his
place.
There was pride in Casey's bearing and a smile on Casey's
face;
And when responding to the cheers he lightly doffed his hat,
No stranger in the crowd could doubt 'twas Casey at the bat.

Ten thousand eyes were on him as he rubbed his hands with
dirt.
Five thousand tongues applauded when he wiped them on his
shirt;
Then when the writhing pitcher ground the ball into his hip,
Defiance glanced in Casey's eye, a sneer curled Casey's lip.

And now the leather-covered sphere came hurtling through
the air,
And Casey stood a-watching it in haughty grandeur there.
Close by the sturdy batsman the ball unheeded sped;
"That ain't my style," said Casey. "Strike one," the umpire said.

From the benches, black with people, there went up a muffled
roar,
Like the beating of the storm waves on the stern and distant
shore.
"Kill him! kill the umpire!" shouted someone on the stand;
And it's likely they'd have killed him had not Casey raised his
hand.

With a smile of Christian charity great Casey's visage shone;
He stilled the rising tumult, he made the game go on;
He signaled to the pitcher, and once more the spheroid flew;
But Casey still ignored it, and the umpire said, "Strike two."

"Fraud!" cried the maddened thousands, and the echo
answered "Fraud!"

But one scornful look from Casey and the audience was awed;
They saw his face grow stern and cold, they saw his muscles strain,
And they knew that Casey wouldn't let the ball go by again.

The sneer is gone from Casey's lips, his teeth are clenched in hate,
He pounds with cruel vengeance his bat upon the plate;
And now the pitcher holds the ball, and now he lets it go,
And now the air is shattered by the force of Casey's blow.

Oh, somewhere in this favored land the sun is shining bright,
The band is playing somewhere, and somewhere hearts are light;
And somewhere men are laughing, and somewhere children shout,
But there is no joy in Mudville—Mighty Casey has struck out!

Ernest Lawrence Thayer

Discussing Issues and Themes

1. What kinds of things made Thayer's time at Harvard especially distinguished? For example, Gardner mentions that Thayer was both student and friend of the American philosopher William James, thereby implying that Thayer was better than the ordinary student. What else was special about Thayer?
2. "Casey at the Bat" might not have been a popular success. For example, had DeWolf Hopper never recited the poem, it might have faded into obscurity. What qualities of the poem, according to Gardner, helped make it so popular after Hopper picked it up?
3. What was the pen name that Thayer wrote under when he first published "Casey at the Bat"? Where did he get the name? What does the choice of such a pen name indicate about Thayer's character?
4. Although "Casey at the Bat" might have brought fame (and money) to its author, Thayer refused to have much to do with it. For example, he refused to be paid for reprintings of the poem and tried to keep aloof from the "constant wrangling about authorship." Does Gardner portray Thayer's lack of interest in the poem as a virtue or a fault? Explain.

5. Gardner ends his tribute to Thayer by asserting that "Thayer's writing career was no strikeout." Do you agree with this judgment? Is one famous poem enough to make a writing career a success?

Discussing Rhetoric and Style

1. Gardner opens his essay with a general anecdote about the late-night clientele of "saloons." How does his opening paragraph set up the rest of the essay, which is largely a biographical tribute to the rather obscure author of "Casey at the Bat"?
2. Gardner quotes Thayer twice—once about the identity of "Casey" and once about Thayer's attitude toward the poem's extraordinary fame. How do these quotations enrich the essay? How does Gardner's portrayal of Thayer enrich the quotations?
3. Gardner builds up Thayer's appeal by citing collegiate honors and prestigious acquaintances. For example, William James is mentioned in the second paragraph, and Thayer's academic laurels are listed in the third. Where else does Gardner build up Thayer's prestige, and how?
4. Gardner's essay begins with a biography and ends with literary criticism—an interpretation of "Casey at the Bat." How does Gardner organize these concerns so that the essay is smoothly coherent?

Ideas for Writing

1. At the end of the essay, Gardner suggests that "Casey" owes its success to "the blend of absurd and tragic" at the heart of the poem. He suggests that the poem dramatizes "the great and glorious poop-out." After reading the poem, do you agree with Gardner's assessment of its appeal? Write a brief paper in which you present your own analysis of the poem, comparing your reading to Gardner's.
2. Gardner suggests that Casey is a symbol, a kind of metaphor, for our American culture. Write an essay in which you examine the symbol of Casey in the light of Robert Frost's comments about metaphor in his essay "Education by Poetry." Frost suggests that all metaphors "break down" somewhere; where does the metaphor of Casey and American culture break down?

STUDENT ESSAY

The Language of Lolita

KIMBERLY MITCHELL

*Kimberly Mitchell, while enrolled in a Nabokov seminar at Rutgers in the Fall of 1989, wrote a critique on the language of one of Nabokov's greatest novels—*Lolita*. Narrowing her discussion to a single scene in order to make her task more manageable, Mitchell discusses the ways in which Humbert the narrator affects the way we perceive Humbert the character. As Mitchell demonstrates, Humbert's tendency to represent everything as ridiculous—even his wife's death—is an attempt to gain mastery over a narrative which, in the end, has control of him.*

From just about the very first page of *Lolita*, Vladimir Nabokov presents his first-person narrator, Humbert Humbert, a middle-aged man who wants the physical and emotional love of a twelve-year-old girl, with desires and situations that are inexpressible within words. However, Humbert tries, and he often tells the reader more about himself through his failures than he could were he successful. For example, after his wife dies and he becomes sole guardian of his step-daughter, Humbert attempts to stage a believable act of mourning, but the reader can only be left feeling amused and almost disgusted rather than sympathetic. The location, situation, people and their reactions, and descriptions provided by Humbert, the author, all rebel against a "normal" scene.

The location is given in the preceding paragraph. Humbert is about to go over the circumstances of his wife's death, as well as how to handle it with the man who ran her over, in his bathroom. This hardly seems the most likely place to discuss the death of one's wife. It is important to keep this location in mind, for it becomes rather symbolic of the further inappropriate actions and ideas that follow. Though Nabokov never has Humbert, the author, mention it, the reader can almost hear the gurgling toilet throughout the rest of the scene, as if it were giggling.

And, giggle one must as Humbert actually begins the scene saying, "Speaking of busybodies, I had another visitor—friend Beale, the fellow who eliminated my wife." Humbert begins with what he typically does; with his choice of often paradoxical words, Humbert tries to create a sense of what he feels. Here he gives within the same sentence, the idea that Beale is a "busybody," "friend," and "man who eliminated my wife" within the same breath. Of course, depending on who Humbert needs to be at the present moment (a cautious pervert, a friendly neighbor or a joyful widower), Beale can be all these things to him.

Humbert, the author, goes on to describe Beale in such a degrading manner (". . . stodgy and solemn, looking like a kind of assistant executioner, with his bulldog jowls, small black eyes, thickly rimmed glasses, and conspicuous nostrils . . ."), that the reader again giggles at the "grotesque" visitor. However, Beale doesn't need Humbert to set him up as ridiculous; Beale does a fine job by himself with his chart of the accident. Again, it is important to think about the literal situation Humbert is setting up for the reader. He gives us a happy widower, thinking joyously of molesting his stepdaughter, while the man who ran his wife down is displaying a diagram of his wife's death, "with all kinds of impressive arrows and dotted lines in varied colored inks" and finally of another man closing the door on the scene "with the utmost tact." The whole scene is outrageously ridiculous. Humbert adds to the disparity between expectations and reality by describing the diagram in his own choice of words, such as "trajectory" and phrases as "dog not shown." Humbert, the author, in retrospect, contributes to our understanding of the outlandish situation he lived through.

Humbert not only adds to *what* is going on, but he also adds to *how* they go on. Beale is not only a jowl-faced bulldog with an asinine diagram, but he is a jowl-faced bulldog "with his hummingbird pencil deftly and delicately flying from one point to another . . . demonstrat[ing] his absolute innocence and the recklessness of [Humbert's] wife." Fred Beale also suggests that Charlotte, as she was slipping on the asphalt with Beale's car racing towards her, should have had enough wits to fall backwards, away from his car, instead of forward, towards his car. Perhaps using Beale's logic, the reader can say Beale should have had enough sense to swerve his car the other way to avoid the dog *and* Charlotte. Of course, the idea is crazy, just as Humbert delights in showing us how Beale's is crazy.

Humbert, the author, not only has fun with Beale, but Humbert, the character, also gets his chance at Beale:

> Breathing violently through tense jet-black nostrils, he shook his head; then, with an air of perfect savoir vivre and gentlemanly generosity, he offered to pay the funeral-home expenses. He expected me to refuse his offer. With a drunken sob of gratitude I accepted it. This took him aback. Slowly, incredulously, he repeated what he had said. I thanked him again, even more profusely than before.

The reader can imagine Beale's little black eyes opening, his jaw dropping, and his jowls hanging, as Humbert "humbly" accepts his most "sincere" offer. The whole scene has rendered Beale so obviously and irretrievably stupid, that the reader can't help but rejoice in Humbert's small victory.

Being this small victory is one of the few Humbert can call and hold onto as his own, it is almost ironic that he should follow it up with a praise of Fate. The reader can imagine Humbert saying, "Oh reader, what a clever Humbert I was to have Charlotte find my journal . . ." but he doesn't. He, instead, seems to say Fate acts upon people. It has made a "hurrying housewife, slippery pavement, a pest of a dog, steep grade, big car and a baboon at its wheel."

The interest in the Fate passage doesn't end there, though. What is equally important to note is the change in tone. Tone tends to drive the wit and ironies of Humbert, but here, for the most part, he becomes sincere and straightforward. Perhaps this is one of the greatest ironies of the book; despite his constant planning and elaborate deceptions, his greatest accomplishment was never his own, but the result of a bunch of freak coincidences. Humbert must cry.

So, the Beale scene, then, has two distinct parts. The first is driven by Humbert—the author's language, which renders the rest of the situation to its most ridiculous state. The second section with Fate, Humbert lowers himself from the role of director he has previously set himself up in. He shows us when he is in absolute control and when he has no control. Thus, he gives the reader another sense of what it is like to be him—to falter by your own actions and succeed solely by fate and coincidence.

Discussing Ideas and Themes

1. According to Mitchell, what are some of the problems Humbert Humbert faces as he tries to articulate his desires? For example, the setting in which Humbert tries to mourn, the bathroom,

seems ridiculous. What other parts of the scene, according to Mitchell, undermine Humbert's attempts to communicate?

2. According to Mitchell, what are Humbert's emotional responses to his wife's death? Why would these responses make it difficult for him to express "normal" grief?
3. What kinds of things does Beale do, according to Mitchell, to make himself seem ridiculous? For example, what is so strange about his chart? What is the fault in Beale's logic?
4. What is Humbert's "victory" over Beale? Reading the passage that Mitchell quotes, do you, too, feel that we "can't help but rejoice in Humbert's small victory"? Explain.
5. How does Humbert's rhetoric about fate undermine his own linguistic mastery in what Mitchell calls the "first part" of the Beale scene? For example, Humbert exerts some control over Beale in the passage that Mitchell has just quoted, but his language about fate evidently doesn't display such control. How does Mitchell suggest we evaluate Humbert after we have read this scene?

Discussing Rhetoric and Style

1. Although this is an "academic" essay, Mitchell often uses casual diction; for example, she opens the first paragraph with the casual phrase, "from just about the very first page." What are the effects of this diction on the context of this kind of essay?
2. Although Mitchell rarely uses figurative language in this piece, she employs a simile and a pun to smooth the transition between the second and third paragraphs. How else does Mitchell make transitions between paragraphs? Are her other transitions as effective as this one?
3. Many essays begin with a quotation, but Mitchell does not quote substantially from Nabokov's text until near the end of her essay. Would you say that her use of quotations, particularly her placement of the longest quotation, is effective? Explain.
4. What kind of appeal does Mitchell make to the reader? How would you describe her overall tone? Be sure to look closely at her essay, considering her diction, sentence structure, and the way she addresses or refers to the reader.

Ideas for Writing

1. Mitchell presents one interpretation of the Beale scene in *Lolita*. Read the scene, and write a brief paper in which you respond to her interpretation with one of your own.
2. Taking Mitchell's analysis of Humbert Humbert's rhetoric as a model, write a paper in which you show that a character's language both reinforces his mastery over life and, in another way, undermines it.

CHAPTER 9

Inspirations for the Life of Writing

The pleasures of reading are often accompanied by a wistful sense that one could never write as well as the authors one admires. Yet this chapter shows that writers are made as well as born, and that simple steps can take anyone a long way toward the goal of being a good writer. The authors who testify here show that writing is not merely reading in reverse—if it were that simple everyone would write easily and well. Rather, writing is a matter of patience and practice, of trying again and again. The essays here are intended to inspire that kind of effort in their readers.

The first two authors suggest ways for the novice to begin. William Safire, a widely syndicated writer on language, tells what keeping a diary can do for your command of life and language. He goes so far as to give rules for the dedicated diarist to follow. "Four are enough," he says.

In "On Keeping a Notebook," Joan Didion takes a more easygoing approach. She distinguishes between keeping a diary and the notes she keeps, giving examples that may inspire some of her readers to adopt both forms of turning life into language.

Columnist Russell Baker records the odd chain of events that led to his becoming a writer. He shows how even under the most unlikely circumstances "something may come along" to provide the kind of inspiration and opportunity that lead to writing as a way of life and perhaps even a way of making a living.

Being dedicated does not get words on the page. How do professional writers face the difficulty every student encounters in getting down to the task of writing? How do writers form a schedule? Essayist Annie Dillard answers these and other questions in "The Writing Life."

Raw material is one thing. Being inspired is another. Turning informal jottings and notes into a coherent piece is still another. But revising until one is satisfied is another thing altogether. Nora Ephron faces these issues in her essay, "Revision and Life." She concludes that her own literary strengths lie not so much in imaginative vision as in patient revision.

Writing is commonly looked on as a way of expressing what you know, but Janet Emig, a famous teacher of writing, tells us about "Writing as a Mode of Learning." Writing, Emig argues, is not simply a matter of expressing thoughts through words. Everyone has thoughts and everyone knows words, yet many find it very difficult to write in a way that satisfies them. Emig suggests that writing is not so much a means of expressing what is already known as one of *discovering* knowledge with the aid of language.

Finally, student writer Susan Sakos advocates the classical technique of imitation as a way to constant improvement in written work.

On Keeping a Diary

WILLIAM SAFIRE

William Safire is probably best known for his popular "On Language" column, which appears each Sunday in the New York Times Magazine. *The author of several books on language, including* Safire's Political Dictionary, Good Advice, *and* I Stand Corrected, *Safire has also won a Pulitzer Prize for distinguished commentary. The following essay is characteristic of his journalistic style. Brief and thoroughly opinionated, it tells in no uncertain terms why diaries are important. "On Keeping a Diary" first appeared in* The New York Times. *For more complete biographical information on Safire, see the introduction to "Bizbuzz" in Chapter 2.*

Diaries are no longer dear; as the invention of the telephone began the decline of letter-writing, the invention of the tape recorder has led to the atrophy of the personal diary. Many of us record our words but few of us record our thoughts.

Why is a diary stereotyped today as the gushing of a schoolgirl or the muttering of a discontented politician, unworthy of the efforts of a busy person? Perhaps because we are out of the habit of writing, or have fallen into the habit of considering our lives humdrum, or have become fearful of committing our thoughts to paper. . . .

Diaries remind us of details that would otherwise fade from memory and make less vivid our recollection. Navy Secretary Gideon Welles, whose private journal is an invaluable source for Civil War historians, watched Abraham Lincoln die in a room across the street from Ford's Theater and later jotted down a detail that puts the reader in the room: "The giant sufferer lay extended diagonally across the bed, which was not long enough for him . . ."

Diaries can be written in psychic desperation, intended to be burned, as a hold on sanity: "I won't give up the diary again," wrote novelist Franz Kafka; "I must hold on here, it is the only place I can." Or written in physical desperation, intended to be read, as in the last entry in Arctic explorer Robert Scott's diary: "For God's sake look after our people."

But what of people who are neither on trial nor freezing to death, neither witnesses to great events nor participants in momentous undertakings? To most of us, a diary presents a terrible challenge: "Write down in me something worth remembering," the neatly dated page says; "prove that this day was not a waste of time."

For people intimidated by their own diaries, here are a handful of rules:

1. *You own the diary, the diary doesn't own you.* There are many days in all our lives about which the less written the better. If you are the sort of person who can only keep a diary on a regular schedule, filling up two pages just before you go to bed, become another sort of person.
2. *Write for yourself.* The central idea of a diary is that you are not writing for critics or for posterity but are writing a private letter to your future self. If you are petty, or wrongheaded, or hopelessly emotional, relax—if there is anybody who will understand and forgive, it is your future self.
3. *Put down what cannot be reconstructed.* You are not a newspaper of record, obligated to record every first time that man walks on the moon. Instead, remind yourself of the poignant personal moment, the remark you wish you had made, your predictions about the outcome of your own tribulations.
4. *Write legibly.* This sounds obvious, but I have pages of scribblings by a younger me who was infuriatingly illiterate. Worse, to protect the innocent, I had encoded certain names and then misplaced my Rosetta Stone; now I will never know who "JW" was in my freshman year at college, and she is a memory it might be nice to have.

Four rules are enough rules. Above all, *write about what got to you that day,* the way a parched John Barrymore did during a trip to Mexico in 1926 when he discovered a bar that to him was an oasis:

> The beer arrived—*draft* beer—in a tall, thin, clean crystal of Grecian proportions, with a creamy head on it. I tasted it. . . . The planets seemed to pause a moment in their circling to breathe a benediction on that Mexican brewer's head. . . . Then the universe went on its wonted way again. Hot Dog! But that *was* a glass of beer!

That is the art of the diarist in its pure form, unafraid, intimate, important in its insignificance, ringingly free. Who can compare Barrymore's frothy recall with the insecure jottings-down of most of us on little expense ledgers?

Wish I still kept a diary. But you see, I get very tired at the end of the day, and besides, nothing interesting happens any more. And so to bed. . . .

Discussing Ideas and Themes

1. What does Safire think diaries do for the diarist? For the rest of the world?
2. What are some of the stereotypes that surround diaries and diary writing today? Write a brief description of someone you think would keep a diary. Does your sketch confirm Safire's hypothesis about stereotypes?
3. Do Safire's four rules seem reasonable to you? Which of the four do you think is the easiest and which the hardest? Would you follow Safire's advice?
4. Do you now keep a diary? Did you as a child? What was the most positive aspect of keeping or not keeping one? The most negative?

Discussing Rhetoric and Style

1. Safire's essay is brief. Is its brevity a plus or a minus?
2. Does Safire really imagine his audience to be full of intimidated diarists? Is his tone appropriate for such an audience? Why or why not?
3. What do the four diary entries presented have in common? What do you think Safire's criteria were in choosing them? Why does he present them in the order that he does?
4. Safire offers four tips for diary writing. How is the list arranged? Is it ordered with the easiest tip first and the most difficult last? Is it ordered from the most general to the most specific? Is there any logical relationship between the four items at all? Are they all equal? Explain.
5. What is the effect of Safire's closing admission that he is too "tired at the end of the day" to keep a diary? Does it reverse the

effect of the rest of the essay, particularly the example from Barrymore?

Ideas for Writing

1. Keep a diary for yourself for one week. Do you find that the diary format accomplishes everything Safire claims for it? Write a brief essay discussing how keeping a diary affects the ways you perceive events in your life.
2. One of the assumptions implicit in this essay is that writing represents life. Write an essay in which you compare Safire's view of language to Nabokov's view in "Good Readers and Good Writers."

On Keeping a Notebook

JOAN DIDION

Born in 1934 and educated at the University of California at Berkeley, Joan Didion has contributed essays to numerous magazines, such as the Saturday Evening Post *and* Harper's. *She is the author of many novels, including* A Book of Common Prayer *and* Democracy; *many of her essays have been collected in* Slouching Towards Bethlehem *and* The White Album. *In the famous and often-reprinted "On Keeping a Notebook," Didion describes her notebook and discusses why keeping a notebook can be an important source of personal identity as well as a safe place to store memories. This essay first appeared in* Slouching Towards Bethlehem.

" 'That woman Estelle,' " the note reads, " 'is partly the reason why George Sharp and I are separated today.' *Dirty crepe-de-Chine wrapper, hotel bar, Wilmington RR, 9:45 a.m. August Monday morning.*"

Since the note is in my notebook, it presumably has some meaning to me. I study it for a long while. At first I have only the most general notion of what I was doing on an August Monday morning in the bar of the hotel across from the Pennsylvania Railroad station in Wilmington, Delaware (waiting for a train? missing one? 1960? 1961? why Wilmington?), but I do remember being there. The woman in the dirty crepe-de-Chine wrapper had come down from her room for a beer, and the bartender had heard before the reason why George Sharp and she were separated today. "Sure," he said, and went on mopping the floor. "You told me." At the other end of the bar is a girl. She is talking, pointedly, not to the man beside her but to a cat lying in the triangle of sunlight cast through the open door. She is wearing a plaid silk dress from Peck & Peck, and the hem is coming down.

Here is what it is: the girl has been on the Eastern Shore, and now she is going back to the city, leaving the man beside her, and all she can see ahead are the viscous summer sidewalks and the 3 A.M. long-distance calls that will make her lie awake and then sleep drugged through all the steaming mornings left in August (1960? 1961?). Because she must go directly from the train to lunch in New York, she wishes that she had a safety pin for the hem of the plaid silk dress, and she also wishes that she could forget about the hem and the lunch and stay in the cool bar that smells of disinfectant and malt and make friends with the woman in the crepe-de-Chine wrapper. She is afflicted by a little self-pity, and she wants to compare Estelles. That is what that was all about.

Why did I write it down? In order to remember, of course, but exactly what was it I wanted to remember? How much of it actually happened? Did any of it? Why do I keep a notebook at all? It is easy to deceive oneself on all those scores. The impulse to write things down is a peculiarly compulsive one, inexplicable to those who do not share it, useful only accidentally, only secondarily, in the way that any compulsion tries to justify itself. I suppose that it begins or does not begin in the cradle. Although I have felt compelled to write things down since I was five years old, I doubt that my daughter ever will, for she is a singularly blessed and accepting child, delighted with life exactly as life presents itself to her, unafraid to go to sleep and unafraid to wake up. Keepers of private notebooks are a different breed altogether, lonely and resistant rearrangers of things, anxious malcontents, children afflicted apparently at birth with some presentiment of loss.

My first notebook was a Big Five tablet, given to me by my mother with the sensible suggestion that I stop whining and learn to amuse myself by writing down my thoughts. She returned the tablet to me a few years ago; the first entry is an account of a woman who believed herself to be freezing to death in the Arctic night, only to find, when day broke, that she had stumbled onto the Sahara Desert, where she would die of the heat before lunch. I have no idea what turn of a five-year-old's mind could have prompted so insistently "ironic" and exotic a story, but it does reveal a certain predilection for the extreme which has dogged me into adult life; perhaps if I were analytically inclined I would find it a truer story than any I might have told about Donald Johnson's birthday party or the day my cousin Brenda put Kitty Litter in the aquarium.

So the point of my keeping a notebook has never been, nor is it now, to have an accurate factual record of what I have been doing or thinking. That would be a different impulse entirely, an instinct for reality which I sometimes envy but do not possess. At no point have I ever been able successfully to keep a diary; my approach to daily life ranges from the grossly negligent to the merely absent, and on those few occasions when I have tried dutifully to record a day's events, boredom has so overcome me that the results are mysterious at best. What is this business about "shopping, typing piece, dinner with E, depressed"? Shopping for what? Typing what piece? Who is E? Was this "E" depressed, or was I depressed? Who cares?

In fact I have abandoned altogether that kind of pointless entry; instead I tell what some would call lies. "That's simply not true," the members of my family frequently tell me when they come up against my memory of a shared event. "The party was *not* for you, the spider was *not* a black widow, *it wasn't that way at all.*" Very likely they are right, for not only have I always had trouble distinguishing between what happened and what merely might have happened, but I remain unconvinced that the distinction, for my purposes, matters. The cracked crab that I recall having for lunch the day my father came home from Detroit in 1945 must certainly be embroidery, worked into the day's pattern to lend verisimilitude; I was ten years old and would not now remember the cracked crab. The day's events did not turn on cracked crab. And yet it is precisely that fictitious crab that makes me see the afternoon all over again, a home movie run all too often, the father bearing gifts, the child weeping, an exercise in family love and guilt. Or that is what it was to me. Similarly, perhaps it never did snow that August in Vermont; perhaps there never were flurries in the night wind, and maybe no one else felt the ground hardening and summer already dead even as we pretended to bask in it, but that was how it felt to me, and it might as well have snowed, could have snowed, did snow.

How it felt to me: that is getting closer to the truth about a notebook. I sometimes delude myself about why I keep a notebook, imagine that some thrifty virtue derives from preserving everything observed. See enough and write it down, I tell myself, and then some morning when the world seems drained of wonder, some day when I am only going through the motions of doing what I am supposed to do, which is write—on that bankrupt morning I will simply open my notebook and there it will all be, a forgotten account with accumulated interest, paid passage back to the world out there: dialogue overheard in hotels and elevators and at the hatcheck counter in Pavillon (one middle-aged man shows his hat check to another and says, "That's my old football number"); impressions of Bettina Aptheker and Benjamin Sonnenberg and Teddy ("Mr. Acapulco") Stauffer; careful *aperçus* about tennis bums and failed fashion models and Greek shipping heiresses, one of whom taught me a significant lesson (a lesson I could have learned from F. Scott Fitzgerald, but perhaps we all must meet the very rich for ourselves) by asking, when I arrived to interview her in her orchid-filled sitting room on the second day of a paralyzing New York blizzard, whether it was snowing outside.

I imagine, in other words, that the notebook is about other people. But of course it is not. I have no real business with what one stranger said to another at the hatcheck counter in Pavillon; in fact I suspect that the line "That's my old football number" touched not my own imagination at all, but merely some memory of something once read, probably "The Eighty-Yard Run." Nor is my concern with a woman in a dirty crepe-de-Chine wrapper in a Wilmington bar. My stake is always, of course, in the unmentioned girl in the plaid silk dress. *Remember what it was to be me:* that is always the point.

It is a difficult point to admit. We are brought up in the ethic that others, any others, all others, are by definition more interesting than ourselves; taught to be diffident, just this side of self-effacing. ("You're the least important person in the room and don't forget it," Jessica Mitford's governess would hiss in her ear on the advent of any social occasion; I copied that into my notebook because it is only recently that I have been able to enter a room without hearing some such phrase in my inner ear.) Only the very young and the very old may recount their dreams at breakfast, dwell upon self, interrupt with memories of beach picnics and favorite Liberty lawn dresses and the rainbow trout in a creek near Colorado Springs. The rest of us are expected, rightly, to affect absorption in other people's favorite dresses, other people's trout.

And so we do. But our notebooks give us away, for however dutifully we record what we see around us, the common denominator of all we see is always, transparently, shamelessly, the implacable "I." We are not talking here about the kind of notebook that is patently for public consumption, a structural conceit for binding together a series of graceful *pensées;* we are talking about something private, about bits of the mind's string too short to use, an indiscriminate and erratic assemblage with meaning only for its maker.

And sometimes even the maker has difficulty with the meaning. There does not seem to be, for example, any point in my knowing for the rest of my life that, during 1964, 720 tons of soot fell on every square mile of New York City, yet there it is in my notebook, labeled "FACT." Nor do I really need to remember that Ambrose Bierce liked to spell Leland Stanford's name "£eland $tanford" or that "smart women almost always wear black in Cuba," a fashion hint without much potential for practical application. And does not the relevance of these notes seem marginal at best?:

> In the basement museum of the Inyo County Courthouse in Independence, California, sign pinned to a mandarin coat:

> "This MANDARIN COAT was often worn by Mrs. Minnie S. Brooks when giving lectures on her TEAPOT COLLECTION."

> Redhead getting out of car in front of Beverly Wilshire Hotel, chinchilla stole, Vuitton bags with tags reading:

> MRS LOU FOX
> HOTEL SAHARA
> VEGAS

Well, perhaps not entirely marginal. As a matter of fact, Mrs. Minnie S. Brooks and her MANDARIN COAT pull me back into my own childhood, for although I never knew Mrs. Brooks and did not visit Inyo County until I was thirty, I grew up in just such a world, in houses cluttered with Indian relics and bits of gold ore and ambergris and the souvenirs my Aunt Mercy Farnsworth brought back from the Orient. It is a long way from that world to Mrs. Lou Fox's world, where we all live now, and is it not just as well to remember that? Might not Mrs. Minnie S. Brooks help me to remember what I am? Might not Mrs. Lou Fox help me to remember what I am not?

But sometimes the point is harder to discern. What exactly did I have in mind when I noted down that it cost the father of someone I know $650 a month to light the place on the Hudson in which he lived before the Crash? What use was I planning to make of this line by Jimmy Hoffa: "I may have my faults, but being wrong ain't one of them"? And although I think it interesting to know where the girls who travel with the Syndicate have their hair done when they find themselves on the West Coast, will I ever make suitable use of it? Might I not be better off just passing it on to John O'Hara? What is a recipe for sauerkraut doing in my notebook? What kind of magpie keeps this notebook? *"He was born the night the Titanic went down."* That seems a nice enough line, and I even recall who said it, but is it not really a better line in life than it could ever be in fiction?

But of course that is exactly it: not that I should ever use the line, but that I should remember the woman who said it and the afternoon I heard it. We were on her terrace by the sea, and we were finishing the wine left from lunch, trying to get what sun there was, a California winter sun. The woman whose husband was born the night the *Titanic* went down wanted to rent her house, wanted to go back to her children in Paris. I remember wishing that I could afford the house, which cost $1,000 a month. "Someday you will," she said lazily. "Someday it all comes." There in the sun on her terrace it seemed easy to believe in someday, but later I had a low-grade afternoon hangover and ran over a black snake on the way to the supermarket and was flooded with inexplicable fear when I heard the checkout clerk explaining to the man ahead of me why she was finally divorcing her husband. "He left me no choice," she said over and over as she punched the register. "He has a little seven-month-old baby by her, he left me no choice." I would like to believe that my dread then was for the human condition, but of course it was for me, because I wanted a baby and did not then have one and because I wanted to own the house that cost $1,000 a month to rent and because I had a hangover.

It all comes back. Perhaps it is difficult to see the value in having one's self back in that kind of mood, but I do see it; I think we are well advised to keep on nodding terms with the people we used to be, whether we find them attractive company or not. Otherwise they turn up unannounced and surprise us, come hammering on the mind's door at 4 A.M. of a bad night and demand to know who deserted them, who betrayed them, who is going to make amends. We forget all too soon the things we thought we could never forget. We forget the loves and the betrayals alike, forget what we whispered and what we screamed, forget who we were. I have already lost touch with a couple of people I used to be; one of them, a seventeen-year-old, presents little threat, although it would be of some interest to me to know again what it feels like to sit on a river levee drinking vodka-and-orange-juice and listening to Les Paul and Mary Ford and their echoes sing "How High the Moon" on the car radio. (You see I still have the scenes, but I no longer perceive myself among those present, no longer could even improvise the dialogue.) The other one, a twenty-three-year-old, bothers me more. She was always a good deal of trouble, and I suspect she will reappear when I least want to see her, skirts too long, shy to the point of aggravation, always the injured party, full of recriminations and little hurts and stories I do not want to hear again, at once saddening me and angering me with her vulnerability and ignorance, an apparition all the more insistent for being so long banished.

It is a good idea, then, to keep in touch, and I suppose that keeping in touch is what notebooks are all about. And we are all on our own when it comes to keeping those lines open to ourselves: your notebook will never help me, nor mine you. *"So what's new in the whiskey business?"* What could that possibly mean to you? To me it means a blonde in a Pucci bathing suit sitting with a couple of fat men by the pool at the Beverly Hills Hotel. Another man approaches, and they all regard one another in silence for a while. "So what's new in the whiskey business?" one of the fat men finally says by way of welcome, and the blonde stands up, arches one foot and dips it in the pool, looking all the while at the cabana where Baby Pignatari is talking on the telephone. That is all there is to that, except that several years later I saw the blonde coming out of Saks Fifth Avenue in New

York with her California complexion and a voluminous mink coat. In the harsh wind that day she looked old and irrevocably tired to me, and even the skins in the mink coat were not worked the way they were doing them that year, not the way she would have wanted them done, and there is the point of the story. For a while after that I did not like to look in the mirror, and my eyes would skim the newspapers and pick out only the deaths, the cancer victims, the premature coronaries, the suicides, and I stopped riding the Lexington Avenue IRT because I noticed for the first time that all the strangers I had seen for years—the man with the seeing-eye dog, the spinster who read the classified pages every day, the fat girl who always got off with me at Grand Central—looked older than they once had.

It all comes back. Even that recipe for sauerkraut: even that brings it back. I was on Fire Island when I first made that sauerkraut, and it was raining, and we drank a lot of bourbon and ate the sauerkraut and went to bed at ten, and I listened to the rain and the Atlantic and felt safe. I made the sauerkraut again last night and it did not make me feel any safer, but that is, as they say, another story.

Discussing Issues and Themes

1. What is the difference between a diary and a notebook? Write a note and a diary entry about something that happened yesterday (try to write one of them in the morning, one in the evening). Do the two entries take you in different directions? Explain.

2. Why doesn't it matter to Didion if her records are factual or not? What is the purpose of keeping a notebook, if not to remember facts of certain events? Cite a passage in the essay that supports your answer.

3. Who is the subject of a notebook such as Didion's? Why is this fact central to her philosophy of notebooks? Would she be likely to keep a notebook about anyone else? Why or why not?

4. Compare Didion's essay with Safire's "On Keeping a Diary." Do the two essays have as much in common as their titles suggest? Pick one area—style or theme, for example—and make a list of at least five ways in which the two essays differ.

Discussing Rhetoric and Style

1. Contrast the grammar of Didion's note in the first paragraph with that of the expanded story in the second and third para-

graphs. What does the author add to make the story fuller? What parts of speech dominate the first paragraph? Which parts of speech are added in the second and third? And what differences does each make?

2. Study the second and third paragraphs of Didion's essay for style. Does her style—choice of syntax, verb tense, and diction, among other things—remind you of the kind of style you would expect to encounter in a novel or story? Why or why not?

3. Didion has written several novels as well as a few travel books. Why might the kind of notes she describes here be particularly helpful for a novelist? For a travel writer? Bear in mind the particular demands of each genre.

4. Why does Didion use so many questions in her essay? Are her questions always rhetorical? When does she use them most—at the beginning, middle, or end of paragraphs? Why?

Ideas for Writing

1. Didion's essay suggests that memory is important in shaping personal identity as well as a sense of continuity within people's lives. Take a memory from your childhood and try to retrace the steps of the notebook process. Write a few paragraphs describing the event, and then break the memory down into the kinds of details—smells, sounds, tastes—that Didion might include in her notebook.

2. Didion writes that "it is a good idea, then, to keep in touch, and I suppose that keeping in touch is what notebooks are all about. . . . We are all on our own when it comes to keeping these lines open to ourselves: your notebook will never help me, nor mine you." Discuss Didion's philosophy of notebook keeping, concentrating on this quotation and one other passage of your choice. What does this passage imply about the aims of writing?

The Making of a Writer

RUSSELL BAKER

Perhaps best known for his "Observer" column in the New York Times Sunday *magazine, Russell Baker is a popular journalist and author of the best-selling* Growing Up *and* The Good Times. *The following essay, a memoir of the adolescent crisis that led to Baker's career in writing, is an excerpt from* Growing Up. *For more complete biographical information on Baker, see the introduction to his essay "New Age Babble" in Chapter 2.*

"Something will come along."

That became my mother's battle cry as I plowed into the final year of high school. Friends began asking her what Russell planned to do when he graduated, and her answer was, "Something will come along." She didn't know what, and nothing was in sight on the horizon, but she'd survived so long now on faith that something always came along for people who did their best. "Russ hasn't made up his mind yet, but something will come along," she told people.

I saw no possibilities and looked forward to the end of school days with increasing glumness. It was assumed I would get a job. Boys of our economic class didn't ordinarily go to college. My education, however, hadn't fitted me for labor. While I was reading the Romantic poets and learning Latin syntax, practical boys had been taking shop, mechanical drawing, accounting, and typing. I couldn't drive a nail without mashing my thumb. When I mentioned my inadequacies to my mother she said, "Something will come along, Buddy."

If, gloomily, I said, "Fat chance," she snapped at me, "For God's sake, Russell, have a little gumption. Look on the bright side."

I didn't mind the prospect of working. Having worked since I was eight, I had acquired the habit of work, but I was stymied about what kind of full-time work I might be fit for. That winter I was trying to muster enthusiasm for a career in the grocery business. Moving from Lombard Street to Marydell Road, I had lost my newspaper route. To make up the lost income I'd taken a Saturday job at a large grocery in the Hollins Market, which paid $14 for twelve hours' work. It was a "self-service" store, a primitive forerunner of the supermarket, the first expression of an idea whose time had not yet come. Situated in a dilapidated old building where groceries had once been sold, old-style, across the counter, it bore little resemblance to the bulging supermonuments to consumption that were to rise after World War II. There was no air-conditioning in summer and little heat in winter. Under the cellar's cobwebbed rafters an occasional rat scurried among sacks of cornmeal and hundred-pound bags of flour. As a stock clerk, I toted merchandise from the cellar, marked its price in black crayon, and stacked it on shelves for Saturday shoppers. The flour sacks were slung over the shoulder and lugged upstairs to be dipped from with an aluminum scoop on demand.

The manager was Mr. Simmons, a bawdy, exuberant slave driver who had learned the business in the days of over-the-counter selling when a manager's personality could attract customers or turn them away. Simmons was a tall, square-shouldered man who affected the breezy style, as though he'd studied his trade under burlesque comedians. His head was as round and hairless as a cannon ball. He wore big horn-rimmed glasses and bow ties, and his mouth, which was wide and frequently open from ear to ear, displayed dazzling rows of teeth so big they would have done credit to a horse.

Throughout the day the store was filled with his roars, guffaws, shouted jokes, and curses. He romped the aisles in Groucho Marx lope, administering tongue lashings when he discovered empty shelves where the canned tomatoes or the Post Toasties or the Ovaltine were supposed to be. Spotting a handsome woman at the meat counter, he might glide behind the hamburger grinder to whisper sotto voce some dirty joke at the butcher's ear, then glare at the woman, part his mouth from ear to ear, and display his magnificent ivory. The store was his stage, and he treated it as if he were its star, director, producer, and owner.

If there was a dull half hour he might creep up behind one of the stock clerks hoisting oatmeal from crate to shelf, goose him with both thumbs, then gallop away roaring with laughter. Many of the customers were black and poor and arrived late on Saturday nights hoping to have their paychecks cashed. With them Simmons played Simon Legree, examining their checks suspiciously, demanding identification papers, then rejecting some damp proffered document as inadequate. "That damn thing is so dirty I don't even want to touch it. You open it up and show it to me." Or, if the credentials were in order:

"I don't know whether I'm going to cash this check or not. How much do you want to buy here?"

Simmons boasted of being a great lecher. In the cellar ceiling he had drilled a small hole through which he could look up the skirts of women customers standing at the cash register overhead. When a woman who pleased his fancy entered the store, he ostentatiously departed for the cellar with some such cry as "Hot damn! I've got to see more of this." Rolling his eyeballs and smacking his lips he plunged into the cellar and could be found there standing on a pile of flour sacks, one eye glued to his peephole.

I wasn't exhilarated by the grocery business, but at least I was getting experience I thought might help me get full-time work at it after high school. For this purpose I wanted to learn to work the cash register so I could become a checker, the most glamorous job in the store except for the manager's. Simmons withheld this prize. At some point I'd made the mistake of trying to show him I was fancily educated, thinking this would move him to promote me from cellar labor. Whether he took me for an overeducated young fool or whether he resented my failure to laugh loudly enough at his jokes, I don't know. Whatever the reason, I waited in vain for my chance to work the cash register. I knew I would never get it when Simmons, desperate one day for help at the cash registers, came down to the cellar, passed me by, and called on Earl to do the job. Earl was black, and black people were contemptible to Simmons but still preferable to me. It made me wonder if I was cut out for the grocery business. But on the other hand, what else was there?

The only thing that truly interested me was writing, and I knew that sixteen-year-olds did not come out of high school and become writers. I thought of writing as something to be done only by the rich. It was so obviously not real work, not a job at which you could earn a living. Still, I had begun to think of myself as a writer. It was the only thing for which I seemed to have the smallest talent, and, silly though it sounded when I told people I'd like to be a writer, it gave me a way of thinking about myself which satisfied my need to have an identity.

The notion of becoming a writer had flickered off and on in my head since the Belleville days, but it wasn't until my third year in high school that the possibility took hold. Until then I'd been bored by everything associated with English courses. I found English grammar dull and baffling. I hated the assignments to turn out "compositions," and went at them like heavy labor, turning out leaden, lackluster paragraphs that were agonies for teachers to read and for me to write. The classics thrust on me to read seemed as deadening as chloroform.

When our class was assigned to Mr. Fleagle for third-year English

I anticipated another grim year in that dreariest of subjects. Mr. Fleagle was notorious among City students for dullness and inability to inspire. He was said to be stuffy, dull, and hopelessly out of date. To me he looked to be sixty or seventy and prim to a fault. He wore primly severe eyeglasses, his wavy hair was primly cut and primly combed. He wore prim vested suits with neckties blocked primly against the collar buttons of his primly starched white shirts. He had a primly pointed jaw, a primly straight nose, and a prim manner of speaking that was so correct, so gentlemanly, that he seemed a comic antique.

I anticipated a listless, unfruitful year with Mr. Fleagle and for a long time was not disappointed. We read *Macbeth*. Mr. Fleagle loved *Macbeth* and wanted us to love it too, but he lacked the gift of infecting others with his own passion. He tried to convey the murderous ferocity of Lady Macbeth one day by reading aloud the passage that concludes

> . . . I have given suck, and know
> How tender 'tis to love the babe that milks me.
> I would, while it was smiling in my face,
> Have plucked my nipple from his boneless gums. . . .

The idea of prim Mr. Fleagle plucking his nipple from boneless gums was too much for the class. We burst into gasps of irrepressible snickering. Mr. Fleagle stopped.

"There is nothing funny, boys, about giving suck to a babe. It is the—the very essence of motherhood, don't you see."

He constantly sprinkled his sentences with "don't you see." It wasn't a question but an exclamation of mild surprise at our ignorance. "Your pronoun needs an antecedent, don't you see," he would say, very primly. "The purpose of the Porter's scene, boys, is to provide comic relief from the horror, don't you see."

Late in the year we tackled the informal essay. "The essay, don't you see, is the . . ." My mind went numb. Of all forms of writing, none seemed so boring as the essay. Naturally we would have to write informal essays. Mr. Fleagle distributed a homework sheet offering us a choice of topics. None was quite so simpleminded as "What I Did on My Summer Vacation," but most seemed to be almost as dull. I took the list home and dawdled until the night before the essay was due. Sprawled on the sofa, I finally faced up to the grim task, took the list out of my notebook, and scanned it. The topic on which my eye stopped was "The Art of Eating Spaghetti."

This title produced an extraordinary sequence of mental images. Surging up out of the depths of memory came a vivid recollection of a night in Belleville when all of us were seated around the supper table—Uncle Allen, my mother, Uncle Charlie, Doris, Uncle Hal—and Aunt Pat served spaghetti for supper. Spaghetti was an exotic treat in those days. Neither Doris nor I had ever eaten spaghetti, and none of the adults had enough experience to be good at it. All the good humor of Uncle Allen's house reawoke in my mind as I recalled the laughing arguments we had that night about the socially respectable method for moving spaghetti from plate to mouth.

Suddenly I wanted to write about that, about the warmth and good feeling of it, but I wanted to put it down simply for my own joy, not for Mr. Fleagle. It was a moment I wanted to recapture and hold for myself. I wanted to relive the pleasure of an evening at New Street. To write it as I wanted, however, would violate all the rules of formal composition I'd learned in school, and Mr. Fleagle would surely give it a failing grade. Never mind. I would write something else for Mr. Fleagle after I had written this thing for myself.

When I finished it the night was half gone and there was no time left to compose a proper, respectable essay for Mr. Fleagle. There was no choice next morning but to turn in my private reminiscence of Belleville. Two days passed before Mr. Fleagle returned the graded papers, and he returned everyone's but mine. I was bracing myself for a command to report to Mr. Fleagle immediately after school for discipline when I saw him lift my paper from his desk and rap for the class's attention.

"Now, boys," he said, "I want to read you an essay. This is titled 'The Art of Eating Spaghetti.' "

And he started to read. My words! He was reading *my words* out loud to the entire class. What's more, the entire class was listening. Listening attentively. Then somebody laughed, then the entire class was laughing, and not in contempt and ridicule, but with openhearted enjoyment. Even Mr. Fleagle stopped two or three times to repress a small prim smile.

I did my best to avoid showing pleasure, but what I was feeling was pure ecstasy at this startling demonstration that my words had the power to make people laugh. In the eleventh grade, at the eleventh hour as it were, I had discovered a calling. It was the happiest moment of my entire school career. When Mr. Fleagle finished he put the final seal on my happiness by saying, "Now that, boys, is an essay, don't you see. It's—don't you see—it's of the very essence of the essay, don't you see. Congratulations, Mr. Baker."

For the first time, light shone on a possibility. It wasn't a very heartening possibility, to be sure. Writing couldn't lead to a job after high school, and it was hardly honest work, but Mr. Fleagle had opened a door for me. After that I ranked Mr. Fleagle among the finest teachers in the school.

My mother was almost as delighted as I when I showed her Mr. Fleagle's A-Plus and described my triumph. Hadn't she always said I had a talent for writing? "Now if you work hard at it, Buddy, you can make something of yourself."

I didn't see how. As the final year of high school neared its end and it began to seem that even the grocery business was beyond me, my mother was also becoming worried. She'd hoped for years that something would come along to enable me to go to college. All those years she had kept the door open on the possibility that she might turn me into a man of letters. When I was in eighth grade she'd spent precious pennies to subscribe to mail-order bargains in the classics. "World's Greatest Literature," retailing at 39 cents a volume, came in the mail every month, books that stunned me with boredom. *The Last of the Mohicans, Ben Hur, Westward Ho, Vanity Fair, Ivanhoe.* Unread, her attempts to cultivate my literary tastes gathered dust under my bed, but it comforted her to know I had them at my fingertips.

She also subscribed on my behalf to the *Atlantic Monthly* and *Harper's*. "The best magazines in America," she said. "That's where you'll find real writers." The best magazines in America also piled up unread and unreadable in my bedroom. I seemed cut out to serve neither literature nor its bastard offspring, journalism, until my great coup in Mr. Fleagle's English class. Then her hopes revived.

"If only something would come along so you could go to college . . ." became, "For somebody with grades as good as yours, Buddy, there must be some way of getting into college."

Delicately, she spoke to Herb [Baker's stepfather]. She could push and haul Herb on matters of household management, but she could scarcely ask him to finance college for me. Grand though his income seemed after her years of poverty, it wasn't big enough to put a boy through college without great sacrifice. There was also a question of taste. I'd done nothing to endear myself to Herb, and she knew it. What's more, with his few years of elementary school education, Herb would have been flabbergasted by the suggestion that a healthy young man should idle away four years in college at vast expense instead of making his own way in the world as he had done.

Still, my mother did speak to Herb, and Herb listened sympathetically. She told me about it next day. "Herb says he thinks he can get you a job as a brakeman on the B&O," she reported.

"Well," I said, "railroad men make good pay."

"Maybe something will come along before school's out," she said.

The idea of becoming a railroad brakeman entertained me for a while that winter. Any job prospect would have interested me then. I was becoming embarrassed about being one of the few boys in class with no plan for the future. The editors of the high-school yearbook circulated a questionnaire among members of the senior class asking each student to reveal his career ambition. I could hardly put down "To be a writer." That would have made me look silly. Boys of the Depression generation were expected to have their hearts set on money-making work. To reply "Ambition: None" was unthinkable. You were supposed to have had your eye on a high goal from the day you left knee pants. Boys who hadn't yet decided on a specific career usually replied that their ambition was "to be a success." That was all right. The Depression had made materialists of us all; almost everybody wanted "to be a success."

I studied the yearbook questionnaire with deepening despair. I wanted the yearbook to record for posterity that I had once had flaming ambition, but I could think of nothing very exciting. Finally I turned to my friend Bob Eckert in the desk behind me.

"What are you putting down for ambition?" I asked.

"Foreign correspondent," Eckert said.

I loved it. It sounded dashing, thrilling. Unfortunately, it was so different, so exciting an "ambition," that I couldn't copy Eckert without looking like a cheat. And so, turning my mind to journalism, I ticked off other glamorous newspaper jobs and after a moment's reflection wrote down, "To be a newspaper columnist."

In fact I hadn't the least interest in journalism and no ambition whatever to be a newspaper columnist. Though City College published an excellent weekly newspaper, during my four years there I was never interested enough to apply for a job, never knew where its office was located, and never cared enough to find out.

Having solved the problem of finding an "ambition" elegant enough for the yearbook, I returned to reality. Was I really sharp enough to make it in the retail grocery business? Should I become a railroad man?

Matters were at this stage in the spring of 1942 when I discovered my great friend and classmate Charlie Sussman filling out a sheaf of forms between classes one day. Sussman was a prodigious bookworm and lover of education. I admired him greatly for the wide range of his knowledge, which far exceeded mine. He understood the distinction between fascism and communism, subjects on which I was utterly ignorant. He was interested in politics and foreign policy, subjects that bored me. He listened to classical music, to which I was completely deaf. He planned to become a teacher and had the instinct for it. It bothered him that there were such great gaps in my education. Like my mother, Sussman wanted to improve me. He tried to awaken me to the beauties of music. "Start with Tchaikovsky," he pleaded. "Tchaikovsky is easy. Everybody likes Tchaikovsky. Then you'll discover the beauty of Beethoven and Mozart."

Now, finding him bent over a strange batch of papers, I asked, "What're you doing Suss?"

"Filling out college application forms," he said.

"What college are you going to?"

"Johns Hopkins," he said.

I knew that Johns Hopkins was a hospital and produced doctors.

"I didn't know you wanted to be a doctor. I thought you wanted to teach."

"Hopkins isn't just for doctors," he said.

"No kidding."

"It's a regular college too," he said. "What college are you going to?"

"I'm not going to college."

Sussman was shocked. Dropping his pen, he glared at me in amazement. "Not going to college?" He said it in outrage. He refused to tolerate this offense to education. "You're got to go to college," he said. "Get some admission forms—they've got them downstairs at the office—and we'll go to Hopkins together."

That would be great, I said, but my family couldn't afford it.

"Apply for a scholarship," he commanded.

"What's that?"

Sussman explained. I was astonished. It seemed that this college, of whose existence I had just learned, was willing to accept a limited number of students absolutely free if they could do well on a competitive examination. Sussman himself intended to take the test in hope of reducing the cost to his parents.

"I'll get you a set of application forms," he said, and he did. He was determined that education would not lose me without a struggle.

My mother was as surprised as I'd been. Just when she had begun to lose faith that something would come along, providence had assumed the shape of Charlie Sussman and smiled upon us. The day of the examination she stopped me as I was going out the door and kissed me.

"I've been praying for you every night," she said. "You'll do great."

She'd been doing more than praying. For three weeks she'd worked with me every night on a home refresher course in mathematics, my weakest subject. Night after night she held the math books and conducted quizzes on geometry and algebra, laboriously checking my solutions against those in the back of the books and, when I erred, struggling along with me to discover where I'd gone wrong. Afterwards, when we were both worn out, she went to bed and prayed. She believed in prayer, in the Lord's intercession, but not in the Lord's willingness to do it all. She and I together had to help. The Lord helped those who helped themselves.

The examination was held on a Saturday in May. I hadn't been to Johns Hopkins before, so I gave myself an extra hour against the possibility of getting lost on the streetcar trip to North Baltimore. My mother had written the directions and put them in my pocket, just in case, but the trip went smoothly, and when I reached the campus I was directed to a huge lecture hall reeking of chemicals. I was dismayed to find the hall filled with boys, each of whom probably wanted one of the few available scholarships as desperately as I did.

Unlike my mother, I had no faith in prayer. From early childhood I had thought of God as a cosmic trick player. Though I'd never told this to my mother and went to church regularly to please her, I'd grown up a fatalist with little faith. Now, though, as I counted the boys in the room and realized the odds against me, I decided it was foolish to leave even the remotest possibility untouched. Closing my eyes, I silently uttered the Lord's Prayer in my head and, to leave no base untouched, followed it with the only other prayer I knew, the one my mother had taught me years ago when putting me to bed in Morrisonville. And so, as the examination papers were being distributed, I sat at my desk silently repeating. "Now I lay me down to sleep, I pray the Lord my soul to keep . . ."

At the end I improvised a single line of my own and prayed, "Dear God, help me with this test." It lasted four hours.

My mother was waiting on the porch when I came back down Marydell Road that afternoon. "How'd it go, Buddy?"

"Don't know," I said, which I didn't.

Two weeks crept slowly past and May neared its end. I had only three weeks left of high school when I arrived home one afternoon to find my mother sitting expressionless in the glider on the front porch. "You got a letter from Hopkins today," she said. "It's on the table."

"Did you open it?"

"I'm not in the habit of opening other people's mail," she said. "You open it and tell me what it says."

We went inside together. The envelope was there on the table. It was a very small envelope. Very small. Hopkins had obviously decided I was not worth wasting much stationery on. Picking it up, I saw that it was also very thin. The message was obviously short and probably not sweet if it could be conveyed in such flimsy form. I ripped the end off the envelope, slid out a piece of note-sized paper, and unfolded it. I saw it was a form letter on which someone had typed a few words in the blank spaces. I read it to myself.

"Well, what does it say?" my mother asked.

I read it aloud to her:

> Sir: I am pleased to inform you that you have been awarded a Hopkins Scholarship for two terms of the academic year 1942–43. This award will entitle you to remission of tuition fees for this period. Please let me know at once if you will accept this award.
>
> Yours very truly,
> Isaiah Bowman
> President

"Let me read it," my mother said. She did, and she smiled, and she read it again; then she said, "Herb is going to be proud of you, Buddy."

"What about you?" I asked.

"Well, I always knew you could do it," she said, heading for the kitchen. "I think I'll make us some iced tea."

She had to do something ordinary, I suppose, or risk fainting with delight. We had helped ourselves, the Lord had helped us in return, and one of her wildest dreams had come true. Something had come along.

Discussing Ideas and Themes

1. Why did Baker think that writing was not real work? What did he think "real work" was, at that point in his life? Do you think this prejudice against writing as a vocation is a common one today?
2. What makes a good teacher? What quality in Mr. Fleagle made him a good teacher, despite his "primness"?
3. What importance does Baker's mother have for the essay? Is she helpful, realistic, comforting? Is her point of view borne out in the end?
4. Why does Baker put down "newspaper columnist" in the "ambition" section of his high school yearbook? What is the irony here?
5. How does Baker develop the themes of hope (which his mother had in abundance), fate (which he seemed to fall into quite a bit), and faith (another province of his mother's)? Do you think that the progress of Baker's early career was as haphazard as he makes it seem?

Discussing Rhetoric and Style

1. Baker's assertion that he had worked since he was eight comes as something of a surprise after the very beginning of the essay. How does Baker set up this surprise? How does this bit of information help establish his personal appeal?
2. How does Baker use description to enliven his anecdote? What makes his descriptions funny as, for example, his descriptions of "Mr. Simmons" or "Mr. Fleagle" are funny?
3. Baker's essay clearly differentiates between the good guys and the bad ones. Mr. Simmons, we know, is bad, and Mr. Fleagle (ineffectual as he seems) is good. How does Baker achieve these characterizations?
4. The essay begins with confusion and despair and ends with order and hope—the classical structure of Comedy. What rhetorical maneuvers does Baker use to bring this order to his seemingly aimless anecdotal narrative?

Ideas for Writing

1. Baker opens by describing his emotional state and his expectations as he neared the end of high school. Write a short essay based on your own personal experience, beginning with your sensations near the end of some significant period in your life, and then telling a meaningful anecdote about how your own confusion was resolved.
2. Baker relates the story of his first successful English composition—an essay about eating spaghetti written for his high school teacher. Take Baker's model of a successful educational experience, and compare it with Reuben Brower's description, in "Reading in Slow Motion," of a model literature class. Write an essay in which you use these two models of education to critique each other.

The Writing Life

ANNIE DILLARD

Annie Dillard, who was born in Pittsburgh in 1945, holds degrees in both English and art from Hollins College and has taught creative writing at various universities. Her first book, Pilgrim at Tinker Creek*—which she has described as a "meteorological journal of the mind"—earned her a Pulitzer Prize for general literature. Her early books include* Tickets for a Prayer Wheel *(poems),* Holy the Firm, Teaching a Stone to Talk, *and* Living By Fiction. *More recently she has written* An American Childhood *(1988) and* The Writing Life *(1989), from which this essay was adapted for* Tikkun, *a Jewish journal of culture and the arts. All of Dillard's writing is somewhat autobiographical, with a strong metaphysical bent, so she is often placed in the company of Henry David Thoreau, the nineteenth-century American philosopher, essayist, and journalist. In the following essay, which ponders the trials and the rewards of the writing life, Dillard recalls some of her early experiences while speculating how a writer can learn to balance a good life with a productive one.*

What if man could see Beauty Itself, pure, unalloyed, stripped of mortality and all its pollution, stains, and vanities, unchanging, divine, . . . the man becoming, in that communion, the friend of God, himself immortal; . . . would that be a life to disregard?

—Plato

I have been looking into schedules. Even when we read physics, we inquire of each least particle, "What then shall I do this morning?" How we spend our days is, of course, how we spend our lives. What we do with this hour, and that one, is what we are doing. A schedule defends from chaos and whim. It is a net for catching days. It is a scaffolding on which a worker can stand and labor with both hands at sections of time. A schedule is a mock-up of reason and order—willed, faked, and so brought into being; it is a peace and a haven set into the wreck of time; it is a lifeboat on which you find yourself, decades later, still living. Each day is the same, so you remember the series afterward as a blurred idyll.

The most appealing daily schedule I know is that of a certain turn-of-the-century Swedish aristocrat. He got up at four and set out on foot to hunt black grouse, wood grouse, woodcock, and snipe. At eleven he met his friends who had also been out hunting alone all morning. They converged "at one of these babbling brooks," he wrote. He outlined the rest of his schedule. "Take a quick dip, relax with a schnapps and a sandwich, stretch out, have a smoke, take a nap or just rest, and then sit around and chat until three. Then I hunt some more until sundown, bathe again, put on white tie and tails to keep up appearances, eat a huge dinner, smoke a cigar and sleep like a log until the sun comes up again to redden the eastern sky. This is living. . . . Could it be more perfect?"

There is no shortage of good days. It is good lives that are hard to come by. A life of good days lived in the senses is not enough. The life of sensation is the life of greed; it requires more and more. The life of the spirit requires less and less; time is ample and its passage sweet. Who would call a day spent reading a good day? But a life spent reading—that is a good life. A day that closely resembles every other day for the past ten or twenty years does not suggest itself as a good one. But who would not call Pasteur's life a good one, or Thomas Mann's?

Wallace Stevens in his forties, living in Hartford, Connecticut, hewed to a productive routine. He rose at six, read for two hours, and walked another hour—three miles—to work. He dictated poems to his secretary. He ate no lunch; at noon he walked for another hour, often to an art gallery. He walked home from work—another hour. After dinner he retired to his study; he went to bed at nine. On Sundays, he walked in the park. I don't know what he did on Saturdays. Perhaps he exchanged a few words with his wife, who posed for the Liberty dime. (One would rather read these people, or lead their lives, than be their wives. When the Swedish aristocrat Wilhelm Blixen shot birds all day, drank schnapps, napped, and dressed for dinner, he and his wife had three children under three. The middle one was Karen, later known as Isak Dinesen.)

Like Stevens, Osip Mandelstam composed poetry on the hoof. So did Dante. Nietzsche, like Emerson, took two long walks a day. "When my creative energy flowed most freely, my muscular activity was always greatest. . . . I might often have been seen dancing; I used to walk through the hills for seven or eight hours on end without a hint of fatigue; I slept well, laughed a good deal—I was perfectly vigorous and patient" (Nietzsche). On the other hand, A. E. Housman, almost predictably, maintained, "I have seldom written poetry unless I was rather out of health." This makes sense, too, because in writing a book you can be too well for your own good.

Jack London claimed to write twenty hours a day. Before he undertook to write, he obtained the University of California course list and all the syllabi; he spent a year reading the textbooks in philosophy and literature. In subsequent years, once he had a book of his own under way, he set his alarm to wake him after four hours of sleep. Often he slept through the alarm, so, by his own account, he rigged it to drop a weight on his head. I cannot say I believe this, though a novel like *The Sea-Wolf* is strong evidence that some sort of weight fell on his head with some sort of frequency—though you wouldn't think a man would claim credit for it. London maintained that every writer needed experience, a technique, and a philosophical position. Perhaps the position need not be an airtight one; London himself felt comfortable with a weird amalgam of Karl Marx and Herbert Spencer. (Marks & Sparks.)

I write these words in my most recent of many studies—a pine shed on Cape Cod. The pine lumber is unfinished inside the study; the pines outside are finished trees. I see the pines from my two windows. Nuthatches spiral around their long, coarse trunks. Sometimes in June a feeding colony of mixed warblers flies through the pines; the warblers make a racket that draws me out the door. The warblers drift loosely through the stiff pine branches, and I follow through the thin long grass between the trunks.

The study—sold as a prefabricated toolshed—is eight feet by ten feet. Like a plane's cockpit, it is crammed with high-tech equipment. There is no quill pen in sight. There is a computer, a printer, and a photocopying machine. My backless chair, a prie-dieu on which I kneel, slides under the desk; I give it a little kick when I leave. There is an air conditioner, a heater, and an electric kettle. There is a low-tech bookshelf, a shelf of gull and whale bones, and a bed. Under the bed I stow paints—a one-pint can of yellow to touch up the window's trim, and five or six tubes of artists' oils. The study affords ample room for one. One who is supposed to be writing books. You can read in the space of a coffin, and you can write in the space of a toolshed meant for mowers and spades.

I walk up here from the house every morning. The study and its pines, and the old summer cottages nearby, and the new farm just north of me, rise from an old sand dune high over a creeky salt marsh. From the bright lip of the dune I can see oyster farmers working their beds on the tidal flats and sailboats under way in the saltwater bay. After I have warmed myself standing at the crest of the dune, I return under the pines, enter the study, slam the door so the latch catches—and then I cannot see. The green spot in front of my eyes outshines everything in the shade. I lie on the bed and play with a bird bone until I can see it.

Appealing workplaces are to be avoided. One wants a room with no view, so imagination can dance with memory in the dark. When I furnished this study seven years ago, I pushed the long desk against a blank wall, so I could not see from either window. Once, fifteen years ago, I wrote in a cinder-block cell over a parking lot. It overlooked a tar-and-gravel roof. This pine shed under trees is not quite so good as the cinder-block study was, but it will do.

"The beginning of wisdom," according to a West African proverb, "is to get you a roof."

* * *

It was on summer nights in Roanoke, Virginia, that I wrote the second half of a book, *Pilgrim at Tinker Creek*. (I wrote the first half in the spring, at home.) Ruefully I noted then that I would possibly look back on those times as an idyll. I vowed to remember the difficulties. I have forgotten them now, however, and I do, in fact, look back on those times as an idyll.

I slept until noon, as did my husband, who was also writing. I wrote once in the afternoon, and once again after our early dinner and a walk. During those months, I subsisted on that dinner, coffee, Coke, chocolate milk, and Vantage cigarettes. I worked till midnight, one, or two. When I came home in the middle of the night I was tired; I longed for a tolerant giant, a person as big as a house, to hold me and rock me. In fact, an exhausted daydream—almost a hallucination—of being rocked and soothed sometimes forced itself upon me, and interrupted me even when I was talking or reading.

I had a room—a study carrel—in the Hollins College library, on the second floor. It was this room that overlooked a tar-and-gravel roof. A plate-glass window, beside me on the left, gave out on a number of objects: the roof, a parking lot, a distant portion of Carvin's Creek, some complicated Virginia sky, and a far hilltop where six cows grazed around a ruined foundation under red cedars.

From my desk I kept an eye out. Intriguing people, people I knew, pulled into the parking lot and climbed from their cars. The cows moved on the hilltop. (I drew the cows, for they were made interestingly; they hung in catenary curves from their skeletons, like two-man tents.) On the flat roof just outside the window, sparrows pecked gravel. One of the sparrows lacked a leg; one was missing a foot. If I stood and peered around, I could see a feeder creek running at the edge of a field. In the creek, even from that great distance, I could see muskrats and snapping turtles. If I saw a snapping turtle, I ran downstairs and out of the library to watch it or poke it.

One afternoon I made a pen drawing of the window and the landscape it framed. I drew the window's aluminum frame and steel hardware; I sketched in the clouds and the far hilltop with its ruined foundation and wandering cows. I outlined the parking lot and its tall row of mercury-vapor lights; I drew the cars, and the graveled rooftop foreground.

If I craned my head, I could see a grassy playing field below. One afternoon I peered around at that field and saw a softball game. Since I happened to have my fielder's glove with me in my study, I thought it would be the generous thing to join the game. On the field, I learned there was a music camp on campus for two weeks. The little boys playing softball were musical whizzes. They could not all play ball, but their patter was a treat. "All right, MacDonald," they jeered when one kid came to bat, "that pizzicato won't help you now." It was slightly better than no softball, so I played with them every day, second base, terrified that I would bust a prodigy's fingers on a throw to first or the plate.

I shut the blinds one day for good. I lowered the venetian blinds and flattened the slats. Then, by lamplight, I taped my drawing to the closed blind. There, on the drawing, was the window's view: cows, parking lot, hilltop, and sky. If I wanted a sense of the world, I could look at the stylized outline drawing. If I had possessed the skill, I would have painted, directly on the slats of the lowered blind, in meticulous colors, a *trompe l'oeil* mural view of all that the blinds hid. Instead, I wrote it.

On the Fourth of July, my husband and our friends drove into the city, Roanoke, to see the fireworks. I begged off; I wanted to keep working. I was working hard, although of course it did not seem hard enough at the time—a finished chapter every few weeks. I castigated myself daily for writing too slowly. Even when passages seemed to come easily, as though I were copying from a folio held open by smiling angels, the manuscript revealed the usual signs of struggle—bloodstains, teeth marks, gashes, and burns.

This night, as on most nights, I entered the library at dusk. The building was locked and dark. I had a key. Every night I let myself in, climbed the stairs, found my way between the tall stacks in the dark, located and unlocked my study's door, and turned on the light. I remembered how many stacks I had to hit with my hand in the dark before I turned down the row to my study. Even if I left only to get a drink of water, I felt and counted the stacks with my hand again to find my room. Once in daylight I glanced at a book on a stack's corner, a book I presumably touched every night with my hand. The book was *The World I Live In,* by Helen Keller. I read it at once: it surprised me by its strong and original prose.

When I flicked on my carrel light, there it all was: the bare room with yellow cinder-block walls; the big, flattened venetian blind and my drawing taped to it; two or three quotations taped up on index cards, and on a far table some books, the fielder's mitt, and a yellow bag of chocolate-covered peanuts. There was the long, blond desk and its chair, and on the desk a dozen different-colored pens, some big index cards in careful, splayed piles, and my messy yellow legal pads. As soon as I saw that desktop, I remembered the task: the chapter, its problems, its phrases, its points.

This night I was concentrating on the chapter. The horizon of my consciousness was the contracted circle of yellow light inside my study—the lone lamp in the enormous, dark library. I leaned over the desk. I worked by hand. I doodled deliriously in the legal-pad margins. I fiddled with the index cards. I reread a sentence maybe a hundred times, and if I kept it I changed it seven or eight times, often substantially.

Now a June bug was knocking at my window. I was wrestling inside a sentence. I must have heard it a dozen times before it registered—before I noticed that I had been hearing a bug knock for half an hour. It made a hollow, bonking sound. Some people call the same fumbling, heavy insects "May beetles." It must have been attracted to my light—what little came between the slats of the blind. I dislike June bugs. Back to work. Knock again, knock again, and finally, to learn what monster of a fat, brown June bug could fly up to a second story and thump so insistently at my window as though it wanted admittance—at last, unthinkingly, I parted the venetian blind slats with my fingers, to look out.

And there were the fireworks, far away. It was the Fourth of July. I had forgotten. They were red and yellow, blue and green and white; they blossomed high in the black sky many miles away. The fireworks seemed as distant as the stars, but I could hear the late banging their bursting made. The sound, those bangs so muffled and out of synch, accompanied at random the silent, far sprays of color widening and raining down. It was the Fourth of July, and I had forgotten all of wide space and all of historical time. I opened the blinds a crack like eyelids, and it all came exploding in on me at once—oh yes, the world.

My working the graveyard shift in Virginia affected the book. It was a nature book full of sunsets; it wholly lacked dawns, and even mornings.

I was reading about Hassidism, among other things. If you stay awake one hundred nights, you get the vision of Elijah. I was not eager for it, although it seemed to be just around the corner. I preferred this: "Rebbe Shmelke of Nickolsburg, it was told, never really heard his teacher, the Maggid of Mezritch, finish a thought because as soon as the latter would say 'and the Lord spoke,' Shmelke would begin shouting in wonderment, 'The Lord spoke, the Lord spoke,' and continue shouting until he had to be carried from the room."

* * *

The second floor of the library, where I worked every night, housed the rare book room. It was a wide, carpeted, well-furnished room. On an end table, as if for decoration, stood a wooden chess set.

One night, stuck on an intractable problem in the writing, I wandered the dark library looking for distraction. I flicked on the lights in the rare book room and looked at some of the books. I saw the chess set and moved white's king's pawn. I turned off the light and wandered back to my carrel.

A few nights later, I glanced into the rare book room and walked in, for black's queen's pawn had moved. I moved out my knight.

We were off and running. Every day, my unseen opponent moved. I moved. I never saw anyone anywhere near the rare book room. The college was not in session; almost no one was around. Late at night I heard the night watchmen clank around downstairs in the dark. The watchmen never came upstairs. There was no one upstairs but me.

When the chess game was ten days old, I entered the rare book room to find black's pieces coming towards me on the carpet. They seemed to be marching, in rows of two. I put them back as they had been and made my move. The next day, the pieces were all pied on the board. I put them back as they had been. The next day, black had moved, rather brilliantly.

Late one night, while all this had been going on, and while the library was dark and locked as it had been all summer and I had accustomed myself to the eeriness of it, I left my carrel to cross the darkness and get a drink of water. I saw a strange chunk of light on the floor between stacks. Passing the stacks, I saw the light spread across the hall. I held my breath. The light was coming from the rare book room; the door was open.

I approached quietly and looked in the room from an angle. There, at the chess table, stood a baby. The baby had blond curls and was wearing only a diaper.

I paused, considering that I had been playing a reasonable game of chess for two weeks with a naked baby. After a while I could make out the sound of voices; I moved closer to the doorway and peered in. There was the young head librarian and his wife, sitting on chairs. I pieced together the rest of it. The librarian stopped by to pick something up. Naturally, he had a key. The couple happened to have the baby along. The baby, just learning to walk, had cruised from the chairs to the table. The baby was holding onto the table, not studying the chess pieces' positions. I greeted the family and played with the baby until they left.

I never did learn who or what was playing chess with me. The game went on until my lunatic opponent scrambled the board so violently the game was over.

* * *

During that time, I let all the houseplants die. After the book was finished I noticed them; the plants hung completely black dead in their pots in the bay window. For I had not only let them die, I had not moved them. During that time, I told all my out-of-town friends they could not visit for a while.

"I understand you're married," a man said to me at a formal lunch in New York that my publisher had arranged. "How do you have time to write a book?"

"Sir?"

"Well," he said, "You have to have a garden, for instance. You have to entertain." And I thought he was foolish, this man in his seventies, who had no idea what you must do. But the fanaticism of my twenties shocks me now. As I feared it would.

Discussing Issues and Themes

1. What difference does Dillard see between the way days are lived and the way a life should be lived? She writes that "a life of good days lived in the senses is not enough." What, according to Dillard, would be enough? Explain.

2. Dillard criticizes some of the people in her anecdotes. For example, after describing Wilhelm Blixen's appealing schedule of

hunting, eating, and sleeping, she notes that "one would rather . . . lead [his] life, than be [his] wife." Find another moment where Dillard seems to reverse tone; discuss the effects of this reversal.

3. What is the difference between Dillard's most recent study (the pine shed on Cape Cod) and the study in which she wrote half of her first book (the study carrel in Hollins College)? Which place does she prefer? How can you tell?
4. Dillard says that she "made a pen drawing of [her study's] window and the landscape it framed" and taped that drawing over the window's blinds. What does Dillard imply here about the process and requirements of making art? Why does she need to do this?
5. At the end of Dillard's essay, what is her attitude toward "the fanaticism of [her] twenties"? She says, for example, that she is shocked by it, but can you discern any other judgments in the tone of her essay as a whole?

Discussing Rhetoric and Style

1. How does Dillard use figures of speech to enrich her essay and to develop her argument? For example, in the opening paragraph Dillard makes a series of metaphors around the concept of schedule and gradually builds up the importance of schedules in relation to "how we spend our lives." Choose another metaphorical passage in her essay, and consider how it works.
2. Choose a paragraph from the essay, and analyze the verbs. For example, in the first paragraph the verb *to be* predominates, causing most of the emphasis in her sentences to fall on the nouns. In other paragraphs, how do the verbs Dillard chooses shape her style?
3. In the opening section of Dillard's essay, she refers to several other people—most of them famous and some of them literary; for example, she opens by describing Wilhelm Blixen's schedule and moves rapidly on to mention Pasteur and Thomas Mann. How do these references enrich her essay and help to establish her own authority as a literary figure?
4. Dillard's essay seems to ramble. For example, she moves from a discussion of her study carrel to an entertaining story about a chess game with an invisible opponent. Can you discern any organization underlying Dillard's seemingly loose structure?

Ideas for Writing

1. Write a brief essay in which you describe a personal experience from your past. Try to imitate Dillard's organization and her style. Dillard's essay ultimately focuses on a few important themes—among them, how one should make art and how one should organize one's life. In telling your story, you should also explore some larger question.

2. Write an essay analyzing the part of Dillard's essay in which she describes the chess game and the encounter with the librarian's baby. Why do you think Dillard includes this episode in her essay? How does it contribute to the essay's thematic development?

Revision and Life

NORA EPHRON

The multitalented Nora Ephron has worked as a reporter, a daily columnist, and an editor as well as having published several collections of essays, a novel, and the screenplays for Heartburn *(starring Jack Nicholson and Meryl Streep) and* When Harry Met Sally . . . *(with Billy Crystal and Meg Ryan). The following essay, written especially for young students and writers, explores the relationship between the way the author writes and the way she lives her life. Revision, she insists, is not only a helpful tool for writers but an inevitable one for anyone who eats, sleeps, dreams, or thinks: It is the way by which we ultimately find meaning in our lives. This essay was written for the* New York Times Book Review.

I have been asked to write something for a textbook that is meant to teach college students something about writing and revision. I am happy to do this because I believe in revision. I have also been asked to save the early drafts of whatever I write, presumably to show these students the actual process of revision. This too I am happy to do. On the other hand, I suspect that there is just so much you can teach college students about revision; a gift for revision may be a developmental stage—like a two-year-old's sudden ability to place one block on top of another—that comes along somewhat later, in one's mid-20s, say; most people may not be particularly good at it, or even interested in it, until then.

When I was in college, I revised nothing. I wrote out my papers in longhand, typed them up and turned them in. It would never have crossed my mind that what I had produced was only a first draft and that I had more work to do; the idea was to get to the end, and once you had got to the end you were finished. The same thinking, I might add, applied in life: I went pell-mell through my four years in college without a thought about whether I ought to do anything differently; the idea was to get to the end—to get out of school and become a journalist.

Which I became, in fairly short order. I learned as a journalist to revise on deadline. I learned to write an article a paragraph at a time—and to turn it in a paragraph at a time—and I arrived at the kind of writing and revising I do, which is basically a kind of typing and retyping. I am a great believer in this technique for the simple reason that I type faster than the wind. What I generally do is to start an article and get as far as I can—sometimes no farther in than a sentence or two—before running out of steam, ripping the piece of paper from the typewriter and starting all over again. I type over and over until I have got the beginning of the piece to the point where I am happy with it. I then am ready to plunge into the body of the article itself. This plunge usually requires something known as a transition. I approach a transition by completely retyping the opening of the article leading up to it in the hope that the ferocious speed of my typing will somehow catapult me into the next section of the piece. This does not work—what in fact catapults me into the next section is a concrete thought about what the next section ought to be about—but until I have the thought the typing keeps me busy, and keeps me from feeling something known as blocked.

Typing and retyping as if you know where you're going is a version of what therapists tell you to do when they suggest that you try changing from the outside in—that if you can't master the total commitment to whatever change you want to make, you can at least do all the extraneous things connected with it, which make it that much easier to get there. I was 25 years old the first time a therapist suggested that I try changing from the outside in. In those days, I used to spend quite a lot of time lying awake at night wondering what I should have said earlier in the evening and revising my lines. I mention this not just because it's a way of illustrating that a gift for revision is practically instinctive, but also (once again) because it's possible that a genuine ability at it doesn't really come into play until one is older—or at least older than 25, when it seemed to me that all that was required in my life and my work was the chance to change a few lines.

In my thirties, I began to write essays, one a month for *Esquire* magazine, and I am not exaggerating when I say that in the course of writing a short essay—1,500 words, that's only six double-spaced typewritten pages—I often used 300 or 400 pieces of typing paper, so often did I type and retype and catapult and recatapult myself, sometimes on each retyping moving not even a sentence farther from the spot I had reached the last time through. At the same time, though, I was polishing what I had already written: as I struggled with the middle of the article, I kept putting the beginning through the typewriter; as I approached the ending, the middle got its turn. (This is a kind of polishing that the word processor all but eliminates, which is why I don't use one. Word processors make it possible for a writer to change the sentences that clearly need changing without having to retype the rest, but I believe that you can't always tell whether a sentence needs work until it rises up in revolt against your fingers as you retype it.) By the time I had produced what you might call a first draft—an entire article with a beginning, middle and end—the beginning was in more like 45th draft, the middle in 20th, and the end was almost newborn. For this reason, the beginnings of my essays are considerably better written than the ends, although I like to think no one ever notices this but me.

As I learned the essay form, writing became harder for me. I was finding a personal style, a voice if you will, a way of writing that looked chatty and informal. That wasn't the hard part—the hard part was that having found a voice, I had to work hard month to month not to seem as if I were repeating myself. At this point in this essay it will not surprise you to learn that the same sort of thing was operating in my life. I don't mean that my life had become harder—but that it was becoming clear that I had many more choices than had occurred to me when I was marching through my twenties. I no longer lost sleep over what I should have said. Not that I didn't care—it was just that I had moved to a new plane of late-night anxiety: I now wondered what I should have done. Whole areas of possible revision opened before me. What should I have done instead? What could I have done? What if I hadn't done it the way I did? What if I had a chance to do it over? What if I had a chance to do it over as a different person? These were the sorts of questions that kept me awake and led me into fiction, which at the very least (the level at which I practice it) is a chance to rework the events of your life so that you give the illusion of being the intelligence at the center of it, simultaneously managing to slip in all the lines that occurred to you later. Fiction, I suppose, is the ultimate shot at revision.

Now I am in my forties and I write screenplays. Screenplays—if they are made into movies—are essentially collaborations, and movies are not a writer's medium, we all know this, and I don't want to dwell on the craft of screenwriting except insofar as it relates to revision. Because the moment you stop work on a script seems to be determined not by whether you think the draft is good but simply by whether shooting is about to begin: If it is, you get to call your script a final draft; and if it's not, you can always write another revision. This might seem to be a hateful way to live, but the odd thing is that it's somehow comforting; as long as you're revising, the project isn't dead. And by the same token, neither are you.

It was, as it happens, while thinking about all this one recent sleepless night that I figured out how to write this particular essay. I say "recent" in order to give a sense of immediacy and energy to the preceding sentence, but the truth is that I am finishing this article four months after the sleepless night in question, and the letter asking me to write it, from George Miller of the University of Delaware, arrived almost two years ago, so for all I know Mr. Miller has managed to assemble his textbook on revision without me.

Oh, well. That's how it goes when you start thinking about revision. That's the danger of it, in fact. You can spend so much time thinking about how to switch things around that the main event has passed you by. But it doesn't matter. Because by the time you reach middle age, you want more than anything for things not to come to an end; and as long as you're still revising, they don't.

I'm sorry to end so morbidly—dancing as I am around the subject of death—but there are advantages to it. For one thing, I have managed to move fairly effortlessly and logically from the beginning of this piece through the middle and to the end. And for another, I am able to close with an exhortation, something I rarely manage, which is this: Revise now, before it's too late.

Discussing Ideas and Themes

1. Why does Ephron think that "revision may be a developmental stage"? What examples does she provide to back up this theory? Do you agree with her speculation?
2. What is revision for you? Is it "typing and retyping"? Is it writing "paragraph by paragraph"? Explain.
3. What does Ephron mean when she says she changes things "from the outside in"? Is this a form of revision, and if it is, why is it helpful?
4. How did Ephron's ideas about revision change in her twenties? In her thirties? In her forties? Do you think they will change again in her fifties? Why or why not?
5. What is the connection between revision and life? Is revision restricted to things that we write, or do we revise our actions, beliefs, memories, and so on? Looking up the etymology of the word *revision* might be helpful.

Discussing Rhetoric and Style

1. What audience is Ephron writing to? Do you find the essay more personally interesting because you are included in its audience? Why or why not?
2. Ephron believes that she has developed "a personal style." List five characteristics of this style, providing examples of each from the essay.
3. Ephron arranges the essay autobiographically, tracking her experience from college to the present and thus slowly unfolding her ideas about revision as they have unfolded themselves to her. How successful do you find this arrangement? Does it effectively help her revise her own ideas—and perhaps yours—about revision? Does the essay seem to be revising itself?
4. Revise the first paragraph of Ephron's essay, deleting all personal pronouns. What is the result?

Ideas for Writing

1. Write a brief essay on the effect that the word processor has had or will eventually have on revision as a technique for discovering ideas and polishing style. What is different about revising on a word processor? Discuss the benefits and drawbacks of word processing.
2. Write an essay that explores the idea of revision as a daily experience and practice. For instance, do children revise their parents' lives as they live their own? Do parents try to revise their own lives by wanting better things for their children? Is memory a form of revision? Is lying? Dreaming? Is revision a natural act for someone who speaks and writes? Is it possible to live and die without revising?

Writing as a Mode of Learning

JANET EMIG

Now a professor of English education at Rutgers University, Janet Emig was born in Cincinnati, Ohio and graduated from Mount Holyoke College, later finishing her M.A. at the University of Michigan and her Ed.D. at Harvard. Having taught around the country in public and private schools, Emig is a highly respected teacher and the author of Writing as Process, *a study of the creative process at the high school level, and* The Web of Meaning: Essays on Writing, Thinking, Teaching, and Learning. *The following essay, which was first collected in* College Composition and Communications, *proposes that writing can be more than just saying what you learned: It can be a means to learning.*

Writing represents a unique mode of learning—not merely valuable, not merely special, but unique. That will be my contention in this paper. The thesis is straightforward. Writing serves learning uniquely because writing as process-and-product possesses a cluster of attributes that correspond uniquely to certain powerful learning strategies.

Although the notion is clearly debatable, it is scarcely a private belief. Some of the most distinguished contemporary psychologists have at least implied such a role for writing as heuristic. Lev Vygotsky, A. R. Luria, and Jerome Bruner, for example, have all pointed out that higher cognitive functions, such as analysis and synthesis, seem to develop most fully only with the support system of verbal language—particularly, it seems, of written language.[1] Some of their arguments and evidence will be incorporated here.

Here I have a prior purpose: to describe as tellingly as possible *how* writing uniquely corresponds to certain powerful learning strategies. Making such a case for the uniqueness of writing should logically and theoretically involve establishing many contrasts, distinctions between (1) writing and all other verbal languaging processes—listening, reading, and especially talking; (2) writing and all other forms of composing, such as composing a painting, a symphony, a dance, a film, a building; and (3) composing in words and composing in the two other major graphic symbol systems of mathematical equations and scientific formulae. For the purpose of this paper, the task is simpler, since most students are not permitted by most curricula to discover the values of composing, say, in dance, or even in film; and most students are not sophisticated enough to create, to originate formulations, using the highly abstruse symbol system of equations and formulae. Verbal language represents the most *available* medium for composing; in fact, the significance of sheer availability in its selection as a mode for learning can probably not be overstressed. But the uniqueness of writing among the verbal languaging processes does need to be established and supported if only because so many curricula and courses in English still consist almost exclusively of reading and listening.

WRITING AS A UNIQUE LANGUAGING PROCESS

Traditionally, the four languaging processes of listening, talking, reading, and writing are paired in either of two ways. The more informative seems to be the division many linguists make between first-order and second-order processes, with talking and listening characterized as first-order processes; reading and writing, as second-order. First-order processes are acquired without formal or systematic instruction; the second-order processes of reading and writing tend to be learned initially only with the aid of formal and systematic instruction.

The less useful distinction is that between listening and reading as receptive functions and talking and writing as productive functions. Critics of these terms like Louise Rosenblatt rightfully point out that the connotation of passivity too often accompanies the notion of receptivity when reading, like listening, is a vital, construing act.

An additional distinction, so simple it may have been previously overlooked, resides in two criteria: the matters of origination and of graphic recording. Writing is originating and creating a unique verbal construct that is graphically recorded. Reading is creating or re-creating *but not* originating a verbal construct that is graphically recorded. Listening is creating or re-creating but not originating a verbal construct that is *not* graphically recorded. Talking is creating *and* originating a verbal construct that is *not* graphically recorded (except for the circuitous routing of a transcribed tape). Note that a distinction is being made between creating and originating, separable processes.

For talking, the nearest languaging process, additional distinctions should probably be made. (What follows is not a denigration of talk as a valuable mode of learning.) A silent classroom or one filled only with the teacher's voice is anathema to learning. For evidence of the cognitive value of talk, one can look to some of the persuasive monographs coming from the London Schools Council project on writing: *From Information to Understanding* by Nancy Martin or *From Talking to Writing* by Peter Medway.[2] We also know that for some of us, talking is a valuable, even necessary, form of pre-writing. In his curriculum, James Moffett makes the value of such talk quite explicit.

But to say that talking is a valuable form of pre-writing is not to say that writing is talk recorded, an inaccuracy appearing in far too many composition texts. Rather, a number of contemporary transdisciplinary sources suggest that talking and writing may emanate from different organic sources and represent quite different, possibly distinct, language functions. In *Thought and Language*, Vygotsky notes that "written speech is separate linguistic function, differing from oral speech in both structure and mode of functioning."[3] The sociolinguist Dell Hymes, in a valuable issue of *Daedalus*, "Language as a Human Problem," makes a comparable point: "That speech and writing are not simply interchangeable, and have developed historically in ways at least partly autonomous, is obvious."[4] At the first session of the Buffalo Conference on Researching Composition (4–5 October 1975), the first point of unanimity among the participant-speakers with interests in developmental psychology, media, dreams and aphasia was that talking and writing were markedly different functions.[5] Some of us who work rather steadily with writing research agree. We also believe that there are hazards, conceptually and pedagogically, in creating too complete an analogy between talking and writing, in blurring the very real differences between the two.

What are these differences?

1. Writing is learned behavior; talking is natural, even irrepressible, behavior.
2. Writing then is an artificial process; talking is not.
3. Writing is a technological device—not the wheel, but early enough to qualify as primary technology; talking is organic, natural, earlier.

4. Most writing is slower than most talking.
5. Writing is stark, barren, even naked as a medium; talking is rich, luxuriant, inherently redundant.
6. Talk leans on the environment; writing must provide its own context.
7. With writing, the audience is usually absent; with talking, the listener is usually present.
8. Writing usually results in a visible graphic product; talking usually does not.
9. Perhaps because there is a product involved, writing tends to be a more responsible and committed act than talking.
10. It can be said that throughout history, an aura, an ambience, a mystique has usually encircled the written word; the spoken word has for the most part proved ephemeral and been treated mundanely (ignore, please, our recent national history).
11. Because writing is often our representation of the world made visible, embodying both process and product, writing is more readily a form and source of learning than talking.

UNIQUE CORRESPONDENCES BETWEEN LEARNING AND WRITING

What then are some *unique* correspondences between learning and writing? To begin with some definitions: Learning can be defined in many ways, according to one's predilections and training, with all statements about learning of course hypothetical. Definitions range from the chemophysiological ("Learning is changed patterns of protein synthesis in relevant portions of the cortex")[6] to transactive views drawn from both philosophy and psychology (John Dewey, Jean Piaget) that learning is the re-organization or confirmation of a cognitive scheme in light of an experience.[7] What the speculations seem to share is consensus about certain features and strategies that characterize successful learning. These include the importance of the classic attributes of re-inforcement and feedback. In most hypotheses, successful learning is also connective and selective. Additionally, it makes use of propositions, hypotheses, and other elegant summarizers. Finally, it is active, engaged, personal—more specifically, self-rhythmed—in nature.

Jerome Bruner, like Jean Piaget, through a comparable set of categories, posits three major ways in which we represent and deal with actuality: (1) enactive—we learn "by doing"; (2) iconic—we learn "by depiction in an image"; and (3) representational or symbolic—we learn "by restatement in words."[8] To overstate the matter, in enactive learning, the hand predominates; in iconic, the eye; and in symbolic, the brain.

What is striking about writing as a process is that, by its very nature, all three ways of dealing with actuality are simultaneously or almost simultaneously deployed. That is, the symbolic transformation of experience through the specific symbol system of verbal language is shaped into an icon (the graphic product) by the enactive hand. If the most efficacious learning occurs when learning is re-inforced, then writing through its inherent re-inforcing cycle involving hand, eye, and brain marks a uniquely powerful multi-representational mode for learning.

Writing is also integrative in perhaps the most basic possible sense: the organic, the functional. Writing involves the fullest possible functioning of the brain, which entails the active participation in the process of both the left and the right hemispheres. Writing is markedly bispheral, although in some popular accounts, writing is inaccurately presented as a chiefly left-hemisphere activity, perhaps because the linear written product is somehow regarded as analogue for the process that created it; and the left hemisphere seems to process material linearly.

The right hemisphere, however, seems to make at least three, perhaps four, major contributions to the writing process—probably, to the creative process generically. First, several researchers, such as Geschwind and Snyder of Harvard and Zaidal of Cal Tech, through markedly different experiments, have very tentatively suggested that the right hemisphere is the sphere, even the *seat*, of emotions.[9] Second—or perhaps as an illustration of the first—Howard Gardner, in his important study of the brain-damaged, notes that our sense of emotional appropriateness in discourse may reside in the right sphere:

> Emotional appropriateness, in sum—being related not only to *what* is said, but to how it is said and to what is *not* said, as well—is crucially dependent on right hemisphere intactness.[10]

Third, the right hemisphere seems to be the source of intuition, of sudden gestalts, of flashes of images, of abstractions occurring as visual or spatial wholes, as the initiating metaphors in the creative process. A familiar example: William Faulkner noted in his *Paris Review* interview that *The Sound and the Fury* began as the image of a little girl's muddy drawers as she sat in a tree watching her grandmother's funeral.[11]

Also, a unique form of feedback, as well as reinforcement, exists with writing, because information from the *process* is immediately and visibly available as that portion of the *product* already written. The importance for learning of a product in a familiar and available medium for immediate, literal (that is, visual) re-scanning and review cannot perhaps be overstated. In his remarkable study of purportedly blind sculptors, Géza Révész found that without sight, persons cannot move beyond a literal transcription of elements into any manner of symbolic transformation—by definition, the central requirement for reformulation and re-interpretation, i.e., revision, that most aptly named process.[12]

As noted in the second paragraph, Vygotsky and Luria, like Bruner, have written importantly about the connections between learning and writing. In his essay "The Psychobiology of Psychology," Bruner lists as one of six axioms regarding learning: "We are connective."[13] Another correspondence then between learning and writing: in *Thought and Language,* Vygotsky notes that writing makes a unique demand in that the writer must engage in "deliberate semantics"—in Vygotsky's elegant phrase, "deliberate structuring of the web of meaning."[14] Such structuring is required because, for Vygotsky, writing centrally represents an expansion of inner speech, that mode whereby we talk to ourselves, which is "maximally compact" and "almost entirely predicative"; written speech is a mode which is "maximally detailed" and which requires explicitly supplied subjects and topics. The medium then of written verbal language requires the establishment of systematic connections and relationships. Clear writing by definition is that writing which signals without ambiguity the nature of conceptual relationships, whether they be coordinate, subordinate, superordinate, causal, or something other.

Successful learning is also engaged, committed, personal learning. Indeed, impersonal learning may be an anomalous concept, like the very notion of objectivism itself. As Michael Polanyi states simply at the beginning of *Personal Knowledge:* "the ideal of strict objectivism is absurd." (How many courses and curricula in English, science, and all else does that one sentence reduce to rubble?) Indeed, the theme of *Personal Knowledge* is that

> into every act of knowing there enters a passionate contribution of the person knowing what is being known, . . . this coefficient is no mere imperfection but a vital component of his knowledge.[15]

In *Zen and the Art of Motorcycle Maintenance,* Robert Pirsig states a comparable theme:

> The Quality which creates the world emerges as *a relationship* between man and his experience. He is a *participant* in the creation of all things.[16]

Finally, the psychologist George Kelly has as the central notion in his subtle and compelling theory of personal constructs man as a scientist steadily and actively engaged in making and re-making his hypotheses about the nature of the universe.[17]

We are acquiring as well some empirical confirmation about the importance of engagement in, as well as self-selection of, a subject for the student learning to write and writing to learn. The recent Sanders and Littlefield study, reported in *Research in the Teaching of English*, is persuasive evidence on this point, as well as being a model for a certain type of research.[18]

As Luria implies in the quotation above, writing is self-rhythmed. One writes best as one learns best, at one's own pace. Or to connect the two processes, writing can sponsor learning because it can match its pace. Support for the importance of self-pacing to learning can be found in Benjamin Bloom's important study "Time and Learning."[19] Evidence for the significance of self-pacing to writing can be found in the reason Jean-Paul Sartre gave last summer for not using the tape-recorder when he announced that blindness in his second eye had forced him to give up writing:

> I think there is an enormous difference between speaking and writing. One rereads what one rewrites. But one can read slowly or quickly: in other words, you do not know how long you will have to take deliberating over a sentence. . . . If I listen to a tape recorder, the listening speed is determined by the speed at which the tape turns and not by my own needs. Therefore I will always be either lagging behind or running ahead of the machine.[20]

Writing is connective as a process in a more subtle and perhaps more significant way, as Luria points out in what may be the most powerful paragraph of rationale ever supplied for writing as heuristic:

> Written speech is bound up with the inhibition of immediate synpractical connections. It assumes a much slower, repeated mediating process of analysis and synthesis, which makes it possible not only to develop the required thought, but even to revert to its earlier stages, thus transforming the sequential

> chain of connections in a simultaneous, self-reviewing structure. Written speech thus represents a new and powerful instrument of thought.[21]

But first to explicate: writing inhibits "immediate synpractical connections." Luria defines *synpraxis* as "concrete-active" situations in which language does not exist independently but as a "fragment" of an ongoing action "outside of which it is incomprehensible."[22] In *Language and Learning,* James Britton defines it succinctly as "speech-cum-action."[23] Writing, unlike talking, restrains dependence upon the actual situation. Writing as a mode is inherently more self-reliant than speaking. Moreover, as Bruner states in explicating Vygotsky, "Writing virtually forces a remoteness of reference on the language user."[24]

Luria notes what has already been noted above that writing, typically, is a "much slower" process than talking. But then he points out the relation of this slower pace to learning: this slower pace allows for—indeed, encourages—the shuttling among past, present, and future. Writing, in other words, connects the three major tenses of our experience to make meaning. And the two major modes by which these three aspects are united are the processes of analysis and synthesis: analysis, the breaking of entities into their constituent parts; and synthesis, combining or fusing these, often into fresh arrangements or amalgams.

Finally, writing is epigenetic, with the complex evolutionary development of thought steadily and graphically visible and available throughout as a record of the journey, from jottings and notes to full discursive formulations.

For a summary of the correspondences stressed here between certain learning strategies and certain attributes of writing see Figure 1.

This essay represents a first effort to make a certain kind of case for writing—specifically, to show its unique value for learning. It is at once over-elaborate and under-specific. Too much of the formulation is in the off-putting jargon of the learning theorist, when my own predilection would have been to emulate George Kelly and to avoid terms like *reinforcement* and *feedback* since their use implies that I live inside a certain paradigm about learning I don't truly inhabit. Yet I hope that the essay will start a crucial line of inquiry; for unless the losses to learners of not writing are compellingly described and substantiated by experimental and speculative research, writing itself as a central academic process may not long endure.

Figure 1
Unique Cluster of Correspondences between Certain Learning Strategies and Certain Attributes of Writing

Selected charactertics of successful learning strategies	Selected attributes of writing, process and product
1. Profits from multi-representational and integrative re-inforcement	1. Represents process uniquely multi-representational and integrative
2. Seeks self-provided feedback:	2. Represents powerful instance of self-provided feedback:
(a) immediate	(a) provides product uniquely available for *immediate* feedback (review and re-evaluation)
(b) long-term	(b) provides record of evolution of thought since writing is epigenetic as process-and-product
3. Is connective:	3. Provides connections:
(a) makes generative conceptual groupings, synthetic and analytic	(a) establishes explicit and systematic conceptual groupings through lexical, syntactic, and rhetorical devices
(b) proceeds from propositions, hypotheses, and other elegant summarizers	(b) represents most available means (verbal language) for economic recording of abstract formulations
4. Is active, engaged, personal—notably, self-rhythmed	4. Is active, engaged, personal—notably, self-rhythmed

REFERENCES

1. Lev S. Vygotsky, *Thought and Language*, trans. Eugenia Hanfmann and Gertrude Vakar (Cambridge: MIT Press, 1962); A. R. Luria and F. Ia. Yudovich, *Speech and the Development of Mental Processes in the Child*, ed. Joan Simon (Baltimore: Penguin, 1971); Jerome S. Bruner, *The Relevance of Education* (New York: W. W. Norton and Co., 1971).
2. Nancy Martin, *From Information to Understanding* (London: Schools Council Project Writing Across the Curriculum, 11–13, 1973); Peter Medway, *From Talking to Writing* (London: Schools Council Project Writing Across the Curriculum, 11–13, 1973).
3. Vygotsky, p. 98.
4. Dell Hymes, "On the Origins and Foundations of Inequality Among Speakers," *Daedalus*, 102 (Summer 1973), 69.
5. Participant-speakers were Loren Barrett, University of Michigan; Gerald O'Grady, SUNY/Buffalo; Hollis Frampton, SUNY/Buffalo; and Janet Emig, Rutgers.
6. George Steiner, *After Babel: Aspects of Language and Translation* (New York: Oxford University Press, 1975), p. 287.
7. John Dewey, *Experience and Education* (New York: Macmillan, 1938); Jean Piaget, *Biology and Knowledge: An Essay on the Relations between Organic Regulations and Cognitive Processes* (Chicago: University of Chicago Press, 1971).
8. Bruner, pp. 7–8.
9. Boyce Rensberger, "Language Ability Found in Right Side of Brain," *New York Times*, 1 August 1975, p. 14.
10. Howard Gardner, *The Shattered Mind: The Person After Brain Damage* (New York: Alfred A. Knopf, 1975), p. 372.
11. William Faulkner, *Writers at Work: The Paris Review Interviews*, ed. Malcolm Cowley (New York: The Viking Press, 1959), p. 130.
12. Géza Révész, *Psychology and Art of the Blind*, trans. H. A. Wolff (London: Longmans-Green, 1950).

13. Bruner, p. 126.
14. Vygotsky, p. 100.
15. Michael Polanyi, *Personal Knowledge: Toward a Post-Critical Philosophy* (Chicago: University of Chicago Press, 1958), p. viii.
16. Robert Pirsig, *Zen and the Art of Motorcycle Maintenance* (New York: William Morrow and Co., Inc., 1974), p. 212.
17. George Kelly, *A Theory of Personality: The Psychology of Personal Constructs* (New York: W. W. Norton and Co., 1963).
18. Sara E. Sanders and John H. Littlefield, "Perhaps Test Essays Can Reflect Significant Improvement in Freshman Composition: Report on a Successful Attempt," *RTE*, 9 (Fall 1975), 145–153.
19. Benjamin Bloom, "Time and Learning," *American Psychologist*, 29 (September 1974), 682–688.
20. Jean-Paul Sartre, "Sartre at Seventy: An Interview," with Michael Contat, *New York Review of Books*, 7 August 1975.
21. Luria, p. 118.
22. Luria, p. 50.
23. James Britton, *Language and Learning* (Baltimore: Penguin, 1971), pp. 10–11.
24. Bruner, p. 47.

Discussing Ideas and Themes

1. What, if anything, is unique about writing as a tool for learning?
2. What similarities and what differences does Emig set up between writing and talking? Make a list of five of each. Can you think of any that Emig does not address?
3. What information does the table in this essay provide? Do you think the table is a helpful addition, or would you rather it had been cut? What do you think the point of charts is in general?
4. Emig discusses "verbal language processes." What are they? Give examples of each kind.

Discussing Rhetoric and Style

1. Emig admits early in the essay that the notion of "writing as a mode of learning" is "clearly debatable." How would you paraphrase the two sides of the debate, and where in her essay—if at all—does Emig address that debate?
2. Who is Emig's audience? Do you find it odd to read an essay that was never intended for you? How can you tell it wasn't intended for you? Use citations from the essay.
3. How would you describe the style of this essay? Pick any sentence at random and study it stylistically—its syntax, diction, and tone, among other things. Then make a list of adjectives that describes Emig as a writer.

4. Consider the range of Emig's examples—say, the vast difference between an example from Faulkner and one from Piaget. What is the effect of mixed examples? Explain.

5. Does Emig draw her conclusions at the end of the essay, or does she present them at the beginning? That is, is her method inductive or deductive? Give examples to support your answer.

Ideas for Writing

1. As an exercise in audience, rewrite Emig's essay, touching on all of her major points but condensing and revising the essay for an audience of students rather than teachers. You may simply stick to Emig's structure and examples, or you may branch out with a new arrangement and examples from your own experience. Whatever you do, remember whom you're writing for.

2. In light of Emig's essay, write an essay that expands Johnson's dictum: "No one but a blockhead ever wrote for anything but money."

STUDENT ESSAY

Imitation
An Approach to Composition

SUSAN SAKOS

Having worked for several years as a full-time nurse, Susan Sakos returned to college to study English. In the following essay, she discusses one of the writing and learning tools she has acquired—imitation, an exercise taught by the classical rhetoricians and by a more contemporary one, Professor Ronald Christ, at Rutgers, where Sakos studied. Offering her own work as an example, Sakos argues that classical rhetoric—and exercises such as imitation—should have their places in the modern curriculum. The essay was written especially for Composition and the English Language.

As if his whole vocation
were endless imitation.

—William Wordsworth

In Advanced Expository Writing, I learned that composition is infinitely more than a mastery of grammar, as painting is more than an ability to mix colors; grammar, syntax and diction are the tools of the writer's trade not the product. All too often, however, my earlier classes in composition focused on rules of grammar (irrefutably as essential as canvas to the painter) or on increasing vocabulary (certainly as indispensable as paint) without offering students models of successful composition to emulate. Art classes have long used imitation as a means of teaching technical skills; imitation should be no less a part of mastering written language, and no less enjoyable than canvas and paint.

The exercise of imitation can be approached in a variety of ways. In ancient Rome, for instance, and later in Renaissance England, schoolboys translated passages from one language to another (Greek to Latin and vice versa), requiring adjustments in style to accommodate grammatical differences in the languages. Today, sadly, few students are proficient enough in more than one language to make such an exercise part of writing studies, but skill building opportunities abound even for the monolinguist.

Imitating a passage noun for noun, comma for comma, trope for trope, forces the novice writer to analyze the total effect of a composition and to examine intimately what elements contribute to that effect. Each word, each punctuation mark, involves a choice, an authorial decision to use a specific word or phrase above all other words or phrases in order to convey an exact meaning or to create a particular effect or style. Imitation, utilizing the foundation and the framework of an example and building upon that structure with new words and new ideas, allows the student to participate in the process of composition. For example, parallelism becomes a means of emphasis and comparison instead of a textbook abstraction, because the student learns to identify and create parallels. Consider the following imitation: the original, written by Irving Howe, and my evocation of the original. Specifically, this passage offers the student an opportunity to create a long, well-organized sentence using complex punctuation.

> Nervous, strewn with knotty or flashy phrases, impatient with transitions and other concessions to dullness, willfully calling attention to itself as a form or at least an outcry, fond of rapid twists, taking pleasure in dispute, dialectic, dazzle—such, at its best or most noticeable, was the essay cultivated by the New York writers.

And the imitation:

> Solitary, littered with sphagnum and fantail fungus, oblivious to mistral and other torments of nature, hauntingly beckoning a sign to me as a prophet or at least a harbinger, torn by vagrant seasons, giving solace in drought, famine, futility—thus, in its dying and near leaflessness was the oak ravaged by the Nebraska plains.

Similarly, exploring the characteristics and possibilities of style can help to sensitize the writer's ear to the rhythms and syncopes of language. Student writers often become all too familiar with the sound of the "official" style from research papers and book reports with little understanding of the elements that contribute to that style: latinate polysyllabic words, convoluted reasoning, and pompous verbosity. An enlightening and enjoyable exercise in style that illustrates how easily the poetic becomes prosaic can be done by translating verses from the King James version of *The Bible* into the official style as shown in the following example:

> In the beginning God created the heaven and the earth. And the earth was without form, and void; and darkness was upon the face of the deep.

Becomes this:

> Prior to the origination of the world as it is known today, at a time henceforth to be referred to as "the beginning," God was involved in the creation of heaven (that area to include those beings not in a state of mortality) and earth (that area to include all living beings). The latter was comprised of amorphous entities, and exhibited the characteristics of nihility; more specifically there was very little resembling illumination.

Although student writers quickly learn to speak of narrative voice and official style, they seldom strip away the bark of academic catch phrases to whittle away at the wood beneath.

Edward P. J. Corbett in his book *Classical Rhetoric for the Modern Student* suggests paraphrasing poetry into prose as a way to explore the process of composition: "Besides teaching students the salient differences between the poetic medium and the prose medium, this exercise made students pay close attention to the potentialities of precise, concrete diction, of emphatic disposition of words, and of figures of speech." Corbett also shows how the process of reworking a model sentence can help students discover the many ways of expressing an idea "partly by the choice of different words, partly by different collocations of words." He offers examples from Erasmus, who produced 150 variations on the sentence (translated from the Latin) "Your letter has delighted me very much."

Rich passages for imitation abound: literature is the student writer's museum, an exhaustive exhibit of masterpieces awaiting exploration line by line, page by page, paragraph by paragraph. As the art student develops technical skills by imitating great painters, so can the student writer begin to unravel the mysteries of composition by imitating great writers.

Discussing Ideas and Themes

1. In her first paragraph, Sakos suggests that writing is like painting. How does she develop this metaphor?
2. What does Sakos assert the values of imitation to be? What, for example, does she think the student can learn from imitating a passage by Irving Howe?
3. Sakos offers both a description and an example of the "official style." She implies that "translating" a passage from poetic language into official language will enlighten the student more than a mere explanation might have done. Do you agree? Do you think this would be a useful exercise? Why or why not?
4. Sakos says that she learned about imitation (and other exercises from classical rhetoric) in an expository writing class. Her essay is geared towards college students, but do you think that these teaching methods could work at other levels—in high school, for example, or preschool? Why or why not?

Discussing Rhetoric and Style

1. What is Sakos's tone in her opening paragraphs? What kind of appeal does she establish? What qualities characterize her voice—her syntax, figures of speech, and diction?
2. What kinds of argument does Sakos employ to defend and elaborate on her thesis? For example, she opens with analogy; what does she do next?
3. Does Sakos's own writing exhibit the qualities of style that she argues imitation will teach a student writer? For example, are her sentences long, suspended, balanced, and so forth?
4. What metaphors, other than the one about painting, does Sakos use to support her argument and enliven her writing? Why do you think she picks these metaphors?
5. Who is the audience for this essay? What do the tone, persuasive purpose, and overall structure suggest?

Ideas for Writing

1. Sakos offers two examples of rhetorical exercises to demonstrate her thesis: an imitation of Irving Howe and a "translation" of a passage in the King James Bible. Do these exercises yourself (imitate the same Howe sentence, but pick a different passage from the Bible to "translate"). Having tried them, write a brief analysis of your own about the effects of these writing exercises.
2. Write an essay in which you advocate something, as Sakos advocates the teaching methods of classical rhetoric. Support your argument with examples, and try, as does Sakos, to make a logical—rather than an emotional—appeal to your reader.

CREDITS *(Continued)*

Chapter 1

Chapter 2

Chapter 3

Chapter 4

Pages 159–161. Adapted from a syndicated column. Copyright © 1988, The Boston Globe Newspaper Company/Washington Post Writers Group. Reprinted by permission.

Pages 163–166. From *The New York Times*, July 29, 1979. Copyright © 1979 by The New York Times Company. Reprinted by permission.

Pages 168–173. Excerpt from *Hunger of Memory* by Richard Rodriguez. Copyright © 1981 by Richard Rodriguez. Reprinted by permission of David R. Godine, Publisher.

Pages 175–182. From *The Speech Teacher*, March 1973. Reprinted by permission of the Speech Communication Association.

Pages 184–190. From *The New Republic*, April 10, 1989. Reprinted by permission of *The New Republic*.

Pages 192–194. From *The Daily Targum*, the Rutgers student newspaper. Copyright © 1989 by Josh Ozersky. Reprinted by permission of the author.

Chapter 5

Pages 199–211. From *Shooting an Elephant and Other Essays* by George Orwell. Copyright 1946 by Sonia Brownell Orwell and renewed 1974 by Sonia Orwell. Reprinted by permission of Harcourt Brace Jovanovich, Inc.

Pages 213–215. From "On the Record" syndicated column, 1939. Reprinted by permission of McIntosh and Otis, Inc., New York.

Pages 218–219. From David B. Wilson's syndicated column in *The Boston Globe*. Reprinted courtesy of *The Boston Globe*.

Pages 221–223. From *Saturday Review*, July/August 1983. Reprinted by permission of Omni Publications International Ltd.

Pages 225–227 From *Playing House* and *Out on a Whim: Some Very Close Brushes with Life*. Copyright © 1983 by Gerald Nachman. Reprinted by permission of the author and the author's agents, Scott Meredith Literary Agency, Inc. (845 Third Avenue, New York, NY 10022).

Pages 229–230. Copyright © 1989 by Catherine J. Barrier. Reprinted by permission of the author.

Chapter 6

Pages 235–240. From *Mauve Gloves & Madmen, Clutter & Vine* by Tom Wolfe. Copyright © 1967, 1976 by Tom Wolfe. Reprinted by permission of Farrar, Straus and Giroux, Inc.

Pages 242–251. From *The Washington Journalism Review*, July/August 1982. Reprinted by permission of *The Washington Journalism Review*.

Pages 254–261. From *College English*, September 1976. Copyright 1976 by the National Council of Teachers of English. Reprinted by permission.

Pages 263–265. From George Will's column of May 8, 1977. Copyright © 1977 by The Washington Post Writers Group. Reprinted by permission of the author.

Pages 267–269. From David B. Wilson's syndicated column in *The Boston Globe*. Reprinted courtesy of *The Boston Globe*.

Pages 271–273. From Bob Swift's syndicated column in the *Miami Herald*, 1985. Reprinted by permission of the *Miami Herald* and the author.

Pages 275–278. Copyright © 1989 by Daniel Moran. Reprinted by permission of the author.

Chapter 7

Pages 283–292. From *Democracy and Its Discontents* by Daniel J. Boorstin. Copyright © 1974 by Daniel J. Boorstin. Reprinted by permission from *Hidden History* (Vintage, 1989).

Pages 294–306. From *New Times*, 1977. Copyright © 1977 by Carol Caldwell. Reprinted by permission of the author.

Pages 308–310. From *And More by Andy Rooney* by Andrew A. Rooney. Copyright © 1982 Essay Productions, Inc. Reprinted by permission of Atheneum Publishers, an imprint of Macmillan Publishing Company.

Pages 312–324. From *Kenyon Review*, Fall, 1979. Copyright © 1979 by Martin Esslin. Reprinted by permission of the author.

Pages 326–328. From *The New York Times*, January 8, 1987. Copyright © 1988 by The New York Times Company. Reprinted by permission.

Pages 330–334. From *The New Republic,* May 11, 1987. Reprinted by permission of *The New Republic.*

Pages 336–337. Copyright © 1989 by George R. Galuschak. Reprinted by permission of the author.

Chapter 8

Pages 341–350. From *Selected Prose of Robert Frost* edited by Hyde Cox and Edward Connery Lathem. Copyright © 1966 by Holt, Rinehart and Winston. Reprinted by permission of Henry Holt and Company, Inc.

Pages 352–357. From *Lectures on Literature* by Vladimir Nabokov. Copyright © 1980 by the Estate of Vladimir Nabokov. Reprinted by permission of Harcourt Brace Jovanovich, Inc.

Pages 359–375. From *Reading for Life* edited by Jacob Price. Copyright © 1959, The University of Michigan Press. Reprinted by permission.

Pages 378–383. Excerpts from *Exercises in Style* by Raymond Quenneau. Copyright © 1947 by Editions Gallimard. Reprinted by permission of New Directions Publishing Corporation.

Pages 385–389. From *The New Yorker,* July 24, 1937. Copyright © 1937, 1965 by The New Yorker Magazine, Inc. Reprinted by permission.

Pages 391–398. From *Edge of Awareness: 25 Contemporary Essays* by Martin Gardner. Copyright © 1989, The University of Chicago Press. Reprinted by permission of the publisher and the author.

Pages 400–402. Copyright © 1989 by Kimberly W. Mitchell. Reprinted by permission of the author.

Chapter 9

Pages 407–409. From *The New York Times,* 1974. Copyright © 1974 by The New York Times Company. Reprinted by permission.

Pages 411–417. From *Slouching Towards Bethelehem* by Joan Didion. Copyright © 1966, 1968 by Joan Didion. Reprinted by permission of Farrar, Straus and Giroux, Inc.

Pages 419–428. From *Growing Up,* copyright © 1982 by Russell Baker. Reprinted by arrangement with Congdon & Weed, Chicago.

Pages 430–437. Excerpts from *The Writing Life* by Annie Dillard. Copyright © 1989 by Annie Dillard. Adapted for and printed in *Tikkun,* vol. 3(6), 1989. Reprinted by permission of HarperCollins Publishers and *Tikkun* (5100 Leona Street, Oakland, CA 94619).

Pages 440–443. Copyright © 1986 by Nora Ephron. First published in the *New York Times Book Review.* Reprinted by permission of International Creative Management, Inc.

Pages 445–454. From *College Composition and Communication,* May 1977. Copyright 1977 by the National Council of Teachers of English. Reprinted by permission.

Pages 456–459. Copyright © 1989 by Susan Sakos. Reprinted by permission of the author.